BENSON and HEDGES
GOLF YEAR

3RD EDITION 1992

NICK EDMUND

Foreword by
Bernhard Langer

PARTRIDGE PRESS

LONDON · NEW YORK · TORONTO · SYDNEY · AUCKLAND

TRANSWORLD PUBLISHERS LTD
61-63 Uxbridge Road, London W5 5SA

TRANSWORLD PUBLISHERS (AUSTRALIA) PTY LTD
15-23 Helles Avenue, Moorebank, NSW 2170

TRANSWORLD PUBLISHERS (NZ) LTD
Cnr Moselle and Waipareira Aves,
Henderson, Auckland

Published 1992 by Partridge Press
a division of Transworld Publishers Ltd
Copyright © Nick Edmund 1992

The right of Nick Edmund to be identified
as author of this work has been asserted in accordance
with sections 77 and 78 of the Copyright Designs and
Patents Act 1988.

A catalogue record for this book is available from the British Library.

ISBN 185225 1433

Photographic editor: DAVE CANNON
All photographic material provided by
Dave Cannon and **Allsport**
Photographers except:
Matthew Harris pp. 18, 19, 23, 24, 26 (main), 34 (right), 38 (main), 63, 71, 74 (bottom), 78 (main), 99 (bottom left), 126, 130, 135, 148, 154, 178 (bottom), 196, 223, 239, 247, 255
Mark Newcombe pp. 116 (right), 121, 123, 172
Keith Hailey p. 16
Lawrence Levy p. 175

This book is sold subject to the Standard Conditions of
Sale of Net Books and may not be resold in the U.K.
below the net price fixed by the publishers for the book.

All rights reserved. No part of this publication may
be reproduced, stored in a retrieval system, or
transmitted in any form or by any means,
electronic, mechanical, photocopying, recording,
or otherwise, without the prior permission of the publishers.

Typeset in Sabon and Gill by Falcon Graphic Art Ltd.

Printed in Great Britain by Richard Clay Ltd, Bungay

CONTENTS

Foreword by Bernhard Langer 5
Sponsor's Message 8
Introduction 9

1 1991: A YEAR TO REMEMBER 11
Highlights and Reflections 12
The Sony Rankings 22

2 THE MAJORS 25
THE US MASTERS 26
Roll of Champions 28
The 1991 US Masters by Nick Edmund 29
Commentary by Colin Callander 36
THE US OPEN 38
Roll of Champions 40
The 1991 US Open by Nick Edmund 41
Commentary by John Hopkins 48
THE OPEN CHAMPIONSHIP 50
Roll of Champions 52
The 1991 Open by Nick Edmund 54
Commentary by Chris Plumridge 64
THE USPGA CHAMPIONSHIP 66
Roll of Champions 68
The 1991 USPGA Championship by Nick Edmund 69
Commentary by David Davies 76

3 THE RYDER CUP 78
Past Results 80
The 1991 Ryder Cup by Nick Edmund 81
Full Result from Kiawah Island 88

4 GLOBAL GOLF 89
EUROPE 90
The PGA European Tour 92
The Dunhill Cup 110
The World Matchplay Championship 113
The WPG European Tour 116

UNITED STATES 126
PGA Tour Review and Results 128
LPGA Tour Review and Results 146
AUSTRALASIA 150
Australian Tour Review 152
Australian PGA Tour Results 153
JAPAN 154
Japanese Tour Review 156
PGA Japan Tour Results 157
REST OF THE WORLD 158
Asia and Africa 160
Four Tours Championship 161
World Cup of Golf 162
SENIOR GOLF
Seniors Review 164
The Senior Majors 166
AMATEUR GOLF
Amateur Review 167
The Amateur Championship 169
The Walker Cup 170
Amateur Roll of Honour 172

5 1992: A YEAR TO SAVOUR 173

Majors Preview by Derek Lawrenson 174
Solheim Cup and Curtis Cup Preview by Lewine Mair 180
Global Golf: January to December 186
USPGA Tour Schedule 198
PGA European Tour Schedule 199

6 GOLF COURSES OF GREAT BRITAIN AND IRELAND 200

ENGLAND 201
SCOTLAND 236
WALES 246
NORTHERN IRELAND 250
IRELAND 252

FOREWORD

by Bernhard Langer

I think many Europeans – perhaps the British in particular – view German people as being a rather cool, unemotional nation. Do you think I had an unemotional year in 1991? I cannot remember a year when I experienced so many emotional highs and lows!

I couldn't put into words (or you couldn't print) how I felt when I missed that putt at Kiawah Island nor can I express the amount of joy I felt when just a week later I won the German Masters title in front of my home fans – a victory which set me up for a great end of season.

I'm sure I could not have recovered so quickly without the immense support I received from my family, my Ryder Cup colleagues and the wonderful European supporters, both those who were able to make the trip and the many millions who watched the events unfold back home.

As the current Benson and Hedges International champion, I am very pleased to provide the foreword to this third edition of the *Benson and Hedges Golf Year*, a book which explores in such colourful detail all the major happenings in 1991 (and the events to come in 1992); not just the Ryder Cup, but the four Major championships, the various men's and women's international tours and all the big amateur and senior tournaments.

I am looking forward greatly to 1992 when the US and British Open Championships are to be played on two of the finest courses in the world: Pebble Beach and Muirfield. I hope I can produce my best form then and, of course, at St Mellion in May when I shall be trying to retain my Benson and Hedges title.

There was a time when I would have climbed trees to win the magnificent gold trophy, now, as I approach my mid-thirties, I am more than content to play my best golf along the rolling fairways of the magnificent Jack Nicklaus Course and to experience the lovely Cornish countryside at ground level.

I wish you all a happy and emotional 1992.

Bernhard Langer

BERNHARD LANGER

A GREAT CHAMPION

SPONSOR'S MESSAGE

Few who follow the game of golf would dispute that 1991 was a special and spectacular year to remember. For three days in September it seemed that the eyes of the world were focused on the Ocean Course at Kiawah Island, where Europe defended its six-year hold on the Ryder Cup. Ultimately, the USA wrenched the trophy from its guests. But only just.

It was a supremely exciting event – and, of course, the real winner was the game of golf.

In 1991 there were many other notable occasions to savour, relish, then commit to memory. Occasions such as Ian Woosnam taking the Green Jacket in the US Masters, or rank outsider Ian Baker-Finch charging to victory in the Open.

Such a packed year of sporting achievement would in itself be enough to make this third edition of the *Benson and Hedges Golf Year* worthy of a place on every golf lover's bookshelf. But it is my pleasure to reveal that you will find a good deal more between these covers.

My thanks and congratulations are due to Editor Nick Edmund, who has – I believe – succeeded in bringing together a number of books in this single volume.

Besides a full review of the game in 1991, this year-book looks forward to a packed calendar of major events – including the women's Solheim Cup, to be staged by Britain for the first time – in the months ahead.

The pages given to statistical information will surely please those who delight in the game's facts and figures. Then to this wealth of material must be added contributions from some of the most respected writers in golf. Well-informed commentaries by Chris Plumridge, John Hopkins, Colin Callander and David Davies give great authority to this book, adding a dimension rarely found in sports compendiums.

Complementing this splendid feast of well-considered words and striking photographs is a fifty-four-page illustrated directory of clubs and courses in Britain and Ireland.

More than ever, the *Benson and Hedges Golf Year* is a comprehensive companion to the game.

I am particularly indebted to Bernhard Langer – a winner on three different continents in 1991 and the current Benson and Hedges International Open champion – for his kind remarks in the foreword of this third edition.

Benson and Hedges looks forward to continuing its long association with golf and will, of course, again stage the Benson and Hedges International Open at St Mellion, Cornwall in 1992.

Enjoy the book – and good golfing!

DEREK STOTHARD
Marketing Manager
Benson and Hedges

INTRODUCTION

I do not think it would be an exaggeration to suggest that watching golf in 1991 wasn't just exciting, it was frequently astonishing.

There is no more thrilling sight in golf than Seve Ballesteros in full flow: whenever and however he plays he always generates excitement, but in the early part of last season the way Seve suddenly recovered his form after a lengthy slump was nothing short of astonishing. In the middle of the year, Ian Baker-Finch amazed us all by playing the first nine holes of his final round in the Open at Birkdale in twenty-nine strokes. Then, just three weeks later, John Daly, a name few were familiar with, took everyone's breath away not only by winning a Major championship but by the awesome nature of his play. To make up a four, there was, of course, the incredible Ryder Cup in September; an event which could fairly be described as exciting, astonishing, amazing, breath-taking and a few more things beside!

Perhaps the chief aim of the third edition of the *Benson and Hedges Golf Year* is to record and relive the many great moments of 1991. A second intention is to whet the 1992 appetite by peering into golf's crystal ball and previewing all this season's major events.

For easy reference the 256 pages have been divided into six sections. Chapter One, 1991: A Year to Remember, offers a general review of the year in which various highlights are selected and reflected upon. This is followed in Chapter Two, by an in-depth and colourful look at how The Masters at Augusta, the US Open at Hazeltine, The Open at Birkdale and the USPGA at Crooked Stick were won and lost. This section includes four excellent commentaries and as editor I must immediately thank Colin Callander for enabling us to wallow in the extraordinary second-round performances of Nicklaus and Watson at Augusta; John Hopkins for explaining why Payne Stewart has always dressed so outrageously and now plays golf so brilliantly; Chris Plumridge who retraces Ian Baker-Finch's Queensland background and David Davies who helps us get a little closer to the phenomenal force of John Daly.

In Chapter Three we journey to Kiawah Island and remember the epic 29th Ryder Cup encounter. 'Global Golf' comes next. This includes results from all over the world — men's and women's, professional and amateur — all of which are drawn together and presented in simple format. There are reviews on the major tours and reports on the World Matchplay Championship, the Dunhill, Walker and World Cups.

The penultimate section, Chapter Five, 1992: A Year to Savour, is where the book looks ahead to what promises to be another thrilling year. Again we have sought the help of two of golf's leading journalists, Derek Lawrenson and Lewine Mair and at the end of the chapter there is an illustrated global calendar. Finally, there is a detailed Directory, listing all the golf clubs in Great Britain and Ireland, complete with telephone numbers, addresses and course yardages.

If there is one thing that makes this *Benson and Hedges Golf Year* stand out from all other golfing year books it is surely the extent and quality of its photographic content. I am especially grateful, therefore, to Dave Cannon and his colleagues at Allsport who have provided most of the pictures for this edition, and to Matthew Harris.

I would also like to say how much I appreciate the efforts of the publishers, Partridge Press, in particular, Debbie Beckerman, Alison Tulett and Bipin Patel and all other persons responsible for the book's production. Last, but by no means least, I thank my wife Teresa for her unfailing support and encouragement at all times.

Nick Edmund
1st January 1992

I
1991
A YEAR TO REMEMBER

HIGHLIGHTS AND REFLECTIONS ON A GOLFING SEASON

How quickly the scene changes: April 1991 at Augusta and there was no question about it – 'the two best golfers in the world are British.' Well, wasn't Nick Faldo, the reigning Open champion and Masters winner in 1989 and 1990, about to slip a green blazer over the shoulders of Ian Woosnam, the player who in the past four years had won twenty tournaments worldwide and had led the Sony Rankings even before he teed up at Augusta? No question at all then. Yet at the end of September, less than six months after The Masters, it was a different story: 'there's no doubt about it – the two best golfers in the world are Spanish!' As the 'invincible' Faldo and Woosnam partnership crumbled in the sandy wastelands of Kiawah Island, Ballesteros and Olazabal alone kept alive European hopes of retaining the Ryder Cup. When the Americans began to boast 'one European team cannot beat four American teams', they were as good as conceding that they couldn't beat the Spaniards. And they couldn't: they were a class apart.

Looking back at 1991 through European-tinted spectacles, the performances of Ian Woosnam at The Masters and of Ballesteros and Olazabal at the Ryder Cup were probably

Britain's Master golfers, Nick Faldo and Ian Woosnam: out of sorts at Kiawah, but in April Faldo passed the Masters crown to Woosnam.

the two biggest highlights of the season. Both events produced genuine edge-of-the-seat type finishes and the length of putt that needed to be holed in both cases measured about 6 feet. On the first occasion the putt fell to Woosnam who only a few days earlier had claimed he felt 'like jelly' on the slick Augusta greens, and in the second – the irony of ironies – everything rested on the putt of a man who has battled so bravely against the dreaded 'yips' for years and who, as a result, employs one of the most extraordinary putting grips ever seen.

Take away the European-tinted spectacles and I would venture that it is still hard to think of two more memorable weeks of golf than those at Augusta and Kiawah Island. Surely for the last time in a Major championship the golfing world was treated to a Nicklaus and Watson show during the second round of The 1991 Masters. There was Jack Nicklaus – he of all people – succumbing to the watery challenges of Amen Corner before fighting back with a barrage of birdies; and Tom Watson, the symbol of all that's good in American golf, reminding us how wonderfully he used to raise his game whenever the Golden Bear threw down the gauntlet. And then there was the truly nail-biting climax on Sunday afternoon as three players, two of them Europeans out to win their first Major, stood on the 18th tee level at eleven under par.

The 29th Ryder Cup has been described as the greatest golf match of all time. The drama was quite unparalleled, perhaps by any other single sporting occasion in memory. But imagine for a second what the atmosphere would have been like if it had been Ballesteros, the most expressive and most charismatic golfer in the world, who had been centre stage during those final gripping moments. He, of course, was the first to say, 'I would not have made that putt.' Again though, imagine the scenes if he had!

Seve's spectacular return to form in 1991 was a highlight in itself. At the beginning of the year he looked like the proverbial lost soul; he had certainly lost his golf game. Then suddenly, just as people who should have known better began to write him off,

An inspired Ballesteros at the Ryder Cup.

or as he put it, 'You think I am down the side of the hill,' like the Grand Old Duke of York, he came marching back. In the space of five heady weeks in Japan and Europe he finished third, first, second (losing a play-off) first and first. Those latter two victories took place in England towards the end of May. To say that the British public views Seve as an 'adopted Brit' is a gross understatement: he sits on a golfing pedestal. At Wentworth, in the Volvo PGA Championship, dropped shots at the 70th and 71st holes meant that he had to play-off for the Tour's most important title against one of Britain's rising stars, Colin Montgomerie. Robert Green described the mood perfectly when he wrote in *The Sunday Times*, '. . . poor Colin – to be British, playing in England and finding that everyone but your relatives is rooting for a Spaniard. But, as they would chant if Seve were a footballer: there's only one Ballesteros.' It did look as if they were about to do something akin to just that at Royal Birkdale in the Open, as their defeated hero, whose every shot, every

(Previous page) Payne Stewart at Kiawah Island.

gesticulation and every movement they had followed, walked down the final fairway and started to applaud the huge gallery. At least it seems the love affair is mutual.

Gary Player was winning golf tournaments before Ballesteros was born – and the Spanish maestro will be all of thirty-five in April. Another cherished moment of 1991 was the sight of the South African, checked cap and all, playing at St Andrews, not for himself, but for his country in the Dunhill Cup. More than a dozen years had passed since South Africa last competed in any major golf team competition and for a fleeting moment it looked as if Player might be leading his nation to a famous victory. Two down with five to play against Mats Lanner of Sweden in the deciding match, he fought back to all-square but couldn't quite equal his opponent's birdie at the first play-off hole.

Sweden's golfers were, of course, something of a surprise package themselves. Throughout the eighties it had been predicted that they were on the verge of claiming major honours, but it didn't quite happen. Yet within a month of winning the Dunhill Cup, Sweden had captured the World Cup as well, then, just for good measure, Anders Forsbrand and Helen Alfredsson joined forces in the Benson and Hedges Mixed Team Trophy and won that too!

There were, however, many greater shocks than the triple team successes of the Swedes. At Woburn in August, the virtually unknown Penny Grice-Whittaker won the Women's British Open after first having to pre-qualify (she was 100th on the Order of Merit having missed the cut in four out of the five events she'd entered) and despite running up a disastrous nine in her third round. With American rookie John Daly, it wasn't so much a case of having to pre-qualify for the USPGA, as turning up for the championship still thinking he was going to spend the next four days spectating as opposed to playing. That week Daly gave new meaning to the phrase 'super-sub' and he also gave an added dimension to the saying, 'I'm going to knock the cover off the ball'.

While Woosnam powered his way to Masters glory, and Daly blasted his way to victory at Crooked Stick, the year's other two Majors were won with a little more finesse. To be Australian and to have a double-barrelled surname was quite an advantage in British sport last year, that is if golf's Ian Baker-Finch and rugby's Nick Farr-Jones are anything to go by. Baker-Finch chose the final two days of The Open at Royal Birkdale to play the best golf of his life. The way he played the first seven holes of his final round recalled the way fellow Australian Greg Norman began his tremendous final-day charge at Troon two years earlier. The difference now, though, was that Baker-Finch began his final day as joint championship leader, and not seven strokes adrift. But for a dropped shot at the 18th, the six foot, four inch Queenslander would have established a new record for the final thirty-six holes of a Major championship. Still, to

And we all thought Swedes were unemotional! Forsbrand and Johansson celebrate their World Cup success in Rome.

Penny Grice-Whittaker.

Chi Chi Rodriguez.

Payne Stewart.

Greg Norman.

shoot 64-66 with a score of 29 on the front nine holes in the final round of an Open was one amazing achievement.

Shocking pink was the colour Baker-Finch chose for his Sunday afternoon Birkdale onslaught; at the US Open we were subjected to the full spectrum of colours as golf's walking wardrobe, Payne Stewart, overcame Scott Simpson in an extended championship at Hazeltine. Simpson may be a 'born-again Christian' but I have it on good authority that golf photographers the world over were praying for Stewart to win.

Fancy outfits and dramatic gestures aside, the most endearing thing about Payne Stewart is that he, probably more than any of the other leading American players, values the experience of competing in all four corners of the globe. After securing his second Major title in June he played in almost as many tournaments overseas as he did on the USPGA Tour. Not only is such an approach refreshing but it also has to be good for golf.

A second leading American who we in Europe have been fortunate to see quite a bit of lately is Fred Couples. 1991 was a very good year for the player affectionately known as 'Boom Boom' on account of his ability to boom drives into Never Never Land. Although Corey Pavin won the most money on the US Tour, week in, week out, Fred was probably the best player. He won two events in America and had the lowest stroke average; he also won an unofficial event in Paris early in the year, a lucrative Skins Game in South Africa in December, and scored an amazing twelve birdies in a round of 61 in the Scandinavian Masters; moreover he achieved

At the Open they paired America's greatest professional with England's finest amateur.

At The Masters they paired England's finest professional with America's greatest amateur.

the lowest aggregate total for 1991's Major championships. Interestingly in eighth place on that Majors aggregate table was a certain fifty-one-year-old senior, Jack Nicklaus.

As in 1990, Nicklaus played in only a handful of events on the US Seniors Tour but still made a tremendous impact. His brilliant play-off victory over Chi Chi Rodriguez in the US Senior Open was one of the highlights of the American summer. In Britain we saw him at Birkdale making what he has threatened may be his penultimate Open Championship appearance. The 'Golden Bear' seems almost certain to play at Muirfield this year but that could well be his last Open. If this is the case then it really will be the end of a golden era. Between his first win at Muirfield as a twenty-four year old in 1966, and the 1980 championship at Muirfield when he was forty, he never once finished outside of the top six: winning on three occasions and finishing runner-up no fewer than six times.

In the final round at Birkdale Nicklaus partnered Britain's leading amateur (as he then was), Jim Payne, and was most impressed by the twenty-one year old, assuring him that Phil Mickelson, America's great amateur prodigy, had nothing on him. Nick Faldo, who had a disappointing year in the Majors (and elsewhere – winning nothing more than the Irish Open all year), may venture to disagree. He was paired with the twenty-year-old left-hander in the opening round of The Masters and was, by all accounts, 'played off the park' when Mickelson scored a 69 to Nick's 72. Another of 1991's amateurs to keep an eye on is Australian Robert Allenby who last November beat some hardened Aussie professionals by six strokes to win the Victorian Open and a few weeks later very nearly captured the Australian Open at Royal Melbourne.

Some top amateurs take a good while to establish themselves as top professionals, others make an immediate impression. In the latter category is Steven Richardson. In only his second year as a professional he finished second to Ballesteros on the Volvo Order of Merit. In the first half of the season, especially, he was the talk of the Tour. I wonder what odds one would have got at the beginning of 1991 that Steven Richardson would win more tournaments and more money in Europe than Nick Faldo! At twenty-five,

and already a Ryder Cup player, the long-hitting Englishman is clearly a very great prospect, particularly when one considers that the youngest player on the American side at Kiawah Island was thirty-year-old Steve Pate. Of course, we also tend to forget that Olazabal, for the second year running a winner on both sides of the Atlantic, is also still very young – less than six months older than Richardson, in fact.

Finishing third on the European money list, behind Ballesteros and Richardson was the Benson and Hedges International champion, Bernhard Langer. And what a year he had! His victory at St Mellion was his second of the year as in February he won the Hong Kong Open by seven strokes, thanks to a dazzling final round 63. His long awaited win in the Benson and Hedges proved, if nothing else, that he is one of the best bad-weather players in the world, while his play-off success in the German Masters, coming as it did just seven days after the Ryder Cup, was, in the circumstances, nothing less than astonishing. Langer hadn't finished either for in December he destroyed a strong field and established a new tournament record in winning the Sun City Million Dollar Challenge.

With Ballesteros and Langer sharing eight victories worldwide, taking first and third places on the European money list and playing such key roles in the Ryder Cup, it was a little like old times. By 'old times' I mean the mid eighties when, together with Greg Norman, they ruled the golfing world. Four victories in the World Matchplay Championship (two in finals against Langer) was the Spaniard's traditional way of proving the point. It took him six years to equal Gary Player's record of five Wentworth titles, but when he finally managed it last October it was worth waiting for. His thrilling final with Nick Price was reminiscent of his 1988 Open win at Lytham, for there, as at Wentworth, it was the likeable

Seve Ballesteros at Wentworth during the Toyota World Matchplay Championship. (Left) Bernhard Langer.

Double Major winner, Meg Mallon.

Zimbabwean who had the misfortune to come up against the Spaniard at his brilliant best. It was the sixty-fourth victory of Ballesteros' career and the twentieth title he has won in Great Britain and Ireland.

Just as The Masters used to ring in the beginning of the golfing season, so the World Matchplay used to bring the curtain down. Now there is 'no rest for the wicked' with golf events being staged almost up until the end of December. How long will it be, I wonder, before we have a Santa Claus Shoot-Out on Christmas Day? Or a Reindeer Skins Game, perhaps? A lot happened towards the end of 1991. At about the same time as Gary Player and his South African team mates were battling against Sweden in October's Dunhill Cup final, Chip Beck was scoring an amazing 59 in the Las Vegas Invitational. In Australia, double LPGA Major winner Meg Mallon won the Women's World Golf Championship at the wonderfully named Paradise Palms, then flew back to New York to receive the US Women's Sports Foundation's Female Athlete of the Year Award, the first golfer ever to be so honoured. Not many days later we were reminded of how women's golf used to be as Lady Heathcoat-Amery, or Joyce Wethered as the golfing world remembers her best, turned ninety. In her prime she was, according to Bobby Jones, the greatest golfer – man or woman – he had ever seen.

The further we got into 1991 the better Sandy Lyle seemed to play. At the beginning of the year he was co-hosting the Lost Souls Party with Ballesteros; ironically – infuriatingly even – he seemed to start to rediscover his form immediately after Bernard Gallacher declined to chose him as a Wild Card selection to play at Kiawah Island. One week after that decision he birdied the final hole at Walton Heath to finish second in the European Open. A few weeks later – just a fortnight after the Ryder Cup, in fact – he won the BMW International, his first victory in three years, beating two of America's leading Ryder Cup players, Payne Stewart and Paul Azinger, in the process.

There was no Wild Card selection for Sandy and, to most people's surprise and dismay, there wasn't one for Tom Watson either. Nor will there be a need for one when the match returns to The Belfry in 1993, as Watson will be skippering the US side. His appointment as Captain is surely the best possible news for the Ryder Cup. We can be sure that he will not encourage or foster any of the crass War-on-the-Shore type of hype, for he values the traditions and spirit of the contest far too highly.

What else happened towards the end of the year? Moving from West to East, Naomichi Ozaki ended the 1991 season as the new star of Japan, José-Maria Olazabal received acupuncture treatment and Seve Ballesteros lost a play-off for the prestigious Dunlop Phoenix Tournament. In Africa, as mentioned, Bernhard Langer won a million dollars while Down Under, Europe won the Four Tours Championship at Royal Adelaide and Wayne Riley sank a 40 foot putt on the final green to land the Australian Open. Heading back towards the West, Ian Woosnam easily won the inaugural Grand Slam champions event in Hawaii and Payne Stewart pocketed most of the money on offer in America's Skins Game at La Quinta. Then with Christmas only days away the Johnnie Walker World Championship was staged in Jamaica with victory going to the man who finally learnt to win in 1991, Fred '50 ways to leave a leader board' Couples.

Finally, we should end with one of the most prophetic quotes of the year, and, of course, it has to relate to the Ryder Cup. It was uttered by Couples back in March: 'If it's all tied, whoever wins the last hole to win the Ryder Cup, why that would be like being President of the United States for a year.' What a pity he didn't say, 'Chancellor of Germany!'

The 1993 US Ryder Cup Captain, Tom Watson.

THE SONY RANKINGS

31 December 1991

Ian Woosnam.

Pos.	Player	Circuit
1	Ian Woosnam	Eur
2	Nick Faldo	Eur
3	José-Maria Olazabal	Eur
4	Seve Ballesteros	Eur
5	Greg Norman	ANZ
6	Fred Couples	USA
7	Bernhard Langer	Eur
8	Payne Stewart	USA
9	Paul Azinger	USA
10	Rodger Davis	ANZ
11	Ian Baker-Finch	ANZ
12	Mark McNulty	Afr
13	Hale Irwin	USA
14	Mark O'Meara	USA
15	Lanny Wadkins	USA
16	Tom Kite	USA
17	Craig Parry	ANZ
18	Corey Pavin	USA
19	Bruce Lietzke	USA
20	Mark Calcavecchia	USA
21	Craig Stadler	USA
22	Chip Beck	USA
23	Davis Love III	USA
24	Nick Price	Afr
25	Curtis Strange	USA
26	Mike Harwood	ANZ
27	Steve Pate	USA
28	Eduardo Romero	SAm
29	Tom Purtzer	USA
30	Masashi Ozaki	Jpn
31	Larry Mize	USA
32	Steven Richardson	Eur
33	Tom Watson	USA
34	Fuzzy Zoeller	USA
35	Larry Nelson	USA
36	Colin Montgomerie	Eur
37	Mark James	Eur
38	Ray Floyd	USA
39	Wayne Levi	USA
40	Jodie Mudd	USA
41	Scott Hoch	USA
42	David Feherty	Eur
43	Ronan Rafferty	Eur
44	Steve Elkington	ANZ
45	John Cook	USA
46	Tim Simpson	USA
47	John Daly	USA
48	Sandy Lyle	Eur
49	Billy Andrade	USA
50	Peter Jacobsen	USA
51	Wayne Grady	ANZ
52=	Ben Crenshaw	USA
52=	Scott Simpson	USA
54	Frank Nobilo	ANZ
55	Sam Torrance	Eur
56	Steve Jones	USA
57	Gil Morgan	USA
58	Nolan Henke	USA
59	Rocco Mediate	USA
60	Mike Hulbert	USA

José-Maria Olazabal.

The winners of three out of the four Majors in 1991: Ian Baker-Finch (left), Payne Stewart (centre) and Ian Woosnam.

2
THE MAJORS

THE US MASTERS
THE US OPEN
THE OPEN
THE USPGA

THE MASTERS

THE MASTERS
ROLL OF CHAMPIONS

1934	Horton Smith	1965	Jack Nicklaus
1935	*Gene Sarazen	1966	*Jack Nicklaus
1936	Horton Smith	1967	Gay Brewer
1937	Byron Nelson	1968	Bob Goalby
1938	Henry Picard	1969	George Archer
1939	Ralph Guldahl	1970	*Billy Casper
1940	Jimmy Demaret	1971	Charles Coody
1941	Craig Wood	1972	Jack Nicklaus
1942	*Byron Nelson	1973	Tommy Aaron
1943-5	No tournaments played	1974	Gary Player
1946	Herman Keiser	1975	Jack Nicklaus
1947	Jimmy Demaret	1976	Ray Floyd
1948	Claude Harmon	1977	Tom Watson
1949	Sam Snead	1978	Gary Player
1950	Jimmy Demaret	1979	*Fuzzy Zoeller
1951	Ben Hogan	1980	Seve Ballesteros
1952	Sam Snead	1981	Tom Watson
1953	Ben Hogan	1982	*Craig Stadler
1954	*Sam Snead	1983	Seve Ballesteros
1955	Cary Middlecoff	1984	Ben Crenshaw
1956	Jack Burke	1985	Bernhard Langer
1957	Doug Ford	1986	Jack Nicklaus
1958	Arnold Palmer	1987	*Larry Mize
1959	Art Wall	1988	Sandy Lyle
1960	Arnold Palmer	1989	*Nick Faldo
1961	Gary Player	1990	*Nick Faldo
1962	*Arnold Palmer	1991	Ian Woosnam
1963	Jack Nicklaus		
1964	Arnold Palmer		

* Winner in play-off.

HIGHLIGHTS

Most wins: 6 Jack Nicklaus
          4 Arnold Palmer
Most times runner-up: 4 Ben Hogan
                       Tom Weiskopf
                       Jack Nicklaus
Biggest margin of victory: 9 Jack Nicklaus (1965)
Lowest winning total: 271 Jack Nicklaus (1965)
                             Ray Floyd (1976)
Lowest single round: 63 Nick Price (1986)
Lowest final round by winner: 64 Gary Player (1978)
Oldest champion: Jack Nicklaus, aged 46 (1986)
Youngest champion: Severiano Ballesteros, aged 23 (1980)

THE 1991 US MASTERS

He marked Nick Faldo's card during an epic final round in the previous year's Masters before watching the tall Englishman triumph over Ray Floyd in the play-off to join him as the only back-to-back winner of Bobby Jones' great tournament. Next he saw him come within a whisker of tying the winning score in the US Open at Medinah – just as he had done over the same course fifteen years previously – and then just a month later he witnessed Faldo's emphatic victory in the Open at St Andrews, once again following in his footsteps for he had twice tasted success on the oldest Old Course of all.

He, needless to say, is Jack Nicklaus who, on the eve of the 1991 Masters, expressed the view that Nick Faldo was 'by far the clear favourite' to win the coveted Green Jacket for a third time. Jack's much publicized remark didn't go down too well with an American public hungry for a home-grown Major success: not only had 'overseas' players won three of the past year's four Major championships but not since 1987 had an American won at Augusta.

Perhaps Nick Faldo hadn't prepared for the 1991 Masters as well as he might have wished: a wrist injury had curtailed his early season schedule and this competitive rustiness was compounded when the previous week's tournament was rained off, but then again Major championships have always brought the best out of Faldo. Moreover, the overseas challenge was as strong as ever. Faldo went into the 55th US Masters in third position on the Sony World Rankings; above him were Ian Woosnam and José-Maria Olazabal. And what form these two were in! Woosnam had

'Master golfer' and caddie: Faldo and Sunneson plot an Augusta hat trick.

Bobby Jones' masterpiece: if there is a golf course in heaven...

climbed to the number one spot following early season victories on both sides of the Atlantic and after his win in the USF&G Classic at New Orleans he declared himself to be presently the number one player in the world. No one could really argue with the Welshman and back home James Mossop wrote in the *Sunday Express* on 7 April, 'There is an irresistible feeling that Ian Woosnam is ready to take his first Major tournament.' Olazabal also had a 1991 win under his belt – a six stroke victory in the Catalan Open – while no one in America had forgotten his incredible twelve stroke victory in the 1990 World Series at Firestone. Then there was Bernhard Langer, a former Masters champion, winner of the Hong Kong Open in February and reputed to be returning to his best form, and Australia's Steve Elkington who surprised many by winning America's prestigious Players' Championship in March.

Not so long ago Elkington walked in the shadow of Greg Norman, just as Woosnam walked in the shadow of Sandy Lyle and Olazabal of Seve Ballesteros. So what of the 'Big Three' of yester-year? Greg Norman arrived at Augusta after a week's fishing declaring that he had 'zero desire to play the game right now'. He duly proved it by scoring a 78 in the first round and went on to miss the cut for the second year running. Sandy Lyle had been at sixes and sevens with his game for some time and he also gave conclusive evidence of this with rounds of 77-76. As for the Spaniard, he too was in a slump. His last round in a Major had been an 83 at the infamous Shoal Creek and according to Faldo his game was currently 'a danger to wildlife'. Seve's outward nine of 34 on the first day at Augusta only flattered to deceive for he came home in 41 and although he did make the halfway cut he was never in serious contention.

When the supporters of Ballesteros, Lyle and Norman looked at the leader board at the end of day one, not only did they note that their heroes were miles off the pace but that American players were making much of the early running: Wadkins, McCumber and Gallagher all posted five under par 67s. On 68 were Couples, Ozaki, Olazabal, Nicklaus and Watson. Yes, Nicklaus and Watson who shared twelve birdies and revived memories of old. And more would follow.

Neither Faldo nor Woosnam could get into top gear and each returned opening level par 72s. Faldo was outscored (and outdriven) by the amateur prodigy, Phil Mickelson, while Woosnam said he felt 'like jelly' on the slick Augusta greens – but with a caddy nicknamed 'Wobbly' what could he expect? The most extraordinary finish to a round on Thursday was provided by Langer who took eight at the 15th but still managed a 71 courtesy of a 3-2-3 finish.

On the march, the 'irresistible' Ian Woosnam.

Tom Watson and Jack Nicklaus relive the Glory Years.

On the second day Langer partnered Hale Irwin and outscored the American by two strokes with a fine 68 – Kiawah Island must have seemed a long way off on Augusta Friday! By far the most intriguing pairing on day two was that of Nicklaus and Watson. But before they and their huge gallery could get into their stride Ian Woosnam rediscovered his touch on the greens. It wasn't just his putting, though, as he was regularly hitting it close from the centre of the fairway. A 66 was the result: 'One of the best rounds of my life... I have got a really good chance now,' he enthused. Although a trio of Americans, Wadkins, Calcavecchia and McCumber, would match Woosnam's six under par (138) halfway total only one player would better it. Olazabal perhaps? Birdies at the 1st and 2nd taking him to six under suggested he might but he then contrived to take a horrid quadruple bogey seven at the short 6th – how he would rue that come Sunday afternoon! A strong finish, however, brought the young Spaniard back into contention, one behind Woosnam and Co. and level with Langer on 139. The defending champion, Faldo, could manage no better than a 73 and on 145 he was effectively out of it. Like Jack Nicklaus in 1967 Faldo had found the Masters hat trick to be an impossible dream. The one player who did get ahead of Woosnam was Tom Watson but it could so easily have been Nicklaus as well.

At last Watson was looking and playing like his old self again – the Kansas kid reborn – and perhaps inspired by this sight and memories of Turnberry and Pebble Beach, not to mention the chance of a seventh Green Jacket, Nicklaus kept his old adversary in his sights... at least until he reached the notorious par three 12th. It was here that the Golden Bear appeared to surrender his challenge. Jack took a seven, a 'quad' in American golf-speak and from four under par he dropped back to level. His recovery was breathtaking. He birdied the 13th, 14th, 15th and then the 16th with a brilliant, curling 30-foot putt. To the gallery's amazement and delight Watson, who had just eagled the 15th, followed Nicklaus in from an equally difficult angle and the two walked up the 18th fairway at eight under and four under par respectively, loving every second of it. Just like old times.

So to the weekend. Tom Watson held a two stroke lead but it was nearly eight years since he had won the last of his eight Major championships and since 1984, he could count his total number of tournament victories on one finger. Could Watson really roll back the years and win his third Masters? Everything he did on the Saturday proved it was possible. Watson played very soundly from tee to green, putted well and with a 70 advanced to ten under par. Tom's only problem was that whilst he played soundly Woosnam continued to play sublimely. On the back nine in particular, Woosnam, to use more American golf-speak, 'peppered the flag sticks'. True he missed the odd putt but still scored a 67 and from being level par after the first day was now eleven under par after three rounds and the new tournament leader.

By Saturday afternoon Watson and Woosnam had succeeded in shaking off most of their pursuers but Olazabal, with an excellent 69 and Wadkins (70) still clung doggedly to their coat-tails. Barring something extraordinary it was now a four horse race. Faldo (67) and Ballesteros (69) at last discovered their form but for them it was all too late. So as dusk fell on Masters' Saturday the leader board was headed by Woosnam on 205, followed by Watson on 206, with Olazabal and Wadkins on 208.

When Woosnam entered the locker room on Sunday he found a note waiting for him. It said simply, 'Good luck – go out and win it.' It was from Nick Faldo.

As is widely known, the glorious colours of Augusta are due largely to the site's previous history as a nursery. Magnificent golf holes reflect magnificent surroundings and against such a back drop Olazabal, desperate to win his first Major, set off and birdied the 1st (Tea Olive), the 5th (Magnolia) and the 7th (Pampas) after which he had drawn level with Woosnam. His playing partner, the veteran Wadkins started shakily but recovered two shots just before the end of the front nine. Behind them Woosnam was playing much more steadily than Watson who sadly missed putts of no more than a yard at the 1st and 5th. When Olazabal stumbled around the turn, dropping strokes at the 8th (Yellow Jasmine), the 9th (Carolina Cherry) and 10th (Camellia) to fall back to eight under par, level with Wadkins, things were looking good for Woosnam. They looked even better when Watson slipped to minus seven after making a double bogey five at the 12th. When Woosnam stood on the 13th tee the 1991 Masters was his for the taking. Then all sorts of things started to happen. Up ahead, Olazabal, angered by those three dropped shots got himself together, threw caution to the wind and promptly birdied the 13th (Azalea), the 14th (Chinese Fir) and the 15th (Fire Thorn). Wadkins looked to be back in with a chance when he hit his approach to 3 feet at the 14th but he missed the putt and then drowned his chances by hitting into the water at the next.

Four behind Woosnam with six to play, Watson's hopes looked remote but a wild drive from Woosnam at the 13th and two stunning eagles from the American at the 13th and 15th caused a dramatic change in the scenario: with three holes to play Woosnam, Watson and Olazabal were tied at eleven under par. When all three players parred the 16th and 17th a fourth play-off in five years looked likely.

The 18th is called 'Holly' and for Olazabal it produced a prickly ending. First his tee shot found sand – Lyle's bunker – but his ball came to rest too close to the lip for him to have much hope of reaching the green in two. In fact his attempt found yet more sand and when he failed to get 'up and down' it meant a bogey five and he knew his hopes had very probably disappeared. After two strokes each Watson's ball was lying in the same greenside trap that had scuppered the Spaniard while Woosnam, following a huge drive which he hooked on to the members' practice ground and an 8 iron second, was looking good for a four. Watson's bunker shot was much too strong and he took three putts to hole out.

Two eagles for Watson on Sunday but no green jacket.

Both Wadkins and Olazabal had their chances on the back nine but neither could quite manage to pull it off.

Moments later Woosnam faced a putt of 7 feet for victory. 'This one for the Masters.' How many times had he attempted such a putt in his dreams? Halfway towards the hole he knew it was in and he was punching the air before it dropped.

It had all started with a man named Jones but for the next twelve months at least the rest of the world would have to try to keep up with the Woosnams.

1991 US MASTERS
FINAL SCORES

I. Woosnam	**72**	**66**	**67**	**72**	**277**	**$243,000**
J.-M. Olazabal	68	71	69	70	278	145,800
T. Watson	68	68	70	73	279	64,800
S. Pate	72	73	69	65	279	64,800
B. Crenshaw	70	73	68	68	279	64,800
L. Wadkins	67	71	70	71	279	64,800
J. Mudd	70	70	71	69	280	42,100
I. Baker-Finch	71	70	69	70	280	42,100
A. Magee	70	72	68	70	280	42,100
H. Irwin	70	70	75	66	281	35,150
T. Nakajima	74	71	67	69	281	35,150
B. Mayfair	72	72	72	66	282	26,500
M. Calcavecchia	70	68	77	67	282	26,500
F. Zoeller	70	70	75	67	282	26,500
C. Stadler	70	72	71	69	282	26,500
N. Faldo	72	73	67	70	282	26,500
J. Gallagher Jnr	67	74	71	71	283	18,920
M. McCumber	67	71	73	72	283	18,920
P. Jacobsen	73	70	68	72	283	18,920
R. Floyd	71	68	71	73	283	18,920
L. Mize	72	71	66	74	283	18,920
S. Ballesteros	75	70	69	70	284	12,960
S. Elkington	72	69	74	69	284	12,960
R. Mediate	72	69	71	72	284	12,960
C. Pavin	73	70	69	72	284	12,960
S. Simpson	69	73	69	73	284	12,960
M. O'Meara	74	68	72	71	285	10,200
J.D. Blake	74	72	68	71	285	10,200
J. Sluman	71	71	72	72	286	9,200
J. Huston	73	72	71	70	286	9,200
M. Hatalsky	71	72	70	73	286	9,200
D. Frost	71	73	71	72	287	8,000
B. Langer	71	68	74	74	287	8,000
W. Levi	69	73	70	75	287	8,000
M. McNulty	75	72	74	67	288	6,371
M. Brooks	69	72	74	73	288	6,371
S. Hoch	72	70	73	73	288	6,371
K. Green	70	74	71	73	288	6,371
M. Ozaki	68	77	69	74	288	6,371
F. Couples	68	73	72	75	288	6,371
J. Nicklaus	68	72	72	76	288	6,371
D. Hammond	71	72	73	73	289	4,875
D. Love III	72	72	71	74	289	4,875
C. Strange	71	72	74	72	289	4,875
B.R. Brown	73	74	65	77	289	4,875
P. Mickelson	69	74	73	74	290	(Am.)
J. Sindelar	72	70	70	78	290	4,050
D. Pooley	72	71	69	78	290	4,050
L. Trevino	71	71	72	77	291	3,533
T. Aaron	74	70	74	73	291	3,533
N. Price	74	72	73	72	291	3,533
P. Azinger	72	73	67	80	292	3,300
B. Tennyson	73	78	67	75	293	3,200
N. Henke	77	73	71	72	293	3,200
L. Nelson	75	74	69	76	294	3,100
T. Kite	71	71	75	78	295	3,100
M. Zerman	71	71	77	80	299	(Am.)

Woosnam celebrates his winning putt on the 72nd hole.

1991 US MASTERS: A COMMENTARY

Colin Callander, *Golf Monthly*

It was at exactly 1.59 p.m. on 12 April 1991 that the two legends smiled at each other and left the sanctuary of Augusta's practice putting green to start the second round of the 55th Masters tournament.

Little more than 20 yards separates the undulating practice putting green from the pristine first tee at Augusta but in the time it took for Jack Nicklaus and Tom Watson to amble from one to the other a strange metamorphosis seemed to occur. One moment all one could hear was the babble of thousands of voices. The next instant there was nothing. An eerie silence descended over the throng and it wasn't to break until first Nicklaus and then Watson actually reached the tee.

In times to come when the 55th Masters is discussed most people will recall the manner in which Ian Woosnam held his nerve to win the first Major title of his career. That is quite understandable but to this mind at least the stunning achievement of the Welshman will always be relegated behind the performance which Nicklaus and Watson put on together during the second round.

It was an episode which embodied all that is best in golf in general and in the Masters in particular. It was a time for dreamers to dream and for reminiscers to reminisce. To all intents and purposes it was one of those fabled moments when the gods chose to smile upon us.

When Jack Nicklaus and Tom Watson stepped on to the first tee at Augusta to commence their second round in the 1991 US Masters it was almost as if real life was suspended for a while. Thousands of spectators seemed to climb aboard a time machine and were transported to the 1970s and early 1980s when this pair of golfing gladiators dominated the world stage as no golfer has been able to do since. Forget for a moment the Ballesteros and Faldo eras. Leave aside the crass commercialism which has spread through the game in recent times. For around five hours we had returned to an age when our heroes made us smile.

The strange thing was that the moment match number 41 got underway we all forgot that it had been a decade since either man had been in his prime. The sight of them walking together was enough for us to dispel those thoughts and instead to recall such magic moments as the fabulous Duel in the Sun in the Open at Turnberry and the titanic struggle for the US Open at Pebble Beach in 1982, which wasn't settled until Watson pitched in on the penultimate hole. Even the youngest members of the gallery seemed to have been drip fed on memories of their battles. It was a trip down memory lane and the fact that it was staged at Augusta served merely to embellish all that we set out to watch.

If the truth be told much of the opening action on that delightful afternoon would never have been recorded had it not been Nicklaus and Watson who were perpetrating the shots. During the opening nine holes the golf was seldom as bright as the red trousers that Nicklaus was wearing but still the crowds clung on. We laughed when Nicklaus and Watson laughed and cried out when either of them missed a putt.

'I've never seen anything like this,' said one gnarled veteran of twenty previous Masters tournaments as he stood on the slopes surrounding the 9th green.

'I didn't think I'd ever see something to compare with the finish to the 1986 Masters,' he added in reference to the charge which brought Nicklaus his sixth title. 'But in some ways this is even better, because this time we've got Nicklaus and Watson together.'

A glance at the records reveals that in 1986 when he won the last of his Masters titles Nicklaus didn't come alive until he birdied the 9th hole to bring him within three shots of the pace. He then proceeded to come home in 30 and in the process add a twentieth Major title to a collection which had been started when he won the US Amateur in 1959 and which in the intervening period had grown to include a further US Amateur, six Masters, five USPGAs, four US Opens and three Open titles.

Five years on from his momentous triumph in the 1986 Masters the world's most successful golfer never seemed likely to reproduce such form. Instead it was his misfortune which set the proceedings alight.

The incident occurred on a hole which Nicklaus himself has described as the most treacherous short hole in the world and one on which the unfortunate Tom Weiskopf once required thirteen shots to hole out. Seldom does a Masters tournament pass without some drama or other being re-enacted on the 155 yard 12th hole and on this occasion Nicklaus was to misjudge the swirling wind and run up a quadruple bogey 7.

To a lesser mortal such a mishap would have led to a series of further blunders and resulted in an ignominious failure to make the cut. But Nicklaus has never been one to be restricted by such human frailties and in front of his adoring public he wasn't about to start.

Far from wilting Nicklaus proceeded to play the next four holes as if his life depended on it. He nailed birdie putts on the 13th and the 14th before dispatching a medium iron second shot on to the green on the 500-yard 15th where two putts brought him his third consecutive birdie.

He was competing as if the 7 on the 12th hole had made him see red.

'I hit a 6 iron on 15,' he told the assembled press in the new five million dollar media centre later. 'That's the second shortest club that I've ever hit to that green.'

Nor as it transpired was the Nicklaus barrage over.

On the 170-yard par 3 16th the Golden Bear hit his tee shot over the water and on to the green and then proceeded to hole a curling 30-foot putt which seemed to crawl up the slope which bisects the green before breaking almost 8 feet down the hill and dropping into the hole.

'It was a 30-foot putt which travelled 50 feet,' Nicklaus explained later. 'As I watched it roll I thought that it was going to be pretty good but I didn't expect it to go in.'

When the putt dropped Nicklaus glanced up at the heavens and then covered his head in disbelief. He had just produced a run of form which would have been enough to shatter most partners but Watson wasn't fazed.

During a career in which he has won five Opens, two Masters and a US Open title in addition to a further forty-two tournaments in America and elsewhere around the world, one quality which Watson became famous for was his determination. In this instance far from faltering under the Nicklaus onslaught the man from Kansas proceeded to raise his game.

Watson made his first significant move when he hit the 15th green in two and then holed the putt for an eagle. On the next hole the crowd had hardly settled after the Nicklaus birdie when Watson followed suit.

'I just copied Jack,' Watson said later in the modest tone which has made him so popular both in America and on this side of the Atlantic. 'But my putt didn't have nearly as much break.'

The two 2s were enough to jolt the huge gallery into frenzied celebration. Gone was the reverential manner in which Nicklaus and Watson had been treated for most of the first fifteen holes. In its place was the sort of hero worship seen more often at a Bros or Beatles concert.

Suddenly a simple game of golf had been transformed into pure theatre. For the remaining two holes it almost seemed that Nicklaus and Watson were taking it in turns to acknowledge the adulation of the crowd. The climax came when Nicklaus stopped short of the 18th green and waited for his partner so that they could take the final steps together.

'That was fun,' Nicklaus said to Watson as he slumped into his seat in the press centre after the round, and added, 'Perhaps we might do it again some time . . .'

ND OPEN

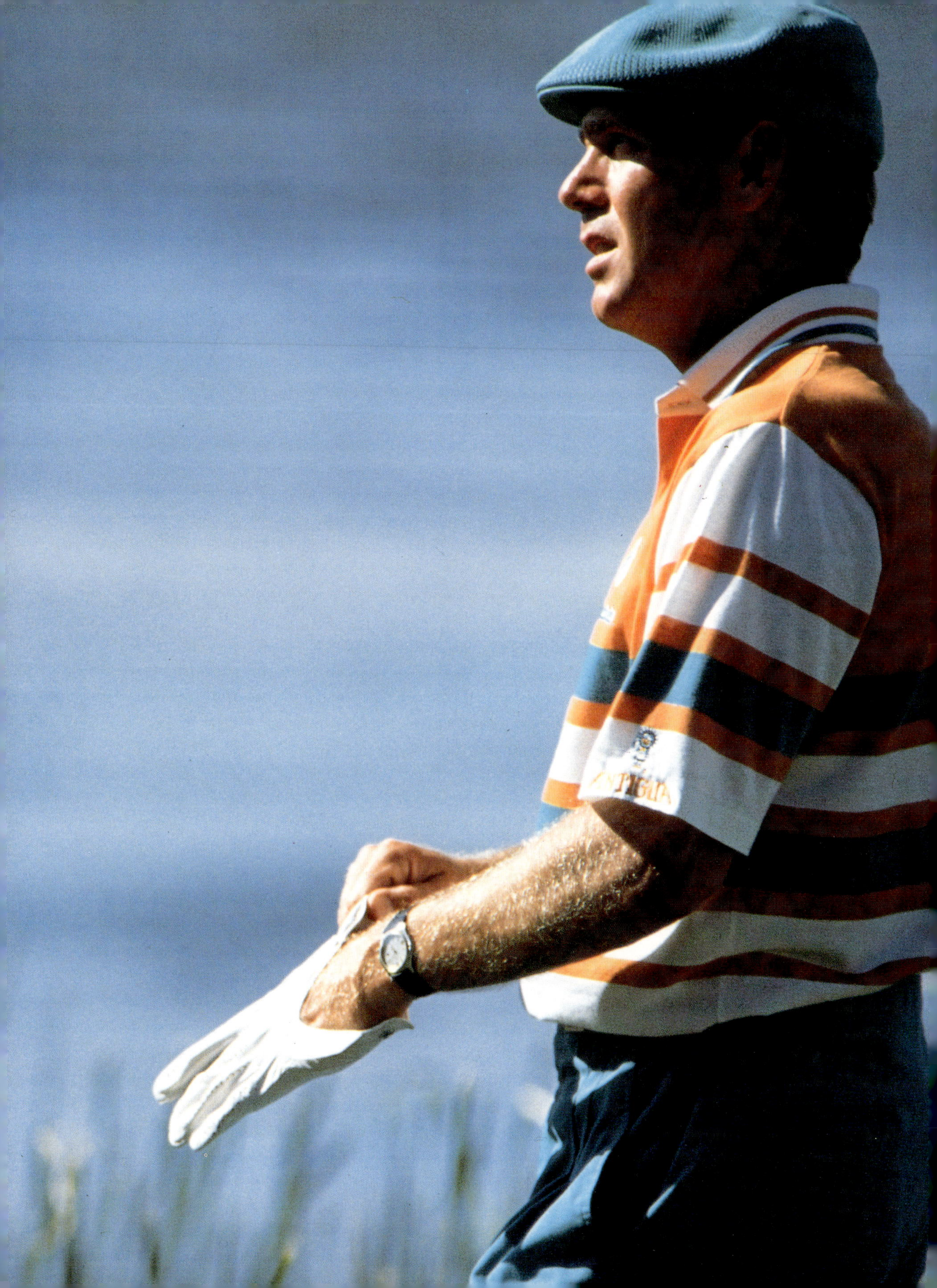

THE US OPEN
ROLL OF CHAMPIONS

Year	Champion	Year	Champion	Year	Champion
1895	Horace Rawlins	1927	*Tommy Armour	1961	Gene Littler
1896	James Foulis	1928	*Johnny Farrell	1962	*Jack Nicklaus
1897	Joe Lloyd	1929	Robert T. Jones	1963	*Julius Boros
1898	Fred Herd	1930	Robert T. Jones	1964	Ken Venturi
1899	Willie Smith	1931	*Billy Burke	1965	*Gary Player
1900	Harry Vardon	1932	Gene Sarazen	1966	*Billy Casper
1901	*Willie Anderson	1933	Johnny Goodman	1967	Jack Nicklaus
1902	Laurie Auchterlonie	1934	Olin Dutra	1968	Lee Trevino
1903	*Willie Anderson	1935	Sam Parks, Jr	1969	Orville Moody
1904	Willie Anderson	1936	Tony Manero	1970	Tony Jacklin
1905	Willie Anderson	1937	Ralph Guldahl	1971	*Lee Trevino
1906	Alex Smith	1938	Ralph Guldahl	1972	Jack Nicklaus
1907	Alex Ross	1939	*Byron Nelson	1973	Johnny Miller
1908	*Fred McLeod	1940	*Lawson Little	1974	Hale Irwin
1909	George Sargent	1941	Craig Wood	1975	*Lou Graham
1910	*Alex Smith	1942-5	No championships played	1976	Jerry Pate
1911	*John McDermott	1946	*Lloyd Mangrum	1977	Hubert Green
1912	John McDermott	1947	*Lew Worsham	1978	Andy North
1913	*Francis Ouimet	1948	Ben Hogan	1979	Hale Irwin
1914	Walter Hagen	1949	Cary Middlecoff	1980	Jack Nicklaus
1915	Jerome Travers	1950	*Ben Hogan	1981	David Graham
1916	Charles Evans, Jr	1951	Ben Hogan	1982	Tom Watson
1917-18	No championships played	1952	Julius Boros	1983	Larry Nelson
1919	*Walter Hagen	1953	Ben Hogan	1984	*Fuzzy Zoeller
1920	Edward Ray	1954	Ed Furgol	1985	Andy North
1921	James M. Barnes	1955	*Jack Fleck	1986	Ray Floyd
1922	Gene Sarazen	1956	Cary Middlecoff	1987	Scott Simpson
1923	*Robert T. Jones	1957	*Dick Mayer	1988	*Curtis Strange
1924	Cyril Walker	1958	Tommy Bolt	1989	Curtis Strange
1925	*W. MacFarlane	1959	Billy Casper	1990	*Hale Irwin
1926	Robert T. Jones	1960	Arnold Palmer	1991	*Payne Stewart

* Winner in play-off.

HIGHLIGHTS

Most wins: 4 Willie Anderson
                Bobby Jones
                Ben Hogan
                Jack Nicklaus
Most times runner-up: 4 Bobby Jones
                        Sam Snead
                        Arnold Palmer
                        Jack Nicklaus
Biggest margin of victory: 9 Willie Smith (1899)
                                Jim Barnes (1921)
Lowest winning total: 272 Jack Nicklaus (1980)
Lowest single round: 63 Johnny Miller (1973)
                        Tom Weiskopf (1980)
                        Jack Nicklaus (1980)
Lowest final round by winner: 63 Johnny Miller (1973)
Oldest champion: Ray Floyd, aged 43 (1986)
Youngest champion: Johnny McDermott, aged 19 (1911)

THE 1991 US OPEN

As the world's golfing élite assembled for the second Major of the year – it was June 1991 and the 91st US Open was about to be staged at Hazeltine National Golf Club, Chaska, Minnesota – we were reminded of how much things had changed in twenty-one years. June 1970 and during the same weekend as Brazil's footballers, Pelé, Jarzihno, Rivelino and Co. destroyed Italy 4–1 in the World Cup final, a young Englishman played the best golf of his life to win the US Open at Hazeltine. Tony Jacklin's stunning seven-stroke victory now seemed worlds away, especially as the golf course that he, and he alone, had mastered had changed out of all recognition.

A very young course in 1970, Hazeltine was severely criticized by many of the leading players of the day. Dave Hill, who finished a distant second to Jacklin, expressed the opinion that 'they ruined a good farm when they built it'. He made a few more scathing comments and was later fined. Such rebellious times! But Hazeltine had done a lot more than grow up in twenty-one years – it had been completely transformed. Tom Watson spoke for many of his fellow professionals when he declared, 'This may be the best US Open course I have seen; it is a superb test.' Beautifully presented perhaps but this new Hazeltine had an almighty sting in its tail.

The three finishing holes, the par four 16th, the par three 17th and par four 18th represented arguably the toughest finishing stretch in US Open history. Reigning champion Hale Irwin reputedly asked golf architect Rees Jones what he needed to do to win again and was told, 'achieve four pars at the 16th.' Although only 384 yards in length it was so difficult that on the third day of the championship not a single player managed to make a birdie three. The green on the 16th is set on the tip of a peninsula – miss the green and Lake Hazeltine beckons, but to have any shot at all at this green a perfectly placed drive fired 200 yards over a bay of swamp grass is essential. Playing the 16th at Hazeltine during US Open week was a bit like trying to guide the proverbial camel through the eye of a needle.

European golf in the twenty-one years since Tony Jacklin's triumph had undergone a seachange in its fortunes. Yet despite the fact that golfers from the 'Old World' had dominated the Masters and the Open Championship in recent years, the only non-American to win the US Open since Jacklin is Australia's David Graham and that was a decade ago.

Nick Faldo, whose game is surely suited to a typically tight US Open type course, and newly crowned Masters champion, Ian Woosnam, had come very close in recent years. Following Europe's 1–2 finish in the Masters, perhaps Hazeltine 1991 was destined to be the time. Unfortunately, with one big exception Europe's top four players were not in particularly good form. Olazabal was still suffering sleepless nights ruing his missed opportunity at Augusta; Woosnam by contrast was probably still not completely back on terra firma after his April trip to Cloud Nine and the Faldo Rolls-Royce engine was still sounding a little like someone had slipped diesel into the petrol tank. The one exception was Ballesteros. After a long barren spell the Spaniard had seemingly rediscovered the old magic: three thrilling victories in his last six starts had him chomping at the bit. The major problem for Seve though was that even at his brilliant best, accuracy and patience had never been his trademarks, yet accuracy and patience are precisely what the US Open is all about. A glance at the list of past champions reveals precious few swashbuckling golfers. Hale Irwin, Scott Simpson, Larry Nelson – these are the sort of men who win US Open Championships – not, it seems, a Seve Ballesteros or a Greg Norman. Even the king of the swashbucklers, Arnold Palmer, could win only one of his 'own' Opens. And so, true to form, the 91st US Open was dominated by straight-hitting Americans.

Plus fours but minus five: Stewart opened his account with a 67.

Woosnam was a serious contender for thirty-six holes.

When the rain stopped, Hazeltine was a picture.

The championship got off to a slow and catastrophic start. A violent thunderstorm, not altogether uncommon in this part of the world at this time of the year, caused a lengthy suspension of play and, tragically, the death of a spectator when lightning struck a tree under which he and several others had been sheltering. Stranded on the course, many players had to complete their rounds the following morning. When the first round was eventually concluded, the 1989 USPGA champion, Payne Stewart, and the little-known Nolan Henke were the joint leaders on 67, five under par. No fewer than twenty-three players finished below par, among them Jack Nicklaus playing in his thirty-fifth consecutive US Open whose 70 was two strokes better than any European could achieve. Faldo and Ballesteros both scored 72s, as did an improving Sandy Lyle, while Woosnam and Olazabal recorded 73s. For the second Major running Greg Norman opened with a 78.

Stewart and Henke continued to make the running on the second day. Playing in the company of Ian Woosnam, the man in plus-fours who had missed much of the season because of a neck injury, advanced to seven under par with a very measured round of 70. Stewart wasn't holing too many putts but then nor was he missing many greens in regulation. After sixteen holes of the second round, Woosnam had got himself to four under par and looked to be putting together a serious challenge for this second leg of the grandslam. At the par three 17th a superbly struck 4 iron appeared to be heading straight for the pin, but in fact Woosnam had hit it too well and it ran through the back of the green. From here it took him three more to get down. It was shades of the previous year's US Open at Medinah where the par three 17th also proved his undoing.

At the end of a long Friday, Payne Stewart, the man with the most colourful wardrobe in

The US Open invariably brings the best out of Scott Simpson.

golf, led the championship on his own on 137. Breathing down Stewart's neck on 138 were three of those straight-hitting Americans: Scott Simpson the US Open specialist, Corey Pavin and Nolan Henke. Woosnam was the best-placed European on 141, Sandy (23 putts) Lyle was only one behind, then came a subdued Olazabal on 144 and a very frustrated Faldo on 146.

The halfway cut fell at 147 and the three other Europeans in the field, Ballesteros ('my putting was terrible'), Langer and Rafferty didn't make it; Rafferty in fact didn't even have the good manners to complete his second round – by the time his playing partners reached the 18th green Ronan was on his way to the airport.

The players awoke on Saturday to discover just how mercurial the Minnesota weather could be. A stiff wind was whistling through the trees, creating the kind of conditions that Ian Woosnam normally relishes. But going in to the championship he had said that his swing was a bit suspect and far from assisting him the wind exposed the flaws in his game. Woosnam ballooned to a 79 in the third round and any dreams of a second Major were blown competely off course. Messrs Pavin and Henke also suffered on a day when only a couple of players, Nick Price and the defending champion, Irwin, scored under par. Stewart and Simpson battled relentlessly throughout the day and by simply playing par golf began to draw away from the field. Following Woosnam's demise, Sandy Lyle found himself in the unfamiliar position of leading the European challenge. In truth though, the 1991 US Open had become a Simpson versus Stewart showdown. When the last putt was holed on windy Saturday they finished level at six under par (210), four strokes ahead of their closest pursuers, Scott Hoch and Nick Price.

Long before the final pair approached the infamous closing stretch on Sunday it was clear that one of them was going to double his tally of Major championship wins. The best performances on the final day came from the 1983 champion, Larry Nelson (68), who tied Fred Couples for third place and the

Dress him up as a Viking and Payne Stewart goes on the rampage.

1984 winner, Fuzzy Zoeller, whose best of the day 67 earned him fifth position. The leading European at the end was Olazabal who finally came on song with a last round 70 to finish joint eighth. Faldo and Lyle tied for sixteenth place, Lyle slipping back after making a double bogey at the 72nd hole and poor Woosnam took one more than on the previous day and finished with a four round total of exactly 300.

From tee to green there was little to choose between Stewart and Simpson as they slugged it out on a beautifully sunny Sunday afternoon. Simpson, however, was the one holing the putts and when Stewart, parading the purple and orange tones of the Minnesota Vikings missed a 5-foot putt for a birdie at the 15th Simpson, a born again Christian who hails from Hawaii, found himself two ahead with three holes to play. Now came the sadistic 16th and for the second day running Simpson bogied. Both parred the

Simpson's hopes of a second US Open title slip away.

17th although Stewart should have drawn level but his brilliant tee shot was followed by another miss from 5 feet and so Simpson arrived at the 18th one ahead.

A par at the 18th would have sealed it for Simpson but an uncharacteristically wayward drive opened the door for Stewart. He seized his chance and so once again at the US Open – for the third time in four years – it was a case of 'do it all again tomorrow please, gentlemen.' They certainly did that and indeed almost produced an action replay. A short putt missed by Stewart on the 15th green again put Simpson two strokes ahead with three holes to play. Yet again Simpson couldn't par the 16th... but this time he couldn't par the 17th or 18th either. Stewart raised his game when it mattered most and proceeded to play the same treacherous holes in one under par including a spectacular birdie at the 16th. It was the mark of a real champion. A US Open champion.

Stewart seals it at the 90th hole.

1991 US OPEN
FINAL SCORES

Player	R1	R2	R3	R4	Total	Prize
P. Stewart	67	70	73	72	282	$235,000
S. Simpson	70	68	72	72	282	117,500
(Stewart won 18-hole play-off 75-77)						
L. Nelson	73	72	72	68	285	62,574
F. Couples	70	70	75	70	285	62,574
F. Zoeller	72	73	74	67	286	41,542
S. Hoch	69	71	74	73	287	36,090
N. Henke	67	71	77	73	288	32,176
R. Floyd	73	72	76	68	289	26,958
J.-M. Olazabal	73	71	75	70	289	26,958
C. Pavin	71	67	79	72	289	26,958
D.A. Weibring	76	71	75	68	290	20,909
D. Love III	70	76	73	71	290	20,909
J. Gallagher Jnr	70	72	75	73	290	20,909
C. Parry	70	73	73	74	290	20,909
H. Irwin	71	75	70	74	290	20,909
T. Watson	73	71	77	70	291	17,186
N. Faldo	72	74	73	72	291	17,186
S. Lyle	72	70	74	75	291	17,186
B.R. Brown	73	71	77	71	292	14,166
P. Persons	70	75	75	72	292	14,166
M. Brooks	73	73	73	73	292	14,166
T. Sieckmann	74	70	74	74	292	14,166
J. Cook	76	70	72	74	292	14,166
C. Stadler	71	69	77	75	292	14,166
N. Price	74	69	71	78	292	14,166
T. Simpson	73	72	76	72	293	11,711
M. Reid	74	72	74	73	293	11,711
B. Tway	75	69	75	74	293	11,711
J. Mudd	71	70	77	75	293	11,711
R. Fehr	74	69	73	77	293	11,711
D. Rummells	72	73	77	72	294	10,133
E. Humenik	72	70	78	74	294	10,133
C. Perry	72	73	75	74	294	10,133
P. Jacobsen	72	73	74	75	294	10,133
L. Ten Broeck	72	73	74	75	294	10,133
B. Kamm	69	73	73	79	294	10,133
T. Purtzer	77	68	77	73	295	8,560
M. Calcavecchia	69	74	78	74	295	8,560
B. Mayfair	72	73	76	74	295	8,560
K. Clearwater	70	76	74	75	295	8,560
T. Kite	71	75	74	75	295	8,560
B. Gardner	74	72	74	75	295	8,560
A. North	71	71	77	76	295	8,560
I. Baker-Finch	77	70	75	74	296	7,477
J. Hallet	72	74	73	77	296	7,477
R. Davis	74	68	81	74	297	6,875
J. Nicklaus	70	76	77	74	297	6,875
B. McCallister	72	72	76	77	297	6,875
S. Pate	72	75	77	74	298	6,033
M. Harwood	71	74	77	76	298	6,033
W. Levi	72	72	76	78	298	6,033
L. Roberts	75	70	74	79	298	6,033
L. Rinker	72	72	77	78	299	5,389
J. Inman	72	72	77	78	299	5,389
P. Mickelson	73	72	80	75	300	(Am.)
L. Mize	73	73	79	75	300	5,164
S. Gotsche	72	75	76	77	300	5,164
S. Elkington	77	69	76	78	300	5,164
I. Woosnam	73	68	79	80	300	5,164
D. Graham	74	71	80	77	302	5,008
S. Utley	73	71	81	78	303	4,958
J. Adams	72	75	78	79	304	4,958
T. Snodgrass	74	73	80	78	305	4,958
L. Wadkins	76	70	80	79	305	4,958
W. Grady	73	74	78	80	305	4,958

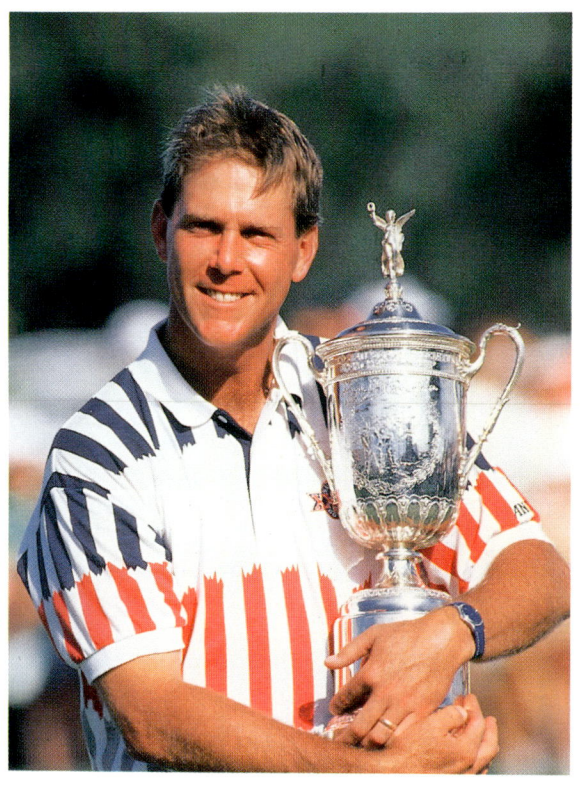

Payne Stewart, US Open champion 1991.

1991 US OPEN: A COMMENTARY

John Hopkins, *Financial Times*

Shut your eyes and think of Payne Stewart. The mental image is of a man in plus-twos wearing a garish shirt, Italian-made white shoes with brass tips, a jaunty, coloured cap, and even a colour-coordinated watch strap. The clothes he wore in the fourth round of the 1990 Open at St Andrews made one journalist suggest Stewart looked as though he was going to be buried at sea. He was, in short, a clothes horse.

It was a characteristic that was handed down to him by his father, along with a tendency to cry. His father, a sales representative, loved brightly coloured sports jackets and wore them with brightly coloured trousers so that he often looked like a collision between three or four paints on an artist's easel. But Bill Stewart stood out as a result and he told his son to do the same.

One day in 1982 while practising, Stewart paused to look around at his fellow toilers belting balls into the distance. 'I was wearing red slacks with a white shirt and white shoes,' he once recalled. 'The guy next to me was wearing red slacks with a white shirt and white shoes. The guy on my right was wearing red slacks with a white shirt and white shoes. I vowed then that I was not going to be another look-alike.'

At Hazeltine, Stewart played such good golf we can never think of him as another look-alike. His victory was his second in the past seven Major championships. Only one other player in the world could match that – Nick Faldo.

Golfers spend years learning how to play, then years learning how to win. The ultimate test is his performance in Major championships and how he plays the closing holes when his stomach is churning and his palms are damp with sweat. It was here, over Hazeltine's fearsome 16th, 17th and 18th, that Stewart came of age and won the 91st US Open.

We saw the maturing of Payne Stewart in Minnesota. On the flat rolling plains of middle America we witnessed the last act in his metamorphosis from a man so used to coming second that he was known as 'Avis', to a man who is so good he could make a habit of winning Major titles.

The talent had always been there, even as a boy when he played round after round with the father he adored, the father who died of cancer in February 1985 just before Stewart won his first professional tournament. Between them they carved up the tournaments in Missouri as Payne was growing up. Bill would win the senior title and Payne the amateur.

Stewart had everything, it seemed. A good, if slightly cocky attitude, a beautiful swing and an enviable consistency. 'The man's game has no weaknesses. He is the next great player,' said Lee Trevino. 'Payne Stewart is the game's next superstar,' said Fred Couples.

The trouble was he couldn't win. He always came second. 'Payne didn't seem to know how to finish a tournament,' said Jack Nicklaus. 'He made the crucial mistake, squandered a lot of opportunities.' In 1986 he had sixteen finishes in the top ten in twenty-nine events. Before 1987 was half over, he had finished in the top ten in six of the thirteen tournaments he entered. Time and again he would get close and then falter.

'I never got to where I hated the heat,' says Stewart. 'That's what we are supposed to live for and a lot of times I thrived on it. But I'd put some form of added pressure on myself. I'd tense up instead of just letting my natural ability do it. I'd be forcing things to happen and when you do that that's when the bad shots creep in. And in the situation when you have a chance to win golf tournaments, it only takes one bad shot. I'd wonder, "Am I going to make something happen or am I going to lose it?"'

He lost it outside the US as well as in his own country. Remember how he missed short putts on the 8th and 9th holes of the 1985 Open at Sandwich? He finished second. At that year's US Open he bogeyed the 18th hole, his 72nd, to dish his chances. A year later, in the US Open again, he held a two-stroke lead with six holes to play only to start noticing the glacial stare of his playing partner, Ray Floyd. The result: Floyd won, Stewart came sixth.

Now Stewart realizes those were bad days for him. At the time, though, he thought they were wonderful. Half a million dollars a year and no pressure. What could be better? 'Even when I wasn't winning, things were great,' says Stewart. 'When I had a good year in 1986 (winning half a million dollars and ending third on the US money list, without a victory) I didn't want to be the number one player. I didn't want the responsibility of having to prove myself every day.'

It wasn't what Tracey, his Australian-born wife, wanted to hear but he didn't know this until he caught the sharp edge of her tongue one day after a tenth-place finish in a tournament. 'You're so complacent with where you're at,' she exploded. 'You're in your comfort zone. You're just happy with a good cheque and a top ten finish! That isn't what your father would be telling you. Your father would be saying, "Hey! You need to be out there winning!" He wouldn't accept that.'

It took time for Stewart to realize that Tracey was right. Meanwhile he carried on being Avis. Between 1984 and 1989 he accumulated fifty-eight top ten finishes, twelve seconds and only three victories.

A combination of factors brought him to his senses. In 1989 he suffered from pains in his lower back, and spending hours having physiotherapy made him realize how transitory his life was as a professional golfer. Like Avis, he vowed to try harder. (He went through the same process this year when a trapped nerve in his neck required him to wear a brace. He had to miss the US Masters in an enforced ten-week absence from golf.) He changed his putter. Most of all, he tackled the greatest problem, which was that he wasn't achieving the kind of results a player of his ability should have been. His reputation was as a player whose ability would get him to within sight of the glittering prize and whose mental attitude would then cause him to screw it up.

In mid-1988 Stewart agreed to work with sports psychologist Dr Richard Coop, a professor of educational psychology at the University of North Carolina. 'Payne's idea of winning was grabbing the golf course by the throat and shaking a win out of it,' says Coop. 'He didn't have that rhythm that guys who are used to winning have – when to reach out and be aggressive, when to lay back and take a par. Payne would try to play over his head because he didn't have a full belief that his normal ability was enough. I told him winning was a by-product. Get into the process of hitting the golf shot; don't be so concerned with the result. The phrase I wanted him to think about was "get lost in your own shotmaking."'

The first time he got lost in his own shotmaking was to finish with four birdies in the last five holes to snatch the 1989 USPGA from a faltering Mike Reid. His loss by one hole to José-Maria Olazabal in the singles in the Ryder Cup a month later was a setback. And so was the way he failed to exert any pressure in the fourth round of the 1990 Open after getting to within two strokes of Faldo with six holes to play.

But at Hazeltine he silenced all the doubters. After his victory he was able to say, with feeling: 'A lot of people said I backed into that one, the PGA. I didn't back into this one. I played my ass off.'

That's one way of putting it. Another is that the man who never wears long trousers when he plays golf has finally grown up.

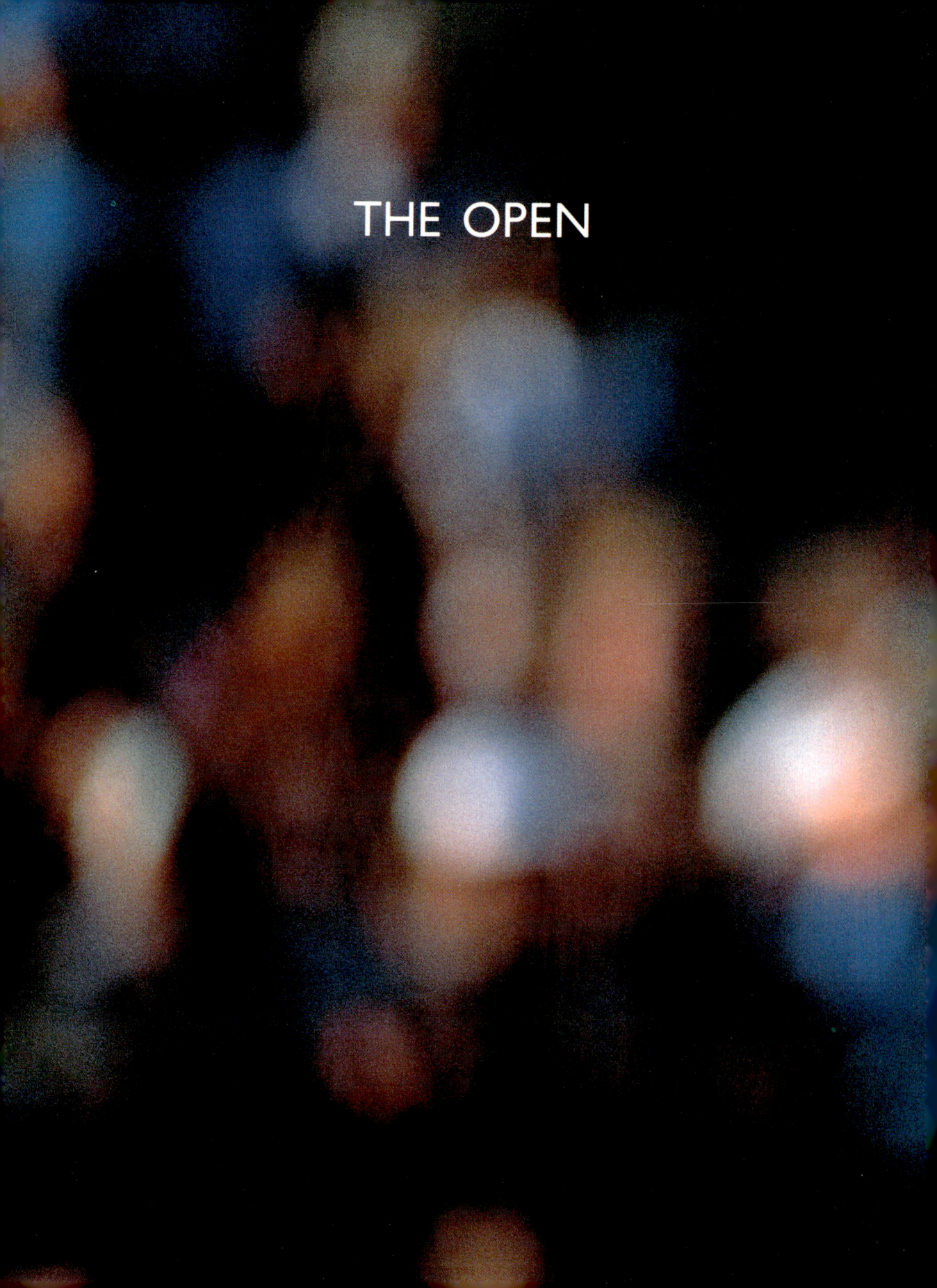

THE OPEN

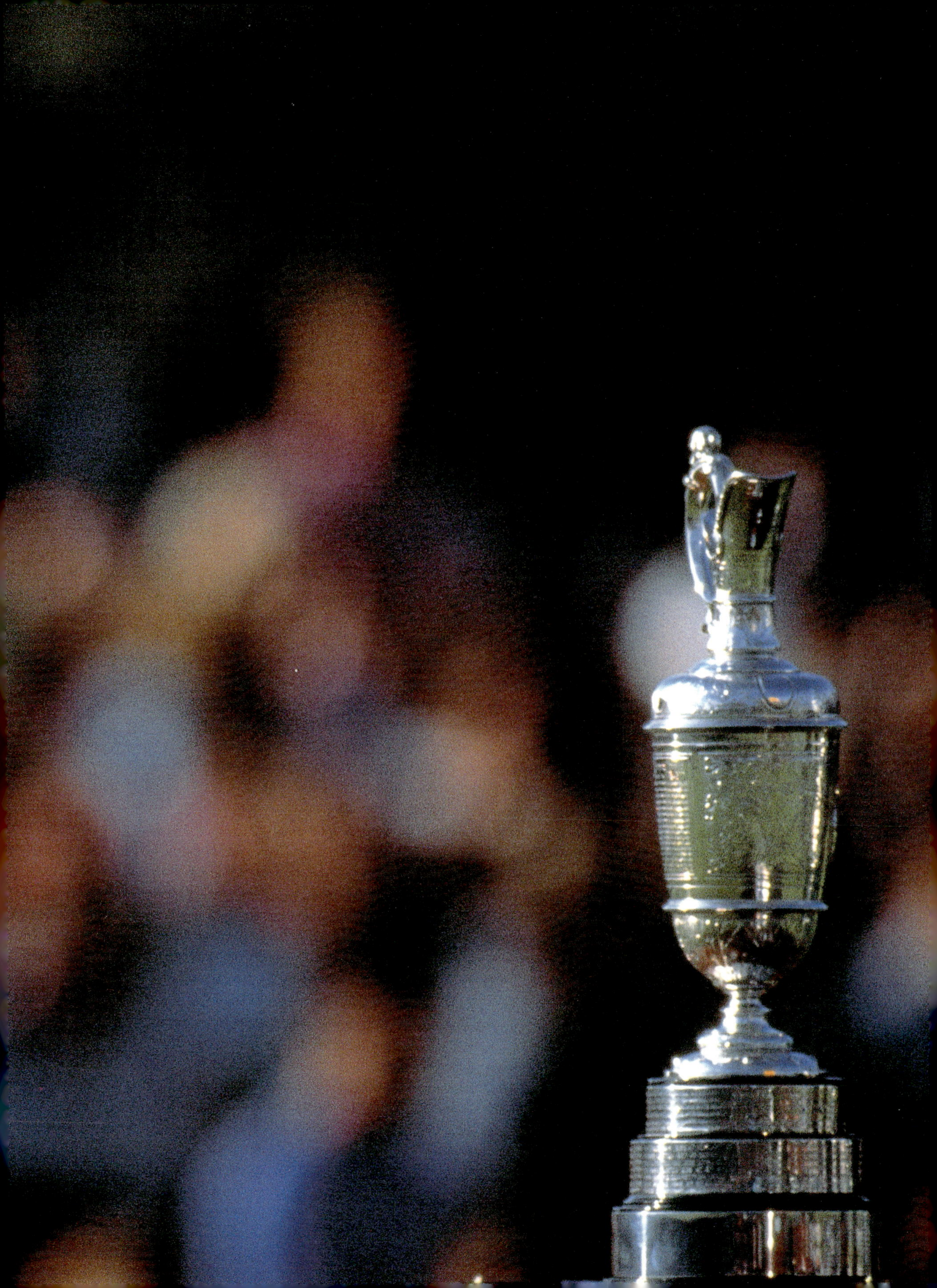

THE OPEN
ROLL OF CHAMPIONS

1860	Willie Park
1861	Tom Morris, Sr
1862	Tom Morris, Sr
1863	Willie Park
1864	Tom Morris, Sr
1865	Andrew Strath
1866	Willie Park
1867	Tom Morris, Sr
1868	Tom Morris, Jr
1869	Tom Morris, Jr
1870	Tom Morris, Jr
1871	No championships played
1872	Tom Morris, Jr
1873	Tom Kidd
1874	Mungo Park
1875	Willie Park
1876	Bob Martin
1877	Jamie Anderson
1878	Jamie Anderson
1879	Jamie Anderson
1880	Robert Ferguson
1881	Robert Ferguson
1882	Robert Ferguson
1883	*Willie Fernie
1884	Jack Simpson
1885	Bob Martin
1886	David Brown
1887	Willie Park, Jr
1888	Jack Burns
1889	*Willie Park, Jr
1890	John Ball
1891	Hugh Kirkaldy
1892	Harold H. Hilton
1893	William Auchterlonie
1894	John H. Taylor
1895	John H. Taylor
1896	*Harry Vardon
1897	Harold H. Hilton
1898	Harry Vardon
1899	Harry Vardon
1900	John H. Taylor
1901	James Braid
1902	Alexander Herd
1903	Harry Vardon
1904	Jack White
1905	James Braid
1906	James Braid
1907	Arnaud Massy
1908	James Braid
1909	John H. Taylor
1910	James Braid
1911	Harry Vardon
1912	Edward Ray
1913	John H. Taylor
1914	Harry Vardon
1915-19	No championships played
1920	George Duncan
1921	*Jock Hutchison
1922	Walter Hagen
1923	Arthur G. Havers
1924	Walter Hagen
1925	James M. Barnes
1926	Robert T. Jones
1927	Robert T. Jones
1928	Walter Hagen
1929	Walter Hagen
1930	Robert T. Jones
1931	Tommy D. Armour
1932	Gene Sarazen
1933	*Denny Shute
1934	Henry Cotton
1935	Alfred Perry
1936	Alfred Padgham
1937	Henry Cotton
1938	R.A. Whitcombe
1939	Richard Burton
1940-45	No championships played
1946	Sam Snead
1947	Fred Daly
1948	Henry Cotton
1949	*Bobby Locke
1950	Bobby Locke
1951	Max Faulkner
1952	Bobby Locke
1953	Ben Hogan
1954	Peter Thomson
1955	Peter Thomson
1956	Peter Thomson
1957	Bobby Locke
1958	*Peter Thomson
1959	Gary Player
1960	Kel Nagle
1961	Arnold Palmer
1962	Arnold Palmer
1963	*Bob Charles
1964	Tony Lema
1965	Peter Thomson
1966	Jack Nicklaus
1967	Roberto DeVicenzo
1968	Gary Player
1969	Tony Jacklin
1970	*Jack Nicklaus
1971	Lee Trevino
1972	Lee Trevino

1973	Tom Weiskopf
1974	Gary Player
1975	*Tom Watson
1976	Johnny Miller
1977	Tom Watson
1978	Jack Nicklaus
1979	Seve Ballesteros
1980	Tom Watson
1981	Bill Rogers
1982	Tom Watson
1983	Tom Watson
1984	Seve Ballesteros
1985	Sandy Lyle
1986	Greg Norman
1987	Nick Faldo
1988	Seve Ballesteros
1989	*Mark Calcavecchia
1990	Nick Faldo
1991	Ian Baker-Finch

* **Winner in play-off.**

HIGHLIGHTS

Most wins: 6 Harry Vardon
          5 John H. Taylor
            James Braid
            Peter Thomson
            Tom Watson
Most times runner-up: 7 Jack Nicklaus
Biggest margin of victory: 13 Old Tom Morris (1862)
Lowest winning total: 268 Tom Watson (1977)
Lowest single round: 63 Mark Hayes (1977)
                    Isao Aoki (1980)
                    Greg Norman (1986)
                    Paul Broadhurst (1990)
                    Jodie Mudd (1991)
Lowest final round by winner: 65 Tom Watson (1977)
                            Severiano Ballesteros (1988)
                              64 Greg Norman (tied but lost play-off in 1989)
Oldest champion: Old Tom Morris, aged 46 (1867)
Youngest champion: Young Tom Morris, aged 17 (1868)
                  Severiano Ballesteros (youngest this century, aged 22 in 1979)

THE 1991 OPEN CHAMPIONSHIP

It started with a whirlwind and finished in a breeze. Was that the weather at Birkdale or the golf? It was both in fact.

The whirlwind that blew across the links on chilly Thursday was of Spanish origin but the gentle giant who breezed home on balmy Sunday came from the other side of the world. The 120th Open Championship was ignited by a sparkling opening 66 from Ballesteros and extinguished by an equally brilliant closing 66 from Baker-Finch. First the Open of 1976 and then the Open of 1984 were relived . . . but on this occasion the tables were dramatically turned.

It was at Birkdale in 1976 that Ballesteros first burst upon the world stage. Aged just nineteen he led the championship for three days before Johnny Miller produced a course-record-equalling 66, playing the kind of golf that made him a genuine, if fleeting, threat to Jack Nicklaus' supremacy in the mid seventies. Ballesteros stumbled to a 74 that day although his round did include a famously audacious eagle-birdie finish. Fifteen years on the thirty-four-year-old Spaniard was now the superstar and was attempting to become only the fourth player to win an Open in three successive decades. By a curious twist of fate his playing partner for the first two rounds of the Open last July was Johnny Miller. This time the scores were exactly reversed although Seve once again finished in thrilling style with an eagle and a birdie for his 66. The 17th at Birkdale measures 525 yards – Ballesteros hit

Vintage Ballesteros: most of the field struggled in the winds on Thursday – Seve simply sizzled. After holing a huge putt on the 18th green for a 66, the mercurial Spaniard moved to the top of the leaderboard.

Both Greg Norman and Payne Stewart had difficulty reading the greens during their first round: Norman returned a 74, Stewart a 72.

a massive drive and 9 iron to 4 feet. At the 18th his birdie putt was all of 40 feet. The stronger the wind blew the better Ballesteros seemed to play. Given the conditions it was a magnificent round: 'I have never seen him play with such control,' said Miller.

Nobody else could score a 66 on Thursday, indeed, with the exception of Nick Faldo, many of the pre-championship favourites struggled in the high winds. Faldo celebrated his thirty-fourth birthday with an encouraging 68 and towards the end of his round strung together a series of superb shots to suggest that he wasn't going to give up the famous trophy without a fight. Woosnam, Olazabal, Stewart and Norman all failed to break 70 and for much of the first day some unfamiliar names hogged the limelight. As Matthew Engel of *The Guardian* observed, 'There was a moment in the morning when the leader board read "Lane, Gates, Marsh, Beck", which sounded like an extract from Wainwright's guide to the Fells.'

Birkdale had, of course, staged one Open Championship in the years since 1976 and that was in 1983 when Tom Watson claimed the fifth of his five championships and the only one on English soil. After coming so close at Augusta, Watson was confident of playing well again at Birkdale. He opened with a fine 69 and on Friday played beautiful golf for seventeen holes. At that point he was just one stroke out of the lead but proceeded to carve his drive deep into the Lancashire undergrowth. It cost him a double bogey six and from that moment on Watson ceased to be a serious contender.

What then of our first round leader? The wind blew as strongly on Friday as it had on Thursday but this time not even two hats (one to keep his head warm and the other to keep the first hat in place!) could prevent Ballesteros getting off to a poor start. After six holes Seve had slipped from four under par to one under; however, he managed to hold it together from then on and finished

The swing is as good as ever, but a sixth Open title remains elusive for Tom Watson.

It wouldn't do for Ascot. Ballesteros wore two hats on Friday and took seven strokes more than on Thursday.

with a 73 for a 139 total. Was he upset? Not at all: 'It is difficult to hold on to a first round lead. I like to be leading on the last day. I am in the best possible position I can be.' That 'position' was just one off the lead, and given that the front runners were the unlikely trio of Hallberg, Harwood and Oldcorn the Spaniard's bravado wasn't entirely misplaced. However, it meant that Ballesteros had almost been caught by a collection of big names. After a 67, Olazabal was only two behind his compatriot, as were Couples and Watson, while Norman, Woosnam, Langer and Baker-Finch were now just three behind Ballesteros and only four off the lead. One further stroke back was a very disgruntled Faldo who had slumped to a disappointing 75. The Nick Faldo of 1991 was a very inferior vintage to the Nick Faldo of 1990.

With Seve coming 'back to the pack', the 120th Open was looking wide open after thirty-six holes and a record number of players survived the halfway cut. Among those who didn't make it through to the weekend were former champions Sandy (No Return) Lyle and Mark (I've given my clubs away) Calcavecchia, plus Corey Pavin, America's leading moneywinner and Ray Floyd.

A strong Australian challenge had been anticipated at Birkdale – Australian players, in fact, went on to occupy five of the top fifteen positions – aside from Norman though, the most widely tipped antipodean to follow in the footsteps of Peter Thomson, who won the Open twice on this great links, was Craig Parry, recent winner of the Scottish Open. Parry did have a good week but when the third round got under way it was another Australian, the man one newspaper tagged, 'Tall, Dark and Hyphenated,' who charged to the fore. Ian Baker-Finch had been on offer at odds of 50–1 on the eve of the championship. Well, what kind of long shot shoots a 64 on the third day of the 1990 Open at St Andrews and repeats the feat twelve months later at Royal Birkdale? A real dark horse!

It was a frustrating week for the defending champion.

Only a week before the Open, in fact at the same time as Craig Parry was winning at Gleneagles, Baker-Finch was finishing runner-up in the New England Classic in America. Fred Couples later described the Australian's form going into the championship as 'awesome'. He certainly demonstrated as much on Open Saturday firing a course record and moving from two over par to four under. At the end of the day the modest Queenslander found himself joint leader of the championship with American Mark O'Meara, whose fine 67 included one of those celebrated eagle-birdie finishes.

One of the factors that enabled Baker-Finch to score a 64 was that the wind dropped considerably on Saturday and it stayed that way throughout the weekend. Eamonn Darcy returned a 66 in the third round to move within a stroke of the two leaders and he was joined by a second six foot, four inch Australian, Mike Harwood. Two behind on two under par was Ballesteros who matched Harwood's 69 and remained firmly convinced that he was going to win his fourth Open Championship. The omens were very good: in each of his three previous victories he had begun the final round two shots off the lead and in one of them, in 1984, Baker-Finch had been a joint leader going into the final day. Of the leading eleven players on Saturday evening only Ballesteros had won a Major championship before, moreover, he was the only player in the top ten of the world rankings at the time within four shots of the lead.

So with one round to go the 'People's Favourite' was also the bookmakers' favourite, or at least joint favourite with Baker-Finch. Ah yes, the Dark Horse who spent his Sunday morning playing with his two-year-old daughter, Hayley. He wasn't letting on but he was very confident too – in his quiet, unassuming way. He had played the supporting role to Ballesteros and Watson in 1984 and to Faldo in 1990: now he reckoned, his time had come.

Before the main event could be decided a 'Mini Championship' had also to be settled. Phil Mickelson, the supremely gifted left-handed American who had already finished leading amateur in both the US Masters and US Open, came to Birkdale to win the final leg of the 'Amateur Grandslam'. But he was thwarted by Lincolnshire golfer Jim Payne who scored 72-72-70-70 to finish four ahead of the young prodigy to claim the prestigious Silver Medal. Payne's partner in the final round at Birkdale was the great man himself, Jack Nicklaus. 'He whupped me,' said Jack after being pipped 70 to 71 by the young Briton. Surely no one ever 'whupped' the Golden Bear.

On a calm day with just that hint of a breeze, someone was likely to 'shoot the lights out' in the final round. The first to have a go was Jodie Mudd, former winner of America's Players' Championship and the man who finished joint fourth in the 1990 Open. Mudd stormed to a 63, equalling the Championship record. After finding the 18th green in two Mudd actually had a putt for a 62 – given that no one has ever scored a 62 in any of the four Major championships Mudd was putting for immortality – he missed, of course, and as he had started the day eight strokes off the pace he never had a realistic chance of winning this championship, but it showed what could be done.

Greg Norman began his final round seven shots behind Baker-Finch and O'Meara, precisely the position he had been in at Troon in 1989 when his stunning 64 enabled him to catch Calcavecchia and Grady. Birdies at the 2nd, 3rd and 5th brought him back to level par but once again his putter let him down at the 8th and 9th. He still had one more go, birdieing the 10th, 14th, 15th and 16th: an eagle-birdie finish could have secured a 63 but it was asking a bit much and when the Great White Shark's birdie attempt slid past the hole from 4 feet at the 17th it was all over. Greg eventually signed for a 66 to finish equal 9th with Langer, who also made up ground in the final round with a 67.

All the real contenders on Sunday were likely to have teed off no more than five

Ian Baker-Finch drives in the third round en route to a brilliant 64.

Mike Harwood was in the frame all week but although he eventually finished runner-up he never really threatened Baker-Finch.

When it really mattered, the putts refused to drop for Ballesteros.

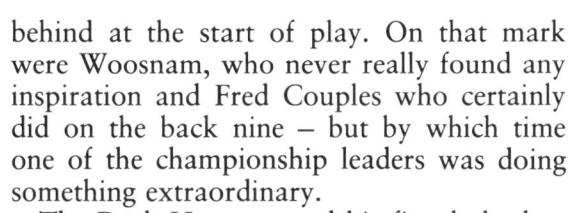

Baker-Finch salutes the crowd on the final green.

behind at the start of play. On that mark were Woosnam, who never really found any inspiration and Fred Couples who certainly did on the back nine – but by which time one of the championship leaders was doing something extraordinary.

The Dark Horse parred his first hole then reeled off five birdies in the next six holes and reached the turn in just 29 strokes. No championship leader had ever done this in the final round of a Major and it left everyone else trailing in his wake. What overnight had appeared to be shaping up as the most open Open in years suddenly became a procession. Not even the famous navy sweater that had guided Seve to three championships could help against this kind of onslaught. Ballesteros didn't make a birdie until the 7th and at that point he had already slipped back to level par and out of contention.

The only player who really threatened Baker-Finch at all on the back nine was Fred Couples who after turning in 32 birdied the 10th, 11th, 12th and 13th thanks to his holing a couple of outrageously long putts. But there were no more birdies after the 12th and Fred's 64 was 'only' good enough for a share of third place with Mark O'Meara – the same position he had finished in the US Open at Hazeltine – and a stroke behind runner-up Harwood who birdied the 16th. From the 7th hole onwards, though, there was only ever going to be one winner.

As two-year-old Hayley Baker-Finch played in the sand bunder beside the 18th green, her daddy held aloft the most famous trophy in golf. And from now on the Dark Horse would be known as the Dark Shark.

1991 OPEN CHAMPIONSHIP
FINAL SCORES

I. Baker-Finch	**71**	**71**	**64**	**66**	**272**	**£90,000**
M. Harwood	68	70	69	67	274	70,000
M. O'Meara	71	68	67	69	275	55,000
F. Couples	72	69	70	64	275	55,000
J. Mudd	72	70	72	63	277	34,166
E. Darcy	73	68	66	70	277	34,166
B. Tway	75	66	70	66	277	34,166
C. Parry	71	70	69	68	278	27,500
G. Norman	74	68	71	66	279	22,833
B. Langer	71	71	70	67	279	22,833
S. Ballesteros	66	73	69	71	279	22,833
M. Sunesson	72	73	68	67	280	17,100
D. Williams	74	71	68	67	280	17,100
V. Singh	71	69	69	71	280	17,100
R. Davis	70	71	73	66	280	17,100
R. Chapman	74	66	71	69	280	17,100
L. Trevino	71	72	71	67	281	10,055
B. Lane	68	72	71	70	281	10,055
N. Faldo	68	75	70	68	281	10,055
C. Beck	67	78	70	66	281	10,055
I. Woosnam	70	72	69	70	281	10,055
P. Broadhurst	71	73	68	69	281	10,055
M. Mouland	68	74	68	71	281	10,055
A. Sherborne	73	70	68	70	281	10,055
P. Senior	74	67	71	69	281	10,055
C. Montgomerie	71	69	71	71	282	6,750
M. Reid	68	71	70	73	282	6,750
W. Grady	69	70	73	70	282	6,750
T. Watson	69	72	72	69	282	6,750
E. Romero	70	73	68	71	282	6,750
M. James	72	68	70	72	282	6,750
G. Hallberg	68	70	73	72	283	5,633
P. Stewart	72	72	71	68	283	5,633
S. Richardson	74	70	72	67	283	5,633
G. Brand Jnr	71	72	69	71	283	5,633
M. Miller	73	74	67	69	283	5,633
C. O'Connor Jnr	72	71	71	69	283	5,633
C. Strange	70	73	69	72	284	4,980
A. Forsbrand	71	72	73	68	284	4,980
P. O'Malley	72	71	70	71	284	4,980
N. Henke	77	71	66	70	284	4,980
M. Poxon	71	72	67	74	284	4,980
J. Payne	72	72	70	70	284	(Am.)
G. Marsh	69	73	72	71	285	4,234
R. Gamez	71	72	72	70	285	4,234
T. Kite	77	71	68	69	285	4,234
S. Elkington	71	68	76	70	285	4,234
F. Allem	70	72	71	72	285	4,234
S. Torrance	72	76	70	67	285	4,234
C. Rocca	68	73	70	74	285	4,234
D. Love III	71	72	69	73	285	4,234
D. Smyth	71	73	73	68	285	4,234
J. Spence	70	73	70	72	285	4,234
J. Nicklaus	70	75	69	71	285	4,234
N. Price	69	72	73	71	285	4,234
D. Hammond	70	75	67	73	285	4,234
G. Levenson	72	73	73	68	286	3,550
A. Magee	71	74	69	72	286	3,550
H. Irwin	74	70	73	69	286	3,550
S. Simpson	74	72	70	70	286	3,550
T. Simpson	72	72	72	70	286	3,550
J. Rivero	74	73	68	71	286	3,550
G. Player	75	71	69	71	286	3,550
M.A. Martin	71	75	71	70	287	3,155
J.D. Blake	75	73	72	67	287	3,155
M. McLean	71	75	72	69	287	3,155
A. Oldcorn	71	67	77	72	287	3,155
M. McNulty	76	71	70	70	287	3,155
S. Jones	70	77	71	69	287	3,155

Ian Baker-Finch: 'Tall, dark and hyphenated'.

Fred Couples produced four successive birdies on the back nine but it was a case of too little, too late.

Plenty of putts dropped for Jodie Mudd, who scored a 63 in his final round.

S. Pate	73	72	74	68	287	3,155
G. Morgan	72	74	74	67	287	3,155
D. Clarke	79	67	68	73	287	3,155
M. Gates	67	75	73	73	288	3,000
P. Jacobsen	75	72	68	73	288	3,000
L. Wadkins	71	75	71	71	288	3,000
F. Nobilo	74	74	71	69	288	3,000
T. Johnstone	69	74	71	74	288	3,000
B. Ogle	73	75	66	74	288	3,000
P. Mickelson	77	67	73	71	288	(Am.)
D. Silva	73	71	75	70	289	3,000
D. Gilford	72	67	73	77	289	3,000
D. Mijovic	70	72	74	73	289	3,000
S. Luna	67	77	72	73	289	3,000
M. Mackenzie	71	73	74	71	289	3,000
M.A. Jimenez	74	74	72	69	289	3,000
B. Crenshaw	71	75	72	71	289	3,000
F. Zoeller	72	72	75	70	289	3,000
M. Brooks	73	74	70	72	289	3,000
J. Bland	71	76	71	71	289	3,000
H. Clark	71	69	73	76	289	3,000
J.-M. Olazabal	74	67	74	74	289	3,000

P. Teravainen	71	72	72	75	290	3,000
R. Gibson	73	75	70	72	290	3,000
B. Marchbank	72	73	75	70	290	3,000
P. Hall	77	71	72	71	291	3,000
C. Sunesson	69	77	69	77	292	3,000
P. Allan	70	71	75	76	292	3,000
A. Webster	73	74	73	72	292	3,000
P. Hedblom	74	74	73	71	292	3,000
J. Hoskison	74	73	74	71	292	3,000
C. Moody	74	71	78	71	294	3,000
C. Stadler	77	71	74	72	294	3,000
T. Weiskopf	74	74	73	73	294	3,000
J. Sluman	71	71	75	77	294	3,000
J. Morse	73	71	77	73	294	3,000
M. Persson	77	71	74	72	294	3,000
S. McAllister	79	69	70	77	295	3,000
E. O'Connell	74	74	74	75	297	3,000
R. Mann	73	74	75	75	297	3,000
J. Oates	77	71	76	75	299	3,000
P. Mayo	71	74	71	83	299	3,000
N. Briggs	73	74	77	76	300	3,000
R. Boxall	71	69	RTD			3,000

1991 OPEN CHAMPIONSHIP: A COMMENTARY

Chris Plumridge, *Sunday Telegraph*

You would be hard pressed to find the scrubland settlement of Peachester on anything but the more intimate maps of Queensland and harder pressed still to find the local course called Beerwah on any list of the great layouts of the world.

Yet it was this remote spot, some sixty miles from Brisbane, which nurtured the first faltering steps of Ian Baker-Finch on a path which was to take him from the backwaters of Beerwah to centre stage at Royal Birkdale. As a boy, Baker-Finch had helped his father clear the land to create the course they christened with that appropriately Australian name, and as he scraped away at the hostile landscape, no doubt the youngster dreamed, as all youngsters do, of one day winning the oldest championship in golf.

Making that dream a reality was a particularly arduous assignment for the man with a name straight out of a P.G. Wodehouse story. Indeed, so far removed is Baker-Finch from the archetypal Aussie that he would fit in comfortably with the chaps at the Drones Club or the weekend set at Blandings Castle. Languages and wines are among the special interests listed against Baker-Finch's name in the United States PGA Tour Book, hardly the hobbies one would normally associate with a nation which prefers its heroes in the Hogan mould (Paul that is, not Ben). Even the Baker-Finch voice did not carry that nasal twang which can so ingratiate but more often than not, just grates. Cultured and charming, Baker-Finch was universally liked but in the cut and thrust of championship golf he was regarded as one of those nice guys who can't help finishing second. Certainly he had had his moments – a host of victories in his native land, a couple of wins in Japan, the Scandinavian Enterprise title in 1985, even a win in his first full season on the US Tour. Sure, the kid could play but for every one of those triumphs there seemed to be at least five times as many near misses, almosts and what might have beens. When it came to the crunch did Baker Flinch? And then there was 1984.

This was the Open Championship which carried Orwellian overtones for a twenty-three-year-old professional who had the temerity to lead the likes of Ballesteros and Watson after three rounds at St Andrews. Big Brother was certainly watching when Baker-Finch teed off on that sunny afternoon but even He may have averted his attention after what followed. What followed a cracking opening drive was a pitch shot so loaded with backspin that when the ball hit the green a few feet from the pin, its final resting place was the Swilcan Burn. This set the pattern for a day when nothing went right. Round in 79, Baker-Finch was inconsolable, believing he had squandered a once-in-a-lifetime opportunity.

What he was unaware of, however, was the irrefutable law of Major championships – you have to lose one before you win one. For some players the time between these two occurrences is short, for others it is a longer learning curve. For Baker-Finch, the Open Championship still beckoned and in 1990, after a third round 64 at St Andrews, he once again found himself in the final pairing on the last day. Although five strokes behind Nick Faldo and acting, as he said, 'just as a marker', he was able to witness at first hand how Faldo focused on the job at hand and another piece of the jigsaw fell into place.

Other pieces had been put in place previously in the form of a re-structured swing under the eye of Mitchell Spearman, one of David Leadbetter's lieutenants, plus some sessions with the noted sports psychologist, Bob Rotella. Just prior to the Open at Birkdale, Rotella had told his 'patient' to go on the course and try to hole every shot from 100 yards down. An unattainable goal certainly, but one which, as Dr Johnson wrote of the man about to be hanged, 'concentrates the mind wonderfully'.

The puzzle at Birkdale was not the course itself, which was universally acclaimed, but the greens. As the week progressed they induced varying degrees of apoplexy from the players, drawing complaints that they were spongy and made holing out from close range something of a nightmare.

One only has to study the list of previous champions to realize that Birkdale's pedigree as an Open course is undeniable. Since it staged its first open in 1954 the winners have been Peter Thomson (twice), Arnold Palmer, Lee Trevino, Johnny Miller and most recently, Tom Watson.

It was generally felt that it was time this American/Australian domination came to an end, particularly as the portents for a British or European victory looked so good. After all, Nick Faldo was defending champion, Ian Woosnam had won the US Masters and Severiano Ballesteros was in towering form. Of these three, only Ballesteros made any kind of showing.

Few people took any notice of Baker-Finch after his two opening rounds of 71 apiece but they sat up after his third round 64 which vaulted him into a share of the lead with the American Mark O'Meara. Mike Harwood supported the Australian challenge only one shot off the lead with Ballesteros a further stroke behind.

The hot money was riding on Ballesteros, the man with five Major championship victories including three Open titles to his name. Aware of the gulf between winners and Major winners, Ballesteros embarked on some psychological warfare after the third round with the reminder that none of the players ahead of him had ever won a Major title.

But the fear factor never materialized as Baker-Finch had two other factors working on his behalf. The first was the domestic routine he had established. A home-cooked meal and a rented video on the Saturday night ensured a solid eight hours sleep. On the Sunday, he spent the morning playing with his daughter, Hayley, who had endeared herself to millions of television viewers after the third round by trying to lick a BBC microphone in the mistaken belief that it was an ice-cream!

The other important factor was his pairing with O'Meara. The two happen to be the closest of friends, live near each other in Florida, possess the same sort of rhythm on the course and have both had to carry the 'too nice to win' tag. They were just going to go out there, have a nice game and see what happened.

What happened was momentous. While ahead of him Ballesteros was struggling, Baker-Finch was confirming his position as the US Tour's most accurate driver and compounding that with the most accurate iron shots and putts. Three birdies in the first four holes quickly became five in the first seven and a four stroke lead.

'Just because you fail, it doesn't make you a failure,' Baker-Finch had said earlier, but he knew that if he threw this one away then he may never recover. Reality delivered the sand-filled sock to the base of the skull in the shape of a bunkered drive on the 10th but thereafter he gave absolutely no quarter. Others made a run at him, notably Fred Couples, but it was Harwood who kept closest order on what was definitely Australia's day.

Even Greg Norman made his by now customary final round surge, and the new champion was quick to pay tribute to his fellow countryman's influence. 'We have a lot to thank Greg for,' he said. 'When you see one person from the same background do well you think, "If he can do it, so can I." You feed off each other's success.'

Waiting by the 18th green with a chilled bottle of champagne was another compatriot, Wayne Grady, but it was some time before he could uncork it as the winner had to run the traditional gauntlet of the crowds milling across the fairway. Bruised, battered but certainly unbowed, Ian Baker-Finch was tasting the sweet wine of success.

Meanwhile, back home in Beerwah the boys were getting in a few 'tinnies' because at Birkdale the man they nicknamed 'Sparrow' was soaring with the eagles.

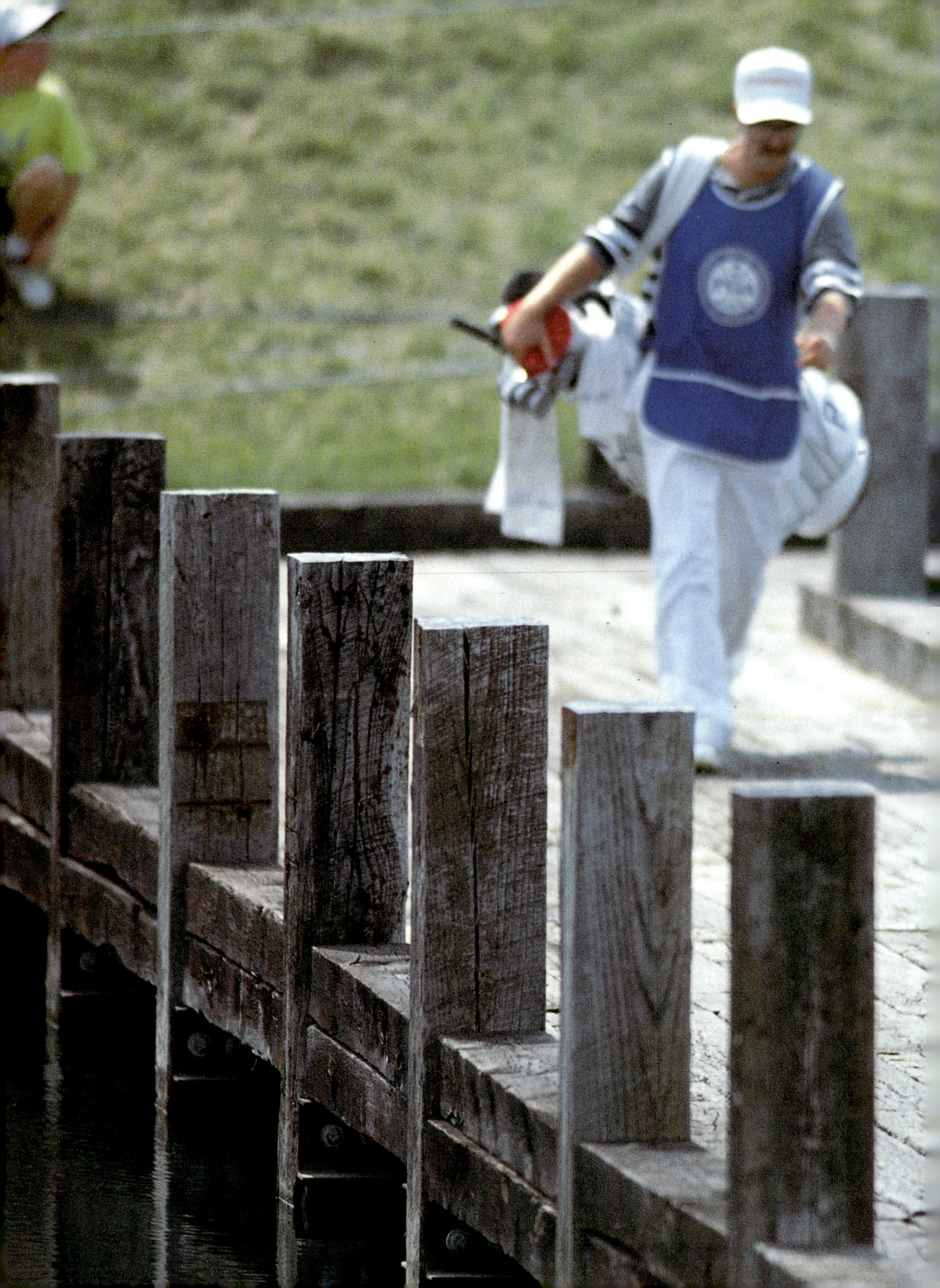

THE USPGA

USPGA CHAMPIONSHIP
ROLL OF CHAMPIONS

1916	James M. Barnes	1943	No championship played	1969	Ray Floyd
1917-18	No championships played	1944	Bob Hamilton	1970	Dave Stockton
1919	James M. Barnes	1945	Byron Nelson	1971	Jack Nicklaus
1920	Jock Hutchison	1946	Ben Hogan	1972	Gary Player
1921	Walter Hagen	1947	Jim Ferrier	1973	Jack Nicklaus
1922	Gene Sarazen	1948	Ben Hogan	1974	Lee Trevino
1923	Gene Sarazen	1949	Sam Snead	1975	Jack Nicklaus
1924	Walter Hagen	1950	Chandler Harper	1976	Dave Stockton
1925	Walter Hagen	1951	Sam Snead	1977	*Lanny Wadkins
1926	Walter Hagen	1952	Jim Turnesa	1978	*John Mahaffey
1927	Walter Hagen	1953	Walter Burkemo	1979	*David Graham
1928	Leo Diegel	1954	Chick Harbert	1980	Jack Nicklaus
1929	Leo Diegel	1955	Doug Ford	1981	Larry Nelson
1930	Tommy Armour	1956	Jack Burke	1982	Ray Floyd
1931	Tom Creavy	1957	Lionel Hebert	1983	Hal Sutton
1932	Olin Dutra	1958	Dow Finsterwald	1984	Lee Trevino
1933	Gene Sarazen	1959	Bob Rosburg	1985	Hubert Green
1934	Paul Runyan	1960	Jay Hebert	1986	Bob Tway
1935	Johnny Revolta	1961	*Jerry Barber	1987	*Larry Nelson
1936	Denny Shute	1962	Gary Player	1988	Jeff Sluman
1937	Denny Shute	1963	Jack Nicklaus	1989	Payne Stewart
1938	Paul Runyan	1964	Bobby Nichols	1990	Wayne Grady
1939	Henry Picard	1965	Dave Marr	1991	John Daly
1940	Byron Nelson	1966	Al Geiberger		
1941	Vic Ghezzi	1967	*Don January		
1942	Sam Snead	1968	Julius Boros		

* Winner in play-off.

HIGHLIGHTS

Most wins: 5 Walter Hagen
                Jack Nicklaus
Most times runner-up: 4 Jack Nicklaus
Biggest margin of victory: 7 Jack Nicklaus (1980)
Lowest winning total: 271 Bobby Nicholls (1964)
Lowest single round: 63 Bruce Crampton (1975)
                        Ray Floyd (1982)
                        Gary Player (1984)
Lowest final round by winner: 65 David Graham (1979)
                                        Jeff Sluman (1988)
Oldest champion: Julius Boros, aged 48 (1968)
Youngest champion: Gene Sarazen, aged 20 (1922)

THE 1991 USPGA CHAMPIONSHIP

To win a USPGA Championship, first you have to hit the ball as straight as an arrow: miss the fairway with your drive and the rough will invariably punish you severely. Second, you have to hole an awful lot of putts — many under immense pressure: no one has or ever will win a Major championship with a cold putter. What chance then a player occupying 185th position on the US Tour's statistics for driving accuracy and 174th position for putting? What chance a twenty-five-year-old Tour rookie who was originally only ninth reserve, who had never played in a USPGA before and who twenty-four hours before the start of the 1991 championship was relaxing with his fiancée in Memphis, some 600 miles from the host golf club, Crooked Stick in Carmel, Indiana? No chance at all, of course. That is why the following week Mitchell Platts writing in The Times was reflecting on, 'possibly the most astonishing triumph in the history of golf.'

Crooked Stick — surely the ultimate name for a golf course! — was designed by Pete Dye, the same architect who constructed Kiawah Island. From the championship tees it measures 7,289 yards, in other words it is a monster. Irishman David Feherty said it felt more like 9,000 yards and that one of the par fives was so long, 'you have to take into consideration the curvature of the earth.' As well as having to hit it straight then, Crooked Stick was always likely to favour a big hitter.

He may be only five foot, four inches tall, but there aren't too many bigger hitters in golf than Ian Woosnam and with a first Major championship win now tucked safely under his belt many fancied his chances at Crooked Stick. Playing alongside Payne Stewart and Ian Baker-Finch, winners of the previous two

Watson and Ballesteros came to Crooked Stick seeking a first USPGA title and they left still seeking a win in golf's fourth Major.

Majors, Woosnam produced a sparkling 67 on the first day. It was seven shots better than both his partners and was equalled only by Kenny (two eagles) Knox. How ironic: here, leading the 1991 PGA Championship was the man who just twelve months earlier had vowed he would never play in the year's final Major again following his experience at Shoal Creek.

Two of Europe's other favourites were playing alongside one another in a second crowd-pulling trio of Seve Ballesteros, Nick Faldo and Tom Watson. Between, them these three had won seventeen Major championships but not one PGA title. Tom Watson is on record as saying that a win in this event would mean more to him than a record equalling sixth Open Championship for it would give him the full set of grandslam championships, a feat that only Gene Sarazen, Ben Hogan, Gary Player and Jack Nicklaus have accomplished. A good performance by the popular American would also have boosted his chances of receiving a Wild Card selection to play in the Ryder Cup at Kiawah. Unfortunately it was to be a case of 'the harder you try the tougher it gets' and poor Tom missed the cut by just two strokes and, of course, narrowly missed the Kiawah boat... a sad conclusion to a Major year that had promised so much at Augusta. Faldo and Ballesteros opened with rounds of 70 and 71 respectively.

Finishing only a shot behind Woosnam and Knox on day one were a quartet of Americans plus Sandy Lyle who completed his round with birdies at the 17th and extremely difficult 18th. David Feherty and Steven Richardson, both playing in their first American Major, performed well, scoring matching two under par 70s.

A new name climbed to the top of the leader board on Friday: John Daly – 'Long John Daly'. A first round 69 by the huge-hitting

Crooked Stick: designed by Pete Dye, devoured by John Daly.

Steven Richardson and David Feherty impressed on their American Majors' début.

young man from Dardanelle, Arkansas was quite an achievement, especially as he had only arrived at his hotel in the early hours of Thursday morning and his first sight of Crooked Stick came only moments before he teed off later that same day. In the second round Daly powered his way to a superb 67 and a halfway total of 136, eight under par. It gave him a two-stroke lead, 'I'll remember this day for the rest of my life,' he told an astonished gathering of the world's press who were frantically trying to find out more about the surprise championship leader. Of course, he had won the Royal Swaziland Sun Classic in 1990 – fancy not remembering that! John Daly was better known in South Africa than America. But not for long.

On Friday evening Daly led Kenny Knox by two strokes and a much more familiar trio of Nick Faldo, Ian Woosnam and Craig Stadler by three. At one point in his second round Faldo had risen to the top of the leader board at seven under but contrived to take a six at the 16th. Woosnam was also annoyed with himself following a level par round of 72 which contained two double bogeys. Both, though, were very much in contention and surely Daly would not be able to cope with the enormous pressure that goes with leading a Major championship?

On Saturday everybody wanted to watch John Daly. Were reports of his long hitting greatly exaggerated? Could he really fly the ball 40 yards past everyone else and hit it so hard that he regularly knocked golf balls out of shape? He certainly could and this week he was not only hitting it straight but he was also putting like a demon. In his first two rounds he used his putter a mere fifty-four times.

It is not only the British who love an underdog, the Americans love one too – especially one who was destroying the strongest overseas challenge ever assembled for a PGA! Huge cheers greeted Daly's birdies at the 4th, 5th and 6th on Saturday as he attempted to pull away from the chasing pack. Faldo continued to battle gainfully and for a fleeting moment it looked as if Ballesteros was

John Daly has the most powerful – and perhaps the most extraordinary – swing in golf: note the length of his backswing.

For three rounds Nick Faldo kept Daly in his sights.

forcing himself into the reckoning. A tremendous back nine of 32 in the second round rescued him from a three over par position and after sixteen holes on Saturday he had advanced to four under par. But Seve wasted an opportunity by dropping shots at both the 17th and 18th. The long 18th was proving a treacherous hole, in fact statistically the hardest on the course, and so when John Daly dropped a shot at the 17th there was some cause for anxiety among his growing band of followers. The 18th measures 445 yards and dog-legs around the edge of a lake; Daly smashed a driver and an 8 iron to 5 feet. Needless to say, he holed the putt for a 69 which gave him a three round total of 205 (eleven under par) and he extended his overnight lead from two to three. Yet more scurrying through the record books. No player had won a PGA at his first attempt since Bob Hamilton in 1944; no player had won a Major in his rookie year since Jerry Pate in 1976; Daly's best finish in a tour event was tied third in the Chattanooga Classic. People started to analyse Daly's swing. Where did the extraordinary power come from? It had to be that never-ending backswing. 'At the top of the backswing the clubhead should be pointing towards the flag': that's what all the coaching manuals say – Daly's points at the ground. Eight of the par fours at Crooked Stick measure in excess of 430 yards: in the third round 'Long John' needed no more than a 7 iron for his second at any of them.

Then there was Daly's putting. He had never putted so well in his life and nobody watching could remember seeing a player waste so little time going about his business. In Daly's book, lining up putts is for wimps. No wonder the crowd loved him – he was Rambo and Roy of the Rovers combined. Of course, Daly hadn't won it yet. After fifty-four holes Knox and Stadler were three behind at eight under par. Knox had won three US Tour events and Stadler, no mean hitter himself, had won a Major – the 1982

It was an encouraging week for Sandy Lyle.

Masters. Bruce Lietzke, a former Ryder Cup player, was four behind and Nick Faldo, the winner of four Majors, was by no means without hope on six under par, five off the pace.

A bogey five at the 1st on Sunday gave his pursuers heart and the way he had pulled his opening tee shot into the trees caused all golf's 'Oldest Members' to mutter, 'I knew this was going to happen.' John's answer was to hit his approach at the second to 5 feet and hole the putt. Ahead of him nobody seemed able to mount a serious challenge and Faldo, surprisingly, was going backwards. Daly gained another birdie at the 5th and when two more followed at the 13th and 15th his lead had become virtually unassailable.

Meanwhile David Feherty and Steven Richardson were closing with excellent rounds of 68 and 69 respectively to finish in the top ten and so win invitations for 1992's Masters and PGA. Faldo eventually finished with a disappointing 76 allowing Fred Couples to claim the best aggregate total for the year's four Major championships.

A double bogey five at the 17th was Daly's only blemish on the closing stretch and it reduced his lead from five to three. One last massive drive, however, at the 18th and the title was his. The reception he received walking down the 18th fairway was almost deafening and quite rightly so. John Daly had just turned the golfing world on its head.

Amazed and amazing. Daly raises his putter in triumph on the 18th green.

1991 USPGA
FINAL SCORES

J. Daly	**69**	**67**	**69**	**71**	**276**	**$230,000**
B. Lietzke	68	69	72	70	279	140,000
J. Gallagher Jnr	70	72	72	67	281	95,000
K. Knox	67	71	70	74	282	75,000
S. Richardson	70	72	72	69	283	60,000
B. Gilder	73	70	67	73	283	60,000
D. Feherty	71	74	71	68	284	38,000
R. Floyd	69	74	72	69	284	38,000
S. Pate	70	75	70	69	284	38,000
H. Sutton	74	67	72	71	284	38,000
J. Huston	70	72	70	72	284	38,000
C. Stadler	68	71	69	76	284	38,000
J.D. Blake	75	70	72	68	285	24,000
P. Stewart	74	70	71	70	285	24,000
A. Magee	69	73	68	75	285	24,000
H. Twitty	70	71	75	70	286	17,000
W. Levi	73	71	72	70	286	17,000
R. Mediate	71	71	73	71	286	17,000
G. Morgan	70	71	74	71	286	17,000
S. Lyle	68	75	71	72	286	17,000
K. Green	68	73	71	74	286	17,000
N. Faldo	70	69	71	76	286	17,000
M. Hulbert	72	72	73	70	287	11,500
J. Nicklaus	71	72	73	71	287	11,500
C. Beck	73	73	70	71	287	11,500
S. Ballesteros	71	72	71	73	287	11,500
L. Roberts	72	74	72	70	288	8,150
F. Couples	74	67	76	71	288	8,150
J. Hallet	69	74	73	72	288	8,150
M. McNulty	75	71	69	73	288	8,150
R. Fehr	70	73	71	74	288	8,150
D. Tewell	75	72	74	68	289	6,000
M. Calcavecchia	70	74	73	72	289	6,000
D. Edwards	71	75	71	72	289	6,000
S. Elkington	74	68	74	73	289	6,000
G. Norman	70	74	72	73	289	6,000
D. Love III	72	72	72	73	289	6,000
T. Purtzer	69	76	71	73	289	6,000
C. Pavin	72	73	71	73	289	6,000
D. Forsman	73	74	68	74	289	6,000
B. Andrade	73	74	68	74	289	6,000
C. Parry	73	70	76	71	290	4,030
S. Hoch	71	75	72	72	290	4,030
L. Wadkins	71	74	72	73	290	4,030
E. Dougherty	75	70	69	76	290	4,030
W. Grady	72	70	71	77	290	4,030
K. Clearwater	72	72	76	71	291	3,175
B. Faxon	72	72	76	71	291	3,175
D. Frost	74	70	75	72	291	3,175
I. Woosnam	67	72	76	76	291	3,175
T. Kite	73	72	75	72	292	2,725
E. Romero	72	75	73	72	292	2,725
T. Sieckmann	68	76	74	74	292	2,725
D. Graham	72	73	73	74	292	2,725
M. McCumber	74	72	71	75	292	2,725
B. McCallister	71	76	77	69	293	2,537
L. Miller	72	72	77	72	293	2,537
N. Henke	74	70	75	74	293	2,537
F. Funk	71	69	72	81	293	2,537
D. Barr	75	72	76	71	294	2,462
J. Sluman	73	73	74	74	294	2,462
B. Wolcott	73	71	79	72	295	2,400
J. Sindelar	74	73	71	77	295	2,400
G. Sauers	75	71	70	79	295	2,400
S. Williams	70	77	76	73	296	2,312
B. Tway	73	71	78	74	296	2,312
D. Pruitt	72	75	73	76	296	2,312
M. Wiebe	72	73	73	78	296	2,312
D. Peoples	74	73	75	75	297	2,225
D. Hepler	71	75	75	76	297	2,225
L. Nelson	74	71	74	78	297	2,225
P. Blackmar	73	72	82	71	298	2,137
B.R. Brown	69	75	79	75	298	2,137
H. Irwin	70	76	74	78	298	2,137
D. Pooley	72	74	72	80	298	2,137
K. Perry	72	73	79	76	300	2,075

John Daly, the 1991 USPGA champion.

1991 USPGA: A COMMENTARY

David Davies, *The Guardian*

There has never been a Major championship like it. The 1991 USPGA was unique in providing a total unknown as its winner and, in the blond John Daly, as unlikely a victor as has ever taken a Major title.

Daly did not just win the thing, he overwhelmed it. He did not just beat the field, he overpowered it. He hit the ball further than it has ever been seen to be hit in a proper competitive event, making the recognized long-hitters, like Greg Norman, Davis Love III or Ian Woosnam look puny. He teed the ball up and at the word of command, from his caddie, of 'Kill', he took the driver back until it pointed directly at the ground. Then he swung it forward as hard as he knew how, crashed Cobra clubhead into ball, and followed through into a position that would have broken the ribs of most of us.

The ball, meanwhile, was behaving like an Inter-Continental ballistic missile, hurtling into the far distance, extracting only incredulous laughter from the awe-struck audiences.

He won, at full bore to the last, by three shots and there then began the competition to find an appropriate nickname. He had been called 'Wild Thing' and 'Macho Man' by his colleagues who had seen at first hand his extravagant hitting and during the course of the championship the Press were not slow to suggest a few more. Dan Jenkins, in *Golf Digest*, said he was 'Terminator 3,' adding, 'and 4 and 5 and 6.' There were others, among them, with reference to his blond mop of hair, 'The Golden Gorilla', or 'The Blond Bazooka' or 'The Ballistic Blond'.

All of them, because of the extraordinary distances he hit the ball, were appropriate. During the USPGA, which had, incidentally, the strongest field of any event in 1991, he averaged 303·6 yards off the tee. That is about 30 yards longer than the likes of Severiano Ballesteros or Sandy Lyle average and Daly has, on one documented tournament occasion, hit the ball 379 yards without assistance from wind or ground. He is, without doubt, the longest hitter in the world, and when, on television, Jack Nicklaus got his first sight of Daly, he too was reduced to disbelief. 'Goodness gracious,' was his involuntary response when he saw a tape of the swing. Then he added admiringly, 'What a coil, what an unleashing of power, unbelievable power.'

Nicklaus, of course, was the last blond prodigy to emerge and set new standards in the distances a golf ball could be hit. In his youth Fat Jack, as they called him then, hit the ball 30 or more yards past the longest of the day. Now Daly was doing the same and Nicklaus went on: 'His hands and arms position at the top is similar to mine when I came out on Tour although he goes much further back. But the right elbow flies, his hands are high and all I can say is I hope everyone leaves him alone and lets him go ahead and have fun with it. I'm sitting here applauding.'

So, on the 72nd green, were thousands of spectators as Daly played the last in a manner befitting a devil-take-the-hindmost golfer. Water runs down the right side of the fairway, making the tee shot perilous. Daly thought about taking a safer club than the driver, but his caddie, Jeff 'Squeaky' Medlin, dismissed the idea from his mind. 'Hell,' he said, 'even if you do knock it in the lake, you'll be so far up that you'll still make the green in three.' So Daly took the driver, 'Squeaky' said, 'Kill,' one last time, and Daly, as he had done all week, knocked it a million miles up the middle of the fairway. It actually carried to the spot where, earlier in the day, Woosnam's well-hit drive had finished.

Minutes later Daly was acknowledging the applause, his fiancée was running on to the green, and the young and unexpected champion was speaking into the microphone thrust under his nose. He did not have much to say but, remembering the endorsement his swing had received from Nicklaus, he blurted forth: 'I just wanna thank you, Jack. You're the greatest.'

But for one week, at least, Daly himself was the greatest, at any rate off the tee. As Bob Verdi, in the *Chicago Tribune*, said: 'He's longer than Fred Couples, he's longer than Greg Norman, he's even longer than *War and Peace*.'

So given that he could do all this, and had been doing it for five or more years, why had no one, prior to the championship, heard of him? The answer to that comes from Daly himself, who admitted afterwards that: 'I've never had a week when I've hit the ball so straight.' That is hardly surprising, for the extreme length of his swing not only gives him his distance, it also provides the opportunity for the fractional deviation that takes the ball into the deep woods. Daly either prospers, or takes lots, and there had been a lot of the latter in his history.

Now that he has his name in the history books, though, there could be the temptation to throttle back, to reduce the length and furious tempo of the swing in order to gain more consistency. That will be a decision for Daly alone, but at the site of the 1991 USPGA he showed the world what can be achieved. Crooked Stick measured 7,289 yards and, before the championship started, Nicklaus called it the hardest course he had ever seen.

Rain made it longer, but easier in that it made the fairways softer and more holding, but it was still a formidable test.

Daly though, wielding his Cobra driver, with its extra-stiff titanium steel shaft, swing-weight C 9, tamed it. He reached the 525-yard-long 9th with a drive and 6 iron and the 468-yard 14th he reduced, in one round, to a drive and wedge. That was particularly impressive because the hole was a dog-leg left and nobody else in the field could make the carry, being forced to play out to the right and hit between 2-5 iron into the green.

Daly showed himself to be a modest young man, at twenty-five years old still very much the rookie. As leader he was, for instance, invited out to dinner with the Crooked Stick President, Michael Browning, on the Saturday night. He had been intending to go to the local American football game involving the Indianapolis Colts and so a compromise was arrived at. They would have dinner, but it would be a Domino's take-away pizza, eaten in the back of Browning's car, as they drove to the Hoosier Dome to watch the match.

Once there, he was introduced to the crowd, to the apprehension of Browning, who was worried that Daly might not be sufficiently well known. He need not have been. Daly's progress up to that point had captured the imagination of the tele-viewers and he got the biggest reception of the entire night.

A day later, after he had won, one of his first actions was to donate $30,000 of the $230,000 he won to 'any charity the USPGA names,' and he has since honoured the obligations that go with being a champion. He went back to Helias High School, in Jefferson City, Missouri where, in 1983, he had won the State High School Championship. He also set a school record in playing 234 tournament holes in a combined total of one over par – early indications of his ability. He told the present-day students that his only advice would be: 'To follow your dream. Do whatever it takes. I've just followed one goal my entire life, and that is to play golf.'

He has made friends, too, with one man who at one stage in the championship looked like he could become Daly's deadliest enemy. Gary Schaal, Vice-President of the USPGA, was the man who had to tell Daly, after his third round 67, that he may be penalized two strokes for his caddie's alleged mistake of touching the line of a putt with the flagstick.

Daly admits: 'When he told me, I couldn't believe it. I got rude with them, I got very rude.'

Schaal said: 'When we explained, John calmed down and acted like a true professional.'

No penalty was imposed, of course, and at the post-championship banquet it was Schaal and Daly who were the last to leave, having shared a few beers until one o'clock in the morning. 'This cat is colourful,' said Schaal. 'He's become a good friend of mine and I hope he wins six tournaments a year.'

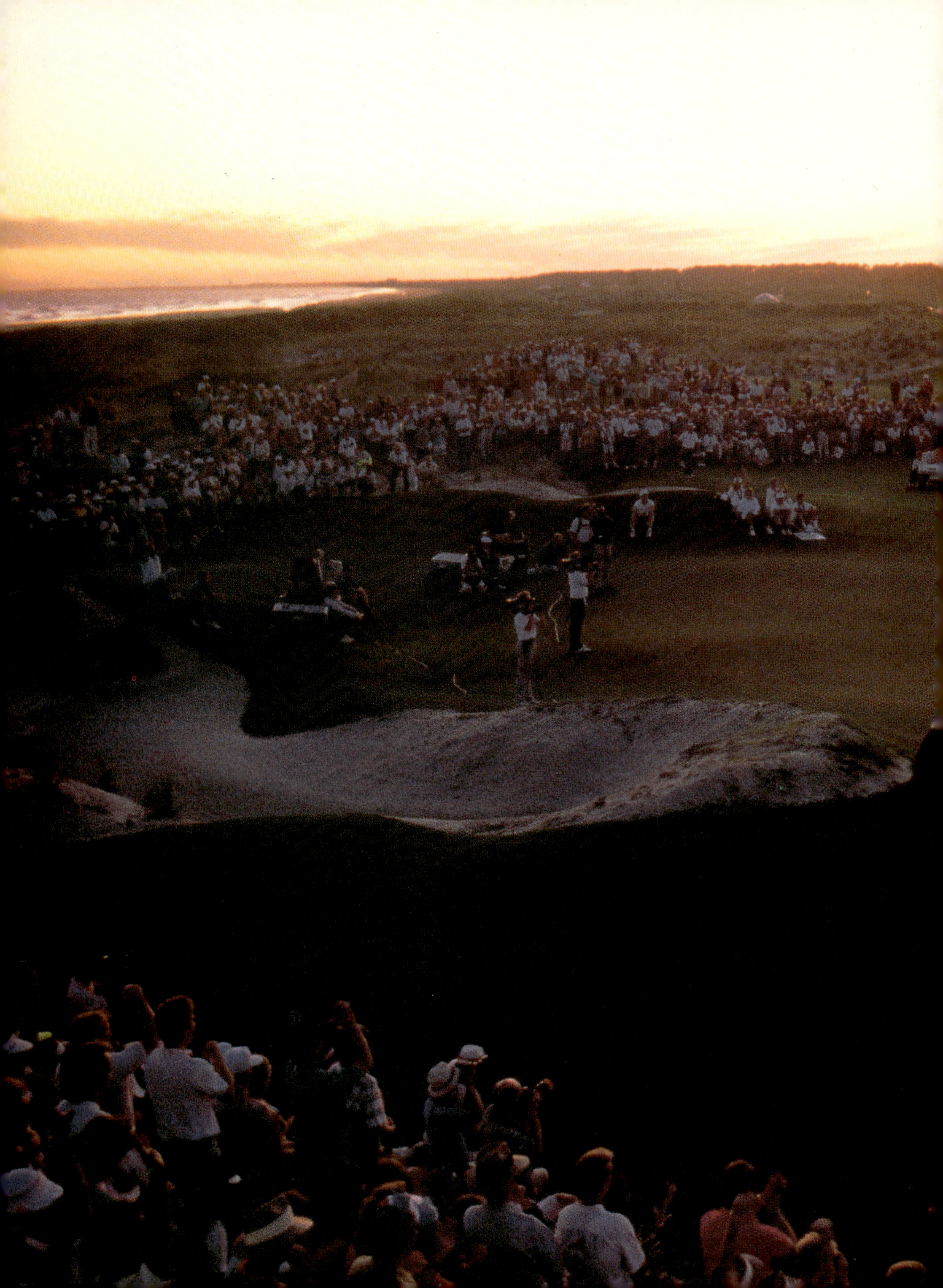

3
THE RYDER CUP

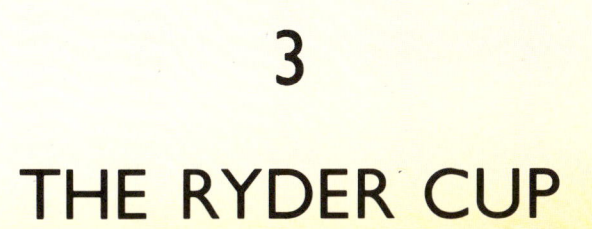

RYDER CUP HISTORY

United States 22, Great Britain/Europe 5, Ties 2

1927	Worcester CC, Worcester, Mass.	US 9½, Britain 2½
1929	Moortown, England	Britain 7, US 5
1931	Scioto CC, Columbus, Ohio	US 9, Britain 3
1933	Southport & Ainsdale, England	Britain 6½, US 5½
1935	Ridgewood CC, Ridgewood, NJ	US 9, Britain 3
1937	Southport & Ainsdale, England	US 8, Britain 4
	Ryder Cup not contested during World War II	
1947	Portland Golf Club, Portland, Ore.	US 11, Britain 1
1949	Ganton GC, Scarborough, England	US 7, Britain 5
1951	Pinehurst CC, Pinehurst, NC	US 9½, Britain 2½
1953	Wentworth, England	US 6½, Britain 5½
1955	Thunderbird Ranch & CC, Palm Springs, Ca.	US 8, Britain 4
1957	Lindrick GC, Yorkshire, England	Britain 7½, US 4½
1959	Eldorado CC, Palm Desert, Ca.	US 8½, Britain 3½
1961	Royal Lytham & St Anne's GC, St Anne's-on-the-Sea, England	US 14½, Britain 9½
1963	East Lake CC, Atlanta, Ga.	US 23, Britain 9
1965	Royal Birkdale GC, Southport, England	US 19½, Britain 12½
1967	Champions GC, Houston, Tex.	US 23½, Britain 8½
1969	Royal Birkdale GC, Southport, England	US 16, Britain 16 (TIE)
1971	Old Warson CC, St Louis, Mo.	US 18½, Britain 13½
1973	Muirfield, Scotland	US 18, Britain 13
1975	Laurel Valley GC, Ligonier, Pa.	US 21, Britain 11
1977	Royal Lytham & St Anne's GC, St Annes-on-the-Sea, England	US 12½, Britain 7½
1979	The Greenbrier, White Sulphur Springs, W. Va.	US 17, Europe 11
1981	Walton Heath GC, Surrey, England	US 18½, Europe 9½
1983	PGA National GC, Palm Beach Gdns, Fla.	US 14½, Europe 13½
1985	The Belfry, Sutton Coldfield, England	Europe 16½, US 11½
1987	Muirfield Village, Ohio	Europe 15, US 13
1989	The Belfry, Sutton Coldfield, England	Europe 14, US 14 (TIE)
1991	Kiawah Island, South Carolina	US 14½, Europe 13½

The 1981 US Ryder Cup team – generally considered to have been the strongest side in Ryder Cup history.

(Previous page) The sun sets over Kiawah Island on Ryder Cup Saturday.

THE 29th RYDER CUP

27–29 September 1991, Kiawah Island

'I couldn't breathe; I couldn't swallow. I could hardly hit the ball.' The words, not of a rookie professional drawn to play with Jack Nicklaus in the first round of an Open at St Andrews, but of a triple US Open champion, a player widely acknowledged as one of golf's toughest competitors. That is what the most emotion-charged finale in Ryder Cup history did to Hale Irwin last September. It melted his inner steel. And if that is what it did to Irwin what must it have been like for Bernhard Langer? To think that after two years of ever-increasing anticipation it all came down to a 6-foot putt on the final green of the final match: unparalleled drama – and in the most extraordinary and magical of settings too.

The Ocean Course at Kiawah Island is like no other course in the world – the perfect choice then for a unique occasion. The golf course – or is it a links? – floats on a bed of sand and scrub; the emerald fairways and greens are the island sanctuaries. Beyond the sandy wasteland there is either sea or marshland: the Atlantic on one flank, alligators on the other. Beautiful? Yes. Monstrously difficult? Yes again.

The United States were desperate to win back the Ryder Cup. For six long years it had resided on the wrong side of 'The Pond'. For six long years Americans had had to stomach pronouncements that its golfers, for so long the dominant force, were now second best. Kiawah Island was where they intended to bury European hegemony.

The opposing teams were like chalk and cheese. The American side reeked of maturity. Three of the team were in their forties, none was under thirty. They lacked an obvious leader in the Nicklaus, Palmer or Watson mould, but all twelve players were ranked among the top forty in the world. By contrast the European side had five players ranked in the world's top ten and seven others ranked somewhere between thirty and one hundred. Theirs was a much younger team with four players still in their twenties. America must be in the land of eternal youth for when US skipper Dave Stockton spoke of selecting a young player and an older one as his two 'Wild Card' choices, for young he meant thirty-five (Chip Beck) – only two of the European side were older than Beck. At thirty-four, Ballesteros is a mere spring chicken (not so much 'El Gran Señor', as 'El Pollo Joven').

Before the first ball was struck, Europe's new captain, Bernard Gallacher, had fewer decisions to make than his American counterpart. Two of his four pairings – for the first day's play at least – had been determined in advance. Nothing and no one was going to split up Ballesteros and Olazabal while logic also suggested that Woosnam and Faldo resume a partnership that had proved so successful in 1987 and 1989.

With the immense benefit of hindsight one can say that Gallacher erred in the morning but struck the right chord in the afternoon (the same could be said of his decisions on Saturday). Putting two rookies together in the first day foursomes was always going to be something of a gamble and unfortunately for Montgomerie and Gilford they had to make their débuts against the formidable pairing of Wadkins and Irwin. They were soundly beaten, but then the experienced Americans did produce some superb golf, birdieing five of the first eight holes – a feat no fourball team could achieve on Friday or Saturday. Langer and James had no luck either against a determined Floyd and Couples – they were four down after ten holes – and at one stage in the morning it looked possible, even probable, that both Europe's leading pairs would also lose. Faldo and Woosnam struggled on the greens and eventually were defeated on the 18th by Calcavecchia and Stewart. As for the Spaniards, when they walked to the 10th tee they were three down to Azinger and Beck, America's strongest pairing from the Belfry. Olazabal then started to play magnificently and Europe won the 10th, 12th, 13th and 15th before Ballesteros holed a 25-foot putt for a two at the 17th to secure Europe's solitary point of the morning. It was a poor start but it could have been a lot worse. After all, Europe had also lost the opening series 3–1 two years earlier.

For the afternoon fourball matches Gallacher brought in Feherty and Torrance in place of Montgomerie and Gilford and rested Langer in favour of big hitting Steven Richardson. The two new pairings gelled nicely: James and Richardson scored a convincing win over Calcavecchia and Pavin and Feherty and Torrance, dubbed the 'Celtic alliance', earned a very useful half against Wadkins and O'Meara.

Ballesteros and Olazabal were once again matched against Azinger and Beck and once again beat them 2 & 1. The Americans didn't play at all badly but they were up against an irresistible force. Again it was Olazabal who played the best golf with Ballesteros adding the occasional touches of brilliance. Robert Green described it nicely in *The Sunday Times*, when he wrote, 'If Ballesteros regularly inspires romantic associations with Don Quixote, for most of Friday's play Olazabal was cast in the role of Rozinante. Not that he played like a feeble horse, but he did carry Seve for much of the day.'

Woosnam and Faldo appeared more irascible than irresistible and were beaten for a second time. On this occasion defeat was inflicted by Butch Cassidy and the Sundance Kid, alias Ray Floyd and Fred Couples, who fired birdies instead of bullets and were nine under par for the sixteen holes played. What a marvellous day it had been for the forty-nine-year-old Floyd who had captained the American side in 1989, and for Couples too,

Ray Floyd and Fred Couples teamed up to win both their matches on Friday.

Who was carrying who? Europe's star performers, Ballesteros and Olazabal.

whose Cup début at the Belfry had ended in tears. So at the end of the first day it was 4½–3½ to the USA.

The matches on Saturday followed a similar pattern to those of the opening day. Europe lost the morning foursomes 3–1 but rallied in the afternoon's fourballs.

After their double failure on the first day, Gallacher felt he had no option but to break up the Woosnam–Faldo partnership, which in any event had come to look decidedly rocky by late Friday afternoon. He decided that Woosnam should sit out the morning's matches and in place of the Welshman he brought in David Gilford. Sadly, Faldo and Gilford proved to be not so much a deadly combination as a dead combination. It didn't work at all and they were trounced 7 & 6 by O'Meara and Azinger. James and Richardson lost by the narrowest of margins to Calcavecchia and Stewart and Feherty and Torrance fell apart on the back nine allowing Wadkins and Irwin to coast to a 4 & 2 victory. Yet again Gallacher's team found itself indebted to the brilliant Spaniards. Irresistible was beginning to look more like invincible as Ballesteros and Olazabal gunned down Floyd and Couples to make it three wins out of three. Between them Olazabal and Ballesteros had won 3 of Europe's 4½ points. The most significant statistic, however, was that the USA now had 7½ points.

It was beginning to look very ominous halfway through the second day . . . 'One European team cannot beat four American teams,' the cynics were saying. Well, the only European pair that didn't win on Saturday afternoon was Ballesteros and Olazabal; but even they managed to halve a thrilling match with Couples and Stewart, a game in which they fought back from two down with six to play and which finished not long before the sun set. The three European successes were James and Richardson (over Wadkins and Levi); Langer and Montgomerie (who defeated Pavin and Pate) and, perhaps most importantly of all, the top match in which Woosnam and Broadhurst (the latter making a belated first appearance) defeated the strong pairing of Azinger and Irwin. Broadhurst was something of a revelation, for though it was Woosnam who delivered the decisive blow – a brilliant bunker shot at the 17th – it was the young Englishman who played the superior golf. When the sun did set on Ryder Cup Saturday the scores were level at 8–8. Olazabal and Ballesteros had emerged from their four matches unbeaten and after the incredible European fightback on the second afternoon it was the players from the Old World who probably slept the more soundly.

Twelve singles matches on Sunday unfortunately became only eleven when the American, Steve Pate, withdrew injured. It meant that the luckless Gilford had to support his team from the sidelines and the first point of the day was shared. Undoubtedly the European player with most to prove was Faldo. He was unquestionably the best player in the world in 1989 and 1990 but his record after two days of the 1991 Ryder Cup read: played three – lost three. Notwithstanding his poor form, Gallacher sent Faldo out first on Sunday and he didn't disappoint. Drawn against Floyd, the player he defeated in the 1990 Masters play-off, Faldo won the first three holes and went four up at the 11th. Playing immediately behind Faldo and Floyd was the match between Feherty and Stewart, one America had clearly expected to win. For fourteen holes Feherty played superbly, in fact he was one under par and thus not

Paul Azinger, America's singles specialist – in 1989 he got the better of Ballesteros and at Kiawah he defeated Olazabal.

How dare it miss! This one got away but Seve remained undefeated in five matches.

Two of Europe's début makers, above: Colin Montgomerie; below: Paul Broadhurst.

Hale Irwin hits a weak pitch to the final green.

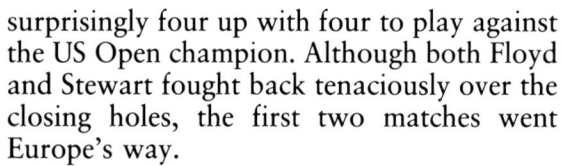

Langer's putt shaves the hole and the Ryder Cup is lost.

surprisingly four up with four to play against the US Open champion. Although both Floyd and Stewart fought back tenaciously over the closing holes, the first two matches went Europe's way.

Three and a half more points were needed for Europe to retain the Ryder Cup. The match between Ballesteros and Levi was only ever likely to have one result, and when Montgomerie snatched a sensational half point from Calcavecchia things were looking good for Gallacher's men. That Montgomerie managed to halve his match was incredible: Calcavecchia held a five hole advantage after the 9th and was still four up after the 14th. Montgomerie played the last four holes in three over par yet won all of them. A distraught 1989 Open champion hit two shots into the water at the 17th and then proceeded to miss a 2 foot putt for the match. He played those last four holes in eight over par.

As the afternoon progressed it looked increasingly as if America was going to win the last three singles matches and so Europe desperately needed to gain some points from its middle order. Surely Messrs Woosnam, Olazabal and Richardson could deliver? Unfortunately, they could not. The young Spaniard, who probably played the best golf of any of the twenty-four players at Kiawah Island, didn't look quite the same force without his inspirational partner at his side and came second in a marvellous 'ding dong' affair with Azinger; Woosnam and Richardson let their matches slip away from them on the back nine, both losing on the 17th to the phlegmatic Beck and the anything but phlegmatic Pavin respectively. Better

This is how you are treated when you captain your side to a famous victory: Stockton gets a ceremonial dunking from Messrs O'Meara, Stewart and Wadkins.

news was that Paul Broadhurst, the star of Saturday afternoon, had once again surprised the Americans by outplaying the hitherto undefeated Mark O'Meara. Faldo, Feherty, Ballesteros and Broadhurst; add the two half points from Montgomerie and Gilford, and Europe still needed one point from the last three matches. They required one point from one match when Torrance and James succumbed to America's two most successful players, Couples and Wadkins. In other words, Bernhard Langer had to beat Hale Irwin for the match to be tied overall – a half wouldn't be good enough.

At two down with four to play – Irwin had been ahead since the 8th – it looked a lost cause. Although the resolute German won the 15th it still seemed improbable when he faced a 7-foot putt to keep Europe's hopes alive on the 16th. But Langer bravely holed it and so the final match went on to the 17th – the 'cauldron of Kiawah'. When Irwin missed a putt of 10 feet the pressure was back on Langer. With an entire golfing continent rooting for him he coolly stroked in another 7 footer. All square – but remember, Langer had to win.

No one will ever forget what happened on the final hole. It was just asking too much of Langer to hole a third crucial putt in succession. As Ballesteros commented, 'Nobody in the world would have made that putt. Not even Jack Nicklaus in his prime. I certainly would not have holed it.' He later said of the match result, 'This hurts a lot. We wish the Ryder Cup was being held again in two weeks time.' What, a return to Pressure Cooker Island . . . was he serious?

THE 29TH RYDER CUP

27-29 September 1991
Kiawah Island

USA	MATCHES	EUROPE	MATCHES
Foursomes: Morning			
P. Azinger & C. Beck	0	S. Ballesteros & J.-M. Olazabal (2 & 1)	1
R. Floyd & F. Couples (2 & 1)	1	B. Langer & M. James	0
L. Wadkins & H. Irwin (4 & 2)	1	D. Gilford & C. Montgomerie	0
P. Stewart & M. Calcavecchia (1 hole)	1	N. Faldo & I. Woosnam	0
Fourballs: Afternoon			
L. Wadkins & M. O'Meara	½	S. Torrance & D. Feherty	½
P. Azinger & C. Beck	0	S. Ballesteros & J.-M. Olazabal (2 & 1)	1
C. Pavin & M. Calcavecchia	0	S. Richardson & M. James (5 & 4)	1
R. Floyd & F. Couples (5 & 3)	1	N. Faldo & I. Woosnam	0
Foursomes: Morning			
L. Wadkins & H. Irwin (4 & 2)	1	D. Feherty & S. Torrance	0
M. Calcavecchia & P. Stewart (1 hole)	1	M. James & S. Richardson	0
P. Azinger & M. O'Meara (7 & 6)	1	N. Faldo & D. Gilford	0
R. Floyd & F. Couples	0	S. Ballesteros & J.-M. Olazabal (3 & 2)	1
Fourballs: Afternoon			
P. Azinger & H. Irwin	0	I. Woosnam & P. Broadhurst (2 & 1)	1
C. Pavin & S. Pate	0	B. Langer & C. Montgomerie (2 & 1)	1
L. Wadkins & W. Levi	0	M. James & S. Richardson (3 & 1)	1
P. Stewart & F. Couples	½	S. Ballesteros & J.-M. Olazabal	½
Singles:			
S. Pate (withdrew injured)	½	D. Gilford	½
R. Floyd	0	N. Faldo (2 holes)	1
P. Stewart	0	D. Feherty (2 & 1)	1
M. Calcavecchia	½	C. Montgomerie	½
P. Azinger (2 holes)	1	J.-M. Olazabal	0
C. Pavin (2 & 1)	1	S. Richardson	0
W. Levi	0	S. Ballesteros (3 & 2)	1
C. Beck (3 & 1)	1	I. Woosnam	0
M. O'Meara	0	P. Broadhurst (3 & 1)	1
F. Couples (3 & 2)	1	S. Torrance	0
L. Wadkins (3 & 2)	1	M. James	0
H. Irwin	½	B. Langer	½
USA 14½		**EUROPE 13½**	

4

GLOBAL GOLF

EUROPE
THE UNITED STATES
AUSTRALASIA
JAPAN
THE REST OF THE WORLD
SENIORS
AMATEURS

EUROPE

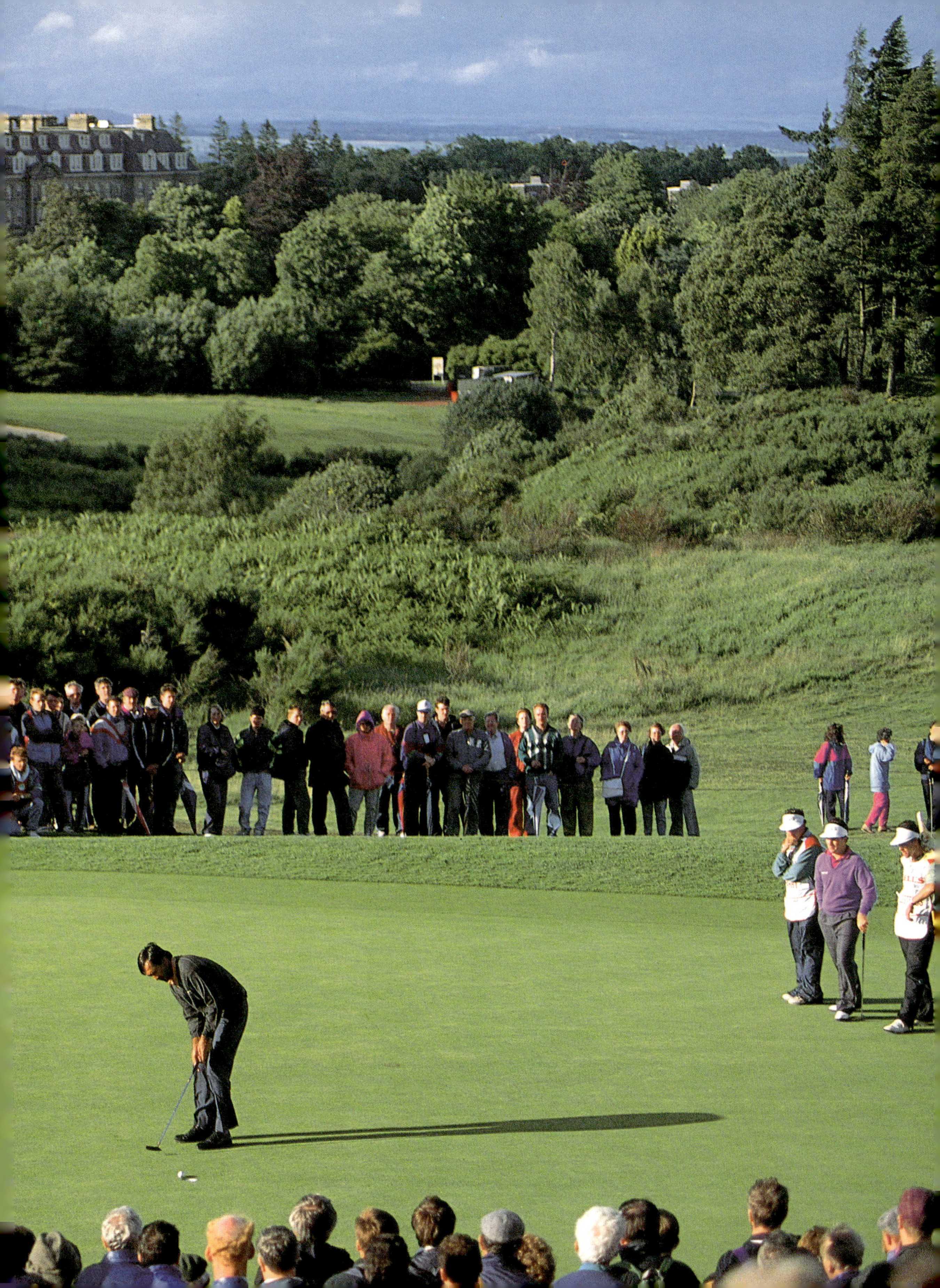

1991 VOLVO (PGA EUROPEAN) TOUR REVIEW

'He's over the hill,' they dared to suggest, 'lost the desire to win, the killer instinct.' They said it when he slumped to eighteenth position on 1990's Order of Merit and they reckoned they had proof when he began 1991's campaign with rounds of 73-75-78 in the Open de Baleares in March, and followed it up by missing the cut in the Catalan Open.

Ballesteros was a far from happy champion in 1990, yet he never doubted that his form would return (and we're proud that the *Benson and Hedges Golf Year* predicted he would 'bounce back in 1991', but how he bounced back!).

Seve's renaissance began during a fortnight's visit to Japan, very soon after his lack-lustre showing in The Masters. He finished third in the Dunlop Open, then won the Chunichi Crowns, one of the top events on the Japanese tour, and returned to Europe full of confidence. For the next few weeks he was simply rampant. He should have won the Spanish Open when a first round 63 put him five ahead of the field, but he eventually lost a play-off to Eduardo Romero at the 7th extra hole. No matter — two weeks later he won the European Tour's flagship event, the Volvo PGA championship at Wentworth, with rounds of 67-69-65-70 and within a week had added the Dunhill British Masters crown, after another devastating display where he scattered a high-class field with opening rounds of 66-66.

Of course he couldn't win every week but his level of play rarely slipped below the plimsoll line of brilliance during the remainder of the year. He easily finished leading moneywinner, amassing £545,353 and also recorded the lowest scoring average of 69.45. We knew this to be the authentic Ballesteros for he mixed dazzling strokeplay with occasional calamities. The great attraction of Ballesteros has always been that we have never been able to predict when he's going to crash a drive into the trees or, more likely, reel off a series of birdies and eagles.

He put together several sensational rounds in 1991 but he also threw away clear opportunities of victory in at least half a dozen tournaments. His above-mentioned 63 in Spain included an eagle-birdie-birdie finish and in the European Masters he concluded his final round of 63 with six successive birdies. There was a 62 in Monte Carlo, a 63 at Gleneagles and a 64 at the Scandinavian Open. He won none of these events and put himself in strong positions in the English, British and European Opens too before falling away on the last day. He didn't fall away, however, in the World Matchplay Championship, instead he produced one of the greatest performances of his life to win a record-equalling fifth title, and then of course there was his heroic, inspirational contribution in the Ryder Cup. In 1991 it was a privilege to watch Ballesteros play.

Back to the real world, who else had a great season in 1991? Financially speaking, many did, with no fewer than forty-three players collecting over £100,000 for their efforts. But perhaps two young players stood out from the crowd in terms of achievement, two who will look back at 1991 and reflect on a year when they not only broke through but made an astonishing impact; one is British, the other Swedish. They are Steven Richardson and Per-Ulrik Johansson.

Before 1991 Richardson had a reputation for hitting the ball the proverbial country mile but for not much else. After joining the Tour in 1990 his best finish of the season came at Valderrama in the final event of the year but he was still an unexpected winner of the opening event of 1991, the Gerona Open. Within

(Previous page) The Scottish Open at Gleneagles.

a month he had won the Portuguese Open as well and while there were no further victories, a string of high finishes throughout the year enabled him to claim second position on the Volvo Order of Merit, behind Ballesteros, but ahead of Faldo, Woosnam, Olazabal et al., with winnings of nearly £400,000.

Ballesteros has described Richardson as 'The next European superstar', and confirmation that he could play equally well overseas came with his top five finish in the USPGA Championship at Crooked Stick and his strong showing in the Ryder Cup. All this from a player who two years earlier wasn't considered good enough for the Walker Cup!

As Richardson was winning the season's curtain raiser at Gerona, Per-Ulrik Johansson was carrying his own bag in his first ever European Tour event. 1991 was Johansson's rookie year but he also mounted the winner's rostrum, winning the Belgian Open after a play-off with Paul Broadhurst (by which time he had earned sufficient kronor to afford the services of a caddie). The twenty-four-year-old Swede finished joint runner-up, with Bernhard Langer, to Payne Stewart in the Dutch Open and only narrowly missed making the Ryder Cup side when Broadhurst grabbed the final place in the last qualifying event. Johansson gained ample consolation when he guided Sweden to a famous Dunhill Cup triumph at St Andrews, his side defeating England (Faldo, Richardson and Broadhurst) *en route*. Nor was that all Johansson achieved last year, for in November he partnered Anders Forsbrand in the World Cup of Golf in Rome and together they snatched the title from under the noses of Seve's Spain and Woosnam's Wales. It was Sweden's first ever win in the event. And where was Johansson two years ago? Studying and playing golf (or perhaps playing golf and studying) in the same American University as US wonder-kid Phil Mickelson.

It was Mickelson who partnered Faldo in his first Major round of the year at Augusta. Not only did Nick fail to achieve a hat trick of wins in the Masters but more surprisingly he didn't really challenge in any of the year's 'Big Four' events. More surprisingly still, his

Per-Ulrik Johannson enjoyed a marvellous first year on Tour.

only European win of the year came in the Irish Open which, for the first time, was staged in the incomparably beautiful setting of Killarney. Some good performances late in the season enabled Faldo to squeeze into the top ten on the Order of Merit but by his exalted standards it was a most disappointing year for the former world number one.

In stark contrast to Faldo was Ian Woosnam. The leading moneywinner in Europe in 1990 had another quite tumultuous year. If his greatest successes occurred overseas, he still managed to win twice on the Volvo Tour in 1991, retaining two of the five titles he had won the previous year, namely the Mediterranean and Monte Carlo Opens.

After Faldo and Woosnam we must turn to Lyle. Surely the most popular tour win of 1991 was Sandy Lyle's triumph in the BMW International. It was his first success anywhere in three years and yet he did it in great style, leading from first to last. He opened with rounds of 65-65 but after a third round of 71 could not have slept too well on Saturday night knowing that the defending champion, Paul Azinger, was only one stroke behind him. He showed great nerve then in shooting a final round of 67 to win by three. The former Open and Masters champion had been hinting for much of the latter part of the season that a return to winning form was imminent: he featured prominently in the USPGA in August, then in September birdied the final hole at Walton Heath to finish second to Mike Harwood in the European Open and a week later fired a fourth round 62 in the European Masters at Crans-sur-Sierre. Lyle's victory may have occurred just a few weeks too late for him to win a trip to Kiawah Island but it must have brought him a wonderful sense of relief all the same.

In addition to Richardson, Faldo, Woosnam and Lyle, six other British golfers won tour events in 1991. Paul Broadhurst has already been mentioned: in fact he lost two play-offs during the year, the second to McNulty in the German Open, but he also registered a runaway seven-stroke victory in the Pro-Celebrity event at Hoylake. David Gilford earned his Ryder Cup spurs following a fine win in the English Open at the Belfry and Sam Torrance and David Feherty were victorious in the more agreeable surrounds of Jersey and Cannes. If Colin Montgomerie's rise to prominence – he finished an excellent fourth on the Order of Merit – was slightly more predictable than that of Richardson, his performances week in and week out were equally outstanding. The big Scot so nearly won the Volvo PGA Championship at Wentworth, losing at the first extra hole to Ballesteros (and only

Former Benson and Hedges International champion, Gordon Brand Jnr, plays out of sand at St Mellion.

The spectacular 10th green on Killarney's Killeen course – venue for the 1991 Irish Open.

then when Seve produced a stroke of pure genius), but gained perfect recompense when he finished one stroke ahead of the charging Spaniard in the Scandinavian Masters – netting a cool £100,000 in the process. Again like Richardson, he proved at Kiawah that Europe needn't be too concerned as to where its next generation of Ryder Cup stalwarts will come from.

The two least predictable British wins on Tour were provided by six foot three inch Westcountryman Andrew Sherborne, whose final round of 66 clinched the Madrid Open, and from Mark Davis who waltzed away with the Austrian Open title at Gut Altentann, an exacting Jack Nicklaus-designed course. There, Davis produced some of the best golf of the year, winning by five strokes and finishing nineteen under par. Although this occurred during Ryder Cup week it is doubtful whether any of Europe's absent 'top twelve' could have bettered his 269 total.

The opening British European Tour event of 1991 was staged on another Nicklaus-built course, his first in Britain. In April, St Mellion staged the twenty-first Benson and Hedges International and the gold trophy was passed from one great European golfer to another. In 1990 José-Maria Olazabal scored a one-stroke victory over Ian Woosnam in St Mellion's first B&H International and last year Bernhard Langer braved some thoroughly unpleasant weather to capture his first win in an event he has long been associated with. Many will recall that it was during the B&H tournament at Fulford ten years earlier that Bernhard went shinning up a tree to play his chip shot to the 17th green. Langer beat a very strong field at St Mellion last year including Faldo, Woosnam, Olazabal and McNulty, who arrived in Cornwall more or less direct from Augusta. The change of climate didn't suit the above four: Olazabal had two 71s but two 77s as well; the normally rock steady McNulty had an 80 in the third round; Faldo posted an 80 and an 82 in his middle two rounds and Woosnam opened with a pair of 82s!

The way in which he mastered St Mellion, it was hard to believe that Langer had also been playing at Augusta. Showing no signs of weariness, he defied the elements and put together rounds of 73-68-75-70 to win by two strokes from the Fijian, Vijay Singh. A back nine of 32 did the business for Bernhard and he finished in the grand manner with a birdie three at the last. Unlike 1990, there were no ducks encircling the green to greet the popular champion – perhaps it was too cold for them. (This year the Benson and Hedges International is to be played in May – hopefully amid brilliant sunshine!)

Langer's other European Tour victory in 1991 came in his 'own' golf tournament, the German Masters, an event he helps to promote. If Langer showed abundant courage and resilience to win at St Mellion, one wonders what words suffice to describe his achievement in winning a top class event the week immediately following the Ryder Cup – only seven days after *that* putt. The famous putt he failed to hole at Kiawah has been estimated at 6 feet; the one he holed to force a play-off with Rodger Davis in the German Masters was at least 12 feet. Langer won the play-off with Davis but fortunately for the Australian it was only three weeks before his turn came, for it was he who triumphed in the end-of-year jamboree at Valderrama.

In 1990 the Volvo Masters had been won by another Australian, Mike Harwood. The tall Queenslander had another successful year in 1991 finishing second in the Open at Birkdale (to an equally tall Queenslander), before going one better at Walton Heath in the European Open. It has been said many times recently that if Australasia could take part in the Ryder Cup they would field a very formidable side. In addition to the antipodean victories of Baker-Finch, Harwood and Davis, Craig Parry claimed two of Europe's national titles, the Scottish and Italian Opens, while

Mark McNulty spent much of the year injured but still retained his German Open title.

Kiwi, Frank Nobilo, took the prestigious Lancôme Trophy in Paris.

The international nature of the tour was further apparent with 'Rest of the World' victories being gained by Argentian Eduardo Romero, winner of both the French and Spanish Opens, and four tournaments by golfers from southern Africa – two by Zimbabweans, Mark McNulty and Tony Johnstone (the latter showing his penchant for Irish stout by

Bernhard Langer has always played some of his best golf surrounded by branches. Two European wins for Langer in 1991.

retaining the Murphy's Cup at Fulford), and two from springbok golfers, Gavin Levenson and Jeff Hawkes.

The sole American victory in Europe was gained by US Open champion Payne Stewart who showed everyone a clean pair of heels (in more ways than one) with a tremendous nine shot win in the Dutch Open at Noordwijk. If Stewart could have produced such blistering form – he compiled rounds of 67-68-62-70 (21 under par) – seven days earlier then he might well have given Baker-Finch a run for his money at Birkdale.

It didn't look as if anyone could equal or better Stewart's margin of victory until Olazabal regained his magical touch late in the season. The young Spaniard had won the Catalan Open in March by six shots but seemed to take a very long time getting over his near miss at Augusta three weeks later. Then, just one week before the Ryder Cup in September, he shot 64-68-67-66 at St Pierre in the Epson Grand Prix tournament. Timely wasn't the word! Moreover his margin of victory would have been a staggering ten shots but for Mark James holing a lengthy putt on the 72nd green. Still, to win a couple of European Tour events by six and nine strokes cannot be too shabby!

Before the season began many people had thought that Olazabal would either win a Major championship or finish number one in Europe; he achieved neither but his outstanding performances in the Ryder Cup proved beyond doubt that he is now a match for anyone. But, in Europe at least, 1991 will go down as the year when 'the other Spaniard', old 'Destino' himself, came back to prove the doubters wrong. And he didn't just prove them wrong, he knocked them for six! Ballesteros has now climbed to the summit of European golf on six occasions: six Vardon Trophies in sixteen seasons.

Can he make it seven in 1992? Don't dare bet against it!

An Argentinian reigns in Spain: Eduardo Romero wins the Spanish Open.

It's a hard life on Tour: Olazabal at Wentworth during the Volvo PGA Championship.

From poetry to farce: the many faces of Seve Ballesteros, Europe's number one.

1991 VOLVO TOUR RESULTS

21-24 February
GIRONA OPEN Club Golf de Pals, Girona

Steven Richardson	71	64	67	70	272	£41,660
Miguel Angel Jimenez	71	66	67	70	274	27,770
Jose Rivero	72	64	72	67	275	15,650
Per-Ulrik Johansson	70	68	71	68	277	12,500
Russell Claydon	71	72	67	68	278	10,600
Keith Waters	70	68	70	71	279	8,750
Miguel Angel Martin	75	69	68	68	280	6,087
Vijay Singh	72	70	68	70	280	6,087
Sam Torrance	70	67	72	71	280	6,087
Bill Longmuir	69	68	71	72	280	6,087

28 February - 3 March
FUJITSU MEDITERRANEAN OPEN Golf d'Esterel – Latitudes Saint Rafael, Nice, France

Ian Woosnam	70	71	71	67	279	£66,660
Michael McLean	66	70	73	71	280	44,440
José-Maria Olazabal	70	75	68	69	282	22,520
Miguel Angel Martin	73	70	68	71	282	22,520
Grant Turner	71	70	71	72	284	16,940
Miguel Angel Jimenez	72	74	71	68	285	10,046
Mark James	70	74	72	69	285	10,046
Guiseppe Cali	70	70	74	71	285	10,046
Chris Moody	71	71	72	71	285	10,046
Jean Van de Velde	74	71	69	71	285	10,046
Daniel Silva	72	76	63	74	285	10,046

7-10 March
OPEN DE BALEARES Santa Ponsa, Majorca

Gavin Levenson	72	74	67	69	282	£45,825
Steven Richardson	71	69	72	71	283	30,530
José-Maria Olazabal	68	72	71	73	284	17,215
Costantino Rocca	70	72	73	70	285	11,676
Miguel Angel Martin	69	71	71	74	285	11,676
Stephen Bennett	73	67	71	74	285	11,676
Malcolm Mackenzie	70	70	76	72	288	6,369
Miguel Fernandez	70	76	70	72	288	6,369
Tony Johnstone	72	73	72	71	288	6,369
Miguel Angel Jimenez	75	71	71	71	288	6,369
Johan Rystrom	73	70	72	73	288	6,369

14-17 March
CATALAN OPEN Club de Golf, Bonmont Terres Noves, Tarragona

José-Maria Olazabal	66	68	64	73	271	£50,000
David Feherty	71	73	61	72	277	33,330
Michael McLean	68	69	68	73	278	18,780
Steven Richardson	72	67	69	71	279	13,850
Eduardo Romero	67	70	70	72	279	13,850
Malcolm Mackenzie	70	71	68	74	283	10,500
Anders Forsbrand	74	71	68	71	284	8,250
Giuseppe Cali	70	70	68	76	284	8,250
Santiago Luna	66	71	73	75	285	6,345
Miguel Angel Jimenez	72	68	68	77	285	6,345
Manuel Moreno	71	73	70	72	286	5,520

21-24 March
PORTUGUESE OPEN Estela, Rio Alto, Oporto, Portugal

Steven Richardson	71	67	71	74	283	£45,825
Vicente Fernandez	73	70	76	67	286	30,530
Jimmy Heggarty	72	76	71	68	287	17,215
Roger Winchester	74	72	72	70	288	11,676
Martin Poxon	73	69	75	71	288	11,676
Brian Barnes	72	72	70	74	288	11,676
Per-Ulrik Johansson	71	69	70	79	289	8,250
Jean Van de Velde	74	67	79	70	290	6,517
Wayne Riley	72	69	77	72	290	6,517
Ronan Rafferty	73	70	81	67	291	5,096
Chris Moody	72	76	70	73	291	5,096
Philip Parkin	75	72	70	74	291	5,096

28-31 March
VOLVO OPEN DI FIRENZE Ugolino, Florence

Anders Forsbrand	71	72	66	65	274	£33,330
Barry Lane	68	69	67	71	275	22,220
Mark Roe	70	73	68	66	277	11,260
Sam Torrance	69	68	69	71	277	11,260
Mats Lanner	70	65	70	73	278	8,470
Johan Rystrom	72	68	70	69	279	7,000
Phil Golding	71	69	71	69	280	5,500
Mark James	77	68	66	69	280	5,500
Santiago Luna	72	71	70	68	281	3,760
Adam Hunter	69	67	73	72	281	3,760
Peter Smith	69	70	69	73	281	3,760
Paul Curry	67	71	69	74	281	3,760
Gordon Brand Jnr	69	72	65	75	281	3,760

11-14 April
JERSEY EUROPEAN AIRWAYS OPEN La Moye, Jersey

Sam Torrance	68	69	69	73	279	£33,330
Mark Davis	72	71	66	71	280	22,220
Mats Lanner	72	69	68	73	282	10,330
Anders Sorensen	70	67	70	75	282	10,330
Jeff Hawkes	70	65	73	74	282	10,330
Christy O'Connor Jnr	75	68	68	73	284	5,615
Colin Montgomerie	71	69	71	73	284	5,615
James Spence	67	73	69	75	284	5,615
Craig Parry	70	65	75	74	284	5,615

18-21 April
BENSON AND HEDGES INTERNATIONAL OPEN, St Mellion Golf & Country Club, Cornwall

Bernhard Langer	73	68	75	70	286	£66,660
Vijay Singh	74	75	69	70	288	44,440
Philip Walton	70	69	77	73	289	22,520
Jose Rivero	72	73	67	77	289	22,520
Mark Roe	74	72	73	71	290	13,235
Craig Parry	75	74	70	71	290	13,235
Gordon Brand Jnr	72	74	69	75	290	13,235
Steven Richardson	73	75	73	69	290	13,235
Costantino Rocca	75	74	73	73	295	8,920
David Feherty	77	73	74	72	296	6,960
Joakim Haeggman	76	75	78	67	296	6,960
Barry Lane	76	73	72	75	296	6,960
Peter Senior	75	76	73	72	296	6,960
Glen Day	75	76	71	74	296	6,960
Christy O'Connor Jnr	71	76	77	73	297	5,640
José-Maria Olazabal	72	77	71	77	297	5,640
Paul Curry	73	77	70	77	297	5,640
David Williams	75	78	75	70	298	4,766
Greg J. Turner	79	73	71	75	298	4,766
Mark McNulty	75	72	80	71	298	4,766
Sandy Lyle	74	82	70	72	298	4,766
Andrew Sherborne	75	74	75	74	298	4,766
Eduardo Romero	72	74	79	73	298	4,766

25-28 April
MADRID OPEN Real Club de la Puerta de Hierro, Madrid

Andrew Sherborne	70	67	69	66	272	£45,825
Miguel Angel Martin	69	67	67	70	273	30,530
Mark James	71	72	67	65	275	17,215
Vijay Singh	71	68	70	67	276	13,750
Mats Lanner	72	66	70	69	277	11,655
Des Smyth	72	69	70	67	278	9,625

Steven Richardson won twice in 1991 and finished second on the Volvo Order of Merit.

Santiago Luna	74	66	71	68	279	7,095
Paul Curry	70	67	74	68	279	7,095
David Feherty	70	68	73	68	279	7,095
Glenn Ralph	71	70	67	72	280	5,280
Darren Clarke	70	71	70	69	280	5,280

2-5 May
CREDIT LYONNAIS CANNES OPEN Cannes Mougins G.C.

David Feherty	69	68	69	69	275	£58,330
Craig Parry	72	71	67	68	278	38,880
Mark McNulty	70	66	70	73	279	21,910
Steven Richardson	72	70	66	72	280	17,500
Eamonn Darcy	70	70	70	71	281	13,540
Jean Ignace Mouhica	68	70	72	71	281	13,540
Costantino Rocca	68	75	68	71	282	9,625
Stephen Hamill	67	70	74	71	282	9,625
Mark Roe	71	69	71	72	283	7,086
Adam Hunter	77	67	70	69	283	7,086
Haydn Selby-Green	72	71	69	71	283	7,086

1991 VOLVO TOUR RESULTS

9-12 May
PEUGEOT SPANISH OPEN *Club de Campo, Madrid*

*Eduardo Romero	68	63	72	72	275	£58,330
Severiano Ballesteros	63	70	67	75	275	38,880
Vijay Singh	68	71	71	70	280	21,910
Ross McFarlane	72	69	70	70	281	16,165
Bernhard Langer	69	73	68	71	281	16,165
Glen Day	70	67	76	70	283	12,250
Steven Richardson	75	69	70	70	284	10,500
Sam Torrance	74	67	70	74	285	8,750
Colin Montgomerie	73	68	71	74	286	7,820
Joakim Haeggman	77	66	70	74	287	5,930
Josie Davila	70	73	72	72	287	5,930
Robert Lee	74	69	74	70	287	5,930
Tony Johnstone	73	73	69	72	287	5,930
Michael McLean	73	71	71	72	287	5,930
Rodger Davis	70	75	72	70	287	5,930

16-19 May
LANCIA-MARTINI ITALIAN OPEN *Castel Conturbia, Nr Milan*

Craig Parry	71	71	67	70	279	£54,212
Ian Woosnam	69	71	73	67	280	36,120
Costantino Rocca	69	73	74	66	282	20,370
Martin Gates	71	71	73	70	285	15,033
David Gilford	70	70	71	74	285	15,033
Stephen McAllister	72	70	73	71	286	10,575
Paul Way	68	73	75	70	286	10,575
Colin Montgomerie	71	72	72	72	287	8,135
José-Maria Olazabal	70	79	73	66	288	6,898
Chris Cookson	72	73	68	75	288	6,898
Wayne Riley	68	75	77	69	289	5,987

24-27 May
VOLVO PGA CHAMPIONSHIP *Wentworth, Surrey*

*Severiano Ballesteros	67	69	65	70	271	£83,330
Colin Montgomerie	69	66	69	67	271	55,550

The shot of the year perhaps? Ballesteros plays his second shot to the 1st green during the PGA Championship play-off with Montgomerie: Seve's 220 yard 5 iron finished 2 feet from the flag.

Eamonn Darcy	69	66	70	67	272	31,300
Bernhard Langer	67	67	69	70	273	25,000
Jesper Parnevik	73	67	65	69	274	19,350
Nick Faldo	69	70	65	70	274	19,350
Gordon Brand Jnr	66	69	71	70	276	15,000
Rodger Davis	71	66	68	72	277	10,710
José Rivero	69	70	69	69	277	10,710
Johan Rystrom	68	69	68	72	277	10,710
Sandy Lyle	71	72	69	65	277	10,710
Ian Woosnam	70	70	66	72	278	8,590
Peter Teravainen	67	71	74	67	279	7,845
David Feherty	70	73	70	66	279	7,845
Anders Forsbrand	71	70	73	66	280	6,760
Wayne Riley	63	71	71	75	280	6,760
Stephen Field	69	68	71	72	280	6,760
Brian Barnes	68	70	68	74	280	6,760
Steven Richardson	69	66	74	71	280	6,760

30 May-2 June
DUNHILL BRITISH MASTERS *Woburn G&CC*

Severiano Ballesteros	66	66	68	75	275	£75,000
Tony Johnstone	67	75	68	68	278	27,096
Eamonn Darcy	69	67	71	71	278	27,096
Sam Torrance	70	68	71	69	278	27,096
Keith Waters	69	67	73	69	278	27,096
David Gilford	72	72	65	69	278	27,096
Ross McFarlane	72	69	72	67	280	13,500
Tony Charnley	73	70	66	72	281	11,250
Ian Woosnam	71	69	71	71	282	9,110
Peter O'Malley	70	69	73	70	282	9,110
Gordon Brand Jnr	68	72	75	67	282	9,110
Brett Ogle	69	71	75	68	283	6,532
Philip Walton	69	70	73	71	283	6,532
Stephen McAllister	74	70	69	70	283	6,532
Brian Barnes	72	72	69	70	283	6,532
Costantino Rocca	70	71	69	73	283	6,532
Vijay Singh	71	70	72	70	283	6,532
Ronan Rafferty	75	67	72	69	283	6,532
Mark Calcavecchia	70	66	74	73	283	6,532

6-9 June
MURPHY'S CUP *Fulford, York*

*Tony Johnstone	10	9	9	12	40	£58,330
Eamonn Darcy	13	9	11	7	40	38,860
Stephen Field	15	12	7	4	38	19,705
Peter O'Malley	10	6	8	14	38	19,705
Ross McFarlane	9	15	8	5	37	13,540
Peter Baker	5	12	10	10	37	13,540
Sam Torrance	8	10	3	14	35	10,500
Martin Poxon	6	6	8	14	34	8,765
Adam Hunter	4	11	8	9	32	7,071
Jay Townsend	2	10	12	8	32	7,071
Colin Montgomerie	7	9	9	7	32	7,071
Ian Woosnam	14	6	4	7	31	5,608
Mike Harwood	13	15	3	0	31	5,608
José Rivero	16	4	4	7	31	5,608

Craig Parry, Australian winner of the Scottish and Italian Open titles.

13-16 June
RENAULT BELGIAN OPEN *Royal Waterloo, Brussels*

*Per-Ulrik Johansson	68	70	70	68	276	£41,660
Paul Broadhurst	67	71	69	69	276	27,770
Chris Williams	70	73	70	64	277	15,650
Jorge Berendt	70	71	70	67	278	12,500
Robert Karlsson	70	69	68	73	280	10,600
Daniel Silva	73	66	71	71	281	7,500
Mats Lanner	75	72	65	69	281	7,500
Bill Longmuir	71	69	72	69	281	7,500
Eoghan O'Connell	74	70	69	69	282	5,300
Costantino Rocca	70	72	70	70	282	5,300

1991 VOLVO TOUR RESULTS

20-23 June
CARROLL'S IRISH OPEN *Killarney, Co. Kerry*

Nick Faldo	68	75	70	70	283	£60,960
Colin Montgomerie	68	72	76	70	286	40,640
Carl Mason	69	73	76	69	287	20,594
Frank Nobilo	72	70	74	71	287	20,594
Ross Drummond	75	75	69	69	288	14,147
José-Maria Olazabal	71	70	75	72	288	14,147
Craig Parry	69	78	72	70	289	10,059
Philip Walton	74	72	72	71	289	10,059
Russell Claydon	69	75	72	74	290	7,123
Eduardo Romero	73	77	71	69	290	7,123
Howard Clark	74	73	75	68	290	7,123
David Feherty	77	73	75	65	290	7,123
Christy O'Connor Jnr	76	70	77	68	291	5,889
Peter O'Malley	71	71	79	71	292	5,486
Mark Davis	69	76	76	71	292	5,486

27-30 June
PEUGEOT FRENCH OPEN *National Golf Club, Paris*

Eduardo Romero	69	69	67	76	281	£66,660
José-Maria Olazabal	74	67	68	74	283	34,740
Sam Torrance	72	70	72	69	283	34,740
Nick Faldo	73	73	67	71	284	20,000
Robert Lee	70	74	74	67	285	16,940
Colin Montgomerie	75	68	73	70	286	11,230
Paul Broadhurst	72	68	74	72	286	11,230
Gordon Brand Jnr	72	70	74	70	286	11,230
Vijay Singh	70	70	73	73	286	11,230
Mark James	79	70	72	66	287	7,170
Steven Richardson	73	72	70	72	287	7,170
Sandy Lyle	71	72	70	74	287	7,170
Santiago Luna	71	72	69	75	287	7,170

3-6 July
TORRAS MONTE CARLO OPEN *Mont Agel, Monte Carlo*

Ian Woosnam	67	66	61	67	261	£66,927
Anders Forsbrand	72	62	66	65	265	44,618
Mats Lanner	67	67	69	63	266	19,071
Peter Mitchell	67	65	67	67	266	19,071
Vijay Singh	68	69	67	62	266	19,071
Rodger Davis	68	62	67	69	266	19,071
Jeff Hawkes	66	65	71	65	267	11,044
Vicente Fernandez	71	66	63	67	287	11,044
Chris Williams	70	66	65	67	268	8,955
Jean Van de Velde	65	69	68	67	269	7,198
Sandy Stephen	65	62	71	71	269	7,198
Johan Rystrom	66	70	65	68	269	7,198
Severiano Ballesteros	62	69	69	69	269	7,198

10-13 July
BELL'S SCOTTISH OPEN *Gleneagles Hotel (King's Course)*

Craig Parry	65	67	69	67	268	£83,330
Mark McNulty	65	68	70	66	269	55,550
David Gilford	68	67	71	65	271	31,300
Danny Mijovic	64	66	73	69	272	25,000
José Rivero	67	68	72	66	273	19,350
Mats Lanner	65	66	72	70	273	19,350
Colin Montgomerie	65	68	72	69	274	15,000
Severiano Ballesteros	63	68	71	73	275	11,825
Rodger Davis	69	69	67	70	275	11,825
Ian Woosnam	69	69	69	69	276	10,000
Mark James	65	70	74	68	277	8,606
David Feherty	69	63	73	72	277	8,606
Jean Van de Velde	69	70	69	69	277	8,606
Barry Lane	66	66	72	74	278	7,500
Nick Faldo	66	69	72	71	278	7,500
Steven Richardson	66	69	78	66	279	6,900
James Spence	69	70	70	70	279	6,900
Gordon Brand Jnr	67	72	71	70	280	6,216
Peter O'Malley	66	71	72	71	280	6,216
Jay Don Blake	70	69	69	72	280	6,216

18-21 July
120TH OPEN CHAMPIONSHIP *Royal Birkdale*
See pp.62-3.

25-28 July
HEINEKEN DUTCH OPEN *Noordwijk*

Payne Stewart	67	68	62	70	267	£83,330
Per-Ulrik Johansson	78	67	62	69	276	43,425
Bernhard Langer	63	71	69	73	276	43,425
Peter Fowler	72	69	66	71	278	23,100
Peter Mitchell	65	71	70	72	278	23,100
Brett Ogle	72	68	65	74	279	12,556
Fred Couples	68	74	69	68	279	12,556
Steven Richardson	67	77	69	66	279	12,556
David Feherty	70	69	71	69	279	12,556
John Hawksworth	71	70	67	71	279	12,556
Danny Mijovic	67	67	70	75	279	12,556
José Rivero	69	71	68	72	280	8,315
Mike Harwood	69	68	72	71	280	8,315
José-Maria Olazabal	67	72	71	71	281	7,500
Johan Rystrom	72	67	69	73	281	7,500

1-4 August
SCANDINAVIAN MASTERS *Drottningholms, Sweden*

Colin Montgomerie	68	65	70	67	270	£100,000
Severiano Ballesteros	70	64	73	64	271	66,660
Robert Karlsson	71	65	68	68	272	33,780
Ian Woosnam	67	69	63	73	272	33,780

David Feherty	71	67	70	65	273	25,400
Brett Ogle	75	66	63	70	274	13,800
Steven Richardson	66	69	71	68	274	13,800
Per-Ulrik Johansson	70	66	71	67	274	13,800
Mark McNulty	71	65	69	69	274	13,800
David James	68	65	68	73	274	13,800
Russell Claydon	70	70	69	65	274	13,800
Fred Couples	74	61	71	68	274	13,800
Paul Broadhurst	65	69	71	69	274	13,800
Klas Eriksson	72	68	66	68	274	(Am.)
Peter Mitchell	70	67	69	69	275	9,000
Rodger Davis	71	68	69	67	275	9,000

8-11 August
EUROPEAN PRO-CELEBRITY *Royal Liverpool, Hoylake*

Paul Broadhurst	67	70	69	66	272	£41,660
Ronan Rafferty	68	72	69	70	279	27,770
Keith Waters	70	70	71	69	280	14,075
Christy O'Connor Jnr	70	67	72	71	280	14,075
Peter Smith	75	67	72	67	281	10,600
Steven Bowman	70	71	71	72	284	8,750
Peter Fowler	72	70	70	73	285	6,450
David A. Russell	70	72	75	68	285	6,450
Fredrik Lindgren	68	75	72	70	285	6,450

15-18 August
NM ENGLISH OPEN *The Belfry G&CC*

David Gilford	70	71	67	70	278	£75,000
Roger Chapman	69	66	74	71	280	50,000
Steven Richardson	71	70	68	73	282	25,335
Severiano Ballesteros	70	71	70	71	282	25,335
Per-Ulrik Johansson	69	73	69	73	284	17,405
Rodger Davis	71	73	71	69	284	17,405
Grant Turner	77	71	70	67	285	13,500
Peter Baker	73	73	69	71	286	9,264
Mark James	66	70	74	76	286	9,264
Craig Parry	74	73	74	65	286	9,264
Glenn Joyner	73	73	68	72	286	9,264
Peter Mitchell	75	69	71	71	286	9,264
Derrick Cooper	74	73	73	67	287	7,240
Jesper Parnevik	68	74	75	71	288	6,340
Magnus Persson	75	72	70	71	288	6,340
Michael McLean	76	71	72	69	288	6,340
James Spence	74	74	74	66	288	6,340
Ronan Rafferty	79	67	71	71	288	6,340

22-25 August
VOLVO GERMAN OPEN *Hubbelrath, Düsseldorf*

*Mark McNulty	68	67	72	66	273	£87,500
Paul Broadhurst	73	67	68	65	273	58,275
Sam Torrance	69	67	69	72	277	29,550

Mark Davis gained his first Tour victory in Austria.

David J. Russell	72	70	69	66	277	29,550
Ronan Rafferty	70	70	67	71	278	18,795
Barry Lane	71	66	73	68	278	18,795
Daniel Silva	72	72	67	67	278	18,795
Rick Hartman	70	67	73	69	279	11,265
Rodger Davis	70	69	69	71	279	11,265
Costantino Rocca	73	70	69	67	279	11,265
Ross McFarlane	69	72	72	66	279	11,265
Vijay Singh	67	71	71	71	280	8,750
Mark James	70	73	67	70	280	8,750

29 August-1 September
GA EUROPEAN OPEN *Walton Heath, Surrey*

Mike Harwood	70	72	70	65	277	£83,330
Sandy Lyle	74	69	69	67	279	51,550
John Bland	69	74	70	67	280	25,833
Payne Stewart	73	69	70	68	280	25,833
Severiano Ballesteros	70	70	70	70	280	25,833
Brett Ogle	76	68	70	67	281	14,037
Paul Broadhurst	71	70	71	69	281	14,037
Craig Parry	70	69	71	71	281	14,037
Peter Fowler	69	69	72	71	281	14,037
Glen Day	70	72	74	66	282	9,595
Rick Hartmann	72	74	68	68	282	9,595
Des Smyth	71	77	68	67	283	7,736
Mark James	71	76	68	68	283	7,736
Martin Poxon	70	73	70	70	283	7,736
Stephen McAllister	70	69	72	72	283	7,736
Costantino Rocca	72	68	69	74	283	7,736
Frank Nobilo	72	74	72	66	284	6,466
Nick Faldo	74	71	70	69	284	6,466
Michael McLean	70	70	74	70	284	6,466

1991 VOLVO TOUR RESULTS

5-8 September
CANON EUROPEAN MASTERS – SWISS OPEN
Crans-sur-Sierre

Jeff Hawkes	68	69	65	66	268	£73,972
Severiano Ballesteros	69	67	70	63	269	49,285
Peter Teravainen	71	68	64	67	270	27,795
Philip Walton	68	71	66	66	271	22,200
Paolo Quirici	72	67	66	67	272	15,895
Patrick Hall	69	67	68	68	272	15,895
Malcolm Mackenzie	69	69	66	68	272	15,895
Carl Mason	68	68	69	68	273	9,524
Jean Van de Velde	71	68	65	69	273	9,524
Mark McNulty	68	68	68	69	273	9,524
Steven Richardson	69	69	66	69	273	9,524
Vijay Singh	70	65	70	69	274	6,449
Lanny Wadkins	70	70	67	67	274	6,449
Howard Clark	67	72	68	67	274	6,449
Gordon Brand Jnr	64	74	69	67	274	6,449
Mats Lanner	69	69	66	70	274	6,449
Glenn Ralph	65	71	72	66	274	6,449
Eduardo Romero	68	65	70	71	274	6,449
Marc Farry	73	65	66	70	274	6,449

12-15 September
LANCOME TROPHY *St Nom-la-Bretèche, La Tuilerie*

Frank Nobilo	65	68	69	65	267	£75,000
David Gilford	67	68	68	65	268	29,932
James Spence	68	68	64	68	268	29,932
Ian Baker-Finch	68	65	68	67	268	29,932
Peter Fowler	66	67	68	67	268	29,932
Colin Montgomerie	64	69	68	68	269	15,750
Ronan Rafferty	67	68	69	66	270	13,500
Jesper Parnevik	73	65	65	68	271	10,100
John Bland	67	68	67	69	271	10,100
Nick Faldo	67	67	68	69	271	10,100
Steven Richardson	68	72	63	69	272	7,676
John Morse	68	68	66	70	272	7,676
Rodger Davis	71	65	65	71	272	7,676

19-22 September
EPSON GRAND PRIX OF EUROPE *St Pierre G&CC, Chepstow*

José-Maria Olazabal	64	68	67	66	265	£75,000
Mark James	70	64	70	70	274	50,000
Miguel Angel Martin	69	68	68	72	277	28,180
Michael McLean	65	73	72	68	278	20,775
Tony Johnstone	71	70	67	70	278	20,775
Peter Teravainen	71	70	69	69	279	14,625
James Spence	67	70	71	71	279	14,825

After three years in the wilderness, Sandy Lyle found his form late in the season to win the BMW International.

José Rivero	70	68	69	73	280	9,270
Russell Claydon	71	68	71	70	280	9,270
Ronan Rafferty	70	69	68	73	280	9,270
Jesper Parnevik	72	71	68	69	280	9,270
Malcolm Mackenzie	71	74	67	68	280	9,270

26-29 September
MITSUBISHI AUSTRIAN OPEN *Gut Altentann G&CC, Salzburg*

Mark Davis	66	66	71	66	269	£41,660
Michael McLean	71	68	71	64	274	27,770
Russell Claydon	68	70	71	66	275	12,916
Marc Farry	66	70	73	66	275	12,916
Vijay Singh	66	68	73	68	275	12,916
Santiago Luna	69	72	70	66	277	8,125
Sandy Lyle	70	69	72	66	277	8,125
Greg J. Turner	67	71	70	70	278	5,925
Craig Parry	71	70	71	66	278	5,925
Tony Johnstone	70	69	72	68	279	5,000

Rodger Davis, winner of the Volvo Masters at Valderrama.

3-6 October
MERCEDES GERMAN MASTERS *Stuttgarter, Monsheim*

*Bernhard Langer	68	72	67	68	275	£83,330
Rodger Davis	73	72	65	65	275	55,550
Nick Faldo	67	71	67	72	277	31,300
Mike Harwood	71	74	62	71	278	21,233
José-Maria Olazabal	71	64	72	71	278	21,233
Jean Van de Velde	68	72	68	70	278	21,233
David Feherty	69	74	69	67	279	12,883
Malcolm Mackenzie	70	67	71	71	279	12,883
Peter Mitchell	70	71	67	71	279	12,883
Vicente Fernandez	67	71	72	70	280	10,000
Paul Way	72	71	68	70	281	8,164
Steven Richardson	67	71	69	74	281	8,164
Brett Ogle	75	70	67	69	281	8,164
Ronan Rafferty	76	71	69	65	281	8,164
Gordon Brand Jnr	72	71	68	70	281	8,164

10-13 October
BMW INTERNATIONAL OPEN *Golfplatz Munchen, Nord-Eichenried, Munich*

Sandy Lyle	65	65	71	67	268	£66,660
Tony Johnstone	67	70	67	67	271	44,440
Peter Fowler	66	69	70	67	272	25,040
Paul Azinger	65	73	64	71	273	15,735
Mark Mouland	69	68	69	67	273	15,735
Tom Purtzer	69	68	68	68	273	15,735
Rodger Davis	67	69	68	69	273	15,735
Peter Baker	69	70	68	67	274	10,000
David Gilford	67	70	68	70	275	7,286
Joakim Haeggman	68	70	70	67	275	7,286
David J. Russell	66	68	70	71	275	7,286
Roger Chapman	68	69	71	67	275	7,286
Magnus Sunesson	65	70	68	72	275	7,286
Martin Gates	68	71	69	67	275	7,286

24-27 October
VOLVO MASTERS *Valderrama, Sotogrande*

Rodger Davis	68	73	68	71	280	£100,000
Nick Faldo	72	70	71	68	281	66,660
Bernhard Langer	70	69	70	74	283	37,560
Severiano Ballesteros	72	73	69	70	284	25,750
Steven Richardson	68	70	76	70	284	25,750
Mark James	67	72	72	73	284	25,750
Costantino Rocca	72	67	72	75	286	18,500
Mark McNulty	71	71	74	71	287	15,500
Craig Parry	71	69	73	75	288	12,560
Sandy Lyle	71	73	73	71	288	12,560
James Spence	70	74	73	71	288	12,560
Frank Nobilo	74	65	75	75	289	10,123
José-Maria Olazabal	73	72	74	70	289	10,123
Barry Lane	71	72	72	74	289	10,123
Gordon Brand Jnr	74	71	72	73	290	9,000
Colin Montgomerie	73	72	72	73	290	9,000

* Winner in play-off.

1991 PGA EUROPEAN TOUR WINNERS SUMMARY

February	*DUNHILL CUP WORLD QUALIFIER	Canada/Paraguay	
	GIRONA OPEN	Steven Richardson	(Eng)
	FUJITSU MEDITERRANEAN OPEN	Ian Woosnam	(Wales)
March	OPEN DE BALEARES	Gavin Levenson	(SA)
	OPEN CATALONIA	José-Maria Olazabal	(Spa)
	PORTUGUESE OPEN	Steven Richardson	(Eng)
	VOLVO OPEN DI FIRENZE	Anders Forsbrand	(Swe)
April	JERSEY EUROPEAN AIRWAYS OPEN	Sam Torrance	(Sco)
	BENSON AND HEDGES INTERNATIONAL OPEN	Bernhard Langer	(Ger)
	MADRID OPEN	Andrew Sherborne	(Eng)
May	CREDIT LYONNAISE CANNES OPEN	David Feherty	(N Ire)
	PEUGEOT SPANISH OPEN	Eduardo Romero	(Arg)
	LANCIA MARTINI ITALIAN OPEN	Craig Parry	(Aus)
	VOLVO PGA CHAMPIONSHIP	Severiano Ballesteros	(Spa)
	DUNHILL BRITISH MASTERS	Severiano Ballesteros	(Spa)
June	MURPHY'S CUP	Tony Johnstone	(Zimb)
	RENAULT BELGIAN OPEN	Per-Ulrik Johansson	(Swe)
	CARROLLS IRISH OPEN	Nick Faldo	(Eng)
	PEUGEOT FRENCH OPEN	Eduardo Romero	(Arg)
July	TORRAS MONTE CARLO GOLF OPEN	Ian Woosnam	(Wales)
	BELL'S SCOTTISH OPEN	Craig Parry	(Aus)
	*SENIORS BRITISH OPEN	Bobby Verwey	(SA)
	120TH OPEN CHAMPIONSHIP	Ian Baker-Finch	(Aus)
	HEINEKEN DUTCH OPEN	Payne Stewart	(USA)
August	SCANDINAVIAN MASTERS	Colin Montgomerie	(Sco)
	EUROPEAN PRO-CELEBRITY	Paul Broadhurst	(Eng)
	NM ENGLISH OPEN	David Gilford	(Eng)
	VOLVO GERMAN OPEN	Mark McNulty	(Zimb)
	GA EUROPEAN OPEN	Mike Harwood	(Aus)
September	CANON EUROPEAN MASTERS-SWISS OPEN	Jeff Hawkes	(SA)
	LANCOME TROPHY	Frank Nobilo	(NZ)
	*EQUITY AND LAW CHALLENGE	Brian Marchbank	(Sco)
	EPSON GRAND PRIX OF EUROPE	José-Maria Olazabal	(Sp)
	*RYDER CUP	USA	
	MITSUBISHI AUSTRIAN OPEN	Mark Davis	(Eng)
October	MERCEDES GERMAN MASTERS	Bernhard Langer	(Ger)
	*DUNHILL CUP	Sweden	
	BMW INTERNATIONAL OPEN	Sandy Lyle	(Sco)
	* UAP UNDER 25s EUROPEAN OPEN	Paul McGinley	(Ire)
	*TOYOTA WORLD MATCH PLAY	Severiano Ballesteros	(Spa)
	TOUR SCHOOL PRE-QUALIFYING II	Andrew Hare	(Eng)
	VOLVO MASTERS	Rodger Davis	(Aus)

* PGA European Tour Approved Special Events

1991 PGA EUROPEAN TOUR

VOLVO ORDER OF MERIT: TOP 100

1	S. Ballesteros (Spain)	£545,353		51	M. A. Jimenez (Spain)	85,951
2	S. Richardson (England)	393,155		52	G. Levenson (S Africa)	85,901
3	B. Langer (Germany)	372,703		53	C. Mason (England)	84,120
4	C. Montgomerie (Scotland)	343,575		54	J. Rystrom (Sweden)	73,975
5	C. Parry (Australia)	328,116		55	D. Williams (England)	73,903
6	R. Davis (Australia)	317,441		56	J. Bland (S Africa)	72,891
7	J.-M. Olazabal (Spain)	302,270		57	P. Way (England)	72,255
8	I. Woosnam (Wales)	257,433		58	B. Ogle (Australia)	71,642
9	D. Gilford (England)	249,240		59	D. Smyth (Ireland)	68,835
10	N. Faldo (England)	245,892		60	S. Luna (Spain)	68,409
11	M. McNulty (Zimbabwe)	230,061		61	G. Day (US)	66,428
12	M. Harwood (Australia)	223,856		62	R. Karlsson (Sweden)	66,428
13	Vijay Singh (Fiji)	221,997		63	D. Mijovic (Canada)	63,370
14	D. Feherty (N. Ireland)	218,389		64	P. Senior (Australia)	62,522
15	P. Broadhurst (England)	217,751		65	M. Poxon (England)	61,990
16	S. Torrance (Scotland)	206,592		66	R. McFarlane (England)	61,011
17	E. Romero (Argentina)	203,303		67	P. Baker (England)	58,888
18	E. Darcy (Ireland)	196,280		68	H. Clark (England)	54,326
19	T. Johnstone (Zimbabwe)	196,015		69	G. Ralph (England)	53,831
20	M. McLean (England)	193,899		70	R. Lee (England)	53,711
21	M. James (England)	189,304		71	P. Price (Wales)	53,047
22	S. Lyle (Scotland)	185,510		72	S. McAllister (Scotland)	52,731
23	P.-U. Johansson (Sweden)	180,161		73	P. Curry (England)	52,062
24	F. Nobilo (NZ)	163,446		74	C. O'Connor Jnr (Ireland)	51,989
25	M. Martin (Spain)	145,512		75	D. Silva (Portugal)	51,799
26	C. Rocca (Italy)	144,861		76	G. Turner (England)	51,065
27	J. Rivero (Spain)	143,174		77	J. Harggman (Sweden)	50,736
28	P. Mitchell (England)	139,708		78	M. Clayton (Australia)	50,119
29	J. Spence (England)	139,198		79	B. Barnes (Scotland)	48,015
30	A. Forsbrand (Sweden)	135,955		80	M. Gates (England)	46,993
31	G. Brand Jnr (Scotland)	135,778		81	C. Williams (England)	44,961
32	P. Fowler (Australia)	133,192		82	R. Drummond (Scotland)	44,899
33	B. Lane (England)	129,809		83	D. Cooper (England)	44,773
34	M. Lanner (Sweden)	124,637		84	A. Sorensen (Denmark)	44,537
35	R. Rafferty (N. Ireland)	118,251		85	C. Moody (England)	43,859
36	J. Hawkes (S. Africa)	117,987		86	J. M. Canizares (Spain)	43,851
37	V. Fernandez (Argentina)	112,707		87	M. Mouland (Wales)	40,497
38	P. Teravainen (US)	110,566		88	G. J. Turner (NZ)	39,962
39	P. Walton (Ireland)	108,415		89	P. Hall (England)	39,953
40	R. Chapman (England)	106,191		90	J. Heggarty (Ireland)	39,699
41	M. Mackenzie (England)	102,966		91	R. Hartmann (US)	39,210
42	J. Van de Velde (France)	102,294		92	M. Farry (France)	38,988
43	A. Sherborne (England)	101,704		93	S. Field (England)	38,671
44	M. Davis (England)	99,733		94	S. Bowman (US)	37,817
45	M. Roe (England)	96,547		95	T. Charnley (England)	37,095
46	K. Walters (England)	95,707		96	P. Smith (Scotland)	37,030
47	R. Claydon (England)	90,466		97	M. Sunnesson (Sweden)	37,007
48	J. Parnevik (Sweden)	90,267		98	B. Marchbank (Scotland)	36,121
49	D. J. Russell (England)	89,382		99	G. Cali (Italy)	35,931
50	P. O'Malley (Australia)	88,944		100	J. Hobday (S Africa)	35,913

THE DUNHILL CUP

10–13 October, St Andrews

Gary Player first came to St Andrews in 1955. He was only nineteen and legend has it he was so broke that he spent his first night sleeping in the dunes – if the truth be known he was probably practising his bunker play. Four years later he was the Open champion and within twenty-five years he'd won nine Major championships. His last grandslam victory was in 1978 at Augusta; a mixed year, therefore, for South African golf for it was also the last year that the country was represented in international team golf – last before the 1991 Dunhill Cup, that is. If it was fitting that South Africa should re-emerge after thirteen years in the golfing wilderness at St Andrews, the 'Home of Golf', then it was even more appropriate that the country should be led by its greatest golfing ambassador, notwithstanding the fact that last October Gary Player was approaching his fifty-sixth birthday.

It was a foggy occasion. The famous St Andrews haar hung over the links for most of the week. But although it interrupted the golf, indeed caused the cancellation of Friday's play, it didn't prevent this seventh Dunhill Cup from being a memorable occasion.

The first day's matches produced a number of shocks and, very nearly, the elimination of many of the favourites. The one big name that did fall was Australia, the joint favourites, who were beaten by the underrated Canadians. Scotland were given a scare by Italy and only went through when Gordon Brand Jnr won his match against Alberto Binaghi on the fifth extra hole and the USA only just overcame Korea following the defeat of double US Open champion, Curtis Strange, by one Choi Sang Ho. South Africa's international return appeared as if it was going to be a very brief one until John Bland holed a 45 foot putt at the second play-off hole to save himself against Paolo Quirci. Fortunately for Messrs Frost and Player, Bland won the next.

The more straightforward first round results were England's victory over Thailand, Sweden's over Taipei, and Ireland's over Paraguay. Finally Wales narrowly overcame Spain (no Ballesteros or Olazabal, sadly) in another match requiring extra holes.

With the second day's play being called off it meant that both the quarter-final and semi-final matches had to be played on the Saturday. Scotland were drawn against Ireland in the morning and trounced them 3–0; it was not a good day for the Irish as, later the same day, just a few miles down the road at Murrayfield, Scotland's rugby team also trounced Ireland in a World Cup quarter-final. England, the losing finalists in 1990, were eliminated by Sweden, the key match being Per-Ulrik Johansson's defeat of Nick Faldo. In a low scoring game Wales got the better of Canada 2–1 but the biggest surprise of the morning was South Africa's 2–1 triumph over the USA. Fred Couples easily beat Gary Player (67–74) but David Frost and John Bland gained single-stroke victories over Steve Pate and Curtis Strange respectively. The Americans had only themselves to blame as it was their decision to match Couples, their best player on current form, with arguably South Africa's weakest link. Of course it also meant that the St Andrews crowd could see no more of Couples' colourful caddie. Dressed from head to toe in shocking pink and carrying her husband's bag was Debbie Couples. 'Truth,' somebody once said, 'is like a torch which gleams through the fog.' On Saturday morning at St Andrews it was Fred's wife.

South Africa were a revelation in the semi-final. Now it was poor Scotland, for there was little they could do as the Springboks scorched around The Old Course in a combined total of thirteen under par. Bland defeated Colin Montgomerie 69–72, Player beat Brand 70–74 while Frost gave Sam Torrance a veritable

Fog at St Andrews, but nothing was going to dampen Gary Player's enthusiasm.

roasting, winning by 64–70. After spending thirteen years on the sidelines, South Africa had made it into the Dunhill Cup final at the first attempt. The three players may have slept contentedly that night but they didn't know who their final opponents were until the following morning. Sweden and Wales fought out a real cliff-hanger on Saturday afternoon. Captain Woosnam beat Johansson 65–68 (Woosnam was twelve under par for his day's golf) but both his team mates' matches finished level, Parkin and Forsbrand each scoring 68s and Price and Lanner, 71s. There was not sufficient light to conclude the ties and unfortunately for Woosnam the Swedes won both play-offs on the Sunday morning.

The conclusion of Saturday's business and the continuing poor weather caused the final to be reduced to eighteen holes. David Frost and John Bland had been playing so well all week that South Africa probably started as slight favourites. Frost was especially on song and he comfortably won his game against Johannson 68–74. His four round total for the week was 272, only two strokes more than Nick Faldo's winning score in the 1990 Open. Forsbrand levelled things by winning his match against Bland on the final green by 68–69; it was a fine game in which both players birdied the 18th – Bland from about 10 inches and Forsbrand, courageously from about 8 feet, knowing he must sink his putt to win.

So it was all down to Player and Lanner. The Swede was in control for most of the round and came into the final stretch two ahead with five to play. But Player refused to surrender (did he ever?) and Lanner still needed to hole a two-and-a-half footer on the 18th for the Cup. Amazingly, Lanner did a Doug Sanders but unlike the American's miss in 1970 it will not be remembered for long as he made an 8-foot putt for a winning birdie at the first play-off hole. Player had come so close; South Africa had come so close; but Sweden had deservedly won its first major international team trophy and, after collecting one hundred thousand pounds each it is reasonable to assume that there were no Swedes sleeping in the dunes that night.

THE DUNHILL CUP

10-13 October, St Andrews (Old Course)

First round

Canada	2	–	1	Australia
South Africa	2	–	1	Switzerland
England	3	–	0	Thailand
Ireland	3	–	0	Paraguay
Scotland	2	–	1	Italy
Wales	2	–	1	Spain
USA	2	–	1	Korea
Sweden	2	–	1	Chinese Team Taipei

First-round losers received £7,500 each

Second round

South Africa	2	–	1	USA
Scotland	3	–	0	Ireland
Sweden	2	–	0	England
Wales	2	–	1	Canada

Second-round losers received £15,000 each

Semi finals

South Africa 3 – 0 Scotland
David Frost (64) beat Sam Torrance (70)
Gary Player (70) beat Gordon Brand Jnr (74)
John Bland (69) beat Colin Montgomerie (72)

Sweden 2 – 1 Wales
Per-Ulrik Johansson (68) lost to Ian Woosnam (65)
Anders Forsbrand (68) beat Philip Parkin (68)
  on the 3rd play-off hole
Mats Lanner (71) beat Philip Price (71)
  on the 5th play-off hole

Play-off for 3rd and 4th places

Scotland 2 – 0 Wales
Sam Torrance (70) beat Ian Woosnam (71)
Colin Montgomerie (69) beat Philip Parkin (70)
Gordon Brand Jnr (69) halved with Philip Price (69)

FINAL

SWEDEN 2 – 1 SOUTH AFRICA
Anders Forsbrand (68) beat John Bland (69)
Per-Ulrik Johansson (74) lost to David Frost (68)
Mats Lanner (74) beat Gary Player (74)
  on the 1st play-off hole

Victory for Sweden as Forsbrand, Johannson and Lanner pose with the Dunhill Cup.

Wales received £26,666 each
Scotland received £36,666 each

South Africa received £50,000 each
Sweden received £100,000 each

TOYOTA WORLD MATCHPLAY CHAMPIONSHIP

17–20 October, Wentworth (West Course)

This was the 28th World Matchplay Championship but the first to be sponsored by Toyota. The field was not as strong as in 1990 – 'What, no Olazabal!' screamed the headlines on the eve of the championship – but it was a class field none the less with five of the top ten in the world rankings present, and a very international field too with the twelve competitors representing eight different countries and five continents. The absence of Olazabal was indeed unfortunate given that he was ranked number two in the world going into the Wentworth event and had proved himself a brilliant head-to-head combatant so recently at Kiawah Island. Commenting on the Spaniard's omission last October, Mitchell Platts wryly remarked in *The Times*, 'Toyota would not expect such an elementary error on its car assembly line.'

The four seeded players, and the ones who therefore received byes into the quarter-finals, were the defending champion and Masters winner, Ian Woosnam (1); Nick Faldo, the winner in 1989 (2); the current Open champion, Ian Baker-Finch (3) and the four-time World Matchplay champion, Seve Ballesteros (4).

Mention of Wentworth in October usually throws up images of glorious autumnal colours accompanied, of course, by glorious Indian summer weather. The colours weren't bad last year but the weather was pretty foul: cold, damp and very windy. It was difficult enough battling against the elements let alone being able to play good golf. The first round matches reflected this and none of the games was close. As expected, Fred Couples always had the upper hand against the Japanese golfer, Naomichi 'Joe' Ozaki, and won comfortably; Billy Andrade, an engaging young American who won twice on the US Tour in 1991, overcame his compatriot, Tom Purtzer, the player voted 'America's sweetest swinger' by his peers; and in a rematch of their epic encounter at Kiawah, Colin Montgomerie crushed Mark Calcavecchia 5 & 4 (he was 8 up at one stage). The best golf of the day was played by Nick Price who defeated Europe's brightest new star, Steven Richardson.

Price's reward for beating Richardson was a quarter-final match with Ian Baker-Finch. So it was to be 1991's Canadian Open champion from Zimbabwe versus its British Open champion from Australia. Baker-Finch was probably a little preoccupied at Wentworth as his wife had recently provided little Hayley Baker-Finch with a sister. In any event, Price was too good for him and always looked in control during a 3 & 2 victory.

American extrovert Billy Andrade beat Ian Woosnam 7 & 6 on Friday.

Billy Andrade surprised everyone, including himself, one suspects, when he went 5 up after ten holes against Ian Woosnam: when Woosnam putts well he's unbeatable; when he putts atrociously . . . he loses 7 & 6. It was a demonstration of how not to defend a title. The player whom Woosnam succeeded as World Matchplay champion in 1990, and as Masters champion in 1991, Nick Faldo, had just enough in reserve to beat Montgomerie at the second extra hole but the quarter-final game most people wanted to see was between Ballesteros and Couples. Although this was Fred's first appearance at Wentworth he was enjoying his best ever year and had been America's top performer in the Ryder Cup; Seve was playing in his sixteenth consecutive World Matchplay but was said to be not feeling too well and arguably Couples started as favourite. Once again, though, it was a case of 'beware the sick golfer' as Seve won 3 & 1. So American hopes of having a first Matchplay champion since Bill Rogers in 1979 rested with Billy Andrade. (Remember Bill Rogers?)

Who should Andrade have to face in the semi-finals but Ballesteros. It was 'Billy versus Bally', although given the winter hats both players donned it looked more like 'Bill versus Ben'. Andrade made many friends with his outgoing, cheery approach but it was the vastly more experienced Spaniard who triumphed 3 & 2. The other semi-final was between the two 'Nicks' – Faldo and Price. At the beginning of the season only a fool would have backed Price to win but there was almost an air of inevitability as the Zimbabwean out-putted (and in most departments of the game outplayed) the Englishman to record an emphatic 5 & 3 victory.

The weather improved for Sunday's final and the quality of the golf certainly stepped up a gear in response to the occasion. Ballesteros versus Price: it was Royal Lytham, 1988 all over again. Few will ever forget that titanic struggle, nor the manner in which Seve emerged victorious to claim his third Open Championship. Now he was after his fifth World Matchplay title and he faced Price who was playing probably the best golf of his life.

Three birdies in the first four holes put Price 3 up; with another at the 7th he was out in 31 and still 3 up. Most players would buckle against such golf but Ballesteros' answer was to come home in 31 for an approximate round of 65 to bring the match back to all square at lunch. After five holes of the afternoon round it was Ballesteros who was 3 up and he had just covered his last fourteen holes in 8 under par. To his credit Price never gave up but Seve didn't drop a stroke to par – something he managed to avoid doing all day – and maintained his lead to win 3 & 2.

Under a heading, 'Ballesteros comes close to perfection', Michael Williams of the *Daily Telegraph* described the Spaniard's golf as 'an exhibition that must rank as one of the finest of even his glittering career.' Seve had waited six years to equal Gary Player's record of five victories in the event; coming one month after his outstanding display in the Ryder Cup it proved beyond doubt that whatever the quality of the field at Wentworth, Seve Ballesteros *is* the world's matchplay champion.

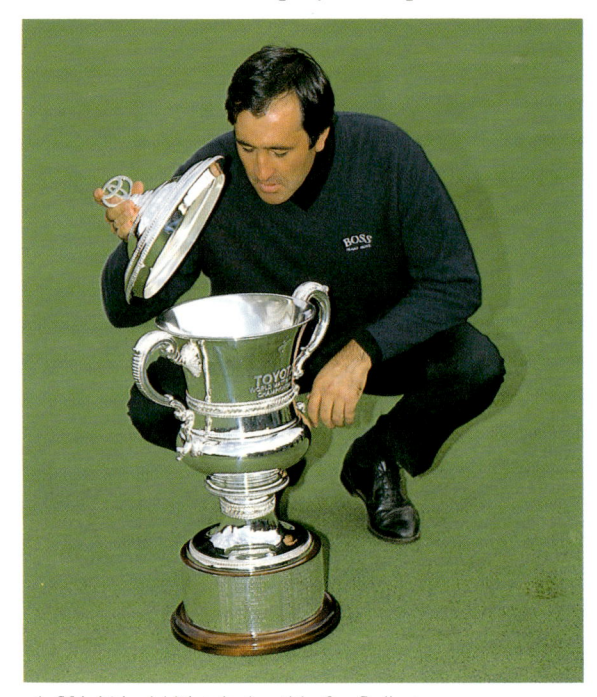

A fifth World Matchplay title for Ballesteros.

TOYOTA WORLD MATCHPLAY CHAMPIONSHIP

17–20 October The Wentworth Club (West Course)

First round
BILLY ANDRADE (USA) beat TOM PURTZER (USA) 3 and 2
FRED COUPLES (USA) beat NAOMICHI 'JOE' OZAKI (Japan) 4 and 3
COLIN MONTGOMERIE (Sco) beat MARK CALCAVECCHIA (USA) 5 and 4
NICK PRICE (Zim) beat STEVEN RICHARDSON (Eng) 5 and 3
   First-round losers received £20,000

Second round
BILLY ANDRADE beat IAN WOOSNAM (Wales) 7 and 6
SEVE BALLESTEROS (Sp) beat FRED COUPLES 3 and 1
NICK FALDO (Eng) beat COLIN MONTGOMERIE at 38TH
NICK PRICE beat IAN BAKER-FINCH (Aus) 3 and 2
   Second-round losers received £25,000

Semi-finals
SEVE BALLESTEROS beat BILLY ANDRADE 3 and 2
NICK PRICE beat NICK FALDO 5 and 3

Play-off for 3rd and 4th places
NICK FALDO beat BILLY ANDRADE 5 and 3
   Faldo received £45,000; Andrade £35,000

FINAL
SEVE BALLESTEROS beat NICK PRICE 3 and 2
   Ballesteros won £150,000, Price received £90,000

Nick Price surrenders to Ballesteros on the 34th hole of their final.

1991 WPG EUROPEAN TOUR REVIEW

To win a British Open championship in 1991 you had to have a double-barrelled name; common, elementary names like Watson or Davies just wouldn't suffice. It is fair to describe Ian Baker-Finch's win in the men's championship at Birkdale as a surprise result; Penny Grice-Whittaker's success at Woburn in the Weetabix-sponsored Women's British Open was nothing short of remarkable. In fact, it was a win of Dalyesque proportions.

The British Open is easily the most sought-after title on the Women's European Tour and from 1992 it is to be accredited 'Major championship' status. Yet on the Monday before last year's championship Grice-Whittaker was playing in the pre-qualifying event. She had up until then, competed in five European Tour events and missed the cut in four of them. Before the first ball was struck in the championship she was the player occupying one hundredth place on the Woolmark Order of Merit. Despite all this she won comfortably – well, by three strokes anyway – and it would have been by a much greater margin had she not run up an horrendous five over par 9 on the 13th hole during the third round. It was the fairy tale, rags to riches story of the year, perhaps of any year.

If you cannot parade a double-barrelled name then to be raised in Queensland, Australia would appear to be the next best thing. Corrine Dibnah, like Baker-Finch, hails from Australia's Sunshine State and Dibnah, too, had a wonderful year in 1991, finishing the season as the tour's leading moneywinner with official earnings of £89,058. The 1988 British Open champion was the only player to win three tournaments and she won them in three different countries: the BMW Masters in Belgium, the La Manga Club Classic

It was a veritable annus mirabilis *for Penny Grice-Whittaker.*

Australia's Corinne Dibnah (right) and Sweden's Helen Alfredsson, Europe's number one and number two in 1991.

in Spain and the Italian Open in Venice.

1991 saw the retirement of Joe Flanagan, the WPGE Tour's Executive Director since 1988 and the appointment in his place, late in the season, of Andrea Doyle. Her major priorities will doubtless be to increase the number of tournaments – in 1991 there were fifteen 'regular' events – and to try to encourage the Tour's 'leading lights' to play as much of their golf in Europe as possible; the one is, of course, heavily dependent on the other.

Among those names one would include in any list of 'leading lights' are Sweden's Helen Alfredsson and Belgium's Florence Descampe, both of whom won their LPGA (American) Tour cards last October.

In only her third season on the European Tour, Alfredsson came second on the Order of Merit and chased Dibnah all the way to the finishing post. She was the year's most consistent golfer with nine top ten finishes in twelve starts. Alfredsson made a fine defence of her British Open title, scoring a final day 69 for a share of second place with Diane Barnard behind Grice-Whittaker, and also won successive events in June: capturing the prestigious Hennessy Cup after an exciting play-off with Dibnah and Marie-Laure de Lorenzi and the Trophee Coconut Skol at St Germain.

Florence Descampe, still only twenty-two, won the Lufthansa German Open with arguably the best round of the year, a course record-equalling closing 64. Her round contained nine birdies, including three in a row at the beginning and two at the end – a finish with a flourish from Florence.

British players were very successful in 1991. Laura Davies won the first event of the season, April's Valextra Classic in Rome (by which time she had already won in America) and came runner-up to Suzanne Strudwick a week later in the AGF Open in Paris. Scotland's Dale Reid had another excellent year, collecting two tour victories, both on English soil. The first of these was in early May when she won the Ford Classic at Woburn after a tremendous tussle with Alison Nicholas (who for once didn't win a tournament but did pick up the Vivien Saunders award for maintaining the lowest scoring average). The second Reid success was a most convincing triumph in the Bloor Homes Eastleigh Classic at Fleming Park; those wins were Reid's twentieth and twenty-first on tour.

During August and September the Tour celebrated a Swedish win in Sweden – Lottie Neumann taking the IBM title in Stockholm – an English victory in the English Open – Katrina Douglas' play-off success over Switzerland's Evelyn Orley – and an Italian win in the Woolmark Matchplay which was staged at Carimate near Milan. Federica Dassu was the very popular local winner of the Matchplay, overcoming Reid by 5 & 4 in the final.

The final event of the season produced a marvellous head-to-head contest between Laura Davies and Penny Grice-Whittaker. The pair pulled away from the field in the second round when Grice-Whittaker scored a superb 63 and Davies holed in one *en route* to a 66. All square going up the 18th on the final day, the new British Open champion rifled a 9 iron to within 3 feet of the flag for a winning birdie. It was a marvellous double-barrelled salvo to finish, and a fitting conclusion to a momentous year for women's golf in Europe ... roll on the Solheim Cup!

Florence Descampe.

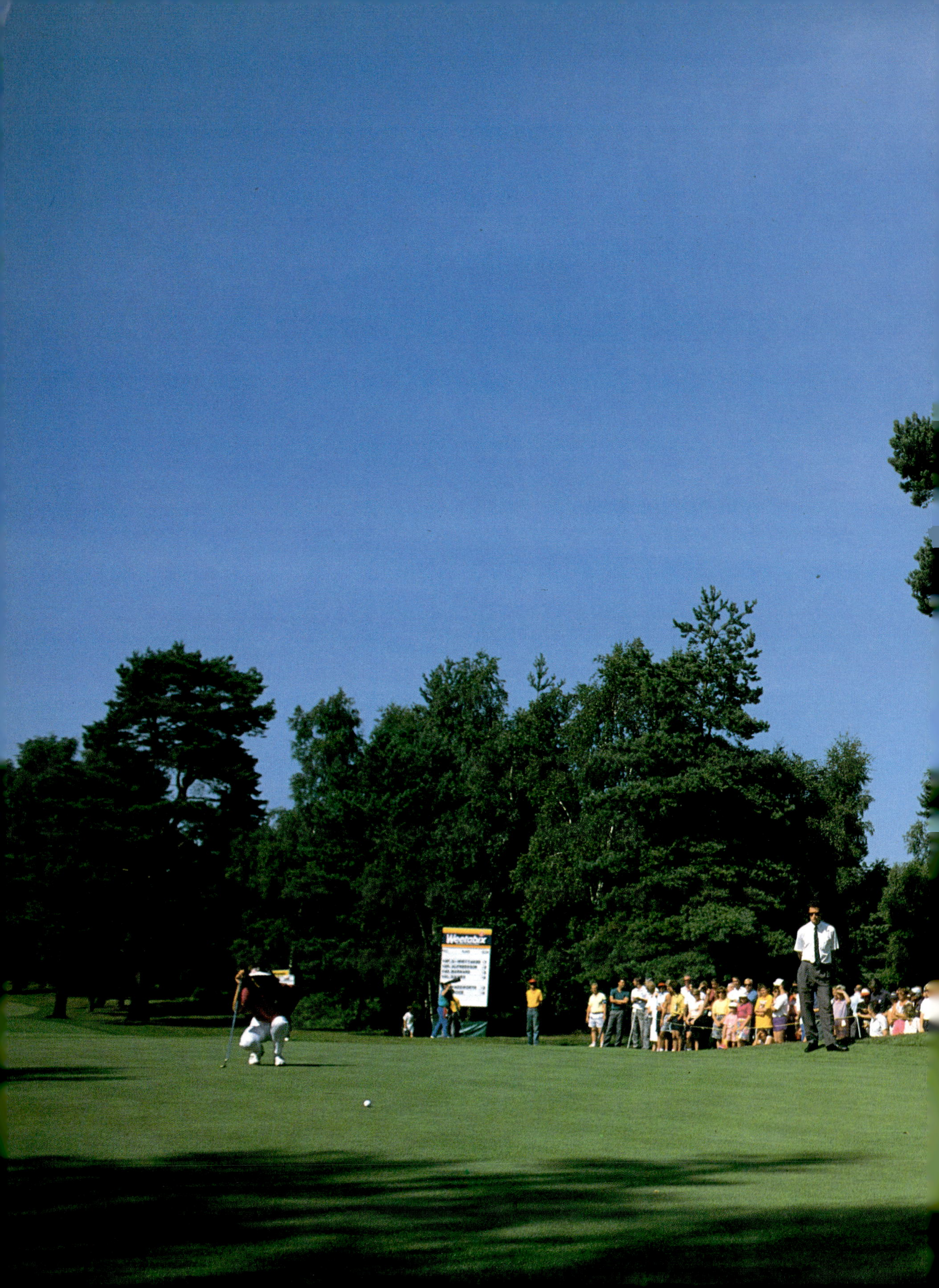
Weetabix

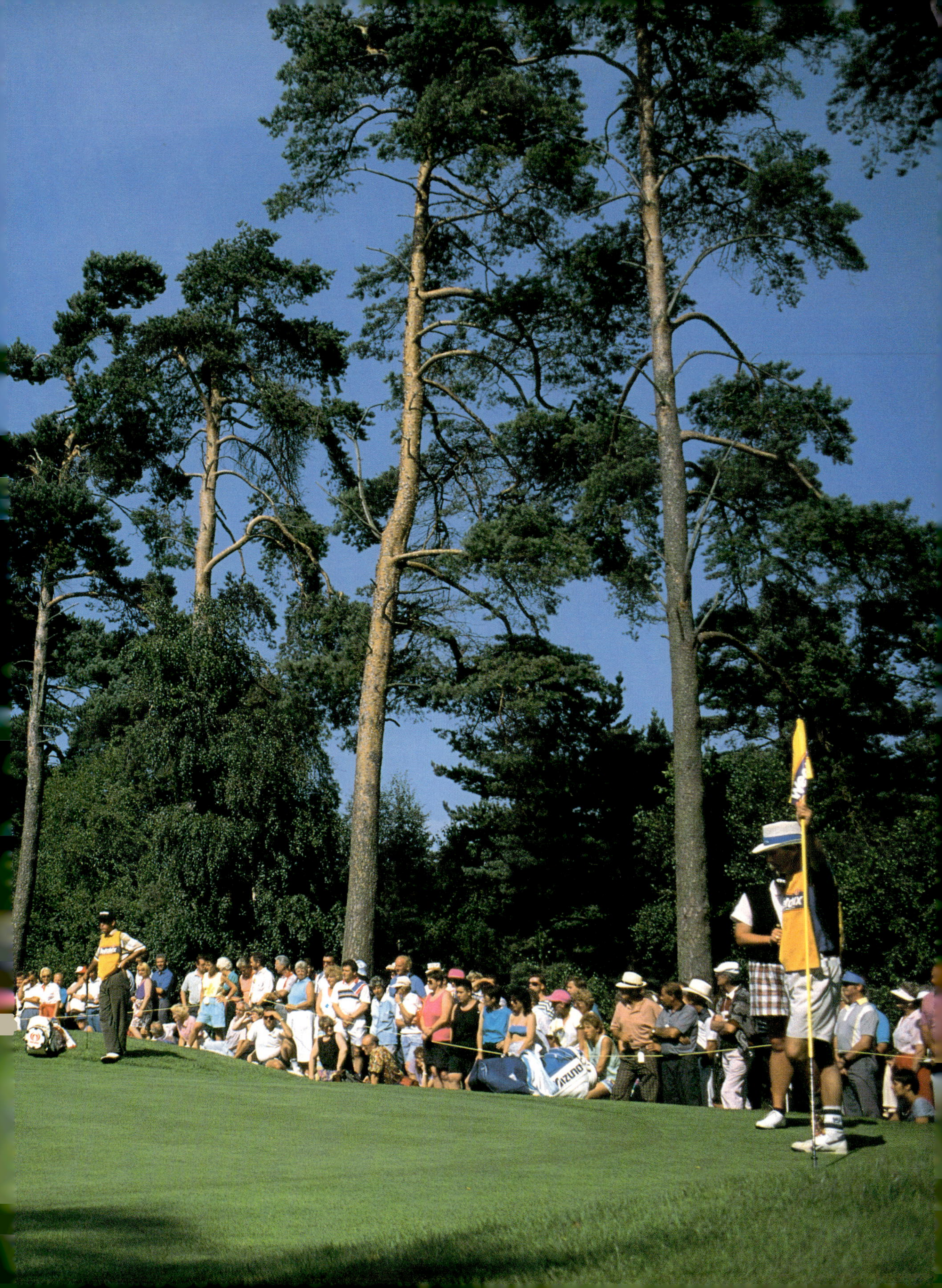

1991 WPG EUROPEAN TOUR RESULTS

18-21 April
VALEXTRA CLASSIC *Olgiata, Rome*

Laura Davies	71	71	70	69	281	£12,000
Tania Abitbol	71	76	70	68	285	8,120
Dale Reid	69	72	72	75	288	4,437
Corinne Soules	72	71	75	70	288	4,437
Catrin Nilsmark	70	74	75	69	288	4,437
Evelyn Orley	75	72	74	69	290	2,800
Corinne Dibnah	74	73	71	73	291	2,200
Li Wen-Lin	73	73	72	73	291	2,200
Regine Lautens	73	71	73	75	292	1,696
Helen Alfredsson	73	72	72	75	292	1,696
Anna Oxenstierna	73	70	76	74	293	1,344
Florence Descampe	73	71	74	75	293	1,344
Anne Marie Palli	77	72	71	73	293	1,344
Muffin Spencer-Devlin	73	72	75	73	293	1,344

25-28 April
AGF LADIES' OPEN DE PARIS *Racing Club de France*

Suzanne Strudwick	70	67	70	71	278	£14,957
Laura Davies	69	71	70	71	281	7,727
Catherine Panton-Lewis	69	74	68	70	281	7,727
Sandrine Mendiburu	69	73	73	67	282	(Am.)
Alison Nicholas	69	73	73	68	283	5,483
Anna Oxenstierna	71	74	68	72	285	3,738
Corinne Soules	74	69	68	74	285	3,738
Gillian Stewart	68	71	74	72	285	3,738
Trish Johnson	68	70	72	76	286	2,367
Martha Nause	73	72	70	71	286	2,367
Tania Abitbol	68	75	72	72	287	1,838
Regine Lautens	74	69	72	72	287	1,838
Florence Descampe	76	72	70	69	287	1,838

2-5 May
FORD LADIES' CLASSIC *Woburn G&CC*

Dale Reid	68	70	71	71	280	£9,750
Alison Nicholas	68	74	68	71	281	6,600
Janice Arnold	70	75	70	68	283	4,550
Stefania Croce	76	75	68	73	292	3,510
Alicia Dibos	74	72	73	74	293	2,756
Diane Barnard	76	73	74	71	294	1,950
Catherine Panton-Lewis	73	71	73	77	294	1,950
Florence Descampe	75	72	75	72	294	1,950
Federica Dassu	74	76	73	72	295	1,317
Li Wen-Lin	73	75	73	74	295	1,317
Helen Alfredsson	77	74	72	72	295	1,317
Rica Comstock	72	73	77	74	296	1,057
Corinne Soules	72	78	72	74	296	1,057
Jean Bartholomew	75	76	72	73	296	1,057

23-26 May
BMW EUROPEAN MASTERS *Golf du Bercuit, Belgium*

Corinne Dibnah	70	71	71	72	284	£19,500
Florence Descampe	71	72	74	70	287	11,147
Catrin Nilsmark	69	73	74	71	287	11,147
Helen Alfredsson	72	71	72	74	289	7,020
Alison Nicholas	72	74	74	72	292	5,031
Julie Larsen	75	72	74	71	292	5,031
Janice Arnold	72	80	71	70	293	3,165
Rae Hast	71	73	73	76	293	3,165
Regine Lautens	73	77	71	72	293	3,165
Joanne Furby	75	72	73	73	293	3,165
Jane Hill	74	72	73	75	294	2,184
Dale Reid	76	74	75	69	294	2,184
Xonia Wunsch-Ruiz	76	74	71	73	294	2,184
Leslie A. Brown	73	72	76	73	294	2,184

6-9 June
LA MANGA CLUB CLASSIC *La Manga, Spain*

*Corinne Dibnah	72	77	69	68	286	£10,500
Laurette Maritz-Atkins	73	71	71	71	286	7,105
Dale Reid	73	72	73	70	288	4,900
Linda Percival	72	72	72	73	289	3,374
Florence Descampe	70	72	71	76	289	3,374
Catrin Nilsmark	74	71	75	70	290	2,450
Marie-Laure de Lorenzi	74	78	69	70	291	1,704
Kitrina Douglas	68	75	76	72	291	1,704
Dennise Hutton	73	75	73	70	291	1,704
Kiernan Prechtl	67	74	79	71	291	1,704
Penny Grice-Whittaker	74	74	74	70	292	1,206
Alison Nicholas	71	79	70	72	292	1,206
Kristal Parker	70	74	75	73	292	1,206

(Previous page) Diane Barnard lines up a putt during the British Open at Woburn.

Laura Davies and Suzanne Strudwick at the AGF Open in Paris.

13-16 June
HENNESSY LADIES' CUP *Golf und Landclub, Köln*

*Helen Alfredsson	70	71	71	68	280	£15,000
Marie-Laure de Lorenzi	69	71	73	67	280	8,575
Corinne Dibnah	71	67	71	71	280	8,575
Sharon Cranmer	70	74	75	67	286	4,820
Kiernan Prechtl	74	71	74	67	286	4,820
Laura Davies	70	72	77	68	287	2,648
Laurette Maritz-Atkins	74	74	69	70	287	2,648
Florence Descampe	70	77	68	72	287	2,648
Alicia Dibos	67	75	70	75	287	2,648
Amy Alcott	69	76	72	70	287	2,648
Kim Saiki	75	70	71	72	288	1,780
Helen Dobson	77	72	73	66	288	1,780
Patricia Gonzales	70	75	72	72	289	1,553
Alison Nicholas	74	69	72	74	289	1,553
Gillian Stewart	71	76	71	71	289	1,553

20-23 June
TROPHEE COCONUT SKOL *Golf de St Germain, Paris*

Helen Alfredsson	71	68	66	71	276	£15,000
Dale Reid	73	68	73	65	279	10,150
Kitrina Douglas	70	69	73	70	282	5,546
Alison Nicholas	70	69	73	70	282	5,546
Corinne Soules	72	71	70	69	282	5,546
Marie-Laure de Lorenzi	71	70	69	75	285	3,250
Gillian Stewart	71	68	71	75	285	3,250
Federica Dassu	69	70	71	76	286	2,370
Maureen Garner	72	72	72	70	286	2,370
Janice Arnold	72	70	70	75	287	1,920
Corinne Dibnah	69	71	76	71	287	1,920

11 July
BLOOR HOMES EASTLEIGH CLASSIC *Fleming Park, Eastleigh*

Dale Reid	63	64	64	58	249	£10,500
Diane Barnard	65	65	63	64	257	7,105
Claire Duffy	65	65	64	64	258	4,340
Li Wen-Lin	66	62	66	64	258	4,340
Xonia Wunsch-Ruiz	64	62	71	62	259	2,968
Tania Abitbol	66	68	59	67	260	1,759
Jane Connachan	58	70	65	67	260	1,759
Gillian Stewart	66	66	63	65	260	1,759
Suzanne Strudwick	65	67	64	64	260	1,759
Joanne Furby	68	66	63	63	260	1,759
Julie Forbes	66	65	62	67	260	1,759

1991 WPG EUROPEAN TOUR RESULTS

25-28 July
LUFTHANSA LADIES' GERMAN OPEN *Worthsee Golf Club, Munich*

Florence Descampe	66	71	71	64	272	£15,000
Liselotte Neumann	70	71	68	66	275	10,150
Mardi Lunn	70	66	70	70	276	6,200
Ayako Okamoto	67	74	70	65	276	6,200
Kelly Leadbetter	70	71	65	71	277	3,870
Dale Reid	68	69	68	72	277	3,870
Trish Johnson	69	71	68	70	278	3,000
Marie-Laure de Lorenzi	69	75	69	66	279	2,370
Laurette Maritz-Atkins	69	69	73	68	279	2,370
Kitrina Douglas	71	70	66	73	280	1,853
Leigh Ann Mills	69	70	68	73	280	1,853
Li Wen-Lin	70	70	67	73	280	1,853

1-4 August
WEETABIX WOMEN'S BRITISH OPEN *Woburn – Duke's Course*

Penny Grice-Whittaker	69	69	77	69	284	£25,000
Diane Barnard	73	72	71	71	287	13,250
Helen Alfredsson	73	69	76	69	287	15,250
Laura Davies	71	74	71	72	288	7,175
Stefania Croce	75	74	70	69	288	7,175
Helen Wadsworth	68	75	72	74	289	5,250
Marie-Laure de Lorenzi	73	70	76	71	290	3,650
Trish Johnson	71	72	76	71	290	3,650
Kristal Parker	73	69	75	73	290	3,650
Evelyn Orley	75	71	72	72	290	3,650
Alison Nicholas	75	73	70	73	291	2,516
Kelley Markette	72	69	77	73	291	2,516
Julie Forbes	74	73	71	73	291	2,516
Kitrina Douglas	73	75	71	73	292	2,280
Rica Comstock	71	75	76	71	293	2,120
Corinne Soules	74	77	72	70	293	2,120
Julie Larsen	77	72	72	72	293	2,120
Jan Stephenson	74	73	71	75	293	2,120

* Winner in play-off.

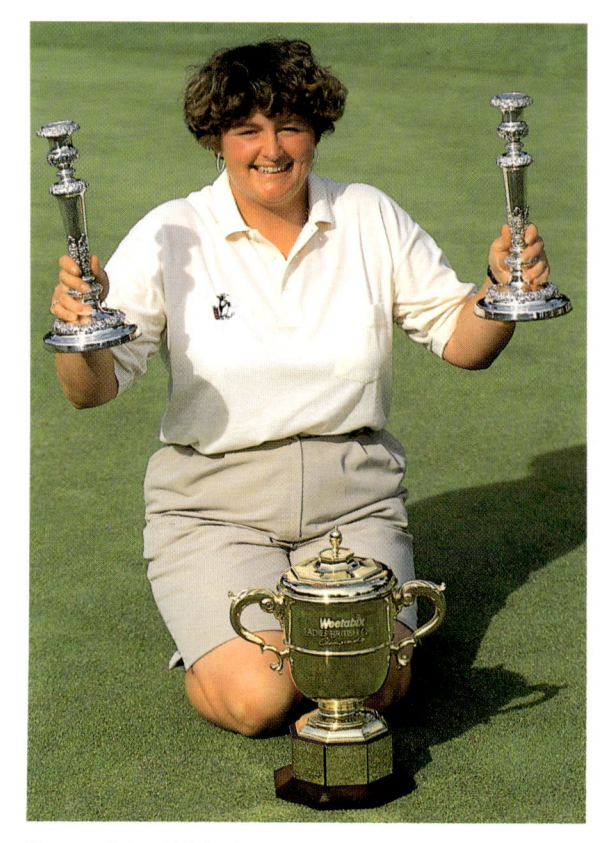

Penny Grice-Whittaker.

15-18 August
IBM LADIES' OPEN *Haninge Golf Club, Nr Stockholm*

Liselotte Neumann	69	70	69	74	282	£12,000
Marie-Laure de Lorenzi	71	75	71	68	285	8,120
Laura Davies	73	73	71	69	286	5,600
Alison Nicholas	77	72	70	68	287	3,856
Helen Alfredsson	75	70	72	70	287	3,856
Corinne Dibnah	72	72	70	74	288	2,600
Lisa Hackney	70	70	73	75	288	2,600
Laurette Maritz-Atkins	72	75	70	74	291	1,797
Dale Reid	73	71	73	74	291	1,797
Catrin Nilsmark	72	75	73	71	291	1,797

19-22 September
BMW ITALIAN LADIES' OPEN *Albarella Golf Club, Nr Venice*

Corinne Dibnah	71	65	69	67	272	£15,000
Florence Descampe	69	69	69	68	275	10,150
Marie-Laure de Lorenzi	68	64	73	71	276	5,546
Mardi Lunn	70	68	68	70	276	5,546
Siobhan Keogh	69	68	67	72	276	5,546
Kitrina Douglas	73	69	65	70	277	3,250
Sandrine Mendiburu	75	64	72	66	277	3,250
Dale Reid	72	70	69	67	278	2,500
Karen Pearce	70	68	70	71	279	2,240

26-29 September
ENGLISH OPEN *The Tytherington Club, Cheshire*

*Kitrina Douglas	72	71	72	70	285	£11,250
Evelyn Orley	69	72	71	73	285	7,610
Corinne Dibnah	70	71	78	70	289	4,650
Helen Alfredsson	76	69	72	72	289	4,650
Jane Hill	74	73	70	74	291	3,180
Suzanne Strudwick	76	71	73	72	292	2,437
Julie Forbes	71	74	69	78	292	2,437
Stefania Croce	73	74	72	74	293	1,875
Laurette Maritz-Atkins	71	73	74	76	294	1,590
Catherine Panton-Lewis	73	73	74	74	294	1,590

Marie-Laure de Lorenzi.

Sweden's Helen Alfredsson.

1991 WPG EUROPEAN TOUR RESULTS

17-20 October
WOOLMARK LADIES' MATCHPLAY CHAMPIONSHIP *Carimate, Nr Milan*

Third Round
F. Dassu beat X. Wunsch
P. Gonazlez beat S. Strudwick
S. Gronberg beat J. Germs
T. Johnson beat H. Dobson
M. Garner beat M. Lunn
P. Wright beat C. Duffy
S. Nicklin beat K. Marshall
D. Reid beat H. Wadsworth
   All third round losers won £1,300

Quarter-Finals
F. Dassu beat P. Gonzalez
T. Johnson beat S. Gronberg
P. Wright beat M. Garner
D. Reid beat S. Nicklin
   All quarter-final losers won £2,600

Semi-Finals
F. Dassu beat T. Johnson
D. Reid beat P. Wright
   All semi-final losers won £5,200

FINAL
F. Dassu beat D. Reid
(£12,000)   (£8,000)

Rookie of the Year, Helen Wadsworth.

24-27 October
LONGINES CLASSIC *Golf Club de Cannes Mandelieu*

Penny Grice-Whittaker	71	63	71	72	277	£16,500
Laura Davies	68	66	69	75	278	9,412
Corinne Dibnah	72	71	66	69	278	9,412
Pamela Wright	73	71	68	68	280	5,302
Helen Wadsworth	69	71	69	71	280	5,302
Florence Descampe	69	69	72	71	281	3,850
Janice Arnold	73	72	65	72	282	3,300
Karine Espinasse	73	69	71	70	283	2,359
Anne Marie Palli	70	71	71	71	283	2,359
Pearl Sinn	73	70	70	70	283	2,359
Helen Alfredsson	73	71	70	69	283	2,359
Kitrina Douglas	73	69	68	74	284	1,754
Sofia Gronberg	74	70	70	70	284	1,754
Susan Moon	69	71	70	74	284	1,754
Corinne Soules	73	66	73	72	284	1,754

1991 WPG EUROPEAN TOUR WINNERS SUMMARY

VALEXTRA CLASSIC	Laura Davies
AGF LADIES' OPEN	Suzanne Strudwick
FORD LADIES' CLASSIC	Dale Reid
BMW EUROPEAN MASTERS	Corinne Dibnah
LA MANGA CLUB CLASSIC	Corinne Dibnah
HENNESSY LADIES' CUP	Helen Alfredsson
TROPHEE COCONUT SKOL	Helen Alfredsson
BLOOR HOMES EASTLEIGH CLASSIC	Dale Reid
LUFTHANSA LADIES' GERMAN OPEN	Florence Descampe
WEETABIX WOMEN'S BRITISH OPEN	Penny Grice-Whittaker
IBM LADIES' OPEN	Liselotte Neumann
ITALIAN OPEN	Corinne Dibnah
ENGLISH OPEN	Kitrina Douglas
WOOLMARK LADIES' MATCHPLAY	Federica Dassu
LONGINES CLASSIC	Penny Grice-Whittaker
BENSON AND HEDGES TEAM TROPHY	Helen Alfredsson and Anders Forsbrand

WOOLMARK ORDER OF MERIT: TOP 60

1	Corinne Dibnah	£89,058	31	Patricia Gonzalez	13,614
2	Helen Alfredsson	75,900	32	Li Wen-Lin	13,424
3	Dale Reid	64,494	33	Julie Forbes	12,564
4	Florence Descampe	54,874	34	Claire Duffy	12,166
5	Laura Davies	49,552	35	Debbie Dowling	12,135
6	Penny Grice-Whittaker	45,904	36	Helen Dobson	11,942
7	Alison Nicholas	37,668	37	Pamela Wright	11,465
8	Marie-Laure de Lorenzi	37,348	38	Joanne Furby	11,036
9	Kitrina Douglas	34,061	39	Julie Larsen	10,757
10	Suzanne Strudwick	30,980	40	Maureen Garner	10,696
11	Diane Barnard	30,591	41	Karine Espinasse	10,227
12	Corinne Soules	27,784	42	Sally Prosser	9,995
13	Catrin Nilsmark	26,041	43	Lisa Hackney	9,760
14	Federica Dassu	25,219	44	Anna Oxenstierna	9,682
15	Liselotte Neumann	23,542	45	Dennise Hutton	9,466
16	Laurette Maritz-Atkins	23,013	46	Rica Comstock	9,273
17	Tania Abitbol	22,040	47	Lora Fairclough	9,252
18	Janice Arnold	18,880	48	Kristal Parker	9,169
19	Trish Johnson	18,155	49	Karen Pearce	9,094
20	Stefania Croce	17,990	50	Susan Moon	8,990
21	Evelyn Orley	17,862	51	Kiernan Prechtl	7,614
22	Helen Wadsworth	17,765	52	Beverley New	7,594
23	Gillian Stewart	17,195	53	Karen Lunn	7,284
24	Catherine Panton-Lewis	17,046	54	Kelly Leadbetter	7,102
25	Mardi Lunn	15,401	55	Allison Shapcott	6,982
26	Alicia Dibos	15,145	56	Rae Hast	6,943
27	Regine Lautens	14,023	57	Nadene Hall	6,904
28	Jane Hill	13,700	58	Muffin Spencer-Devlin	6,757
29	Sofia Gronberg	13,699	59	Maria Navarro Corbachio	6,735
30	Xonia Wunsch-Ruiz	13,630	60	Siobhan Keogh	6,716

THE UNITED STATES

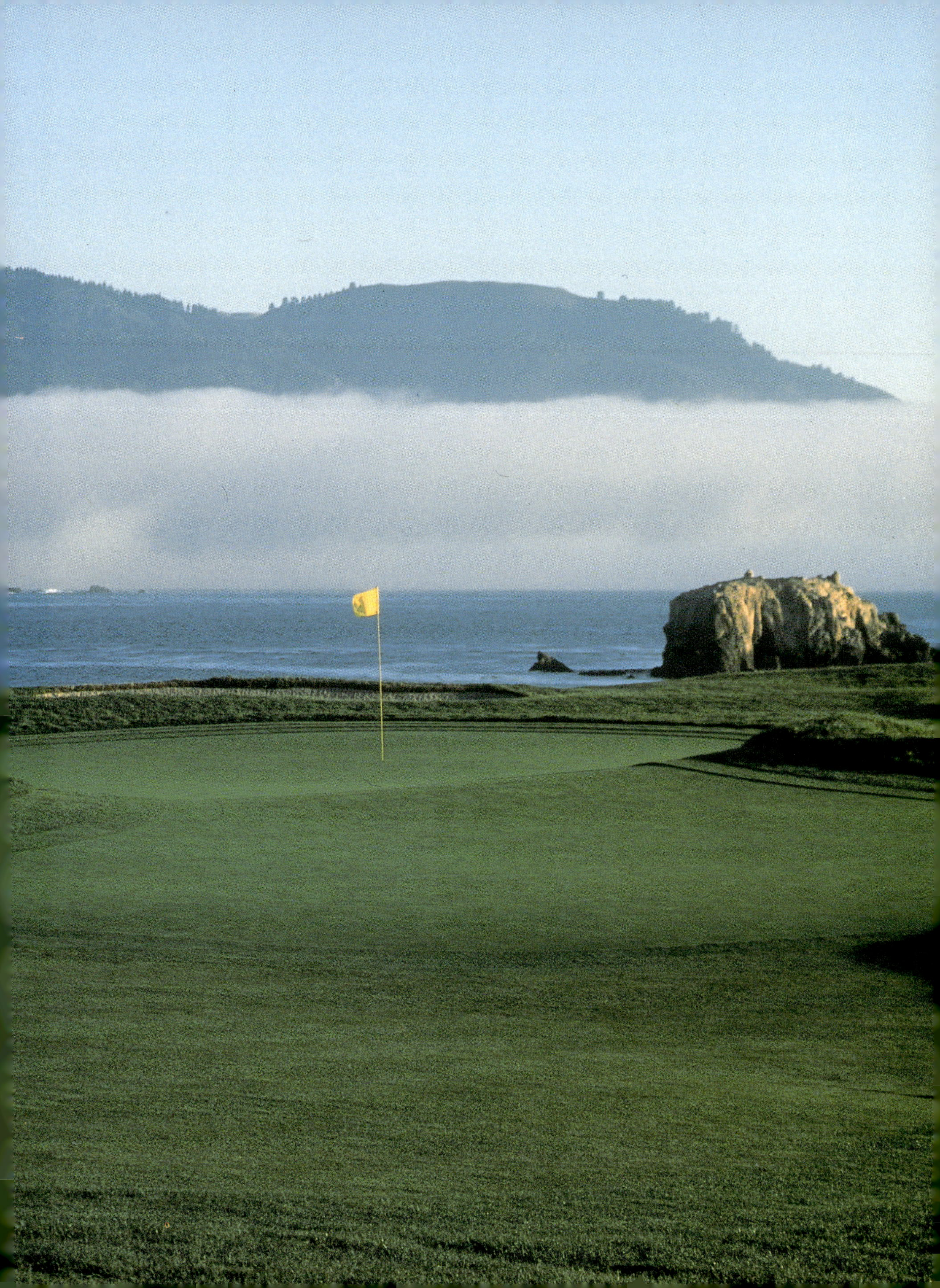

THE 1991 US TOUR

Between 1986 and 1990 Curtis Strange and Greg Norman pretty much dominated things on the US Tour – they didn't dominate in the way Nicklaus and Watson dominated in the 1970s but they were the ones who were rarely out of the picture, rarely out of the frame. Strange was leading moneywinner in 1987 and 1988 while Norman led the way in 1986 and 1990. Yet in 1991 neither the American nor the Australian could win a tournament and they finished forty-eighth and fifty-third respectively on the money list.

Norman's decline, which one desperately hopes is only temporary, was the US Tour's biggest loss in 1991. During the first half of 1990 his golf had been electrifying, especially, it seemed, when everyone was watching – and he made many more watch – on Sunday afternoons. Greg's final round charges were every bit as exciting as those of Arnold Palmer three decades earlier. He didn't always win of course – indeed due to two players holing outrageous shots he only did so twice – but every week he seemed to be launching some kind of dramatic, all-guns-blazing assault on the leaderboard. If he wasn't the cavalry, he was certainly cavalier. Naturally there were flashes of brilliance in 1991 but more often than not he fizzled out. In the Western Open, for instance, six birdies in the first ten holes put Norman five ahead of the field. In what he later described as a 'Jekyll and Hyde round', he then proceeded to drop strokes at the 13th, 14th, 15th, 16th and 18th – needless to say he didn't win. He also led after thirty-six holes in the Honda Classic and the Buick Open but fell away on both occasions and in the Kemper Open he set himself up for victory with rounds of 67-65-64 before slipping to a disappointing 71.

The only tournament Curtis Strange looked like winning was the Doral Ryder Open in March but he lost a play-off to Rocco Mediate when the man with the broom-handled putter rolled in birdie putts at the 71st and 72nd holes and then another at the first extra hole. Later in the season Strange told *Golf Monthly*, 'I'm fed up to the eyeballs with the way I'm playing. I haven't made a putt in six months. I'm just frustrated. I've had it. I'm in a terrible mood but I've earned it.'

The player who succeeded Greg Norman as the US Tour's leading moneywinner in 1991 was Corey Pavin: a fine golfer for sure – ugly swing, great putter – but probably not a person readily recognizable to the man on the Clapham omnibus. He hardly dominated either; he won two tour events, the Bob Hope Chrysler Classic and the Bell South Atlanta Classic but needed extra holes to do so on both occasions.

Corey Pavin, America's leading moneywinner in 1991. (Previous page) Pebble Beach, California.

1991 was a year of unfamiliar names and unfamiliar winners. Included in the top twenty moneywinners were Messrs Purtzer, Magee, Cochran, Brooks, Andrade, Mediate and Gallagher Jnr. Not among the top thirty (aside from Norman and Strange) were Messrs Stewart, Irwin, Kite, Watson, Calcavecchia and Crenshaw. And what of Wayne Levi who won four tournaments and one million dollars in 1990? He finished in 87th place, and, poor chap, won less than $200,000 from twenty-five starts.

Several of the big events on the Tour calendar were won by outsiders. The Players' Championship was won by Steve Elkington; Mediate, as mentioned, won the Doral Ryder, Kenny Perry captured first prize at the Memorial; left-hander Russ Cochran took advantage of Norman's collapse in the Western Open and Tom Purtzer won the Colonial and World Series titles. Joining Purtzer as unexpected double winners were Billy Andrade, Andrew Magee and Mark Brooks.

Play-offs were another feature of life on the US Tour in 1991. There were seventeen in all, and between The Masters in April and the PGA in August, nine of the fifteen events were decided by sudden death.

It is probably fair to say, and the Sony World Rankings concur, that the best three American golfers are presently Payne Stewart, Fred Couples and Paul Azinger. Stewart won the US Open and so didn't really need to do much else, besides, he spent the best part of the early season sidelined with a neck injury. Couples had easily his best season on Tour: he finished third in the money list, for the first time won two tournaments (both fairly comfortably), averaged 69.59 per round to take the Vardon Trophy for maintaining the lowest scoring average and easily headed the US Ryder Cup points list. Paul Azinger? When he wasn't saying silly things he played some excellent golf including winning the AT&T Pebble Beach Pro-Am by four strokes.

Even without any contribution from Greg Norman, overseas golfers captured seven of the forty-three official US Tour events. The 'big ones', of course, were Ian Woosnam's win in The Masters and Aussie Steve Elkington's in the Players' Championship. Woosnam, in fact, won twice, as did Zimbabwean Nick Price. The Welshman's first US victory came when he defeated Jim Hallet in a play-off in the USF&G Classic at New Orleans and Price's two Tour wins were at the Byron Nelson Classic and the Canadian Open – the latter a result of an amazing run of five successive birdies on the back nine in the final round.

The South African, Fulton Allem, was a surprise winner of the Huston Open in October and José-Maria Olazabal took his second US title in two years with a win in the International at Castle Rock in Colorado. If the US Tour order of merit was based on dollars won per tournaments entered then the top ten on the 1991 US Tour would read: 1. Woosnam (GB), 2. Olazabal (Sp), 3. Stadler (US), 4. Pavin (US), 5. Couples (US), 6. Azinger (US), 7.

No US Tour victories for Greg Norman, the top dog in 1990.

Payne Stewart.

Fred Couples.

Spaniard José-Maria Olazabal won The International at Castle Rock in August.

Price (Zmb), 8. Baker-Finch (Aus), 9. Purtzer (US), 10. Leitzke (US). An interesting thought.

Olazabal undoubtedly provided the most sensational week on the US Tour in 1990; in 1991 there were no storming twelve-stoke victories but that is not to say there were no amazing feats. Perhaps two wins and two rounds of golf stand out. The most spectacular victory, because it came in a Major championship, was John Daly's triumph at Crooked Stick in the USPGA Championship (reviewed fully in an earlier section). The other occurred in the second tournament of the year at Tucson. One year earlier, in January 1990, twenty-one-year-old Robert Gamez caused many observers to shake their heads in disbelief when he routed the field to record his first Tour victory only months after turning professional. Last year Phil Mickelson, at twenty, one year younger than Gamez and still an amateur, won at Tucson scoring two 65s in the process. He also holed a 15-foot birdie putt at the last for a victory that had seemed very improbable when he took a triple bogey eight at the 14th.

The two most memorable rounds of golf on the US Tour occurred near the beginning and the end of the season. The first came in the second round of the Doral Ryder Open, the event Curtis Strange should have won, and it was by Jack Nicklaus. Proving that there is still 'life in the old Bear yet', Jack stormed around Miami's revered Blue Monster Course in sixty-three strokes to lead the tournament after thirty-six holes. In response to the obvious question he told a captivated press, 'Of course I surprised myself. Are you kidding? I surprised myself, the other players, my wife too.' The fifty-one year old then added, tongue in cheek, 'I was trying to shoot my age – I'm getting closer!'

In the second week of October Chip Beck did what every golfer on the Tour had been trying to do since June 1977 – match Al Geiberger's record score of 59. He did it in style too (not that it would be easy to shoot 59 unstylishly) by birdieing seven of his first eight holes and finishing with three straight birdies. There were three more in the middle of his round making a total of thirteen birdies and five pars in eighteen holes. At the beginning of the season the Hilton Hotel Group had promised to pay $500,000 to the first golfer to break 60 in a US Tour event and a further $500,000 to the PGA Tour charity. So it was one million dollars payout time and where did all this take place? Why, in Las Vegas of course.

1991 is a year Curtis Strange will want to forget.

1991 USPGA TOUR RESULTS

3-6 January
INFINITI TOURNAMENT OF CHAMPIONS
Carlsbad, California

T. Kite	68	67	68	69	272	$144,000
L. Wadkins	65	67	73	68	273	86,400
C. Beck	68	69	70	69	276	41,600
F. Couples	70	68	67	71	276	41,600
W. Levi	70	71	69	66	276	41,600
T. Armour	72	71	72	66	281	26,800
G. Norman	70	71	73	67	281	26,800
B. Tway	73	67	70	71	281	26,800
B. Crenshaw	74	70	67	71	282	21,275
W. Grady	69	72	72	69	282	21,275
N. Henke	72	72	70	68	282	21,275
M. O'Meara	72	69	70	71	282	21,275

10-13 January
NORTHERN TELECOM TUCSON OPEN *Tucson, Arizona*

P. Mickelson	65	71	65	71	272	(Am.)
T. Purtzer	70	70	66	67	273	144,000
B. Tway	64	70	71	68	273	144,000
C. Stadler	69	64	72	70	275	68,000
J. Cook	66	69	75	66	276	39,375
J. Maggert	68	69	70	69	276	39,375
D. Peoples	70	67	66	73	276	39,375
B. Tennyson	69	65	73	69	276	39,375
S. Hoch	68	66	70	73	277	27,000
N. Lancaster	70	68	72	67	277	27,000
R. Mediate	67	69	70	71	277	27,000
C. Pavin	67	67	69	74	277	27,000
D. Rummells	71	71	67	68	277	27,000

17-20 January
UNITED HAWAIIAN OPEN *Waialae, Honolulu*

L. Wadkins	69	67	69	65	270	$198,000
J. Cook	64	66	69	75	274	118,800
E. Dougherty	70	68	66	71	275	74,800
C. Beck	66	66	70	74	276	41,470
P. Blackmar	66	70	71	69	276	41,470
M. Calcavecchia	68	67	72	69	276	41,470
H. Irwin	66	69	68	73	276	41,470
G. Morgan	66	66	69	75	276	41,470
M. Lye	66	70	71	70	277	25,457
C. Stadler	67	73	66	71	277	25,457
B. Bryant	70	66	70	71	277	25,457
F. Funk	69	64	71	73	277	25,457
B. Gardner	68	65	72	72	277	25,457
L. Mize	64	70	70	73	277	25,457
D. Rummells	67	70	65	75	277	25,457

24-27 January
PHOENIX OPEN *Scottsdale, Arizona*

N. Henke	65	66	66	71	268	$180,000
G. Morgan	66	67	70	66	269	74,666
T. Watson	68	68	68	65	269	74,666
C. Strange	64	67	71	67	269	74,666
J. D. Blake	68	66	70	66	270	35,125
M. Hulbert	68	72	65	65	270	35,125
B. Lietzke	67	68	68	67	270	35,125
A. Magee	72	65	67	66	270	35,125
R. Mediate	70	68	68	65	271	27,000
G. Sauers	65	69	68	69	271	27,000
B. Tway	65	69	68	69	271	27,000
F. Funk	71	65	66	70	272	19,000
S. Jones	63	70	70	69	272	19,000
S. Lyle	65	70	70	67	272	19,000

31 January-3 February
AT&T PEBBLE BEACH NATIONAL PRO-AM
Monterey, California

P. Azinger	67	67	73	67	274	$198,000
B. Claar	66	73	71	68	278	96,800
C. Pavin	71	71	69	67	278	96,800
R. Mediate	69	67	69	74	279	45,466
M. Smith	70	73	71	65	279	45,466
D. Love III	67	70	69	73	279	45,466
J. Haas	68	70	74	68	280	34,283
J. Cook	66	72	69	73	280	34,283
L. Mize	71	66	73	70	280	34,283
M. Calcavecchia	71	72	71	67	281	29,700
C. Beck	70	70	69	74	283	24,200
J. Inman	72	69	72	70	283	24,200
H. Sutton	71	74	68	70	283	24,200
B. Wadkins	73	70	73	67	283	24,200

Paul Azinger, winner at Pebble Beach in 1991 – how he'd love to do the same in June this year.

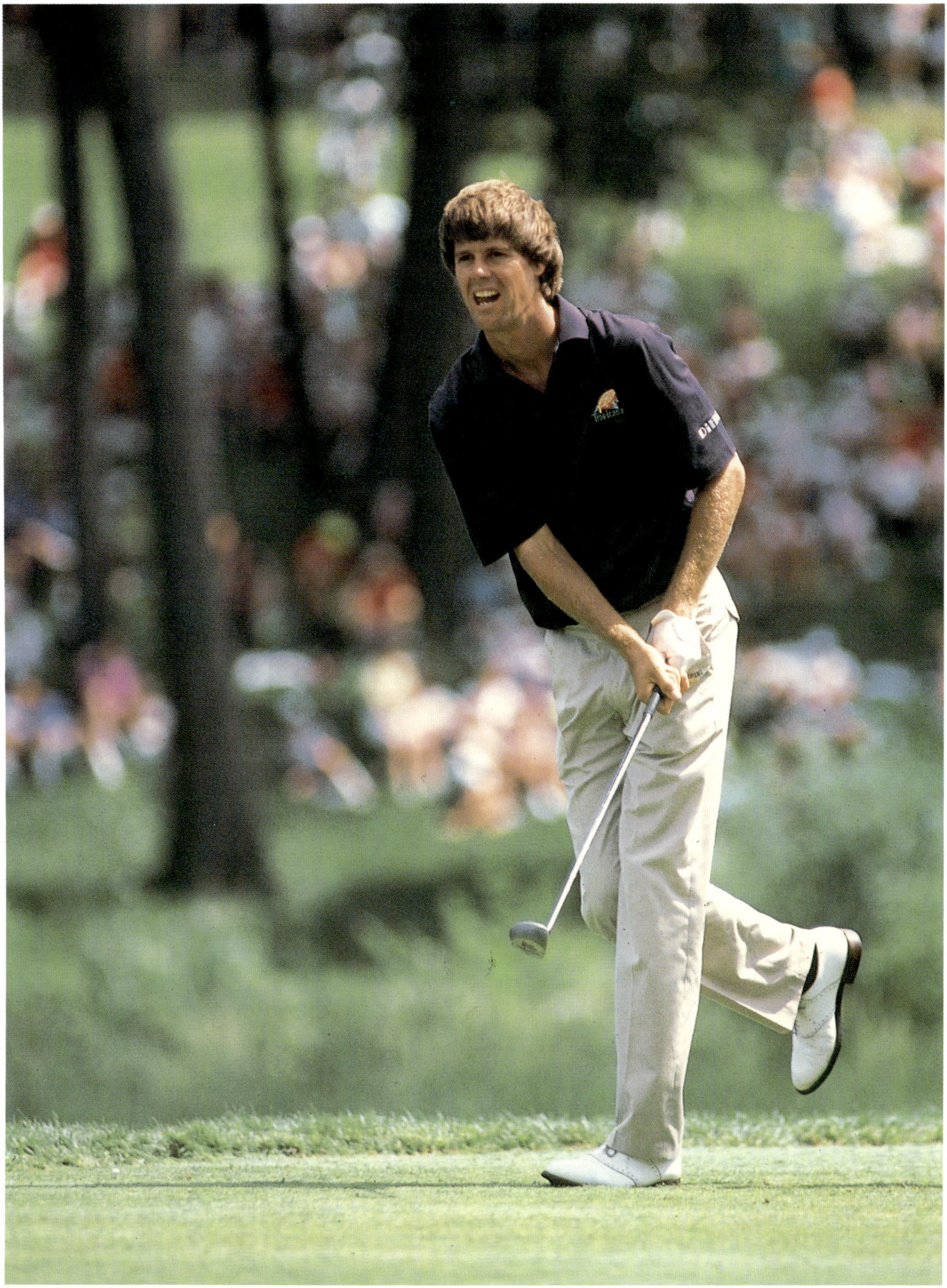

1991 USPGA TOUR RESULTS

6-10 February
BOB HOPE CHRYSLER CLASSIC, La Quinta, California

*C. Pavin	65	69	66	66	65	331	$198,000
M. O'Meara	66	65	66	67	67	331	118,800
T. Simpson	67	64	66	68	67	332	74,800
R. Floyd	71	68	66	64	64	333	52,800
F. Couples	67	69	64	67	67	334	44,000
B. McCallister	66	70	63	68	68	335	39,600
B. Tway	66	68	71	68	64	337	34,283
S. Hoch	72	64	69	63	69	337	34,283
J. Sluman	71	65	69	67	65	337	34,283
J. Hallet	67	70	70	67	64	338	27,500
B. Lohr	69	68	68	69	64	338	27,500
J. McGovern	66	67	69	69	67	338	27,500

14-17 February
SHEARSON LEHMAN BROTHERS OPEN La Jolla, California

J. D. Blake	69	65	67	67	268	$180,000
B. Sander	68	65	71	66	270	108,000
D. Forsman	68	64	71	68	271	68,000
B. Crenshaw	65	68	70	69	272	48,000
J. Hallet	68	69	66	70	273	36,500
S. Pate	67	65	67	74	273	36,500
R. Wrenn	68	66	68	71	273	36,500
B. Faxon	69	64	67	74	274	29,000
D. Hart	68	70	71	65	274	29,000
E. Humenik	69	70	68	67	274	29,000

21-24 February
NISSAN LOS ANGELES OPEN Pacific Pallisades, California

T. Schulz	69	66	69	68	272	$180,000
J. Sluman	66	69	68	70	273	108,000
B. Lietzke	70	63	70	71	274	52,000
D. Love III	70	65	69	70	274	52,000
C. Stadler	66	71	71	66	274	52,000
R. Mediate	70	69	66	70	275	33,500
S. Randolph	72	65	69	69	275	33,500
S. Simpson	71	68	67	69	275	33,500
R. Fehr	68	69	71	68	276	27,000
A. Magee	66	69	70	71	276	27,000
D. Waldorf	66	72	72	66	276	27,000

28 February-3 March
DORAL RYDER OPEN Miami, Florida

*R. Mediate	66	70	68	72	276	$252,000
C. Strange	69	68	72	67	276	151,200
A. Bean	68	68	67	74	277	81,200
R. Cochran	69	67	68	73	277	81,200
D. Love III	71	68	68	72	279	53,200
J. Nicklaus	71	63	75	70	279	53,200
M. Calcavecchia	68	70	69	73	280	46,900
L. Wadkins	71	67	70	73	281	43,400
W. Levi	67	70	71	74	282	40,600
T. Sieckmann	68	72	71	72	283	37,800
B. Gardner	72	70	70	72	284	30,800
M. Hulbert	70	73	67	74	284	30,800
M. O'Meara	67	69	74	74	284	30,800
M. Smith	70	72	70	72	284	30,800

Rocco Mediate and his giant putter swept to victory in the Doral Ryder Open in March.

7-10 March
HONDA CLASSIC *Coral Springs, Florida*

S. Pate	69	65	70	75	279	$180,000
P. Azinger	68	67	75	72	282	88,000
D. Halldorson	67	67	78	70	282	88,000
B. Andrade	68	72	75	68	283	41,333
J. Daly	68	68	76	71	283	41,333
B. Lietzke	72	67	70	74	283	41,333
B. Bryant	69	71	72	72	284	33,500
D. Barr	70	66	74	75	285	31,000
A. Bean	70	71	73	72	286	26,000
D. Love III	74	70	68	74	286	26,000
A. Magee	70	71	71	74	286	26,000
B. McCallister	69	70	73	74	286	26,000
G. Norman	69	66	77	75	287	21,000

Aussie Steve Elkington wins the Players' Championship.

14-17 March
THE NESTLE INVITATIONAL *Bay Hill, Orlando, Florida*

A. Magee	68	69	66	203	$180,000
T. Sieckmann	70	65	70	205	108,000
M. Calcavecchia	66	69	71	206	58,000
S. Pate	72	66	68	206	58,000
M. O'Meara	68	69	70	207	40,000
J. D. Blake	69	69	70	208	36,000
B. Tway	70	71	68	209	28,083
I. Woosnam	70	70	69	209	28,083
N. Faldo	67	71	71	209	28,083
S. Hoch	70	66	73	209	28,083
B. Langer	70	69	70	209	28,083
R. Mediate	68	69	72	209	28,083

21-24 March
USF&G CLASIC *New Orleans, Louisiana*

*I. Woosnam	73	67	68	67	275	$180,000
J. Hallet	69	71	65	70	275	108,000
T. Sieckmann	71	68	70	68	277	68,000
J. Huston	72	70	68	68	278	48,000
R. Black	68	74	66	71	279	36,500
J. Edwards	73	71	64	71	279	36,500
T. Simpson	71	72	71	65	279	36,500
C. Byrum	72	72	68	68	280	29,000
K. Knox	68	75	66	71	280	29,000
T. Watson	67	72	73	68	280	29,000

28–31 March
THE PLAYERS' CHAMPIONSHIP *Ponte Vedra, Florida*

S. Elkington	66	70	72	68	276	$288,000
F. Zoeller	68	68	69	72	277	172,800
P. Azinger	67	68	69	74	278	83,200
P. Blackmar	67	72	69	70	278	83,200
J. Cook	71	73	69	65	278	83,200
B. Langer	70	70	71	69	280	53,600
B. Lietzke	71	72	68	69	280	53,600
C. Strange	71	68	70	71	280	53,600
B. Lohr	68	71	68	74	281	41,600
N. Price	68	75	67	71	281	41,600
G. Sauers	68	74	68	71	281	41,600
B. Wadkins	68	74	69	70	281	41,600
J. Delsing	71	71	71	69	282	32,000
M. McCumber	70	72	69	71	282	32,000
K. Clearwater	72	72	70	69	283	25,600
J. Huston	72	71	70	70	283	25,600
R. Mediate	69	74	68	72	283	25,600
C. Parry	70	74	69	70	283	25,600
I. Woosnam	72	69	70	72	283	25,600

1991 USPGA TOUR RESULTS

11-14 April
THE MASTERS Augusta, Georgia
See p. 35.

11-14 April
DEPOSIT GUARANTY CLASSIC Hattiesburg, Mississippi

*L. Silveira	66	66	71	63	266	$54,000
R. Cochran	69	65	69	63	266	26,400
M. Nicolette	65	65	68	68	266	26,400
F. Funk	66	67	68	66	267	14,400
B. Chamblee	71	67	64	66	268	11,400
J. Haas	66	69	66	67	268	11,400

Ian Woosnam at The Masters.

18-21 April
MCI HERITAGE CLASSIC Hilton Head Island, South Carolina

D. Love III	65	68	68	70	271	$180,000
I. Baker-Finch	75	64	65	69	273	108,000
L. Wadkins	68	68	70	68	274	68,000
P. Stewart	68	68	70	69	275	41,333
H. Irwin	70	70	66	69	275	41,333
M. O'Meara	68	69	68	70	275	41,333
F. Funk	69	69	68	71	277	31,166
B. Mayfair	68	72	66	71	277	31,166
C. Beck	68	64	73	72	277	31,166
B. Clampett	72	66	67	73	278	27,000
J. Delsing	73	68	68	70	279	24,000
J. Huston	69	70	70	70	279	24,000

25-28 April
K-MART GREATER GREENSBORO OPEN
Greensboro, North Carolina

*M. Brooks	71	70	70	64	275	$225,000
G. Sauers	70	64	72	69	275	135,000
J. Huston	74	68	69	65	276	72,500
B. Wolcott	67	69	68	72	276	72,500
B. Britton	70	70	69	68	277	43,906
M. Hulbert	70	70	69	68	277	43,906
J. Sluman	69	67	70	71	277	43,906
L. Wadkins	69	65	72	71	277	43,906
M. Dawson	71	71	69	67	278	33,750
D. Love III	75	67	67	69	278	33,750
L. Roberts	71	71	68	68	278	33,750

2-5 May
GTE BYRON NELSON CLASSIC Irving, Texas

N. Price	68	64	70	68	270	$198,000
C. Stadler	68	66	70	67	271	118,800
R. Floyd	67	69	67	69	272	52,800
C. Pavin	68	66	69	69	272	52,800
S. Simpson	68	68	68	68	272	52,800
H. Sutton	68	68	67	69	272	52,800
L. Wadkins	66	71	68	68	273	36,850
P. Blackmar	70	66	66	73	275	30,800
T. Kite	68	66	66	75	275	30,800
L. Roberts	71	68	66	70	275	30,800
T. Watson	65	69	70	71	275	30,800

9-12 May
BELL SOUTH ATLANTA CLASSIC Marietta, Georgia

*C. Pavin	68	67	67	70	272	$180,000
S. Pate	68	70	68	66	272	108,000
H. Irwin	71	69	67	66	273	52,000
T. Kite	64	68	67	74	273	52,000
M. Springer	68	63	69	73	273	52,000
D. Edwards	70	68	68	68	274	34,750
F. Funk	62	77	67	68	274	34,750
J. D. Blake	68	73	68	66	275	29,000
J. Mudd	69	69	68	69	275	29,000
L. Thompson	70	69	67	69	275	29,000
I. Baker-Finch	72	68	67	69	276	21,200
L. Mize	69	68	69	70	276	21,200

16-19 May
MEMORIAL TOURNAMENT *Muirfield Village, Dublin, Ohio*

*K. Perry	70	63	69	71	273	$216,600
H. Irwin	73	69	65	66	273	129,600
C. Pavin	66	71	67	71	275	81,600
M. Hulbert	73	67	72	67	279	52,800
C. Stadler	71	70	70	68	279	52,800
I. Baker-Finch	69	73	69	69	280	41,700
C. Beck	70	66	74	70	280	41,700
A. Bean	69	69	72	71	281	30,000
J. D. Blake	69	71	72	69	281	30,000
J. Cook	72	72	69	68	281	30,000
D. Frost	69	71	73	68	281	30,000
L. Mize	72	69	73	67	281	30,000
T. Schulz	69	71	67	74	281	30,000
D. Tewell	69	69	72	71	281	30,000
J. Nicklaus	71	68	69	74	282	20,400
T. Watson	68	73	70	71	282	20,400
F. Zoeller	68	69	75	70	282	20,400

23-26 May
SOUTHWESTERN BELL COLONIAL *Fort Worth, Texas*

T. Purtzer	70	66	67	64	267	$216,000
D. Edwards	66	68	68	68	270	89,600
S. Hoch	67	67	70	66	270	89,600
B. Lohr	68	68	63	71	270	89,600
M. Calcavecchia	65	68	68	70	271	45,600
F. Funk	65	68	68	70	271	45,600
I. Baker-Finch	70	65	71	66	272	36,150
W. Grady	68	67	67	70	272	36,150
S. Utley	68	64	69	71	272	36,150
T. Watson	68	66	69	69	272	36,150
K. Clearwater	68	64	69	72	273	27,600
J. Hallet	66	72	64	71	273	27,600
S. Simpson	70	67	67	69	273	27,600

30 May-2 June
KEMPER OPEN *Potomac, Maryland*

*B. Andrade	68	64	64	67	263	$180,000
J. Sluman	70	64	64	65	263	108,000
B. Britton	67	67	66	66	266	68,000
M. Brooks	67	67	68	65	267	41,333
G. Norman	67	65	64	71	267	41,333
H. Sutton	66	65	64	72	267	41,333
S. Hoch	69	69	65	65	268	33,500
S. Jones	71	65	65	68	269	30,000
S. Utley	68	70	64	67	269	30,000
D. Edwards	68	69	66	67	270	27,000

6-9 June
BUICK CLASSIC *Westchester, Rye, New York*

B. Andrade	68	68	69	68	273	$180,000
B. Bryant	66	70	68	71	275	108,000
N. Henke	69	70	67	70	276	58,000
H. Irwin	67	69	67	73	276	58,000
S. Ballesteros	70	67	69	71	277	36,500
W. Levi	71	72	67	67	277	36,500
L. Rinker	68	73	65	71	277	36,500
F. Allem	66	69	70	73	278	30,000
R. Floyd	69	68	69	72	278	30,000
F. Couples	70	65	72	72	279	24,000
G. Norman	70	68	70	71	279	24,000
L. Roberts	68	73	67	71	279	24,000
H. Twitty	70	70	70	69	279	24,000

13-16 June
US OPEN *Hazeltine, Chaska, Minnesota*

See p. 47

20-23 June
ANHEUSER-BUSCH CLASSIC *Williamsburg, Virginia*

*M. Hulbert	66	67	65	68	266	$180,000
K. Knox	67	69	62	68	266	108,000
I. Baker-Finch	62	68	68	69	267	58,000
F. Zoeller	67	69	66	65	267	58,000
B. Claar	68	68	62	71	269	38,000
B. Gilder	63	68	70	68	269	38,000
B. Fabel	66	67	68	70	271	33,500
J.D. Blake	67	68	70	68	273	25,000
B. Britton	69	69	68	67	273	25,000
K. Clearwater	69	66	69	69	273	25,000
M. Donald	66	64	68	75	273	25,000
K. Perry	67	68	68	70	273	25,000
D. Pohl	64	67	65	77	273	25,000
N. Price	67	69	69	68	273	25,000

27–30 June
FEDERAL EXPRESS ST JUDE CLASSIC *Germantown, Tennessee*

F. Couples	68	67	66	68	269	$180,000
R. Fehr	64	70	71	67	272	108,000
D. Canipe	69	69	70	65	273	58,000
J. Haas	70	65	73	65	273	58,000
R. Cochran	66	67	73	68	274	40,000
M. Brooks	68	66	69	72	275	32,375
N. Price	71	65	69	70	275	32,375
D. Tewell	68	71	66	70	275	32,375
R. Thompson	67	72	69	67	275	32,375
B. Gilder	68	74	67	67	276	25,000
G. Ladehoff	70	71	67	68	276	25,000
P. Persons	67	70	65	74	276	25,000

1991 USPGA TOUR RESULTS

4-7 July
CENTEL WESTERN OPEN, *Lemont, Illinois*

R. Cochran	66 72 68 69 275	$180,000
G. Norman	69 66 71 71 277	108,000
F. Couples	70 68 68 72 278	68,000
B. Gilder	70 71 70 70 281	48,000
D. Barr	70 74 68 70 282	32,750
G. Hallberg	67 71 70 74 282	32,750
J. Huston	72 70 71 69 282	32,750
K. Knox	73 69 70 70 282	32,750
N. Price	71 71 70 70 282	32,750
D.A. Weibring	71 72 73 66 282	32,750
J. Gallagher Jnr	76 67 69 71 283	22,000
L. Janzen	67 71 73 72 283	22,000
A. Magee	69 69 70 75 283	22,000
M. Springer	70 70 68 75 283	22,000

11-14 July
THE NEW ENGLAND CLASSIC *Pleasant Valley, Massachusetts*

*B. Fleisher	64 67 73 64 268	$180,000
I. Baker-Finch	66 68 66 68 268	108,000
G. Sauers	67 67 66 69 269	68,000
T. Schulz	65 69 71 67 272	48,000
C. Bowles	68 68 71 66 273	35,125
E. Dougherty	69 67 70 67 273	35,125
B. Faxon	70 68 65 70 273	35,125
B. Jaeckel	70 65 68 70 273	35,125
J. Adams	69 68 67 70 274	28,000
L.T. Broeck	70 66 72 66 274	28,000

18-21 July
CHATTANOOGA CLASSIC *Hixson, Tennessee*

D. Pruitt	66 65 65 64 260	$126,000
L.T. Broeck	64 65 66 67 262	75,600
J. Daly	65 66 67 66 264	33,600
J. Gallagher Jnr	64 68 65 67 264	33,600
S. Lowery	63 65 69 67 264	33,600
D. Rummells	69 66 68 61 264	33,600
P. Arthur	67 64 67 67 265	21,087
R. Cochran	68 66 67 64 265	21,087
B. Fabel	67 65 66 67 265	21,087
K. Knox	70 63 67 65 265	21,087

25-28 July
CANON GREATER HARTFORD OPEN, *Cromwell, Connecticut*

*B.R. Brown	67 72 65 67 271	$180,000
R. Fehr	68 67 66 70 271	88,000
C. Pavin	65 67 70 69 271	88,000
L. Roberts	68 69 68 67 272	41,333
B. Andrade	72 66 66 68 272	41,333
J. Gallagher Jnr	68 65 70 69 272	41,333
D. Pohl	70 69 67 67 273	31,166
M. Reid	71 69 68 65 273	31,166
L. Rinker	71 66 66 70 273	31,166

1-4 August
BUICK OPEN *Grand Blanc, Michigan*

*B. Faxon	66 68 71 66 271	$180,000
C. Beck	67 67 68 69 271	108,000
J. Cook	68 73 66 65 272	52,000
S. Hoch	63 70 72 67 272	52,000
S. Pate	68 69 69 66 272	52,000
N. Faldo	68 69 65 71 273	32,375
G. Sauers	67 68 69 69 273	32,375
H. Sutton	69 69 66 69 273	32,375
H. Twitty	71 66 66 70 273	32,375
B. Britton	69 69 65 71 274	23,000
M. Dawson	66 70 64 74 274	23,000
W. Grady	68 66 71 69 274	23,000
G. Norman	67 65 71 71 274	23,000
T. Simpson	72 68 64 70 274	23,000

8-11 August
USPGA CHAMPIONSHIP *Crooked Stick, Carmel, Indiana*

See p. 75.

15-18 August
THE INTERNATIONAL *Castle Rock, Colorado*

J.-M. Olazabal	+10	$198,000
B. Lohr	+7	82,133
I. Baker-Finch	+7	82,133
S. Gump	+7	82,133
B. Clampett	+6	38,637
L. Mize	+6	38,637
T. Schulz	+6	38,637
T. Watson	+6	38,637
K. Clearwater	+5	30,800
R. Mediate	+5	30,800
R. Kawagishi	+4	27,500
B. Estes	+3	23,100
P. Senior	+3	23,100
C. Stadler	+3	23,100

23-25 August
NEC WORLD SERIES OF GOLF *Firestone, Akron, Ohio*

*T. Purtzer	72	69	67	71	279	$216,000
J. Gallagher Jnr	72	68	70	69	279	105,600
D. Love III	72	66	72	69	279	105,600
M. Brooks	72	64	74	70	280	52,800
F. Couples	74	70	69	67	280	52,800
J. Ozaki	72	70	68	72	282	38,850
N. Price	72	70	71	69	282	38,850
D. Pruitt	71	66	68	77	282	38,850
J. Sindelar	70	68	73	71	282	38,850
S. Elkington	71	70	71	71	283	30,000
A. Magee	73	68	70	72	283	30,000
C. Pavin	72	68	74	69	283	30,000

29 August-1 September
GREATER MILWAUKEE OPEN *Franklin, Wisconsin*

M. Brooks	63	67	70	70	270	$180,000
R. Gamez	61	66	74	70	271	108,000
S. Jones	71	66	69	67	273	68,000
J. Maggert	65	65	71	73	274	48,000
J. Adams	68	68	72	68	276	38,000
N. Lancaster	67	66	73	70	276	38,000
N. Price	72	67	72	66	277	31,166
D.A. Weibring	67	67	72	71	277	31,166
H. Sutton	65	66	74	72	277	31,166

5-8 September
CANADIAN OPEN *Glen Abbey, Oakville, Ontario*

N. Price	71	69	67	66	273	$180,000
D. Edwards	69	69	68	68	274	108,000
F. Couples	69	69	68	69	275	58,000
K. Green	68	69	68	70	275	58,000
J. Sluman	69	72	72	64	277	38,000
D.A. Weibring	69	64	69	75	277	38,000
J. Benepe	64	67	75	72	278	33,500
B. Kamm	65	67	74	73	279	30,000
N. Lancaster	70	70	70	69	279	30,000
P. Azinger	70	68	70	72	280	24,000
I. Baker-Finch	68	72	71	69	280	24,000
B. Lohr	69	69	71	71	280	24,000
R. Stewart	68	69	70	73	280	24,000

12-15 September
HARDEE'S CLASSIC *Coal Valley, Illinois*

D.A. Weibring	68	67	68	64	267	$180,000
P. Azinger	65	65	70	68	268	88,000
P. Jacobsen	65	66	72	65	268	88,000
S. Hoch	69	65	69	66	269	41,333
G. Norman	64	67	70	68	269	41,333
L. Thompson	67	62	73	67	269	41,333
B. Fabel	68	69	67	66	270	31,166
S. Jones	68	69	64	69	270	31,166
S. Lowery	65	66	70	69	270	31,166

Canadian Open champion, Nick Price.

19-22 September
BC OPEN *Endicott, New York*

F. Couples	66	67	68	68	269	$144,000
P. Jacobsen	68	68	68	68	272	86,400
B. Faxon	65	64	71	73	273	46,400
B. McCallister	64	68	72	69	273	46,400
D. Peoples	69	70	66	69	274	32,000
L. Janzen	73	68	65	69	275	28,800
M. Lye	70	70	70	66	276	25,800
S. Pate	68	70	68	70	276	25,800
P. Broadhurst	66	69	71	71	277	20,800
J. Haas	70	70	70	67	277	20,800
M. McCullough	70	70	66	71	277	20,800
G. Twiggs	71	68	69	69	277	20,800

1991 USPGA TOUR RESULTS

26-29 September
BUICK SOUTHERN OPEN Columbus, Georgia

D. Peoples	67	71	72	66	276	$126,000
R. Gamez	71	70	66	70	277	75,600
L. Nelson	69	68	70	72	279	40,600
D. Sutherland	67	71	70	71	279	40,600
B. Gardner	73	69	71	69	282	25,550
D. Hart	71	72	69	70	282	25,550
M. Hatalsky	71	70	69	72	282	25,550
D. Canipe	73	72	71	67	283	20,300
S. Hoch	70	72	73	68	283	20,300
B. Lohr	71	70	71	71	283	20,300

3-6 October
H.E.B. TEXAS OPEN San Antonio, Texas

*B. McCallister	66	64	69	70	269	$162,000
G. Hallberg	70	65	65	69	269	97,200
B. Britton	66	68	68	71	273	43,200
B. Claar	68	66	72	67	273	43,200
B. Crenshaw	67	68	68	70	273	43,200
B. Lohr	68	67	69	69	273	43,200
M. Calcavecchia	65	71	68	70	274	25,275
J. Cook	67	67	66	74	274	25,275
B. Estes	69	68	67	70	274	25,275
L. Janzen	71	68	69	66	274	25,275
J. Sluman	70	67	68	69	274	25,275
B. Wadkins	71	64	70	69	274	25,275

9-13 October
LAS VEGAS INVITATIONAL Las Vegas, Nevada

* A. Magee	69	65	67	62	66	329	$270,000
D.A. Weibring	70	64	65	64	66	329	162,000
C. Beck	65	72	59	68	67	331	78,000
J. Gallagher Jnr	69	65	69	61	67	331	78,000
T. Schulz	65	68	67	66	65	331	78,000
B. Lietzke	68	63	65	67	69	332	54,000
E. Humenik	66	69	68	64	66	333	48,375
M. McCumber	69	64	67	66	67	333	48,375
K. Green	70	65	67	67	65	334	42,000
D. Thompson	70	68	68	61	67	334	42,000
R. Cochran	68	70	66	65	67	336	37,500

16-19 October
WALT DISNEY WORLD/OLDSMOBILE CLASSIC
Lake Buena Vista, Florida

M. O'Meara	66	66	71	64	267	$180,000
D. Peoples	68	67	68	65	268	108,000
P. Azinger	72	65	65	67	269	68,000
S. Elkington	65	71	67	67	270	48,000
J Cook	69	69	68	65	271	36,500
S. Gump	71	67	66	67	271	36,500
D. Love III	71	66	66	68	271	36,500
R. Gamez	68	71	68	65	272	28,000
K. Green	69	68	67	68	272	28,000
N. Henke	67	70	69	66	272	28,000
L. Nelson	65	70	70	67	272	28,000

23-27 October
INDEPENDENT INSURANCE AGENT OPEN
Houston, Texas

F. Allem	71	69	67	66	273	$144,000
B.R. Brown	67	67	69	71	274	59,733
M. Hulbert	68	69	66	71	274	59,733
T. Kite	69	73	64	68	274	59,733
M. Springer	71	70	69	65	275	30,400
D. Waldorf	67	67	72	69	275	30,400
G. Hallberg	68	69	70	69	276	23,280
D. Hammond	69	68	66	73	276	23,280
S. Jones	65	74	70	67	276	23,280
B. Norton	70	70	69	67	276	23,280
M. Reid	67	68	68	73	276	23,280

31 October-3 November
TOUR CHAMPIONSHIP Pinehurst, North Carolina

*C. Stadler	68	68	72	71	279	$360,000
R. Cochran	68	69	71	71	279	216,000
J. Daly	68	76	68	70	282	138,000
B. Lietzke	71	69	72	71	283	96,000
C. Beck	72	70	72	71	285	71,000
J. Gallagher Jnr	71	74	69	71	285	71,000
N. Henke	69	70	74	72	285	71,000
N. Price	70	67	75	73	285	71,000
S. Elkington	69	75	71	71	286	60,000
I. Baker-Finch	68	76	71	72	287	54,000
C. Pavin	74	69	72	72	287	54,000
J. Sluman	74	71	69	73	287	54,000

* Winner in play-off.

(Right) Craig Stadler.

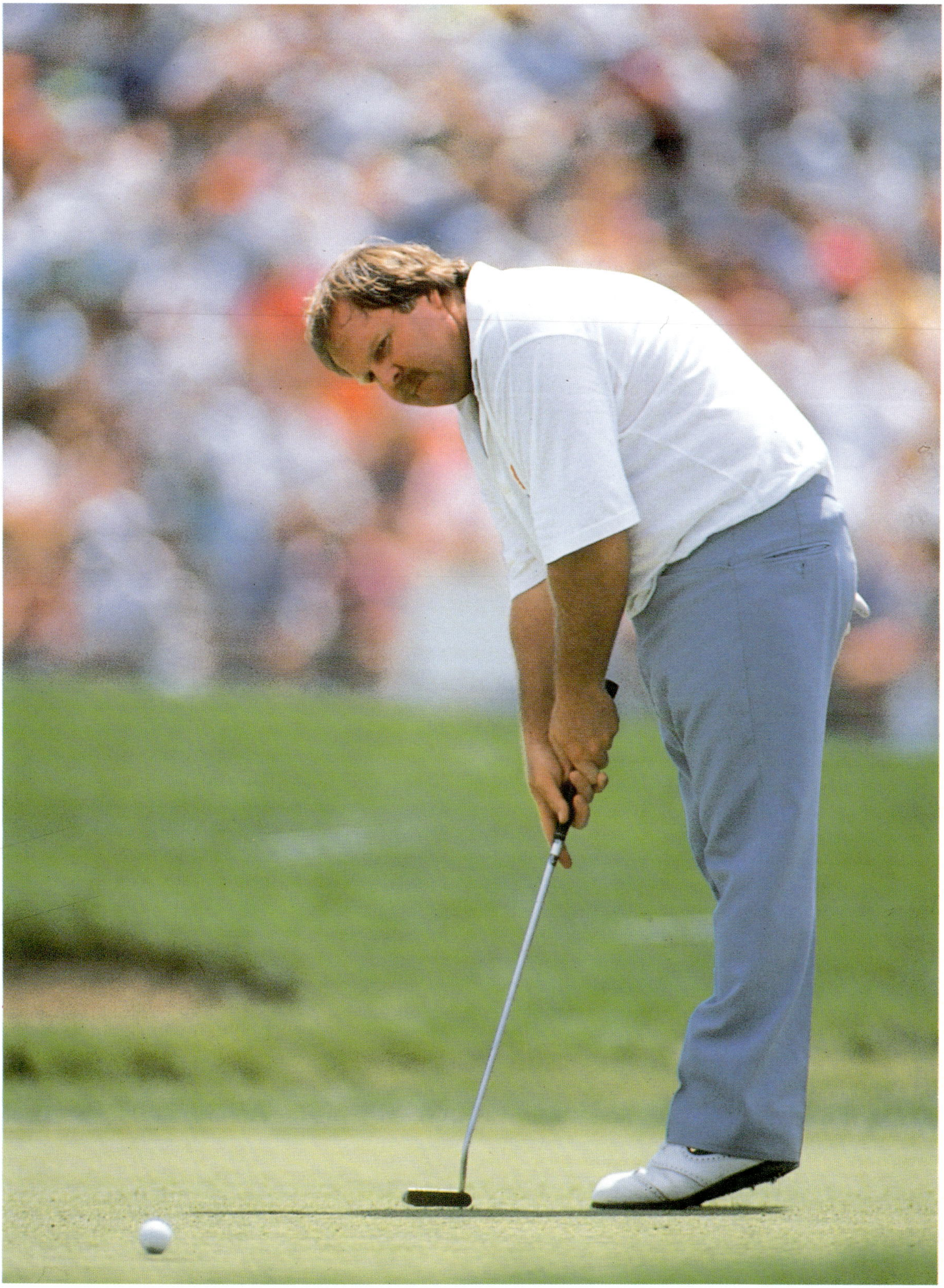

1991 USPGA TOUR WINNERS SUMMARY

Month	Tournament	Winner	Country
January	INFINITI TOURNAMENT OF CHAMPIONS	T. Kite	(US)
	NORTHERN TELECOM TUCSON OPEN	P. Mickelson	(US)
	UNITED HAWAIIAN OPEN	L. Wadkins	(US)
	PHOENIX OPEN	N. Henke	(US)
	AT&T PEBBLE BEACH NATIONAL PRO-AM	P. Azinger	(US)
February	BOB HOPE CHRYSLER CLASSIC	C. Pavin	(US)
	SHEARSON LEHMAN BROTHERS OPEN	J. D. Blake	(US)
	NISSAN LOS ANGELES OPEN	T. Schulz	(US)
	DORAL RYDER OPEN	R. Mediate	(US)
March	HONDA CLASSIC	S. Pate	(US)
	THE NESTLE INVITATIONAL	A. Magee	(US)
	USF&G CLASSIC	I. Woosnam	(GB)
	THE PLAYERS' CHAMPIONSHIP	S. Elkington	(Aus)
April	THE MASTERS	I. Woosnam	(GB)
	DEPOSIT GUARANTY CLASSIC	L. Silveira	(US)
	MCI HERITAGE CLASSIC	D. Love III	(US)
	K-MART GREATER GREENSBORO OPEN	M. Brooks	(US)
May	GTE BYRON NELSON CLASSIC	N. Prize	(Zmb)
	BELL SOUTH ATLANTA CLASSIC	C. Pavin	(US)
	MEMORIAL TOURNAMENT	K. Perry	(US)
	SOUTHWESTERN BELL COLONIAL	T. Purtzer	(US)
	KEMPER OPEN	B. Andrade	(US)
June	BUICK CLASSIC	B. Andrade	(US)
	US OPEN	P. Stewart	(US)
	ANHEUSER BUSCH CLASSIC	M. Hulbert	(US)
	FEDERAL EXPRESS ST JUDE CLASSIC	F. Couples	(US)
July	CENTEL WESTERN OPEN	R. Cochran	(US)
	NEW ENGLAND CLASSIC	B. Fleischer	(US)
	CHATTANOOGA CLASSIC	D. Pruitt	(US)
	CANON GREATER HARTFORD OPEN	B.R. Brown	(US)
August	BUICK OPEN	B. Faxon	(US)
	USPGA CHAMPIONSHIP	J. Daly	(US)
	THE INTERNATIONAL	J.-M. Olazabal	(Sp)
	NEC WORLD SERIES OF GOLF	T. Purtzer	(US)
	GREATER MILWAUKEE OPEN	M. Brooks	(US)
September	CANADIAN OPEN	N. Price	(Zmb)
	HARDEE'S CLASSIC	D.A. Weibring	(US)
	BC OPEN	F. Couples	(US)
	BUICK SOUTHERN OPEN	D. Peoples	(US)
October	HEB TEXAS OPEN	B. McCallister	(US)
	LAS VEGAS INVITATIONAL	A. Magee	(US)
	WALT DISNEY WORLD/OLDSMOBILE CLASSIC	M. O'Meara	(US)
	INDEPENDENT INSURANCE AGENT OPEN	F. Allem	(S. Afr)
	TOUR CHAMPIONSHIP	C. Stadler	(US)

1991 USPGA TOUR

MONEY LIST TOP 100:

1	Corey Pavin		$979,430	51	Scott Simpson	322,936
2	Craig Stadler		827,628	52	Bob Tway	322,931
3	Fred Couples		791,749	53	Greg Norman	320,196
4	Tom Purtzer		750,568	54	Steve Jones	294,961
5	Andrew Magee		750,082	55	Rick Fehr	288,983
6	Steve Pate		727,997	56	Ray Floyd	284,897
7	Nick Price		714,389	57	Bill Britton	282,894
8	Davis Love III		686,361	58	Loren Roberts	281,174
9	Paul Azinger		685,603	59	Robert Gamez	280,349
10	Russ Cochran		684,851	60	Larry Mize	279,061
11	Mark Brooks		667,263	61	Tom Sieckmann	278,598
12	Lanny Wadkins		651,495	62	Gary Hallberg	273,546
13	Ian Baker-Finch		649,513	63	Dillard Pruitt	271,861
14	Billy Andrade		615,765	64	Peter Jacobsen	263,180
15	Rocco Mediate		597,438	65	Ken Green	263,034
16	Chip Beck		578,535	66	Bob Gilder	251,683
17	John Daly		574,783	67	Brian Claar	251,309
18	Jim Gallagher Jnr		570,627	68	Jeff Maggert	240,940
19	Bruce Lietzke		566,272	69	Keith Clearwater	239,727
20	Mark O'Meara		563,896	70	Gill Morgan	232,913
21	Jay Don Blake		563,854	71	Fulton Allem	229,702
22	D.A. Weibring		558,648	72	Lee Janzen	228,242
23	Jeff Sluman		552,979	73	Fred Funk	226,915
24	Mike Hulbert		551,750	74	Howard Twitty	226,426
25	Steve Elkington		549,120	75	Ben Crenshaw	224,563
26	John Cook		546,984	76	Bruce Fleisher	219,335
27	Scott Hoch		520,038	77	Phil Blackmar	218,838
28	Nolan Henke		518,811	78	Dan Forsman	214,175
29	Ted Schulz		508,058	79	Dave Rummells	213,627
30	Ian Woosnam		485,023	80	Scott Gump	207,809
31	Payne Stewart		476,971	81	Bobby Wadkins	206,503
32	Kenny Knox		423,025	82	Ed Dougherty	201,958
33	Hale Irwin		422,652	83	Buddy Gardner	201,700
34	Brad Faxon		422,088	84	Jay Haas	200,637
35	David Peoples		414,346	85	Tim Simpson	196,582
36	Blaine McAllister		412,974	86	Duffy Waldorf	196,081
37	Gene Sauers		400,535	87	Wayne Levi	195,861
38	David Edwards		396,695	88	Andy Bean	193,609
39	Tom Kite		396,580	89	Billy Mayfair	185,668
40	John Huston		395,853	90	Neal Lancaster	180,037
41	Bob Lohr		386,759	91	Mike Springer	178,587
42	Fuzzy Zoeller		385,139	92	Mark McCumber	173,852
43	José-Maria Olazabal		382,124	93	David Frost	171,262
44	Kenny Perry		368,784	94	Joey Sindelar	168,352
45	Tom Watson		354,877	95	Dan Pohl	163,438
46	Billy Ray Brown		348,082	96	Larry Nelson	160,543
47	Hal Sutton		346,411	97	Dan Halldorson	158,743
48	Curtis Strange		336,333	98	Mike Reid	152,678
49	Jim Hallet		333,010	99	Brad Bryant	152,202
50	Mark Calcavecchia		323,621	100	Jay Delsing	149,775

1991 LPGA TOUR REVIEW

Pat Bradley played almost as superbly on the LPGA Tour in 1991 as she had in 1986 (when she won three of the four LPGA Majors) and as Betsy King and Beth Daniel had done in 1989 and 1990. She won four tournaments, including three in the space of four weeks in September, and close to three quarters of a million dollars. The third of those wins in September was her thirtieth career victory, so earning her a place in the LPGA Hall of Fame; in May she won the richest prize in the LPGA Tour's history, the Centel Classic and she also won an event in Japan by ten strokes. During the course of the season she became the first player to win four million dollars on the Tour – just as she had been first to the two-million-dollar and three-million-dollar marks. The only thing Bradley didn't do in 1991 was win a Major championship.

For all Pat Bradley's brilliance there was one person on the LPGA Tour who had an even more momentous year. At the beginning of February, twenty-eight-year-old Meg Mallon won the Oldsmobile Classic, her first victory on Tour, indeed her first win since the 1983 Michigan Amateur. In June she won a Major, the LPGA Championship, edging out the vastly more experienced duo of Bradley and Japan's Okamoto. She did it in their presence too, holing a winning birdie putt at the 18th from 12 feet for a 67 to win by a single stroke. To everyone's astonishment, a month later in the sweltering heat and humidity of southern Texas she added the US Women's Open title as well. Again she pushed Bradley into second place, overtaking her on the last day with another magnificent 67 (see results on page 148). It was unbelievable stuff. She hadn't quite finished either, for in October Mallon travelled to Australia and won the Daikyo Women's World Championship at the extremely demanding Paradise Palms course near Cairns, beating a strong field by five strokes.

Bradley and Mallon will almost certainly be playing for the US in the Solheim Cup this October – as should King, Daniel, Lopez and Sheehan. A frightening prospect! Not that the Europeans didn't make an impression on the LPGA Tour in 1991, mind you. Laura Davies gained her fifth win in America with a four-stroke victory in the Inamori Classic in March and Sweden's Lottie Neumann, like Davies a former US Women's Open champion, won the Mazda Japan Classic in the last event of the season. In 1992, Davies, Neumann and the other Europeans already playing the LPGA Tour are due to be joined by Florence Descampe and Helen Alfredsson who both won 'tour cards' last October. As an illustration of how good Bradley was last year, in the Rail Charity Classic in September Laura Davies scored an amazing ten under par 62 in the first round and led by five; she then added solid rounds of 70 and 72 but still lost to Bradley by seven. Bradley's three rounds were 67-65-65 – not bad on a course measuring 6,403 yards!

Beth Daniel (leading moneywinner in 1990) and Betsy King (US Women's Open champion in 1989 and 1990) both won twice in 1991. However, by their standards, it was perhaps a slightly disappointing year. A word also for Nancy Lopez who as an expectant mum missed much of the season yet still managed a victory in the Sara Lee Classic.

In addition to the LPGA Championship and the Women's US Open, the two other LPGA Majors, the Nabisco Dinah Shore and the Du Maurier Classic, were won respectively by Amy Alcott (by the huge margin of eight strokes after which she dived into the lake beside the 18th green taking Dinah Shore with her) and by Nancy Scranton (née Brown) whose win was her first ever on tour. The good news at the Du Maurier in September was that Trish Johnson, Pam Wright and Laura Davies, three members of the 1990 European Solheim Cup team, tied for third place.

Pat Bradley was the leading money winner and captured four titles on the LPGA Tour in 1991.

THE 1991 LPGA MAJORS

28-31 March
NABISCO DINAH SHORE, *Mission Hills, Rancho Mirage, California*

A. Alcott	67	70	68	68	273	$90,000
D. Mochrie	70	71	71	69	281	55,500
P. Bradley	70	72	73	67	282	36,000
P. Sheehan	71	71	70	70	282	36,000
L. Garbacz	73	71	70	70	284	25,500
C. Keggi	72	70	73	70	285	17,100
A. Okamoto	72	68	74	71	285	17,100
N. Brown	74	69	70	72	285	17,100
M. Nause	71	72	69	73	285	17,100
O. H. Ku	69	72	73	72	286	12,600
B. King	72	75	71	69	287	9,704
D. Ammaccapane	75	70	71	71	287	9,704
A. Benz	73	70	73	71	287	9,704
V. Fergon	70	76	69	72	287	9,704
J. Dickinson	71	75	67	74	287	9,704
T. Green	73	71	68	75	287	9,704

27-30 June
MAZDA LPGA CHAMPIONSHIP, *Bethesda, Maryland*

M. Mallon	68	68	71	67	274	$150,000
P. Bradley	68	68	71	68	275	80,000
A. Okamoto	70	64	73	68	275	80,000
B. Daniel	71	70	68	69	278	52,500
D. Richard	67	70	72	70	279	38,750
B. Bunkowsky	70	68	70	71	279	38,750
B. King	69	75	67	70	281	29,500
J. Carner	71	70	70	71	282	26,000
J. Inkster	72	70	71	70	283	23,500
A. Alcott	69	70	71	74	284	21,000
Leading European scores:						
L. Neumann	72	73	71	69	285	17,158
P. Wright	73	70	71	72	286	12,604

11-14 July
US WOMEN'S OPEN, *Colonial, Fort Worth, Texas*

M. Mallon	70	75	71	67	283	$110,000
P. Bradley	69	73	72	71	285	55,000
A. Alcott	75	68	72	71	286	32,882
L. Kean	70	76	71	70	287	23,996
D. Mochrie	73	76	68	71	288	17,642
C. Johnson	76	72	68	72	288	17,642
J. Pitcock	70	72	72	75	289	14,623
K. Albers	76	70	71	73	290	12,252
J. Anschutz	73	72	72	73	290	12,252
B. Burton	75	71	69	75	290	12,252
B. Daniel	74	76	75	66	291	9,738
T. Barrett	74	74	72	71	291	9,738
D. Massey	72	72	75	72	291	9,738
J. Carner	73	72	73	73	291	9,738
Leading European scores:						
L. Neumann	74	72	74	72	292	7,665
A. Nicholas	77	72	71	74	294	5,323
L. Davies	77	72	71	79	299	3,563
C. Pierce	79	72	75	74	300	3,125
M. Figueras-Dotti	76	75	77	73	301	2,797

12-15 September
DU MAURIER CLASSIC, *Vancouver G.C., B.C., Canada*

N. Scranton	72	75	64	68	279	$105,000
D. Massey	67	70	72	73	282	64,750
L. Davies	71	71	71	71	284	37,916
T. Johnson	67	71	73	73	284	37,916
P. Wright	72	69	69	74	284	37,916
D. Coe	68	77	71	70	286	17,966

Meg Mallon with the Women's US Open trophy.

UNITED STATES LADIES PGA TOUR

1991 TOURNAMENT WINNERS

Jamaica Classic: Jane Geddes
Oldsmobile Classic: Meg Mallon
Phar-Mor Inverrary Classic: Beth Daniel
Orix Hawaiian Open: Patty Sheehan
Kemper Open: Deb Richard
Inamori Classic: Laura Davies
Desert Inn International: Penny Hammel
Standard Register Ping: Danielle Ammaccapane
Nabisco Dinah Shore: Amy Alcott
Ping/Welch's Championship: Chris Johnson
Sara Lee Classic: Nancy Lopez
Crestar-Farm Fresh Classic: Hollis Stacy
Centel Classic: Pat Bradley
Corning Classic: Betsy King
Rochester International: Rosie Jones
Atlantic City Classic: Jane Geddes
Lady Keystone Open: Colleen Walker

McDonald's Championship: Beth Daniel
Mazda LPGA Championship: Meg Mallon
Jamie Farr Toledo Classic: Alice Miller
US Women's Open: Meg Mallon
JAL Big Apple Classic: Betsy King
Bay State Classic: Juli Inkster
Phar-Mor Youngstown: Deb Richard
Stratton Mountain Classic: Melissa McNamara
Northgate Computer Classic: Cindy Rarick
Chicago Sun-Times Shoot-Out: Martha Nause
Rail Charity Classic: Pat Bradley
Ping-Cellular One Championship: Michelle Estill
Du Maurier Ltd. Classic: Nancy Scranton
Safeco Classic: Pat Bradley
MBS Classic: Pat Bradley
Daikyo World Championship: Meg Mallon
Mazda Japan Classic: Liselotte Neumann

1991 LPGA ORDER OF MERIT

1	Pat Bradley	$763,118	26	Nancy Lopez	153,772
2	Meg Mallon	633,802	27	Liselotte Neumann	151,367
3	Dottie Mochrie	477,767	28	Barb Bunkowsky	150,719
4	Beth Daniel	469,501	29	Vicki Fergon	146,695
5	Deb Richard	376,640	30	Martha Nause	143,702
6	Danielle Ammaccapane	361,925	31	Kristi Albers	139,982
7	Ayako Okamoto	349,437	32	Tina Barrett	138,232
8	Patty Sheehan	342,204	33	Chris Johnson	135,416
9	Betsy King	341,785	34	Sally Little	134,859
10	Jane Geddes	315,240	35	Ok-Hee Ku	134,771
11	Colleen Walker	294,845	36	Kris Monaghan	134,753
12	Rosie Jones	281,089	37	Laurel Kean	133,659
13	Amy Alcott	258,269	38	Kris Tschetter	129,532
14	Judy Dickinon	251,017	39	Debbie Massey	127,308
15	Tammie Green	237,073	40	Michelle McGann	121,663
16	Nancy Scranton	223,677	41	Cindy Figg-Currier	121,558
17	Juli Inkster	213,096	42	Alice Miller	118,344
18	Caroline Keggi	208,534	43	Jody Anschutz	118,300
19	Cindy Rarick	201,342	44	Lynn Connelly	118,010
20	Laura Davies	200,831	45	Hollis Stacy	114,731
21	Elaine Crosby	181,610	46	Missie McGeorge	113,959
22	Brandie Burton	176,412	47	Missie Berteotti	106,459
23	Michelle Estill	171,475	48	Marta Figueras-Dotti	104,896
24	Sherri Steinhauer	165,568	49	Alice Ritzman	102,576
25	Dawn Coe	158,013	50	Pam Wright	96,904

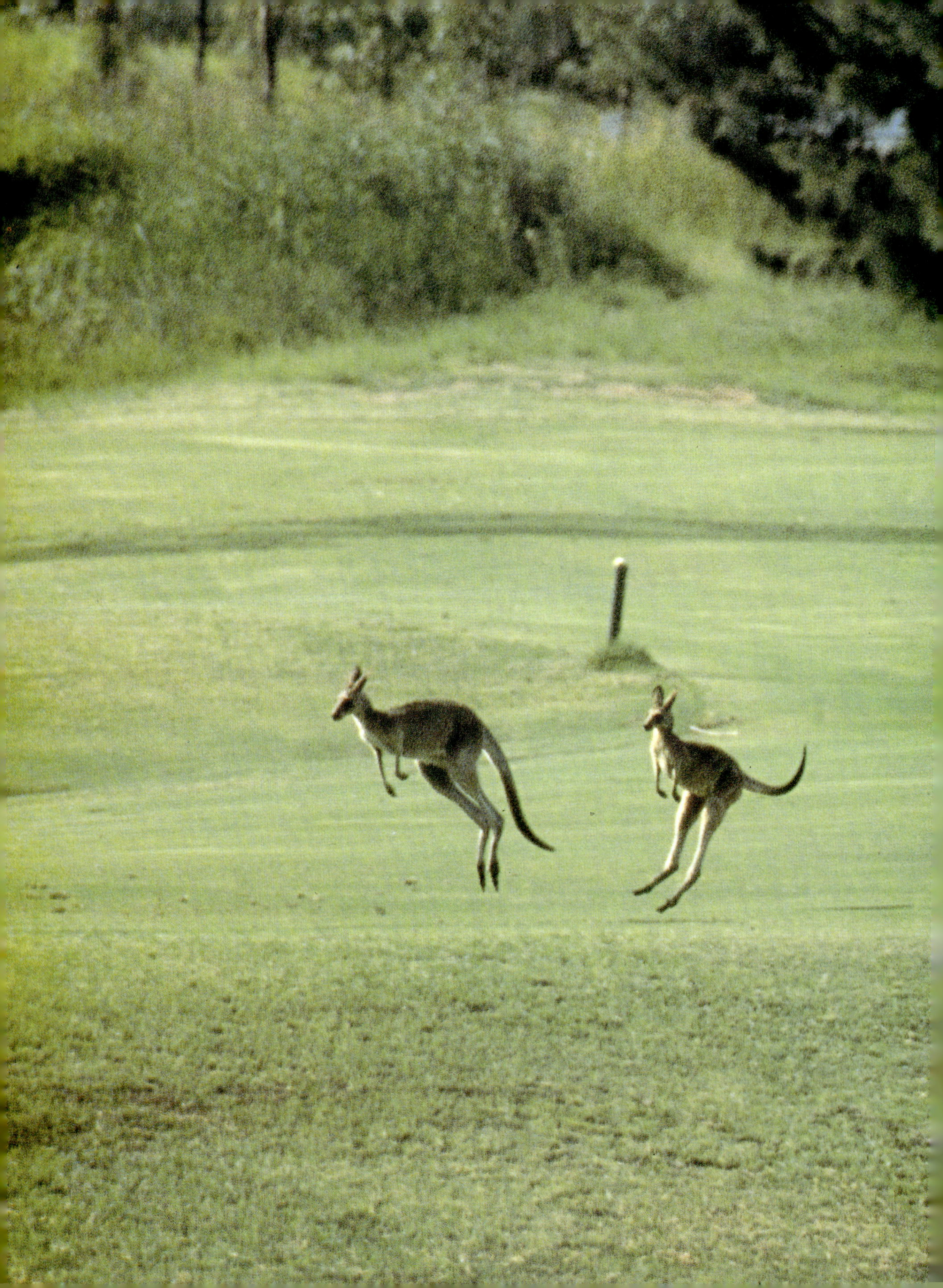

AUSTRALASIA

AUSTRALIAN TOUR REVIEW

Australian golfers won all over the world in 1991: Ian Baker-Finch claimed his first Major championship success in the Open at Royal Birkdale; Steve Elkington won the prestigious Players' Championship, golf's so called 'fifth Major', in Florida; Roger Mackay starred in Japan, winning three titles, including the Taiheiyo Masters; while in Europe Craig Parry and Rodger Davis both finished in the top six on the Volvo Order of Merit and in addition to finishing runner-up to Baker-Finch in the Open, Mike Harwood won the European Open.

The Australian Tour is a tour of two halves: it runs from January to March, then takes a long break before starting up again in October. Like the European Tour it stages events beyond its continent as a handful of South-East Asian events are now part of the Australian PGA Tour. The first two tour events of 1991 were both held on the Gold Coast: the Palm Meadows Cup won by Kiwi Greg Turner (who scored a 62 in the second round) and the Sanctuary Cove Classic, won by Rodger Davis on the resort's magnificent Pines Course (seven weeks later Davis also captured the New Zealand Open title). Greg Norman played in the first of these, Palm Meadows being his 'home club', and came second. In February Norman was runner-up again, this time to Peter Senior in the Australian Masters. It was an event Norman appeared to have completely sewn up as he led by 2 with four holes to play but contrived to drop shots at the 15th, 17th and 18th holes. Only two days earlier he had looked irresistible when he played the 10th to the 14th holes in his second round at Huntingdale with scores of birdie-birdie-birdie-birdie-eagle.

After the long break, and the 'mini tour' of Malaysia and Singapore, twenty-year-old amateur Robert Allenby raised many an eyebrow by winning the Victorian Open by six strokes. He would appear to have a great future; especially as he went on to finish runner-up in the Australian Open before turning professional last December. Great things have also been predicted for Brett Ogle, much of whose 1991 was wiped out owing to a freak injury he sustained at the 1990 Australian Open when a ball hit him after ricocheting off a tree. Ogle began to re-establish himself in November by winning the South Australian Open, then a week later came second to Wayne Grady in the Australian PGA Championship.

Greg Norman returned to Australia at the end of November to play in the Australian Open Championship at Royal Melbourne and the Johnnie Walker Classic at the Lakes, Sydney. After opening rounds of 76 (in the former) and 74 (in the latter) he never really featured in either event. Both titles were won by Australians though, as first Wayne Riley, then Peter Senior swept to victory with the aid of broom-handled putters. Perhaps it's time Greg paid a visit to his local hardware store.

Greg Norman.

(Previous page) Kangaroos on a fairway at the Kooralbyn Country Club in Queensland.

THE 1991 AUSTRALIAN PGA TOUR

14-17 February
AUSTRALIAN MASTERS *Huntingdale, Melbourne*

Player	R1	R2	R3	R4	Total	Prize
P. Senior	68	71	69	70	278	$A90,000
G. Norman	70	67	71	71	279	54,000
M. Clayton	67	71	74	69	281	29,700
P. O'Malley	72	68	71	70	281	29,700
D. Delong	71	70	73	68	282	19,000
I. Baker-Finch	74	70	69	69	282	19,000
R. Davis	71	68	72	71	282	19,000
J. Woodland	71	67	73	72	283	14,900
R. Allenby	74	70	70	71	285	(Am.)
J. Morse	71	74	72	68	285	13,500
T. Power	72	74	69	71	286	11,800
W. Riley	74	72	71	70	287	9,600
F. Nobilo	73	68	71	75	287	9,600
C. Parry	76	69	76	68	289	7,300
J. Clifford	75	71	72	71	289	7,300
P. Lonard	70	73	73	73	289	7,300
S. Ginn	72	71	70	76	289	7,300
G. Boros	71	72	74	73	290	6,150
T. Price	74	70	70	76	290	6,150

21-24 November
AUSTRALIAN PGA *Concord, Sydney*

Player	R1	R2	R3	R4	Total	Prize
W. Grady	66	68	68	69	271	$A45,000
B. Ogle	70	70	67	67	274	27,000
S. Richardson	67	67	70	73	277	14,850
N. Kerry	67	68	71	71	277	14,850
W. Smith	65	70	70	73	278	10,400
J. Spence	71	69	69	70	279	7,640
S. Owen	73	68	69	69	279	7,640
C. Parry	67	70	71	71	279	7,640
C. Warren	69	71	69	70	279	7,640
M. Clayton	69	72	67	71	279	7,640

28 November-1 December
AUSTRALIAN OPEN *Royal Melbourne.*

Player	R1	R2	R3	R4	Total	Prize
W. Riley	72	74	71	68	285	$A126,000
R. Allenby	70	78	70	68	286	(Am.)
R. Davis	72	70	70	75	287	75,600
B. Ogle	71	72	73	72	288	37,427
J. Spence	70	72	72	74	288	37,427
S. Richardson	72	70	70	76	288	37,427
C. Parry	74	70	72	73	289	26,740
H. Baron	72	68	74	76	290	22,400
M. Lanner	67	73	74	76	290	22,400
F. Nobilo	70	78	74	69	291	14,024
R. Rafferty	75	73	74	69	291	14,024
G. Waite	68	78	71	74	291	14,024
M. Bradley	71	75	72	73	291	14,024
A. Forsbrand	72	74	71	74	291	14,024
J. Kay	72	76	68	75	291	14,024

Peter Senior.

1991 WINNERS SUMMARY

Palm Meadows Cup	G. Turner
Sanctuary Cove Classic	R. Davis
The Vines Classic	B. McCallister
Australian Matchplay	C. Patton
Qantas Superskins	W. Grady
Australian Masters	P. Senior
AMP New Zealand Open	R. Davis
Tasmanian Open	C. Gray
Malaysian Masters	S. Ginn
Perak Masters	T. Power
Singapore PGA	P. Teravainen
Queensland PGA	W. Case
Victorian Open	R. Allenby
Air New Zealand Open	J. Morse
South Australian Open	B. Ogle
Australian PGA	W. Grady
Australian Open	W. Riley
Johnnie Walker Classic	P. Senior

JAPAN

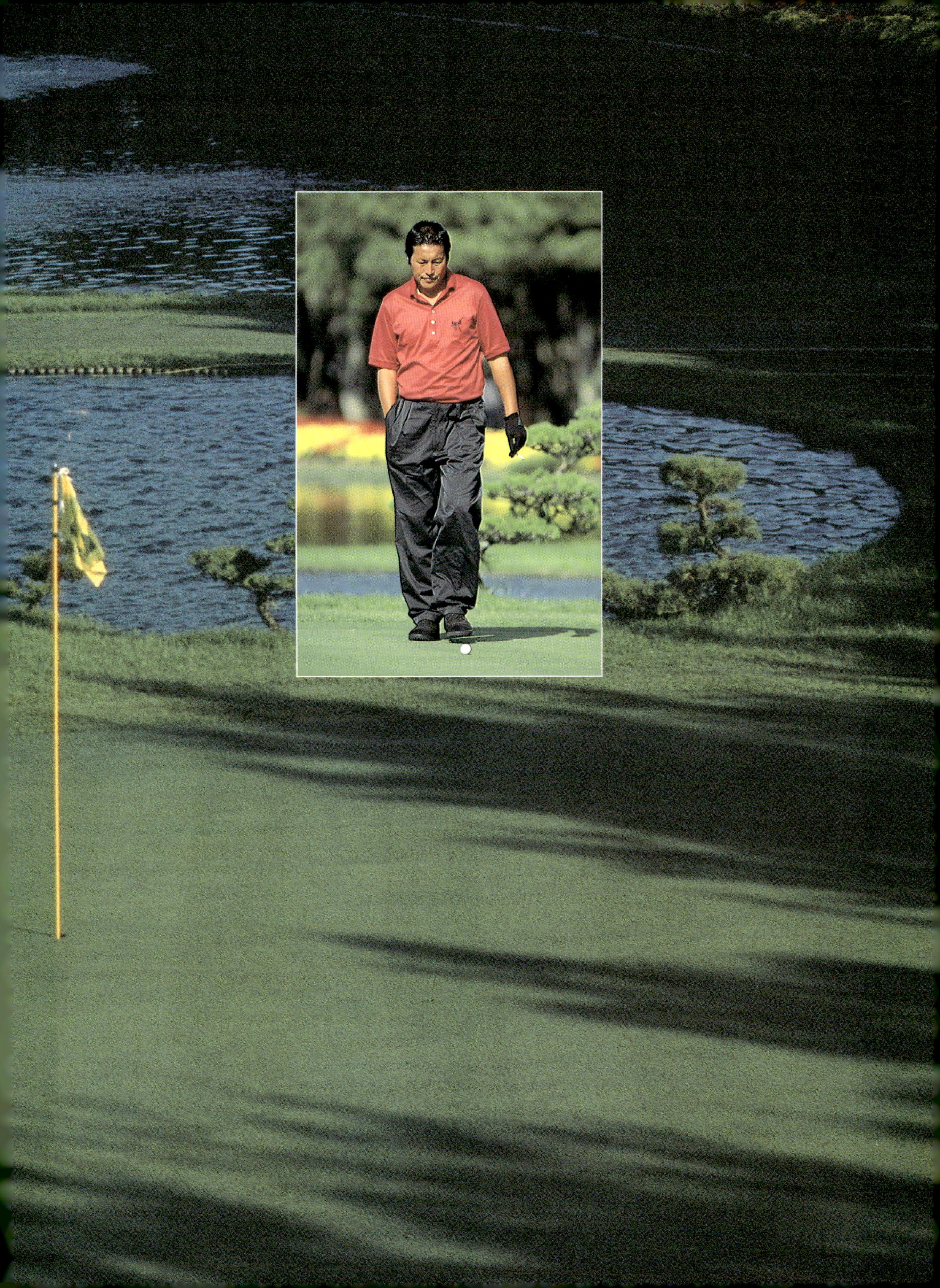

JAPANESE TOUR REVIEW

Tommy Nakajima won the Japan Open for the fourth time in October – the forty-sixth tournament success of his career.

1991 was meant to be the year when Ryoken (Ricky) Kawagishi took over from Masashi (Jumbo) Ozaki and Tsuneyuki (Tommy) Nakajima as Japan's leading player, but it didn't happen; in fact, after a brilliant Rookie season in 1990, twenty-four-year-old Kawagishi was a little disappointing, winning just once on the 1991 Japanese PGA Tour. Nor for that matter was Jumbo his usual, dominant self either but he did gain a spectacular victory in the important Japanese PGA Championship, coming from two strokes behind to win by 6 courtesy of a magnificent 61 in the final round.

Tommy Nakajima confirmed that his slump towards the end of the 1980s is now well and truly behind him by successfully defending the Japan Open title at Shimonoseki in October, defeating Noboru Sugai in a play-off. It was Nakajima's fourth win in Japan's most important (if not its most lucrative) event. Forty-nine-year-old Isao Aoki finished strongly to miss the play-off by a single stroke and Jumbo finished a further stroke back.

The aforementioned Aoki, who is eligible to make his début on the US Seniors Tour in 1992, continues to belie his years; he won the Bridgestone Tournament last Autumn after several near misses earlier in the year and very nearly scooped the huge first prize of thirty-six million yen (about £150,000) in the November Dunlop Phoenix tournament.

The 'Phoenix' is one of Japan's three end of season International Tour events, traditionally dominated by visiting American and European players whose home tours have just concluded. The first of the three, the Visa Taiheiyo Masters was won by Australian Roger Mackay, who thus prevented Olazabal from claiming a hat trick of 'red jackets'. Mackay also featured prominently in the Dunlop Phoenix a week later, an event Ballesteros ought really to have won but the Spaniard missed a 10-foot birdie putt at the last for the title. Seve joined Aoki and two Americans in a play-off and it was one of those Americans, Larry Nelson, who eventually triumphed.

Ballesteros did win, however, in Japan in 1991, his sixth Japanese Tour victory, as back in May he holed a putt twice as long as the one he missed at the Dunlop Phoenix to win the Chunichi Crowns tournament; a win which set him up for a brilliant summer in Europe.

Two of the last three titles of the year, including the prestigious Casio World Open, were claimed by Naomichi 'Joe' Ozaki, Jumbo's younger brother, who as a result overtook Mackay to finish the 1991 season as leading moneywinner.

THE 1991 PGA JAPAN TOUR

JAPAN'S INTERNATIONAL TOUR

14-17 November
VISA TAIHEIYO MASTERS *Taiheiyo, Gotemba*

R. Mackay	70	69	65	68	272	Y27,000,000
Y. Kaneko	68	70	68	68	274	15,000,000
T. Nakajima	70	65	68	72	275	10,200,000
J.-M. Olazabal	69	71	68	69	277	7,200,000
J. Sluman	71	72	70	66	279	6,000,000
F. Couples	70	71	70	69	280	5,400,000
B. Jones	73	73	67	68	281	4,350,000
Y. Hagawa	70	71	71	69	281	4,350,000
P. Senior	71	69	71	70	281	4,350,000
I. Aoki	71	71	74	66	282	3,450,000

21-24 November
DUNLOP PHOENIX *Phoenix, Miyazaki*

*L. Nelson	70	71	67	68	276	Y36,000,000
S. Ballesteros	68	69	69	70	276	14,400,000
I. Aoki	73	68	69	66	276	14,400,000
J.D. Blake	69	71	68	68	276	14,400,000
M. Reid	70	69	69	69	277	8,000,000
N. Henke	67	72	69	70	278	6,800,000
M. Brooks	66	68	71	73	278	6,800,000
C. Stadler	72	68	67	72	279	5,500,000
R. Mackay	69	70	67	73	279	5,500,000
S. Lyle	68	74	72	66	280	4,300,000
M. Harwood	71	70	71	68	280	4,300,000
M. Ozaki	71	76	66	68	281	3,386,666

28 November - 1 December
CASIO WORLD OPEN *Ibusuki, Kagashima*

N. Ozaki	71	67	64	68	270	Y25,200,000
H. Meshiai	69	67	70	66	272	14,000,000
L. Nelson	70	64	69	70	273	9,520,000
M. Ozaki	68	68	71	68	275	6,160,000
M. Kuramoto	65	71	74	65	275	6,160,000
W. Grady	68	71	70	67	276	4,760,000
T. Watanabe	74	65	70	67	276	4,760,000
N. Yuhara	70	67	70	70	277	3,850,000
K. Yoshimura	74	70	65	68	277	3,850,000

* Winner in play-off

TOURNAMENT WINNERS

Daiichi Fudosan Cup S. Fujiki
Imperial Tournament Y. Hagawa
Shizuoka Open Y. Hagawa
Taylor Made TSB M. Kimura
Pocarisweat Open R. Kawagishi
Bridgestone Aso Open K. Murota
Chunichi Crowns S. Ballesteros
Fujisankei Classic S. Fujiki
Japan PGA Matchplay S. Higashi
Pepsi Ube Tournament T. C. Chen
Mitsubishi Galant K. Suzuki
JCB Sendai Classic T. Ueno
Sapporo Tokyo Open R. Gibson
Yomiuri Open T. Nakajima
Mizuno Open R. Mackay
Yonex Hiroshima Open E. Itai
Takeda Cup H. Hamano
NST Nigata Open A. Yokoyama
Japan PGA Championship M. Ozaki
Maruman Open T. Nishikawa
Daiwa KBC Augusta R. Floyd.
Suntory Open N. Ozaki
ANA Sapporo Open A. Omachi
Gene Sarazen Classic M. Ozaki
Tokai Classic E. Itai
Japan Open Championship T. Nakajima
Asahi Beer Golf Digest H. Hamano
Bridgestone Tournament I. Aoki
Lark Cup Y. Yokoshima
Acom Stableford M. Kuramoto
Visa Taiheiyo Masters R. Mackay
Dunlop Phoenix L. Nelson
Casio World Open N. Ozaki
Nippon Series N. Ozaki
Daikyo Open H. Makino

Leading Money Winners

1	N. Ozaki	Y118,976,374
2	R. Mackay	113,137,135
3	T. Nakajima	107,799,213
4	M. Ozaki	99,050,539
5	I. Aoki	74,237,850

(Previous page) Unmistakably Japanese – the Dunlop Phoenix tournament and (inset) Masashi 'Jumbo' Ozaki.

(Overleaf) The beautiful Tanah Merah Country Club, Tanimur – venue for the 1991 Singapore Open.

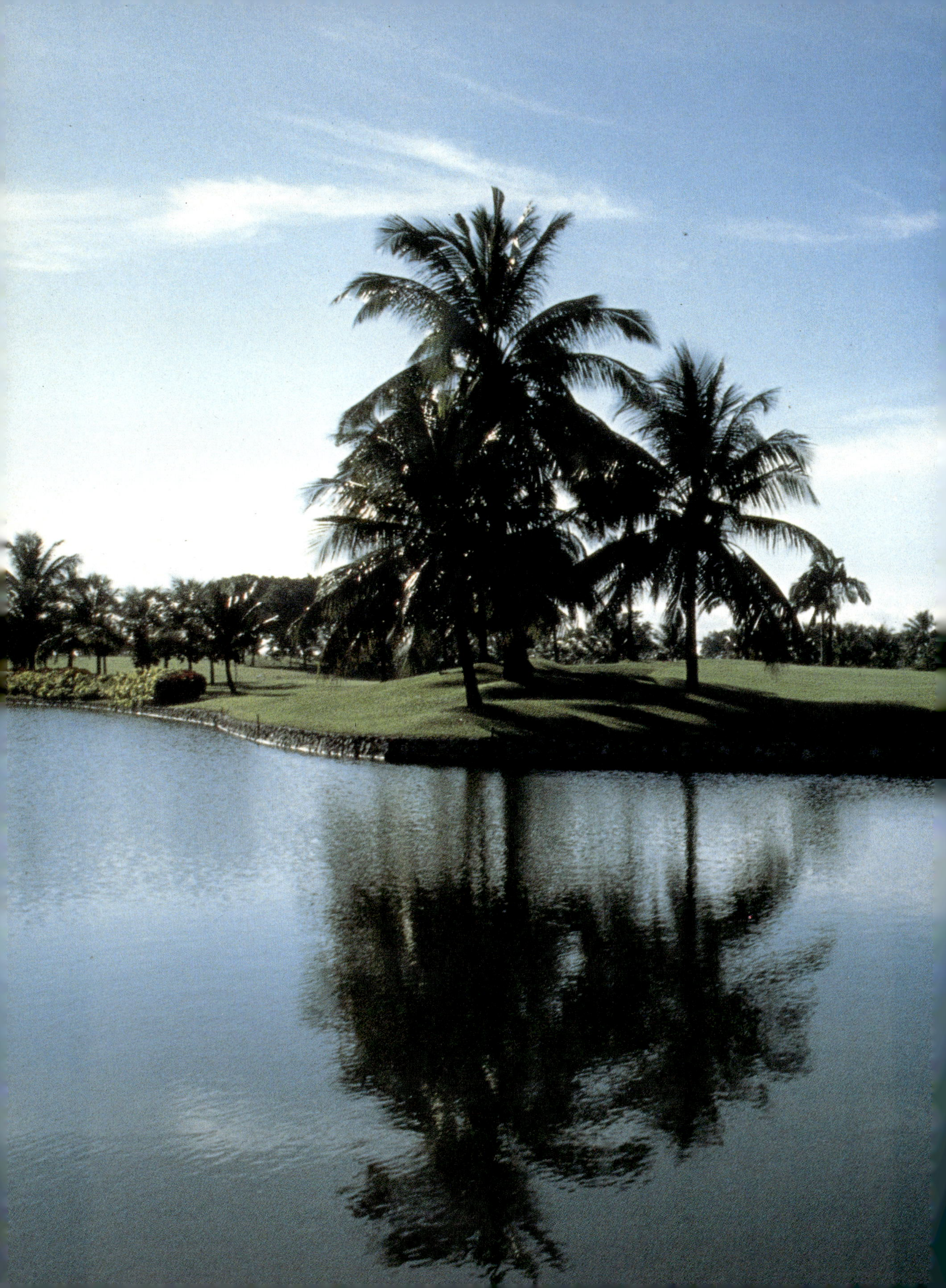

THE REST OF THE WORLD

ASIA and AFRICA

ASIAN TOUR 1991

Tournament winners

Hong Kong Open	B. Langer
Philippine Open	D. Paulson
Singapore Open	J. Kay
Malaysian Open	R. Gibson
Indonesian Open	L. H. Chen
Indian Open	A. Sher
Thailand Open	S. Meesawat
Republic of China Open	J. Jacobs
Maekyung Open	S. H. Choi
Dunlop Open	R. Mackay

1991 ASIAN ORDER OF MERIT WINNER
Rick Gibson (Canada)

JOHNNIE WALKER ASIAN CLASSIC

1990 Winner – N. Faldo
1991 No Tournament
1992 30 Jan – 2 Feb

SOUTH AFRICA (SUNSHINE) TOUR

1990-91 Order of Merit

1	John Bland	R333,637
2	Fulton Allem	190,090
3	Wayne Westner	168,158
4	Hugh Baiocchi	155,409
5	Tony Johnstone	146,918

1991 SOUTH AFRICAN OPEN – W. Westner

SUN CITY MILLION DOLLAR CHALLENGE

1989 winner – D. Frost
1990 winner – D. Frost
1991 winner – B. Langer

SAFARI TOUR

1990-91 Tournament winners

Nigerian Open	W. Stephens
Ivory Coast Open	D. Llewellyn
Zimbabwe Open	K. Waters
Zambia Open	D. Jones
Kenya Open	J. Robinson

Bernhard Langer, winner of the Hong Kong Open.

John Bland led the South African Tour in 1991.

ASAHI GLASS FOUR TOURS WORLD CHAMPIONSHIP

7-10 November, Royal Adelaide, Australia

FIRST DAY
PGA European Tour beat Australian PGA Tour 8–4
Ronan Rafferty (77) halved with Roger Mackay (77)
Paul Broadhurst (71) beat Craig Parry (75)
Steven Richardson (76) halved with Graham Marsh (76)
Sam Torrance (73) beat Ian Baker-Finch (79)
David Feherty (78) lost to Mike Harwood (75)
Colin Montgomerie (73) beat Rodger Davis (79)

USPGA Tour beat PGA Japan 8–4
Jim Gallagher Jnr (74) beat Ricky Kawagishi (77)
Tom Purtzer (73) beat Tsukasa Watanabe (74)
Billy Mayfair (79) lost to Yoshinori Kaneko (76)
Lanny Wadkins (75) beat Hideki Kase (76)
Bob Tway (80) lost to Hiroshi Makino (78)
Fred Couples (73) beat Noburo Sugai (76)

SECOND DAY
PGA European Tour halved with PGA Japan 6–6
Ronan Rafferty (70) beat Tsukasa Watanabe (73)
Sam Torrance (72) halved with Ricky Kawagishi (72)
David Feherty (73) lost to Yoshinori Kaneko (71)
Steven Richardson (74) halved with Hideki Kase (74)
Paul Broadhurst (72) beat Hiroshi Makino (74)
Colin Montgomerie (73) lost to Noboru Sugai (71)

Australian PGA Tour beat USPGA Tour 7–5
Ian Baker-Finch (76) lost to Fred Couples (70)
Graham Marsh (70) beat Billy Mayfair (72)
Rodger Davis (73) halved with Jim Gallagher Jnr (73)
Roger Mackay (71) beat Bob Tway (78)
Craig Parry (71) beat Tom Purtzer (72)
Mike Harwood (77) lost to Lanny Wadkins (70)

THIRD DAY
PGA European Tour halved with USPGA Tour 6–6
Ronan Rafferty (73) lost to Bob Tway (71)
Steven Richardson (74) lost to Billy Mayfair (69)
Sam Torrance (70) beat Tom Purtzer (72)
David Feherty (71) lost to Fred Couples (70)
Colin Montgomerie (66) beat Lanny Wadkins (71)
Paul Broadhurst (70) beat Jim Gallagher Jnr (72)

Australian PGA Tour beat PGA Japan 8–4
Rodger Davis (73) beat Ricky Kawagishi (74)
Ian Baker-Finch (76) lost to Tsukasa Watanabe (72)
Mike Harwood (74) lost to Yoshinori Kaneko (72)
Graham Marsh (71) beat Hideki Kase (74)
Roger Mackay (73) beat Hiroshi Makino (74)
Craig Parry (68) beat Noboru Sugai (78)

TOTAL POINTS AFTER 54 HOLES ROUND-ROBIN
PGA European Tour 20 points
Australian Tour 19 points
USPGA Tour 19 points
PGA Japan 14 points
Australian PGA Tour qualified for the final by virtue of beating USPGA Tour on the second day

Play-Off for 3rd and 4th places
USPGA Tour halved with PGA Japan 6–6

*PGA of Japan won on count-back

FINAL
PGA European Tour beat Australian PGA Tour 8–4
Colin Montgomerie (74) lost to Mike Harwood (72)
Ronan Rafferty (65) beat Rodger Davis (70)
David Feherty (71) beat Graham Marsh (74)
Steven Richardson (73) lost to Roger Mackay (71)
Sam Torrance (72) beat Craig Parry (73)
Paul Broadhurst (69) beat Ian Baker-Finch (74)

LEADING INDIVIDUAL SCORES

Paul Broadhurst	71	72	70	69	282
Ronan Rafferty	77	70	73	65	285
Colin Montgomerie	73	73	66	74	286
Sam Torrance	73	72	70	72	287
Craig Parry	75	71	68	73	287
Tom Purtzer	73	72	72	70	287
Lanny Wadkins	75	70	71	72	288
Fred Couples	73	70	70	75	288

THE 37th WORLD CUP OF GOLF

31 October – 3 November, Rome, Italy

For the second year running, the World Cup produced a surprise European winner. In 1990 at Grand Cypress, Florida, it was Germany who stunned the golfing world, or, more especially, it was Torsten Giedeon who stunned the golfing world, by playing the best golf of his life to partner Bernhard Langer to a memorable three-stroke victory over England.

In 1991 the World Cup was staged in Italy at La Querce G.C. on the outskirts of Rome; Langer and Giedeon were back but the favourites were England and Spain, led respectively by Nick Faldo and Seve Ballesteros. For the first two days England, Spain and Germany battled for the lead; a resurgent Woosnam then thrust Wales in to contention but it was Sweden, represented by Anders Forsbrand and Per-Ulrik Johansson, who eventually stole the show.

It all sounds a very European affair and to a large extent it was. Australian players have lately become the talk of golf in all four corners of the globe but Rodger Davis and Mike Harwood never remotely challenged for the title and the United States, who once dominated this event, could finish no better than joint twelfth behind Switzerland. To be fair to Uncle Sam, the World Cup clashed with the US Tour's grand finale at Pinehurst and so the best pairing they could muster was Wayne Levi and Joey Sindelar – not exactly the kind of partnership likely to put the fear of God into the opposition.

After the first round England's Faldo and Richardson looked the team to beat but they followed their first day total of 137 (68 for Faldo and 69 for Richardson) with a pair of 73s, allowing Spain (Ballesteros, 68-69 and Rivero, 73-69) to take over the lead.

The Spanish pair played steadily on the third day, without doing anything spectacular, but as England and Germany started to fall away Wales and Sweden made their moves. After nine holes of the third round the Swedes were 9 shots behind Ballesteros

Spanish smiles in Rome, but Ballesteros and Rivero couldn't hold on to their lead.

and Rivero but they then began to play magnificently: Forsbrand came home in 31 for a 65 and Johansson in 33 for a 69, reducing Spain's lead to just 2. Woosnam's 67 lifted Wales to within a stroke of Sweden, so setting up an exciting final day's play.

Most eyes were on Ballesteros and Woosnam as the teams teed off on Sunday but it was Forsbrand who was scoring all the birdies. He, remember, had played his final nine holes on Saturday in 31; on Sunday he did the same on the front nine – eighteen holes in sixty-two strokes! With the Spaniards struggling and Johanssson playing a strong supporting role to Forsbrand that should have settled it but Woosnam and Price made the Swedes fight all the way to the finishing line – and, but for Woosnam incurring an unfortunate penalty stroke at the 15th when he lifted his ball on the green but forgot to put down a marker, the teams might have finished level.

So just three weeks after winning the Dunhill Cup, Sweden had won the World Cup and Woosnam had to settle for the consolation of finishing Leading Individual.

LEADING TEAM SCORES

SWEDEN	**563**						
A. Forsbrand	73	73	65	68	279		
P.-U. Johansson	69	75	69	71	284	£68,846 each	
WALES	**564**						
I. Woosnam	70	69	67	67	273		
P. Price	72	75	72	72	291	34,423 each	
SCOTLAND	**567**						
S. Torrance	71	71	66	73	281		
C. Montgomerie	73	70	74	69	286	25,243 each	
ENGLAND	**570**						
N. Faldo	68	73	74	71	286		
S. Richardson	69	73	74	68	284	16,351 each	
GERMANY	**570**						
B. Langer	69	69	71	67	276		
T. Giedeon	69	75	78	72	294	16,351 each	
NEW ZEALAND	**571**						
F. Nobilo	73	69	71	72	285		
G. J. Turner	73	71	70	72	286	10,040 each	
SPAIN	**571**						
S. Ballesteros	68	69	71	72	280		
J. Rivero	73	69	72	77	291	10,040 each	
IRELAND	**574**						
R. Rafferty	76	70	72	68	286		
E. Darcy	71	69	74	74	288	5,546 each	
JAPAN	**574**						
S. Higashi	73	71	73	67	284		
N. Serizawa	69	74	72	75	290	5,546 each	
CANADA	**574**						
D. Barr	72	72	70	70	284		
D. Halldorson	72	75	69	74	290	5,546 each	
SWITZERLAND	**575**						
A. Bossert	71	71	70	68	280		
P. Quirici	72	75	70	78	295	4,016 each	
AUSTRALIA	**578**						
R. Davis	74	70	69	71	284		
M. Harwood	76	75	72	71	294	2,868 each	
ITALY	**578**						
C. Rocca	72	70	74	70	286		
G. Cali	78	73	67	74	292	2,868 each	
USA	**578**						
W. Levi	72	70	72	73	287		
J. Sindelar	75	73	70	73	291	2,868 each	
FRANCE	**579**						
M. Farry	74	73	70	70	287		
J. Van De Velde	72	74	73	73	292	2,008 each	
NORWAY	**582**						
G. Midivage	76	73	70	71	290		
P. Haugsrud	72	71	77	72	292	2,008 each	
MEXICO	**583**						
R. Alarcon	77	68	74	71	290		
C. Espinosa	73	71	75	74	293	2,008 each	
REP OF KOREA	**584**						
S. Choi	74	75	68	73	290		
N. Park	69	80	72	73	294	2,008 each	
DENMARK	**584**						
A. Sorensen	69	73	69	72	283		
J. Rasmussen	73	78	73	77	301	2,008 each	
ARGENTINA	**585**						
E. Romero	70	71	72	73	286		
R. Alvarez	74	71	79	75	299	2,008 each	
HOLLAND	**585**						
C. Van De Velde	73	69	69	75	286		
W. Swart	74	75	76	74	299	2,008 each	

LEADING INDIVIDUAL SCORES

I. Woosnam	70	69	67	67	273	£43,029
B. Langer	69	69	71	67	276	28,686
A. Forsbrand	73	73	65	68	279	22,948
A. Bossert	71	71	70	68	280	14,343
S. Ballesteros	68	69	71	72	280	14,343
S. Torrance	71	71	66	73	281	8,605
A. Sorensen	69	73	69	72	283	
R. Davis	74	70	69	71	284	
S. Higashi	73	71	73	67	284	
S. Richardson	69	73	74	68	284	
D. Barr	72	72	70	70	284	
P.-U. Johansson	69	75	69	71	284	

SENIORS REVIEW

Not for the first time, and probably not for the last time either, it was the Year of the Bear. Several players won more money than Jack Nicklaus on the 1991 US Seniors Tour and one or two won more tournaments, but the fifty-one-year-old part-time Senior, who only entered a handful of events, made by far the biggest impression on Senior golf in 1991. Nicklaus has always measured his form against the yardstick of Major championships, well, last year he won two of the four so-called 'Senior Majors' and another of those, the Seniors British Open, he didn't enter anyway.

Jack, in fact, didn't play in his first Senior Tour event until April, although he did take part in the Senior Skins game in Hawaii in January along with four of his greatest sparring partners from times past: Arnold Palmer, Gary Player, Lee Trevino and Chi Chi Rodriguez. Who won the most loot? Nicklaus did, of course. He claimed the Bear's share of $310,000 and a 35-foot putt at the final hole was worth the outrageous sum of $285,000 – more than he has ever won for winning a full tournament!

When Nicklaus teed up to defend his Tradition title at Desert Mountain in April, Lee Trevino had already won three Senior tournaments yet it was Nicklaus who emerged victorious despite falling twelve strokes behind Phil Rodgers after thirty-six holes. Rounds of 66–67 enabled him to effect a remarkable comeback. Two weeks later he maintained his form to win the PGA Seniors Championship at Palm Beach, Florida. Playing in his 'own backyard' he destroyed the opposition and left them scrambling for second place as he compiled rounds of 66-66-69-70 to win by six (his lead had been as much as 10 with seven holes to play).

Nicklaus' other Senior Tour victory of 1991 was in the most important over fifties event, the US Senior Open at Oakland Hills, Michigan. It came after a play-off with Chi Chi Rodriguez who described the contest on the eve of the eighteen extra holes as 'The Big Bear versus the Little Mouse from Puerto Rico'. The 'Little Mouse' had actually captured four Tour victories and headed the money list but Nicklaus shot a 65 on the Monday and that, frankly, was that.

Jack Nicklaus has won three of the six Senior Majors that he's entered.

Despite a number of successes, Lee Trevino had a slightly frustrating year in 1991. He started the season very strongly but then seemed to find finishing second much easier than finishing first. He was rarely out of the frame all year but certainly didn't dominate week in, week out as he had done in 1990 when he won seven tournaments and a million dollars in prize money. Rodriguez, Mike Hill and George Archer were just as successful as 'Super Mex', moreover Trevino failed to win a Senior Major despite leading after three rounds in two of them. He relinquished his US Senior Open crown with a 74 to finish two strokes behind Nicklaus and Rodriguez, but his collapse in the Senior Players' Championship was much more spectacular, as can be gleaned from scores of 70-67-69-78. Jim Albus, a virtually unknown club professional from Long Island, was the chief beneficiary of Trevino's amazing final round generosity.

With neither Nicklaus nor Trevino choosing to play in the Seniors British Open at Royal Lytham & St Annes, the two favourites were Gary Player and Bob Charles. Both had won the event before, indeed had shared the spoils since 1988, and both had won Open Championships on the famous Lancashire links – Charles in 1963 and Player in 1974. In the event, Charles was joint leader after the first round and Player sole leader after two rounds but while both finished in the top five, the title was claimed by a third golfer from the Southern hemisphere, South African Bobby Verwey. The result must have produced mixed feelings for the Player family as Verwey just happens to be Mrs Player's brother – Gary's brother-in-law!

'Super-Mex', Lee Trevino.

THE 1991 SENIOR MAJORS

18-21 April
USPGA SENIORS CHAMPIONSHIP, *PGA National, West Palm Beach, Florida*

J. Nicklaus	66 66 69 70	271	$85,000
B. Crampton	72 67 70 68	277	55,000
B. Charles	72 71 68 71	282	40,000
H. Blancas	70 72 70 71	283	30,000
G. Archer	68 74 68 74	284	25,000
R. Thompson	72 72 72 69	285	18,725
J. Dent	71 66 75 73	285	18,725
O. Moody	72 72 70 72	286	14,150
G. Player	73 73 68 72	286	14,150
J. Colbert	73 67 72 74	286	14,150
L. Trevino	72 72 72 71	287	12,000
C. C. Rodriguez	73 72 70 73	288	10,500
L. Laoretti	74 69 69 76	288	10,500

6-9 June
SENIOR PLAYERS CHAMPIONSHIP, *T.P.C. at Michigan*

J. Albus	66 74 69 70	279	$150,000
B. Charles	69 71 73 69	282	73,333
D. Hill	71 68 70 73	282	73,333
C. Coody	71 69 70 72	282	73,333
J.P. Cain	71 73 69 70	283	41,333
T. Dill	74 69 68 72	283	41,333
D. Bies	68 75 66 74	283	41,333
M. Hill	69 71 72 72	284	27,350
D. Douglass	74 72 67 71	284	27,350
J. Colbert	70 71 69 74	284	27,350
L. Trevino	70 67 69 78	284	27,350

11–14 July
SENIORS BRITISH OPEN, *Royal Lytham & St Annes, Lancashire*

B. Verwey	70 74 71 70	285	£25,000
B. Charles	69 76 74 67	286	12,775
T. Horton	69 76 71 70	286	12,775
C. Green	72 75 72 70	289	(Am.)
G. Player	70 73 73 74	290	7,350
D. Butler	75 75 70 72	292	6,150
N. Coles	73 75 73 72	293	4,071
A. Proctor	72 76 72 73	293	4,071
B. Waites	73 74 72 74	293	4,071
H. Muscroft	74 73 75 71	293	4,071
P. Butler	69 75 72 78	294	2,795
B. Hunt	71 76 76 71	294	2,795
C. Mehok	73 77 72 73	295	2,560
A. Palmer	72 77 75 74	298	2,370
B. Rose	71 74 74 79	298	2,370

25-28 July
US SENIOR OPEN, *Oakland Hills, Birmingham, Michigan*

J. Nicklaus	72 69 70 71	282	$110,000
C.C. Rodriguez	73 68 70 71	282	55,000
(J. Nicklaus won play-off 65-69)			
A. Geiberger	71 70 72 70	283	33,137
J. Dent	73 72 72 67	284	21,604
L. Trevino	70 72 68 74	284	21,604
D. Bies	72 69 72 73	286	15,633
C. Coody	78 68 69 71	286	15,633
B. Charles	72 70 73 72	287	12,346
G. Player	69 73 73 72	287	12,346
M. Hill	68 74 71 74	287	12,346
B. Crampton	75 69 72 73	289	9,813
H. Henning	73 73 70 73	289	9,813
B. Nichols	71 73 74 71	289	9,813
K. Still	76 71 72 70	289	9,813

South African Bobby Verwey.

AMATEUR REVIEW

Not for thirty years has there been an amateur golfer with as big a reputation as Phil Mickelson, and yes, there are no prizes for guessing who that amateur was. Perhaps there is a special interest because Mickelson is left-handed and among Americans there may be a prejudiced opinion as they desperately search for a superstar to succeed Nicklaus and Watson. But Mickelson is undoubtedly a great talent and his achievement last January of winning a US Tour event, the Tucson Open, with rounds of 65-71-65-71 sent the biggest shock waves around the world of professional golf since Jack Nicklaus scorched around Merion in the 1960 Eisenhower Trophy, shooting 66-67-68-68. Jack was only twenty at the time; Mickelson was twenty when he won in Tucson.

Golf enthusiasts on this side of the Atlantic had two opportunities to watch Mickelson in 1991, firstly at the Open where he didn't play his best but still produced a second round 67 and secondly at the Walker Cup at Portmarnock where he inspired the visiting team to regain the trophy they had lost at Peachtree in 1989. He displayed several flashes of genius at Portmarnock, one of which, a marvellous recovery shot at the par three 15th (captured by the photographer Dave Cannon and reproduced below), will long be remembered by all those who witnessed its sheer audacity. The Walker Cup is reviewed briefly ahead.

Mickelson finished leading amateur in both The Masters and the US Open but was denied an 'Amateur Grandslam' by Lincolnshire's

Phil Mickelson plays a brilliant pitch to the 15th green at Portmarnock.

Jim Payne, widely acknowledged as Britain's top amateur in 1991. Payne won the British Youths and European Amateur Championships last year but has since turned professional, as have a high proportion of the players from both Walker Cup teams. Included in this number is Worthing golfer Gary Evans who finished joint second in the European Tour qualifying school in November and earlier won the Lytham Trophy. He also tied for first place in the English Amateur Strokeplay – just as he had done in 1990. Payne and Evans will be joined on the 1992 Volvo Tour by McGinley and White from the Great Britain and Ireland side but not, surprisingly, by Ricky Willison, an emphatic winner of the English Amateur Championship at Formby but who failed to gain one of the forty prized Tour cards.

One week after the clash at Portmarnock the 1991 Amateur Championship was staged at Ganton. Eight of America's winning team played in the championship, but sadly not Mickelson who had been playing truant from college for too long. An American win was expected, especially when two of their best, Dave Duval and Bob May, reached the semifinals, but thirty-one-year-old Gary Wolstenholme from Bristol & Clifton had other ideas. Playing the best golf of his life he fired nine birdies and an eagle in the thirty-six hole final to defeat a bewildered Bob May 8 and 6. For Wolstenholme it not only gave him the thrill of seeing his name engraved upon the same trophy as the greatest of all amateurs, Bobby Jones, but also a place in the 1992 Masters at Augusta. Quite a bonus!

The Women's British Amateur Championship was staged not a million miles away from Ganton at Pannal on the outskirts of Harrogate. There, Valerie Michaud became the first French winner of the championship since the celebrated Catherine Lacoste in 1969. Michaud is another golfer keen to join the professional ranks and would seem to have all the credentials to become the next Marie-Laure de Lorenzi. The most successful British amateur woman in 1991 was Janet Morley who won both the English and British Strokeplay titles. Another double winner

Jim Payne.

of big events was Nicola Buxton who captured the English Women's Championship and the English Girls' Championship, while Vicki Thomas will be able to look back at 1991 as the year she won a record seventh Welsh Women's Amateur Championship at Royal St Davids.

Among the seniors, Charlie Green and Angela Uzielli retained their British Senior titles, for Green it was his fourth victory in succession, while the most outstanding homegrown junior players of 1991 were England's Iain Pyman and Scotland's Janice Moodie. Finally, a young Spanish golfer to make a note of is Francisco Valera. He won the 1991 British Boys' Championship and is perhaps a natural successor to the 1983 champion, one José-Maria Olazabal.

THE 1991 AMATEUR CHAMPIONSHIP

September 10-15, Ganton G.C., North Yorkshire

Fourth round
D. Duval beat P. Wood 3 and 2
I. Pyman beat F. Valera 2 and 1
S. Twynholm beat S. Lovey at 19th
B. May beat J. Sigel 7 and 5
K. Miller beat C. O'Carroll 4 and 3
G. Wolstenholme beat M. Florioli 6 and 5
W. Bryson beat M. Pullan at 19th
G. Zahringer III beat J. Hodgson 4 and 3

Quarter-finals
D. Duval beat I. Pyman 3 and 2
B. May beat S. Twynholm 2 and 1
G. Wolstenholme beat K. Miller 2 and 1
W. Bryson beat G. Zahringer 3 and 2

Semi-finals
B. May beat D. Duval 3 and 2
G. Wolstenholme beat W. Bryson 5 and 4

FINAL (36 holes)
G. Wolstenholme beat B. May 8 and 6

Gary Wolstenholme.

PAST CHAMPIONS
Post 1945

1946 J. Bruen	1962 R. Davies	1979 J. Sigel
1947 W. Turnesa	1963 M. Lunt	1980 D. Evans
1948 F. Stranahan	1964 G. Clark	1981 P. Ploujoux
1949 S. McCready	1965 M. Bonallack	1982 M. Thompson
1950 F. Stranahan	1966 R. Cole	1983 P. Parkin
1951 R. Chapman	1967 R. Dickson	1984 J.-M. Olazabal
1952 E. Ward	1968 M. Bonallack	1985 G. McGimpsey
1953 J. Carr	1969 M. Bonallack	1986 D. Curry
1954 D. Bachli	1970 M. Bonallack	1987 P. Mayo
1955 J. Conrad	1971 S. Melnyk	1988 C. Hardin
1956 J. Beharrell	1972 T. Homer	1989 S. Dodd
1957 R. Reid-Jack	1973 R. Siderowf	1990 R. Muntz
1958 J. Carr	1974 T. Homer	
1959 D. Beaman	1975 M. Giles	
1960 J. Carr	1976 R. Siderowf	
1961 M. Bonallack	1977 P. McEvoy	
	1978 P. McEvoy	

Most victories
John Ball (8) between 1888 and 1912

THE 33rd WALKER CUP

5–6 September, Portmarnock, Dublin

As the crow flies, Peachtree, near Atlanta, and Portmarnock, near Dublin, are about 3,500 miles apart. In golfing terms they belong to different worlds. The former is one of the most beautifully manicured courses in America; a wonderful test of inland golf and though overshadowed it is in no way outclassed by the most celebrated course in Georgia, good ol' Augusta.

Portmarnock is one of the great seaside courses of the world, some would say the greatest. Spectacularly situated on a peninsula north of Dublin, it has all the characteristics of pure links golf, including, when the mood takes it, a devilish wind. If Great Britain and Ireland could win the Walker Cup at Peachtree then surely they could successfully defend the trophy at Portmarnock? That is one way of looking at it, another, to take an American viewpoint, is to look at the overall match score which read, pre-Portmarnock: Played 32: Wins for USA 28, Wins for GB & Ireland 3, Tied matches 1: Peachtree was just a blip.

After the first morning of the two-day match last September the New World view of things was looking entirely accurate. The visitors led 4–0 after winning all four of the foursomes matches. It could so easily have been 2–2 as the home side were up in two of the matches until they reached the closing stretch where they were first caught after seventeen holes then beaten on the 18th green. One of the matches, Payne and Evans (1 up with three to play) versus Duval and Sposa, was lost when the Americans holed a 25-foot putt for a birdie; the other, McGimpsey and Willison (2 up with four to play) versus Voges and Eger, went west when the home side contrived to three putt from 25 feet. Surely not even with the support of a large, partisan Irish crowd could a team come back from 4–0 down against a side led by the mighty Mickelson? Well, they gave it a darned good try.

The eight afternoon singles matches were shared making the overall score 8–4 to the USA but the following morning GB and Ireland grabbed three of the four foursomes matches: Milligan and McGimpsey beating Voges and Eger; Evans and Coltart getting the better of Langham and Scherrer and most significantly, White and McGinley triumphing over Mickelson and May by one hole.

The Americans' lead had been cut back to 7–5 and GB and Ireland were still in with a chance. They needed to win five of the eight singles matches to retain the Cup – a tall order but not impossible. At one point in the afternoon it looked a distinct possibility, but the Americans rallied and when Mickelson turned around his match with Milligan, the hero of 1989, an American victory was virtually assured. In the end it was they who won five of the eight matches and the final result was 14–10 to the visitors. The four-point margin they had established on the first morning had indeed proved decisive.

Beaten, but only just, the British and Irish players could hold their heads high and reflect that if they, and not the Americans, had won the 18th hole in those two key foursomes matches on the first morning the Walker Cup would not be heading across the water ... besides, where was that devilish wind?

Gary Evans gained two points from his four matches.

THE 33RD WALKER CUP

5-6 September, Portmarnock, Dublin

FIRST DAY

Foursomes (GB and Ire names first)
J. Milligan and G. Hay lost to P. Mickelson and B. May 5 and 3
J. Payne and G. Evans lost to D. Duval and M. Sposa 1 hole
G. McGimpsey and R. Willison lost to M. Voges and D. Eger 1 hole
P. McGinley and P. Harrington lost to J. Sigel and A. Doyle 2 and 1
Great Britain and Ireland 0 **USA** 4

Singles
A. Coltart lost to Mickelson 4 and 3
Payne beat F. Langham 2 and 1
Evans beat Duval 2 and 1
Willison lost to May 2 and 1
McGimpsey beat Sposa 1 hole
McGinley lost to Doyle 6 and 4
Hay beat T. Scherrer 1 hole
L. White lost to Sigel 4 and 3
Great Britain and Ireland 4 **USA** 8

SECOND DAY

Foursomes
Milligan and McGimpsey beat Voges and Eger 2 and 1
Payne and Willison lost to Duval and Sposa 1 hole
Evans and Coltart beat Langham and Scherrer 4 and 3
White and McGinley beat Mickelson and May 1 hole
Great Britain and Ireland 7; **USA** 9

Singles
Milligan lost to Mickelson 1 hole
Payne beat Doyle 3 and 1
Evans lost to Langham 4 and 2
Coltart beat Sigel 1 hole
Willison beat Scherrer 3 and 2
Harrington lost to Eger 3 and 2
McGimpsey lost to May 4 and 3
Hay lost to Voges 3 and 1

MATCH RESULT: USA 14 GREAT BRITAIN AND IRELAND 10

The Walker Cup goes West! The victorious American side at Portmarnock.

AMATEUR ROLL OF HONOUR 1991

British Amateur G. Wolstenholme (GB) bt B. May (US) 8 & 6
English Amateur R. Willison bt M. Pullan 10 & 8
Scottish Amateur G. Lowson bt L. Salariya 4 & 3
Welsh Amateur S. Pardoe bt A. Jones 7 & 5
Irish Amateur G. McNeil bt N. Goulding 3 & 1
British Boys F. Valera (Sp) bt R. Walton (Eng) 2 & 1
British Youths J. Payne
British Seniors C. Green
English Amateur Strokeplay G. Evans/M. Pullan (tied)
Scottish Amateur Strokeplay A. Coltart
Welsh Amateur Strokeplay A. Jones

English Boys (Carris Trophy) I. Pyman
Scottish Boys C. Hislop
Welsh Boys B. Dredge
European Amateur J. Payne
US Amateur M. Voges bt M. Zerman 7 & 6

Leading Amateur in the Open J. Payne
Leading Amateur in the US Open P. Mickelson
Leading Amateur in The Masters P. Mickelson

British Womens Amateur V. Michaud (Fr) bt. W. Doolan (Aus) 3 & 2
British Womens Strokeplay J. Morley

English Womens Amateur N. Buxton
Scottish Womens Amateur C. Lambert
Welsh Womens Amateur V. Thomas
Irish Womens Amateur C. Hourihane
British Girls M. Hjorth (Sw) bt J. Moodie (Sco) 3 & 2
English Girls N. Buxton
Scottish Girls J. Moodie
Welsh Girls S. Boyes

British Womens Seniors A. Uzielli
European Womens Amateur D. Bourson (Fr)
US Womens Amateur A. Fruhwirth bt. H. Voorhees 5 & 4

Home Internationals Ireland
European Team Championship England
European Womens Team Championships England

Valerie Michaud, the British Women's Amateur Champion.

5

1992
A YEAR TO SAVOUR

1992 MAJORS PREVIEW

Derek Lawrenson, *Birmingham Post*

Such is the power and the glory of the Ryder Cup it is clearly now the sport's equivalent of the Lord Mayor's Show and so pity the season that has to follow in its wake. What can 1992 possibly offer that can douse the obvious surface feelings of anticlimax?

Well, quite a lot actually. For starters, if you haven't got Augusta, Pebble Beach and Muirfield all nestling among your top twenty golf courses in the world, then take up hockey. These mighty venues, sublime examples of links and inland golf, and the game in the lap of nature's luxury, will host the first three and the most important Major championships of the year. In order: The Masters, the US Open, and the Open.

So vast and sprawling is the golf season that it is quite possible for a player to deposit cheques worth $750,000 before he reaches the year's traditional starting point, Augusta National. After all Sandy Lyle did it four years ago, and prize money has moved up another escalator since then.

But for European audiences in particular the Masters remains golf's opening shot, the day it loosens the hold of hibernation.

It has been this way since players like Ian Woosnam, Sandy Lyle and Nick Faldo were schoolboys, and pestered their parents to let them stay up late to watch the splendour of the tournament unfold.

Like all of us they would have dreamt

Nick Faldo at Augusta's treacherous par three 12th hole.

of pulling on the winner's green jacket, the only difference being, of course, that they went out and captured the dream. Thanks to this great triumvirate, Augusta has become a small British holding.

The locals are getting restless too. It brought almost unbearable sadness to report last year that standing on the 14th tee, a Southern boy whistled loudly: 'This is not a links course, Woosnam. This is Augusta.'

Pull the red mist over Woosnam's eyes and the best front runner in the game becomes omnipotent. Tom Watson, Woosie's partner at the time, never had a chance from thereon in.

But Watson remains the sport's classiest act and there was a period in the late seventies, early eighties when he could have walked through fire and still made birdies when the crunch moments came.

His finest hour was his win in the 1977 Open at Turnberry when he and Jack Nicklaus turned the event into a matchplay jamboree. But his greatest hit came five years later, at Pebble Beach in the US Open. The mighty Nicklaus once more shadowed Watson's stride to the point that when the latter stepped on to the par three 17th, there was nothing between them. There was after his tee shot. It wasn't just advantage Nicklaus, it appeared game, set and match. Watson had hooked a 2 iron into what seemed an impenetrable area of rough.

As if the recovery shot was not hard enough, the flag was cut no more than 12 feet from the edge of the green where Watson was playing from, so drastically reducing his chances of getting down in two. In fact, there was not one analyst who believed he could get the ball closer than 20 feet.

It says everything about Watson's state of mind, and the aura of self-belief that he had constructed around him, that when he saw how the ball was lying he said to his caddy that he believed he could chip the ball into the hole.

It's a wonder the caddy didn't reply: 'Mmm, and I guess that when you've done it, you'll pull a rabbit out of the hole with the ball.'

Tom Watson wins the US Open in 1982.

Watson's optimism centred around the ball lying on a tuft of grass, enabling him to get it out fast. He also knew that if he missed the pin, such were the contours of the green, that it would mean a long and winding putt for a par.

A couple of short, sharp practice swings and then the chip shot that shook Nicklaus to the core. Watson knew the ball would disappear below ground as soon as he hit it. He birdied the last as well and Nicklaus, in the clubhouse, could only watch and applaud his rival's two-stroke victory.

A few weeks later, Watson and a group of friends strolled out to that 17th green and tried to duplicate the chip shot. There were six or seven of them, including the architect Robert Trent Jones, and each of them had three or four attempts at holing it. No one came close.

It was hailed at the time as one of the great US Opens, and the sepia tint has done nothing but enhance its standing. The surroundings helped. The author, Robert Louis Stevenson, once called the Monterey Peninsula the most perfect piece of shoreline in the world and Pebble Beach glistens there, alongside its fabled neighbour, Cypress Point.

It's an authentic links course then, and so one that must give the European contingent heart. For the first time since Shinnecock Hills in 1986, the US Open will not be held on an inland track with savage rough that eliminates the art of the shotmaker.

Pebble Beach is a test of golf that asks questions of a player not normally found in this championship, and so surely presents the best opportunity yet for the Europeans to end a barren run that stretches back to Tony Jacklin's victory at Hazeltine in 1970.

This is the third US Open to be held at Pebble Beach and if we believe the old cliché that great courses produce great champions, then the fact that the other name alongside Watson's belongs to Nicklaus says everything. Nicklaus indeed, has won five tournaments at Pebble Beach, the others being three Bing Crosby pro-ams, and the US Amateur Championship.

A month after his win in 1982, Watson went to Troon for the Open and won there as well. What a double act he had completed, and one that for many confirmed him as the greatest purveyor of links golf that we have seen.

Two years earlier in 1980 Watson had also triumphed in the Open Championship at Muirfield and the Open returned to the home of the Honourable Company of Edinburgh golfers in 1987 when all Britain celebrated its second Open champion within three years.

One shot stood out there too. The last hole on the last day, and Nick Faldo looked over a 5 iron stroke to the home green. Seventeen pars he had compiled to that point and now he knew he needed one more to place the Open within his grasp.

It is this type of shot that decides a player's place in the grand scheme of things, and for Faldo, the odds were raised even higher. This was nothing less than the shot over which he had dedicated his life.

For a good player had decided there was no way he could become a great one with a swing that he believed would wither under pressure. So Faldo underwent two years of purgatory, as he pursued his insatiable goal of becoming not one of the world's top ten players but number one full stop.

He had to go down before he could go up and in the interim the Press gave voice to the public's worries: what is he doing?

Over his favourite Open course, Faldo showed what he had been doing. The 5 iron never left the flag for a second. It became the first of a number of great shots that Faldo has produced under pressure, which has fully vindicated the changes he made. He got his par, and when his nearest challenger, Paul Azinger, ran up a bogey, Faldo had emulated his great rival, Sandy Lyle, the winner of the Open at Royal St George's two years earlier.

There should be more than enough excitement then to sustain us for the first half of the year, and the prospects of European success in these Majors has got to be high.

It will be in the fourth as well, as the PGA Championship goes to St Louis, Missouri, and the Bellerive Country Club.

Last year, the PGA of America broke the habit of a lifetime and invited more than a dozen Europeans to compete. Their enterprise was rewarded as David Feherty and Steven Richardson introduced themselves to American audiences with top ten finishes.

There is every hope that a similar contingent will be asked to make the trip on this occasion, and, of course, the more that are allowed to compete the more chance there is of a European winning this event for what would be an historic first triumph in modern times.

Nick Faldo at Muirfield in 1987.

Bellerive is a typical Robert Trent Jones design with big bunkers and large, undulating greens. The US Open was held there in 1965 and dominated by the overseas players, with the South African, Gary Player, winning, and the Australian, Kel Nagle, second. An omen there perhaps?

And the winners of these Major championships? Put down Faldo for one, Fred Couples for a second, and José-Maria Olazabal a third. As for who will win what, and the name of the fourth man, it really would be a case of after the Lord Mayor's show to reveal everything.

A first Major for Fred Couples in 1992? Bellerive Country Club, venue for the 1992 USPGA Championship.

The magnificent 8th hole at Pebble Beach.

Much is expected of Olazabal in 1992.

SOLHEIM CUP AND CURTIS CUP PREVIEW

Lewine Mair, *Daily Telegraph*

The news that Laura Davies was to be seen shaking on Lake Nona's first tee in the 1990 Solheim Cup went a long way towards capturing the atmosphere at that inaugural clash between the women of America and Europe.

'If Laura shakes,' said one among the Continentals, 'the tension has to be in a different league to anything we know on the regular tour.'

It is a tension they all long to taste and, well before the end of the 1991 season, the conversation on the women's professional circuit was peppered with references to the 1992 return match at Dalmahoy from 2-4 October.

Helen Wadsworth, Rookie of the Year in 1991, suggested that the Solheim Cup label was one they all wanted after their names. 'Career-wise, it would mean so much,' said this elegant newcomer, who still feels that she is too short on experience to be in with a chance of making the 1992 instalment.

Xonia Wunsch, a beautifully organized little Spaniard who won the Italian Open of '89, talked of how she had put too much pressure on herself to make the side in 1990. 'Now,' she said, 'I try to put it out of my mind but it's not easy.'

For the purposes of the first Solheim Cup, when the sides were eight-strong as opposed to the ten-strong affairs they will be this year, four players were taken from the European money-list and two from the American money-list, with two Wild Cards.

That system has now been changed. For 1992, the ten will be made up of the top seven on the European Order of Merit, with three Wild Cards to be dealt by the captain, Mickey Walker.

The dropping of automatic berths for those playing on the American tour was something demanded by European tour regulars who deemed it unfair. In their view, anyone looking for a place in a European side should play in Europe.

The attitude is one which would no doubt be best for the tour *per se* but, in the shorter term, it could certainly adversely affect our Solheim Cup chances.

To give some idea of how the team was shaping after the final event of the 1991 season, the top seven on the Solheim Cup points list – a list which started in August '91 and will be finalized at the beginning of August '92 – were as follows: Penny Grice-Whittaker, Kitrina Douglas, Laura Davies, Marie-Laure de Lorenzi, Florence Descampe, Federica Dassu and Dale Reid.

If that septette is the same when the list closes, players such as Helen Alfredsson, Trish Johnson, Pam Wright and Alison Nicholas will all be looking for one of those three Wild Cards.

No doubt some among this group will make their way up the points list during the early tournaments of 1992. But, bearing in mind that Wright plays 90 per cent of her golf in America and Alfredsson, Davies and Johnson plan to divide their time between both tours, there could be a problem.

The Americans, it has to be said, would not find it too difficult to get by with less than their optimum team, but no one could imagine that we are in a position to do likewise. 'The European tour simply does not have the same strength in depth,' said Wright, who had a never-to-be-forgotten half against the US Open champion, Betsy King, at Lake Nona.

Meanwhile, there was much the same brand of critical conversation in amateur circles as the Ladies' Golf Union bedded down for the winter having named the seventeen-strong squad from which they will choose the eight players for the Curtis Cup to be held at the Royal Liverpool Golf Club, Hoylake on 5-6 June.

No one denied that the selectors had come up with a strong seventeen, but why was Mary McKenna not among them? How could there be seventeen better candidates than a player who, only last year, was good enough to reach the semi-finals of the British Women's Championship at Pannal?

The selectors will argue that the Irish player's Curtis Cup record could be better and that she had an unproductive week at the Home Internationals at Aberdovey. However, the fact is that those who play in her company recognize her as one forty-one year old who has so far come up with better golf in this decade than ever she did in the 1970s and 1980s.

With Anne Sander having played in the 1990 American Curtis Cup side at the age of fifty-two and Belle Robertson having turned out for the Great Britain and Ireland side when she was similarly over fifty, McKenna was not having any wild ideas when, a couple of winters ago, she decided to aim her game at one more Curtis Cup. That was all she needed to bring her record in line with Joe Carr's ten Walker Cups and Christy O'Connor's ten Ryder Cups.

She spent two thousand pounds and more in taking herself off for a fortnight's lessons from David Leadbetter in Florida and, on her return, was swinging the club better than at any stage in her career.

That her refurbished action was one which could stand up to pressure was readily apparent when, with her lead having dwindled to one hole in her quarter-final match with Vicki Thomas in the aforementioned British Championship at Pannal, she caught that most elusive of 17th greens with her driver *en route* to taking her place in the last four. Pre-Leadbetter, that drive could have gone anywhere.

If the selectors are not going to pick McKenna for their eight-strong side, who are they going to pick?

Catriona Lambert, a Stirling University student and the 1991 Scottish Champion, would have to be the first player on their list, with Joanne Morley, the *Daily Telegraph*'s Player of the Year in 1991, a close second.

Julie Hall and Vicki Thomas will, one imagines, be required to lend experience to the team, while Nicola Buxton, the 1991 English Champion, and Caroline Hall, with

Sweden's Helen Alfredsson may need to rely on a Wild Card selection to make the Solheim Cup side in 1992.

Lake Nona, Florida: spectacular venue of the inaugural Solheim Cup match in 1990.

The contrast with Lake Nona is staggering! The links at Hoylake, where the 1992 Curtis Cup will be contested.

Somerset Hills, 1990 – where Great Britain and Ireland lost the Curtis Cup.

Laura Davies and Alison Nicholas performed heroically at Lake Nona in 1990.

whom she played so well in the European Team Championships, are two more who will presumably have been pencilled in side by side.

Janice Moodie, a wonderfully cool young Scot, and Elaine Farquharson, a fully qualified lawyer, could well complete the party.

Just as Dalmahoy, with its new country club surrounds and proximity to Edinburgh, adds up to precisely the right venue for the American and European professionals, so Hoylake, as rich in history as the Curtis Cup itself, is perfect for the amateurs.

Both Mickey Walker and Liz Boatman, who will captain the amateurs, have proved themselves in the realm of captaincy. Walker, the first of the British women professionals to have a top three finish on America's LPGA tour, captained the last Solheim Cup side and is quietly convincing in everything she does.

Boatman, for her part, is so consistently open and honest that she automatically creates a happy working environment for those around her.

Curtis Cup apart, she has captained everything there is to be captained. A former English international, she has the respect of all the players while, as a former chairman of her country, she has what it takes to identify with officialdom.

With all four of the Ryder, Walker, Solheim and Curtis Cups currently in American hands, it is Boatman who must kick off in the bid to turn things around.

Having examined the way the scoring worked in each of the Walker and Ryder Cups, she is hell bent on her players getting off to a good start. The last thing she wants is a bad first morning and an uphill struggle.

In 1990, our Solheim and Curtis Cup golfers were criticized for their short games. Still painfully clear in the mind's eye is the memory of how, at Lake Nona, the European players were still getting the feel of the greens at a time when the Americans were already down to the business of holing 30-footers. Time and time again the home side had the confidence to make the crucial early putts.

At Somerset Hills, the British players were lost on the particularly slick and swirling putting surfaces – so much so that Jill Thornhill, the 1990 captain who was England's chairman last year, called for faster greens at all the clubs the English Ladies' Golf Association visited in 1991.

Vast crowds are expected at both matches. Indeed, International Management Group, who are organizing the Solheim Cup, are so confident of their match's spectator appeal that they are putting a 10,000-a-day ceiling on the number of tickets sold.

All of which prompts a pleasing picture of two weeks in the 1992 season in which the men's tour will be eclipsed by the distaff side of the game.

May the women make the most of it.

THE 26TH CURTIS CUP

28 – 29 July 1990, Somerset Hills, New Jersey

FIRST DAY

Foursomes (GB and I names first)
H. Dobson (Seacroft) and C. Lambert (North Berwick) lost to V. Goetze and A. Sander 4 and 3
J. Hall (Felixstowe Ferry) and K. Imrie (Monifieth) beat K. Noble and M. Platt 2 and 1
E. Farquharson (Deeside) and H. Wadsworth (Royal Cinque Ports) lost to C. Semple-Thompson and R. Weiss 3 and 1
Great Britain and Ireland 1   USA 2

Singles (GB and I names first)
Hall beat Goetze 2 and 1
Imrie lost to K. Peterson 3 and 2
Farquharson lost to B. Burton 3 and 1
L. Fletcher (Almouth) lost to Weiss 4 and 3
Lambert lost to Noble 1 hole
V. Thomas (Pennard) beat Thompson 1 hole
Great Britain and Ireland 2   USA 4

SECOND DAY

Foursomes (GB and I names first)
Hall and Imrie lost to Goetze and Sander 3 and 1
Lambert and Dobson beat Noble and Platt 1 hole
Farquharson and Wadsworth lost to Peterson and Burton 5 and 4
Great Britain and Ireland 1   USA 2

Singles (GB and I names first)
Dobson lost to Goetze 4 and 3
Lambert lost to Burton 4 and 3
Imrie lost to Peterson 1 hole
Hall lost to Noble 2 holes
Farquharson lost to Weiss 2 and 1
Thomas lost to Semple-Thompson 3 and 1
Great Britain and Ireland 0   USA 6

MATCH RESULT: GREAT BRITAIN AND IRELAND 4   USA 14

THE 1st SOLHEIM CUP

16 – 18 November 1990, Lake Nona, Orlando, Florida

Foursomes (US names first)
C. GERRING and D. MOCHRIE beat P. WRIGHT (Sco) and L. NEUMANN (Swe) 6 and 5
P. SHEEHAN and R. JONES beat D. REID (Sco) and H. ALFREDSSON (Swe) 6 and 5
P. BRADLEY and N. LOPEZ lost to L. DAVIES (Eng) and A. NICHOLAS (Eng) 2 and 1
B. DANIEL and B. KING beat T. JOHNSON (Eng) and M.-L. DE LORENZI (Fr) 5 and 4
USA 3   Europe 1

Fourball (US names first)
P. SHEEHAN and R. JONES beat T. JOHNSON and M.-L. DE LORENZI 2 and 1
P. BRADLEY and N. LOPEZ beat D. REID and H. ALFREDSSON 2 and 1
B. DANIEL and B. KING beat L. DAVIES and A. NICHOLAS 4 and 3
C. GERRING and D. MOCHRIE lost to P. WRIGHT and L. NEUMANN 4 and 2
USA 3   Europe 1

Singles (US names first)
C. GERRING beat H. ALFREDSSON 4 and 3
R. JONES lost to L. DAVIES 3 and 2
B. DANIEL beat L. NEUMANN 7 and 6
N. LOPEZ beat A. NICHOLAS 6 and 4
B. KING halved with P. WRIGHT
P. SHEEHAN lost to D. REID 2 and 1
D. MOCHRIE beat M.-L. DE LORENZI 4 and 3
P. BRADLEY beat T. JOHNSON 8 and 7
USA 5½ Europe 2½

MATCH RESULT: USA 11½ EUROPE 4½

JANUARY

Spyglass Hill, Monterey, California.

As we in Britain shiver at the prospect of the next winter stableford, halfway round the world the cream of American golf (and a few wealthy celebrities) enjoy the privilege of playing the magnificent courses of the Monterey peninsula in the AT&T Pebble Beach Pro-am. One of these courses, Spyglass Hill, is pictured above. The AT&T isn't the first event of the US Tour (traditionally the Tournament of Champions at Carlsbad) but it is certainly the most glamorous of the early tournaments. Not so many years ago the European Tour did not get under way until after The Masters had been staged in April; in 1991 the curtain rises in the last week of January with the Johnnie Walker Asian Classic in Bangkok. Better rename it the Eurasian tour.

FEBRUARY

The Emirates Golf Club, Dubai.

At the beginning of February the European Tour starts to move towards Europe with the Emirates Classic in Dubai. The above photograph offers an interesting bird's-eye view of the extraordinary Emirates clubhouse and the adjacent double green for the 9th and 18th holes. The Hong Kong Open takes place in February; last year Bernhard Langer won the tournament by seven strokes. But perhaps the most prestigious event of the month takes place at Huntingdale on the outskirts of Melbourne where in 1992, Greg Norman is likely to be challenging for a seventh Australian Masters' 'Gold Jacket'. South Africa's Sunshine Tour starts to wind down late in February while the US Tour moves from California to Florida and the European Tour basks in the Mediterranean.

MARCH

The famous par three 17th at the TPC at Sawgrass, Florida.

There really is golf in all four corners of the globe in March. The US Tour is in full flow and its much vaunted Players' Championship at Sawgrass is staged during this month although there are several other big events in Florida – most on courses looking very similar to the TPC at Sawgrass. The European Tour continues to zig-zag its way around southern Europe, visiting Majorca, mainland Spain and Italy and the Japanese PGA Tour awakens from its brief winter slumber. By the end of March tournament golf has effectively petered out in Australia but is still flourishing in South-East Asia.

APRIL

Augusta, Georgia.

For many golfers April means just one thing: The Masters. It used to be more commonly known as the US Masters but with eight overseas victories since 1978 it is beginning to suffer an identity crisis. Perhaps in 1992 an American will win at Augusta for the first time since Larry Mize chipped it in 1987 to deny Greg Norman a deserved Green Jacket? Perhaps Norman will win at last? One thing is for sure: no tournament is more eagerly awaited. The week after The Masters is the Heritage Classic at Hilton Head while in Europe the Volvo Tour visits Jersey and Cannes and the Women's Tour gets under way with Australia's Corinne Dibnah aiming to retain her leading moneywinner's crown.

MAY

Bernhard Langer at St Mellion in the 1991 Benson and Hedges International.

The European Tour's star-studded ship at last sails towards Britain in early May and drops anchor, most appropriately, near Plymouth at St Mellion. Bernhard Langer (pictured above on the 18th green) is due to defend his Benson and Hedges International Open Trophy. There are two other big events in Britain during May: the Volvo PGA Championship at Wentworth, which is sure to draw huge Bank Holiday crowds and, following immediately after, the Dunhill British Masters at Woburn where in 1991 Ballesteros cruised to his third win in four starts. On the other side of 'The Pond' the Colonial tournament is held in May and on the Japanese Tour there is a touch of the traditional with the PGA Matchplay Championship.

JUNE

Pebble Beach, California.

We began this global calendar with a picture of Spyglass Hill. Pebble Beach is a close neighbour on the Monterey peninsula: little wonder that Robert Louis Stevenson described this part of the Californian coast as 'the finest meeting of land and sea in the world.' Dave Cannon's photograph was taken from beside the 18th green where in June this year a new US Open champion will be crowned. America's premier championship has been played here twice before, in 1972 when Jack Nicklaus won, and in 1982, when Tom Watson won. It must be the turn of Ballesteros! Seve has never won a US Open, nor for that matter has any European since Tony Jacklin in 1970. Earlier in the month there is the Memorial Tournament in Ohio while back in the Old World, June brings the Irish, French and Austrian Opens.

JULY

The par five 17th at Muirfield.

Edinburgh is the only place to be this summer. Not only is there the magnificent annual festival in August but in July, just down the road there is the greatest festival of golf, otherwise called the Open Championship. It last visited Muirfield in 1987 when Nick Faldo reeled off eighteen straight pars in the final round which so frustrated Paul Azinger that he contrived to bogey the 17th and 18th holes to lose to the Englishman by one. He seems to have had it in for Europeans ever since. Also in Scotland during July is the popular Bell's Scottish Open at Gleneagles. Elsewhere in Europe the Volvo Tour hosts the Dutch Open and the Scandinavian Masters and the Women's WPGE Tour is in mid season. In America there is the Western Open, the US Senior Open and on the LPGA Tour, the Women's US Open.

AUGUST

John Daly wins the 1991 USPGA Championship.

When you are ranked 223rd in the world nobody cares if you can hit the ball 350 yards but when you win a Major championship the whole world wants to either hug you or take your picture. John Daly's win in the 1991 USPGA Championship at Crooked Stick was, in his words, 'the greatest story ever'. The venue for the PGA in 1992 is the Bellerive Country Club, scene of Gary Player's victory in the 1965 US Open. The PGA is followed by The World Series (won by Olazabal in 1990) and The International (won by Olazabal in 1991). There are two events in Germany in August and at the end of the month, the English Open now sponsored by Murphy's at the Belfry. So in 1992 the European Tour will have an English Open sponsored by an Irish company, Japanese sponsors of the Austrian Open, French sponsors of the Spanish Open and Swedish sponsors of the German Open.

SEPTEMBER

Crans-sur-Sierre, Switzerland.

With the Major season over and no Ryder Cup in 1992, Europe's top golfers will be able to focus their intentions fully on the European Tour in September when there are several important events. The first of these is the Canon European Masters at Crans-sur-Sierre. In 1991 Ballesteros birdied the last six holes but couldn't quite catch South African Jeff Hawkes. A wonderful contrast to the beautiful Alpine scenery comes a week later with the GA European Open at Sunningdale. Pure Switzerland followed by pure England! And then it is pure Paris with the Lancôme Trophy. The premier event on the US Tour in September is the Canadian Open at Glen Abbey, not far from Toronto. During the final week of September Woburn hosts the Weetabix Women's British Open.

OCTOBER

The United States, winners of the 1st Solheim Cup in 1990.

Remember Edinburgh? It was the only place to be in July and now, as summer turns to autumn at the Dalmahoy Country Club, just to the south of Scotland's capital, the ten best women golfers in Europe take on the ten best women golfers of America in the eagerly awaited 2nd Solheim Cup. The powerful Americans are certain to start as firm favourites. Also in October Bernhard Langer can be expected to put up a good defence of the German Masters, Ballesteros the World Matchplay Championship – he will surely be gunning for a record sixth victory – and Sweden the Dunhill Cup. On the other side of the world the Australian PGA Tour starts up again after its winter break and in Japan Tommy Nakajima will be attempting to win a third successive Japan Open title.

NOVEMBER

A very international field is always assembled for Japan's Dunlop Phoenix Tournament.

The European Tour officially finishes on 1 November, the final day of the Volvo Masters at Valderrama in southern Spain. On the same day the US Tour will also reach a climax with the Tour Championship at Pinehurst, North Carolina. The golfing season is hardly over though for the leading European and American players: many make their way to Japan to compete in one or more of the lucrative events that comprise the Japanese PGA's 'International Tour'. There are also a number of events in Australia, by far the most important of which is the Australian Open, won in years past by Arnold Palmer, Gary Player, Jack Nicklaus, Tom Watson and Greg Norman. There is plenty of team golf in November including the World Cup of Golf in Spain and the Four Tours Championship in Japan.

DECEMBER

Magnificent Royal Melbourne celebrated its centenary in 1991.

Royal Melbourne is unquestionably the best golf course in Australia, almost certainly the best in the southern hemisphere and quite possibly the best in the world. Hyperbole? No – according to Ray Floyd, Ben Crenshaw and Greg Norman it is worthy of the latter accolade. No wonder it regularly hosts the Australian Open Championship (as it did towards the end of last year) and other important events on the Australian PGA Tour. December is mid summer and mid season in Australasia but in other parts of the world the major tours have either finished before December or do so well before Christmas. Now is the season of Skins Games, World Championships and Million Dollar Challenges. Quite what Bobby Jones would have made of it all, Lord only knows!

USPGA TOUR 1992

JANUARY
9-12 **Tournament of Champions**, Carlsbad, California
15-19 **Bob Hope Chrysler Classic**, La Quinta, California
23-26 **Phoenix Open**, TPC at Scottsdale, Arizona
39-2 February **AT & T Pebble Beach National Pro-Am**, Pebble Beach, California

FEBRUARY
6-9 **United Airlines Hawaiian Open**, Waialae CC, Honolulu
13-16 **Northern Telecom Open**, Tucson National GC and TPC at StarPass, Tucson, Arizona
20-23 **Buick Invitational of California**, Torrey Pines GC, La Jolla, California
27-1 March **Nissan Los Angeles Open**, Riviera CC, Pacific Palisades, California

MARCH
5-8 **Doral Ryder Open**, Doral Resort & CC, Miami, Florida
12-15 **Honda Classic**, Weston Hills CC, Fort Lauderdale, Florida
19-22 **Nestlé Invitational**, Bay Hill Club & Lodge, Orlando, Florida
26-29 **The Players' Championship**, TPC at Sawgrass, Jacksonville, Florida

APRIL
2-5 **Freeport-McMoRan Classic**, English Turn G & CC, New Orleans, Louisiana
9-12 **The Masters**, Augusta National GC, Augusta, Georgia
9-12 **Deposit Guaranty Golf Classic**, Hattiesburg CC, Hattiesburg, Missouri
16-19 **MCI Heritage Classic**, Harbour Town GL, Hilton Head Island, South Carolina
23-26 **K-Mart Greater Greensboro Open**, Forest Oaks CC, Greensboro, North Carolina
30-3 May **Shell Houston Open**, TPC at The Woodlands, Texas

MAY
7-10 **Bell South Classic**, Atlanta CC, Marietta, Georgia
14-17 **GTE Byron Nelson Classic**, TPC at Las Colinas, Irving, Texas
21-24 **Southwestern Bell Colonial**, Colonial CC, Fort Worth, Texas
28-31 **Kemper Open**, TPC at Avenel, Potomac, Maryland

JUNE
4-7 **The Memorial Tournament**, Muirfield Village GC, Dublin, Ohio
11-14 **Federal Express St Jude Classic**, TPC at Southwind, Memphis, Tennessee
18-21 **US Open**, Pebble Beach, California
25-28 **Buick Classic**, Westchester CC, Rye, New York

JULY
2-5 **Centel Western Open**, Cog Hill GC, Lemont, Illinois
9-12 **Anheuser-Busch Golf Classic**, Kingsmill GC, Williamsburg, Virginia
16-19 **Chattanooga Classic**, Council Fire G & CC, Chattanooga, Tennessee
23-26 **New England Classic**, Pleasant Valley CC, Sutton, Massachusetts
30-2 August **Canon Greater Hartford Open**, TPC at River Highlands, Cromwell, Connecticut

AUGUST
6-9 **Buick Open**, Warwick Hills G & CC, Flint, Michigan
13-16 **USPGA Championship**, Bellerive CC, St Louis, Missouri
20-23 **The International**, Castle Pines GC, Castle Rock, Colorado
27-30 **NEC World Series of Golf**, Firestone CC, Akron, Ohio

SEPTEMBER
3-6 **Greater Milwaukee Open**, Tuckaway CC, Franklin, Wisconsin
10-13 **Canadian Open**, Glen Abbey GC, Oakville, Ontario
17-20 **Hardee's Golf Classic**, Oakwood CC, Coal Valley, Illinois
24-27 **BC Open**, En-Joie GC, Endicott, New York

OCTOBER
1-4 **Buick Southern Open**, Calloway Gardens Resort, Pine Mountain, Georgia
7-11 **Las Vegas Invitational**, TPC at Summerlin, Las Vegas CC, Desert Inn CC, Las Vegas, Nevada
15-18 **Walt Disney World/Oldsmobile Classic**, Magnolia, Palm & Buena Vista Courses, Lake Buena Vista, Florida
22-25 **HEB Texas Open**, Oak Hills CC, San Antonio, Texas
29-1 November **TOUR Championship**, Pinehurst, North Carolina

VOLVO (PGA EUROPEAN) TOUR 1992

JANUARY
30-2 February **Johnnie Walker Asian Classic**, Bangkok, Thailand

FEBRUARY
6-9 **Dubai Dessert Classic**, Emirates, Dubai
13-16 **Turespana Masters**, TBA
27-Mar 1 **Mediterranean Open**, Valencia

MARCH
5-8 **Open de Baleares**, Santa Ponsa
12-15 **Catalan Open**, Barcelona
19-22 **Portuguese Open**, TBA
26-29 **Volvo Open de Firenze**, Ugolino, Florence

APRIL
9-12 **Jersey European Airways Open**, La Moye Golf Club, Jersey
16-19 **Moroccan Open**, Rabat
23-26 **Credit Lyonnais Cannes Open**, Cannes Mougins
30-May 3 **Lancia Martini Italian Open**, Montecello

MAY
7-10 **Benson and Hedges International**, St Mellion
14-17 **Peugeot Spanish Open**, Club de Campo, Madrid
22-25 **Volvo PGA Championship**, Wentworth
28-31 **Dunhill British Masters**, Woburn

JUNE
4-7 **Irish Open**, Killarney
11-14 **Austrian Open**, Salzburg
18-21 **Lyons Open**, Lyon
25-28 **Peugeot French Open**, National Club, Paris

JULY
1-4 **Monte Carlo Open**, Mont Agel
8-11 **Bell's Scottish Open**, Gleneagles
16-19 **121st Open Championship**, Muirfield
23-26 **Heineken Dutch Open**, Noordwijk
30-Aug 2 **Scandinavian Masters**, Malmo

AUGUST
6-9 **BMW International**, Munich
13-16 **European Pro-Celebrity**, TBA
20-23 **Volvo German Open**, Dusseldorf
28-31 **Murphy's English Open**, The Belfry

SEPTEMBER
3-6 **Canon European Masters**, Crans-sur-Sierre
10-13 **GA European Open**, Sunningdale
14-15 ***Equity & Law Challenge**, Royal Mid-Surrey
17-20 **Lancôme Trophy**, St Nom la Breteche
24-27 **Belgian Open**, TBA

OCTOBER
1-4 **Mercedes German Masters**, Stuttgart
8-11 **Toshiba PC Open**, Gutkaden, Hamburg
8-11 ***Toyota World Matchplay**, Wentworth
15-18 ***Dunhill Cup**, St Andrews
22-25 **Iberia Madrid Open**, Puerta de Hierro
29-Nov 1 **Volvo Masters**, Valderrama

NOVEMBER
5-8 ***World Cup of Golf by Philip Morris**, Spain
5-8 ***Four Tours Championship**, TBA

*PGA European Tour Approved Special Events

TBA: to be announced

6

GOLF COURSES OF GREAT BRITAIN AND IRELAND

ENGLAND
SCOTLAND
WALES
NORTHERN IRELAND
IRELAND

ENGLAND

AVON

Bath G.C.
(0225) 463834
Sham Castle, North Road, Bath
(18) 6369 yards

Bristol and Clifton G.C.
(0272) 393474
Beggar Bush Lane, Failand, Bristol
(18) 6294 yards

Chipping Sodbury G.C.
(0454) 319042
Chipping Sodbury
(18) 6912 yards

Clevedon G.C.
(0272) 874057
Castle Road, Clevedon
(18) 5835 yards

Filton G.C.
(0272) 694169
Golf Course Lane, Filton, Bristol
(18) 6227 yards

Fosseway C.C.
(0761) 412214
Charlton Lane, Midsomer Norton
(9) 4246 yards

Henbury G.C.
(0272) 500044
Henbury Hill, Westbury-on-Trym, Bristol
(18) 6039 yards

Knowle G.C.
(0272) 770660
Brislington, Bristol
(18) 6016 yards

Lansdown G.C.
(0225) 422138
Lansdown, Bath
(18) 6267 yards

Long Ashton G.C.
(0272) 392316
Long Ashton, Bristol
(18) 6051 yards

Mangotsfield G.C.
(0272) 565501
Carsons Road, Mangotsfield
(18) 5337 yards

Mendip G.C.
(0749) 840570
Gurney Slade, Bath
(18) 5982 yards

Saltford G.C.
(0225) 873220
Manor Road, Saltford
(18) 6081 yards

Shirehampton Park G.C.
(0272) 822083
Park Hill, Shirehampton, Bristol
(18) 5943 yards

Tracy Park G. & C.C.
(027582) 2251
Bath Road, Wick
(18) 6613 yards
(9) 5200 yards

Weston-Super-Mare G.C.
(0934) 621360
Uphill Road, Weston-Super-Mare
(18) 6225 yards

Worlebury G.C.
(0934) 623214
Worlebury Hill Road, Weston-Super-Mare
(18) 5945 yards

BEDFORDSHIRE

Aspley Guise & Woburn Sands G.C.
(0908) 583596
West Hill, Aspley Guise
(18) 6248 yards

Beadlow Manor G. & C.C.
(0525) 60800
Shefford
(18) 6231 yards
(9) 3297 yards

Bedford & County G.C.
(0234) 52617
Green Lane, Clapham, Bedford
(18) 6347 yards

Bedfordshire G.C.
(0234) 53241
Bromham Road, Biddenham, Bedford
(18) 6172 yards

Dunstable Downs G.C.
(0582) 604472
Whipsnade Road, Dunstable
(18) 6184 yards

John O'Gaunt G.C.
(0767) 260252
Sutton Park, Sandy, Biggleswade
(18) 6513 yards (John O'Gaunt)
(18) 5869 yards (Carthagena)

Leighton Buzzard G.C.
(0525) 373811
Plantation Road, Leighton Buzzard
(18) 5959 yards

Millbrook G.C.
(0525) 402269
Millbrook, Ampthill
(18) 6473 yards

Mowsbury G.C.
(0234) 771042
Kimbolton Road, Bedford
(18) 6514 yards

South Beds G.C.
(0582) 591500
Warden Hill, Luton
(18) 6342 yards
(9) 4954 yards

Stockwood Park G.C.
(0582) 413704
London Road, Luton
(18) 5964 yards

Tilsworth G.C.
(0525) 210721
Dunstable Road, Tilsworth
(9) 5443 yards

Wyboston Lakes G.C.
(0480) 212501
Wyboston
(18) 5688 yards

BERKSHIRE

Bearwood G.C.
(0734) 760060
Mole Road, Sindlesham
(9) 5628 yards

The Berkshire G.C.
(0344) 21496
Swinley Road, Ascot
(18) 6356 yards (Red)
(18) 6258 yards (Blue)

Calcot Park G.C.
(0734) 27124
Bath Road, Calcot
(18) 6283 yards

Downshire G.C.
(0344) 424066
Easthampstead Park, Wokingham
(18) 6382 yards

East Berkshire G.C.
(0344) 772041
Ravenswood Avenue, Crowthorne
(18) 6315 yards

Goring & Streatley G.C.
(0491) 873229
Rectory Road, Streatley-on-Thames
(18) 6255 yards

Hawthorn Hill G.C.
(0628) 75588
Drift Road, Maidenhead
(18) 6212 yards

Hurst G.C.
(0734) 345143
Hurst, Wokingham
(9) 3015 yards

Maidenhead G.C.
(0628) 24693
Shoppenhangers Road,
Maidenhead
(18) 6344 yards

Newbury & Crookham G.C.
(0635) 40035
Greenham, Newbury
(18) 5880 yards

Reading G.C.
(0734) 472909
Kidmore End Road, Reading
(18) 6283 yards

Royal Ascot G.C.
(0990) 25175
Winkfield Road, Ascot
(18) 5653 yards

Sonning G.C.
(0734) 693332
Duffield Road,
Sonning-on-Thames
(18) 6355 yards

Sunningdale G.C.
(0344) 21681
Ridgemount Road,
Sunningdale
(18) 6341 yards (Old)
(18) 6676 yards (New)

Sunningdale Ladies G.C.
(0344) 20507
Cross Road, Sunningdale
(18) 5622 yards

Swinley Forest G.C.
(0344) 20197
Coronation Road,
South Ascot
(18) 6001 yards

Temple G.C.
(062882) 4795
Henley Road, Hurley
(18) 6206 yards

West Berks G.C.
(04882) 574
Chaddleworth, Newbury
(18) 7053 yards

Winter Hill G.C.
(06285) 27613
Grange Park, Cookham,
Maidenhead
(18) 6432 yards

BUCKINGHAMSHIRE

Abbey Hill G.C.
(0908) 563845
Two Ash, Milton Keynes
(18) 6505 yards

Beaconsfield G.C.
(0494) 676545
Seer Green, Beaconsfield
(18) 6469 yards

Buckingham G.C.
(0280) 815566
Tingewick Road,
Buckingham
(18) 6082 yards

Burnham Beeches G.C.
(06286) 61448
Green Lane, Burnham
(18) 6415 yards

Chesham & Ley Hill G.C.
(0494) 784541
Ley Hill, Chesham
(9) 5147 yards

Chiltern Forest G.C.
(0296) 631267
Halton, Aylesbury
(9) 5724 yards

Datchet G.C.
(0753) 43887
Buccleuch Road, Datchet
(9) 5978 yards

Denham G.C.
(0895) 832022
Tilehouse Lane, Denham
(18) 6439 yards

Ellesborough G.C.
(0296) 622114
Butler's Cross, Aylesbury
(18) 6207 yards

Farnham Park G.C.
(0753) 64332
Park Road, Stoke Poges
(18) 5847 yards

Flackwell Heath G.C.
(06285) 20929
High Wycombe
(18) 6150 yards

Gerrards Cross G.C.
(0753) 885300
Chalfont Park,
Gerrards Cross
(18) 6305 yards

Harewood Downs G.C.
(02404) 2185
Cokes Lane, Chalfont St Giles
(18) 5958 yards

Hazlemere G. & C.C.
(0494) 714722
Penn Road, Hazlemere
(18) 5855 yards

Iver G.C.
(0753) 655615
Hollow Hill Lane, Iver
(9) 6214 yards

Little Chalfont G.C.
(02404) 4877
Lodge Lane, Little Chalfont
(9) 5852 yards

Stoke Poges G.C.
(0753) 526385
Park Road, Stoke Poges
(18) 6654 yards

Weston Turville G.C.
(0296) 24084
New Road, Weston Turville,
Aylesbury
(18) 6782 yards

Wexham Park G.C.
(02816) 3217
Wexham Street, Wexham
(18) 5836 yards
(9) 2383 yards

Whiteleaf G.C.
(08444) 3097
Whiteleaf, Aylesbury
(9) 5391 yards

Windmill Hill G.C.
(0908) 78623
Tattenhoe Lane, Bletchley,
Milton Keynes
(18) 6773 yards

Woburn G. & C.C.
(0908) 370756
Bow Brickhill,
Milton Keynes
(18) 6883 yards Duke's
(18) 6616 yards Duchess

CAMBRIDGESHIRE

Abbotsley G.C.
(0480) 215153
Eynesbury Hardwicke,
St Neots
(18) 6214 yards

**Cambridgeshire
Moat House Hotel G.C.**
(0954) 80555
Bar Hill, Cambridge
(18) 6734 yards

Ely City G.C.
(0353) 662751
Cambridge Road, Ely
(18) 6686 yards

Girton G.C.
(0223) 276169
Dodford Lane, Cambridge
(18) 5927 yards

Gog Magog G.C.
(0223) 247626
Shelford Bottom, Cambridge
(18) 6354 yards (Old)
(9) 5833 yards (New)

The Isle of Purbeck, Dorset.

St George's Hill, Surrey.

March G.C.
(0354) 52364
Grange Rd, March
(9) 6278 yards

Orton Meadows G.C.
(0733) 237478
Ham Lane, Peterborough
(18) 5800 yards

Peterborough Milton G.C.
(0733) 380489
Milton Ferry, Peterborough
(18) 6431 yards

Ramsey G.C.
(0487) 812600
Abbey Terrace, Ramsey
(18) 6136 yards

St Ives G.C.
(0480) 68392
St Ives, Huntingdon
(9) 6052 yards

St Neots G.C.
(0480) 72363
Crosshall Rd, St Neots
(18) 6027 yards

Thorpe Wood G.C.
(0733) 267701
Nene Parkway, Peterborough
(18) 7086 yards

CHESHIRE

Alderley Edge G.C.
(0625) 585583
Brook Lane, Alderley Edge
(9) 5839 yards

Astbury G.C.
(0260) 272772
Peel Lane, Astbury, Congleton
(18) 6269 yards

Birchwood G.C.
(0925) 818819
Kelvin Close, Birchwood, Warrington
(18) 6666 yards

Chapel-en-le-Frith G.C.
(0298) 813943
The Cockyard,
Manchester Road, Chapel-en-le-Frith
(18) 6065 yards

Chester G.C.
(0244) 677760
Curzon Park, Chester
(18) 6487 yards

Congleton G.C.
(0260) 273540
Biddulph Road, Congleton
(18) 6221 yards

Crewe G.C.
(0270) 584099
Fields Road, Haslington, Crewe
(18) 6277 yards

Davenport G.C.
(0625) 877319
Worton Hall,
Middlewood Road, Higher Poynton
(18) 6006 yards

Delamere Forest G.C.
(0606) 882807
Station Road, Delamere, Northwich
(18) 6287 yards

Eaton G.C.
(0244) 680474
Eaton Park, Eccleston, Chester
(18) 6446 yards

Ellesmere Port G.C.
(051) 339 7689
Chester Road, Hooton
(18) 6432 yards

Helsby G.C.
(09282) 5457
Towers Lane, Helsby, Warrington
(18) 6262 yards

Knights Grange G.C.
(06065) 52780
Grange Lane, Winsford
(9) 6210 yards

Knutsford G.C.
(0565) 3355
Mereheath Lane, Knutsford
(9) 6288 yards

Leigh G.C.
(092576) 2943
Kenyon Hall,
Culcheth, Warrington
(18) 5853 yards

Lymm G.C.
(092575) 5020
Whitbarrow Road, Lymm
(18) 6304 yards

Macclesfield G.C.
(0625) 23227
The Hollins, Macclesfield
(9) 5974 yards

Malkins Bank G.C.
(0270) 765931
Betchton Road, Sandbach
(18) 6178 yards

Mere G. & C.C.
(0565) 830219
Mere, Knutsford
(18) 6849 yards

Mottram Hall Hotel G.C.
(0625) 878135
Mottram St Andrews

New Mills G.C.
(0663) 43816
Shaw Marsh, New Mills
(9) 5924 yards

Poulton Park G.C.
(0925) 812034
Cinnamon Brow, Warrington
(9) 5512 yards

Prestbury G.C.
(0625) 828241
Macclesfield Road, Prestbury
(18) 6359 yards

Runcorn G.C.
(09285) 74214
Clifton Road, Runcorn
(18) 6012 yards

Sandbach G.C.
(0270) 762117
Middlewich Road, Sandbach
(9) 5533 yards

Sandiway G.C.
(0606) 883247
Chester Road, Sandiway
(18) 6435 yards

Shrigley Hall G.C.
(0625) 575757
PO4 Shrigley, Nr Prestbury
(18) 6500 yards

The Tytherington Club
(0625) 434562
Macclesfield
(18) 6737 yards

Upton-by-Chester G.C.
(0244) 381183
Upton Lane, Chester
(18) 5875 yards

Vicars Cross G.C.
(0244) 335174
Littleton, Chester
(18) 5804 yards

Walton Hall G.C.
(0925) 66775
Higher Walton, Warrington
(18) 6843 yards

Warrington G.C.
(0925) 61775
Appleton, Warrington
(18) 6217 yards

Widnes G.C.
(051) 424 2995
Highfield Road, Widnes
(18) 5719 yards

Widnes Municipal G.C.
(051) 424 2995
Dundalk Road, Widnes
(9) 5982 yards

Wilmslow G.C.
(056587) 2148
Great Warford, Mobberley, Knutsford
(18) 6500 yards

CHANNEL ISLANDS

Alderney G.C.
(048182) 2835
Routes des Carriers, Alderney
(9) 2528 yards

La Moye G.C.
(0534) 43401
La Moye, St Brelade
(18) 6464 yards

Royal Guernsey G.C.
(0481) 47022
L'Ancresse, Guernsey
(18) 6206 yards

Royal Jersey G.C.
(0534) 54416
Grouville, Jersey
(18) 6106 yards

St Clements G.C.
(0534) 21938
St Clements, Jersey
(9) 3972 yards

CLEVELAND

Billingham G.C.
(0642) 554494
Sandy Lane, Billingham
(18) 6430 yards

Castle Eden & Peterlee G.C.
(0429) 836220
Castle Eden, Hartlepool
(18) 6297 yards

Cleveland G.C.
(0642) 483693
Queen Street, Redcar
(18) 6707 yards

Eaglescliffe G.C.
(0642) 780098
Yarm Road, Eaglescliffe
(18) 6275 yards

Hartlepool G.C.
(0429) 836510
Hart Warren, Hartlepool
(18) 6325 yards

Middlesborough G.C.
(0642) 316430
Marton, Middlesborough
(18) 6106 yards

Middlesborough Municipal G.C.
(0642) 315533
Ladgate Lane, Middlesborough
(18) 6314 yards

Saltburn-by-the Sea G.C.
(0287) 22812
Hob Hill, Saltburn-by-the-Sea
(18) 5803 yards

Seaton Carew G.C.
(0429) 266249
Tees Road, Seaton Carew
(18) 6604 yards

Teeside G.C.
(0642) 616516
Acklam Road, Thornaby
(18) 6472 yards

Wilton G.C.
(0642) 465265
Wilton Castle, Redcar
(18) 5774 yards

CORNWALL

Bodmin G. & C.C.
(0208) 73600
Bodmin
(18) 6500 yards

Bude & North Cornwall G.C.
(0288) 352006
Burn View, Bude
(18) 6202 yards

Budock Vean Hotel G.C.
(0326) 250288
Mawnan Smith, Falmouth
(9) 5007 yards

Carlyon Bay Hotel G.C.
(072681) 4228
Carlyon Bay, St Austell
(18) 6463 yards

Clovelly G. & C.C.
(0787) 313424
Woolsery, Bideford
(18) 5640 yards

Falmouth G.C.
(0326) 40525
Swanpool Road, Falmouth
(18) 5581 yards

Isles of Scilly G.C.
(0720) 22692
St Mary's, Isles of Scilly
(9) 5974 yards

Launceston G.C.
(0566) 3442
St Stephen, Launceston
(18) 6409 yards

Looe G.C.
(05034) 239
Widegates, Looe
(18) 5875 yards

Lostwithiel G. & C.C.
(0208) 873550
Lostwithiel
(18) 6098 yards

Mullion G.C.
(0326) 240685
Curry, Helston
(18) 5616 yards

Newquay G.C.
(0637) 874354
Tower Road, Newquay
(18) 6140 yards

Perranporth G.C.
(0872) 573701
Budnick Hill, Perranporth
(18) 6208 yards

Praa Sands G.C.
(0736) 763445
Germoe Cross, Penzance
(9) 4036 yards

St Austell G.C.
(0726) 74756
Tregongeeves Lane, St Austell
(18) 5875 yards

St Enodoc G.C.
(020886) 2402
Rock, Wadebridge
(18) 6188 yards
(18) 4151 yards

St Mellion G. & C.C.
(0579) 50101
St Mellion, Saltash
(18) 6626 yards (Nicklaus)
(18) 5927 yards

Tehidy Park G.C.
(0209) 842208
Camborne
(18) 6222 yards

Trevose G. & C.C.
(0841) 520208
Constantine Bay, Padstow
(18) 6608 yards
(9) 1367 yards

Truro G.C.
(0872) 78684
Treliske, Truro
(18) 5347 yards

West Cornwall G.C.
(0736) 753401
Lelant, St Ives
(18) 6070 yards

Whitsand Bay Hotel G.C.
(0503) 30276
Portwrinkle, Torpoint
(18) 5512 yards

CUMBRIA

Alston Moor G.C.
(0498) 381675
The Hermitage, Alston
(9) 5380 yards

Appleby G.C.
(0930) 51432
Blackenber Moor, Appleby-in-Westmoreland
(18) 5913 yards

Barrow G.C.
(0229) 24174
Hawcoat, Barrow-in-Furness
(18) 6209 yards

St Enodoc, Cornwall.

Brampton G.C.
(06977) 2255
Talkin Tarn, Brampton
(18) 6426 yards

Carlisle G.C.
(0228) 34856
Aglionby, Carlisle
(18) 6278 yards

Cockermouth G.C.
(059681) 223
Embleton, Cockermouth
(18) 5496 yards

Dunnerholme G.C.
(0229) 62675
Duddon Road, Askam-in-Furness
(10) 6118 yards

Furness G.C.
(0229) 41232
Central Drive, Barrow-in-Furness
(18) 6374 yards

Grange Fell G.C.
(04484) 2536
Fell Road, Grange-over-Sands
(9) 5278 yards

Grange-over-Sands G.C.
(05395) 32536
Meathop Road, Grange-over-Sands
(18) 5660 yards

Kendal G.C.
(0539) 724079
The Heights, Kendal
(18) 5533 yards

Keswick G.C.
(07687) 72147
Threlkeld Hall, Keswick
(18) 6175 yards

Kirkby Lonsdale G.C.
(0468) 71483
Casterton Road, Kirkby Lonsdale
(9) 4058 yards

Maryport G.C.
(0900) 812605
Bank End, Maryport
(18) 6272 yards

Penrith G.C.
(0768) 62217
Salkeld Road, Penrith
(18) 6026 yards

St Bees School G.C.
(0946) 812105
Station Road, St Bees
(9) 5082 yards

Seascale G.C.
(09467) 28662
The Banks, Seascale
(18) 6372 yards

Sedbergh G.C.
(0587) 20993
Sedburgh
(9) 4134 yards

Silecroft G.C.
(0657) 4250
Silecroft, Millom
(9) 5627 yards

Silloth-on-Solway G.C.
(06973) 31304
Silloth-on-Solway, Carlisle
(18) 6343 yards

Stony Holme Municipal G.C.
(0228) 34856
St Aidans Road, Carlisle
(18) 5773 yards

Ulverston G.C.
(0229) 52806
Bardsea Park, Ulverston
(18) 6092 yards

Windermere G.C.
(09662) 3123
Cleabarrow, Windermere
(18) 5006 yards

Workington G.C.
(0900) 3460
Branthwaite Road,
Workington
(18) 6202 yards

DERBYSHIRE

Alfreton G.C.
(0773) 832070
Wingfield Road,
Oakerthorpe
(9) 5012 yards

Allestree Park G.C.
(0332) 550616
Allestree Hall, Derby
(18) 5749 yards

Ashbourne G.C.
(0335) 42077
Clifton, Ashbourne
(9) 5388 yards

Bakewell G.C.
(062981) 2307
Station Road, Bakewell
(9) 5240 yards

**Breadsall Priory
G. & C.C.**
(0332) 832235
Moor Road, Morley, Derby
(18) 6402 yards
(9) 3300 yards

Burton-on-Trent G.C.
(0283) 44551
Ashby Road East, Burton-on-Trent
(18) 6555 yards

**Buxton &
High Peak G.C.**
(0298) 3453
Fairfield, Buxton
(18) 5954 yards

Cavendish G.C.
(0298) 25052
Gadley Lane, Buxton
(18) 5833 yards

Chesterfield G.C.
(0246) 566032
Walton, Chesterfield
(18) 6326 yards

**Chesterfield
Municipal G.C.**
(0246) 273887
Crow Lane, Chesterfield
(18) 6044 yards

Chevin G.C.
(0332) 841864
Golf Lane, Duffield
(18) 6057 yards

Derby G.C.
(0332) 766462
Shakespeare Street,
Sinfin, Derby
(18) 6183 yards

Erewash Valley G.C.
(0602) 322984
Stanton-by-Dale, Ilkeston
(18) 6487 yards

**Glossop &
District G.C.**
(04574) 3117
Sheffield Road, Glossop
(11) 5726 yards

Ilkeston G.C.
(0602) 320304
West End Drive, Ilkeston
(9) 4116 yards

Kedleston Park G.C.
(0332) 840035
Kedleston, Quarndon
(18) 6636 yards

Matlock G.C.
(0629) 582191
Chesterfield Road, Matlock
(18) 5871 yards

Mickleover G.C.
(0332) 512092
Uttoxeter Road, Mickleover
(18) 5621 yards

**Ormonde Fields
G. & C.C.**
(0773) 42987
Nottingham Road,
Codnor, Ripley
(18) 6007 yards

Pastures G.C.
(0332) 513921
Pastures Hospital,
Mickleover
(9) 5005 yards

Renishaw Park G.C.
(0246) 432044
Station Road,
Renishaw
(18) 6253 yards

Shirlands G. & S.C.
(0773) 834935
Lower Delves,
Shirland
(18) 6021 yards

Sickleholme G.C.
(0433) 51306
Bamford
(18) 6064 yards

Stanedge G.C.
(0246) 566156
Walton, Chesterfield
(9) 4867 yards

DEVON

Axe Cliff G.C.
(0297) 20499
Axemouth, Seaton
(18) 4998 yards

Bigbury G.C.
(0548) 810207
Bigbury-on-Sea,
Kingsbridge
(18) 6038 yards

Chulmleigh G.C.
(0769) 80519
Leigh Road, Chulmleigh
(18) 1440 yards

Churston G.C.
(0803) 842751
Churston, Brixham
(18) 6201 yards

Downes Crediton G.C.
(03632) 3025
Hookway, Crediton
(18) 5858 yards

East Devon G.C.
(03954) 3370
North View Road,
Budleigh Salterton
(18) 6214 yards

**Elfordleigh Hotel
G. & C.C.**
(0752) 336428
Plympton, Plymouth
(9) 5609 yards

Exeter G. & C.C.
(0392) 874139
Countess Wear, Exeter
(18) 5702 yards

Holsworthy G.C.
(0409) 253177
Kilatree, Holsworthy
(18) 5935 yards

Honiton G.C.
(0404) 44422
Honiton
(18) 5900 yards

Ilfracombe G.C.
(0271) 62176
Hele Bay, Ilfracombe
(18) 6227 yards

**Manor House Hotel G. &
C.C.**
(0647) 40355
Princetown Road,
Moretonhampstead
(18) 6016 yards

**Newton Abbot (Stover)
G.C.**
(0626) 62078
Bovey Road, Newton Abbot
(18) 5724 yards

Okehampton G.C.
(0837) 2113
Okehampton
(18) 5307 yards

Royal North Devon G.C.
(0237) 473817
Westward Ho!, Bideford
(18) 6449 yards

Saunton G.C.
(0271) 812436
Saunton, Braunton
(18) 6703 yards (East)
(18) 6356 yards (West)

Sidmouth G.C.
(0395) 513451
Cotmaton Road, Sidmouth
(18) 5188 yards

Staddon Heights G.C.
(0752) 402475
Plymstock, Plymouth
(18) 5861 yards

Tavistock G.C.
(0822) 612049
Down Road, Tavistock
(18) 6250 yards

Teignmouth G.C.
(0626) 773614
Exeter Road, Teignmouth
(18) 6142 yards

Thurlestone G.C.
(0548) 560405
Thurlestone, Kingsbridge
(18) 6337 yards

Tiverton G.C.
(0884) 252187
Post Hill, Tiverton
(18) 6227 yards

Torquay G.C.
(0803) 314591
St Marychurch,
Torquay
(18) 6251 yards

Torrington G.C.
(0805) 22229
Weare Trees, Torrington
(9) 4418 yards

Warren G.C.
(0626) 862255
Dawlish Warren
(18) 5968 yards

Wrangaton G.C.
(03647) 3229
Wrangaton, South Brent
(9) 5790 yards

Yelverton G.C.
(0822) 852824
Golf Links Road, Yelverton
(18) 6288 yards

DORSET

Ashley Wood G.C.
(0258) 452253
Wimborne Road,
Blandford Forum
(9) 6227 yards

Boscombe G.C.
(0202) 36817
Queen's Park, Bournemouth
(18) 6505 yards

Bridport & West Dorset G.C.
(0308) 22597
East Cliff, West Bay, Bridport
(18) 5246 yards

Broadstone G.C.
(0202) 692595
Wentworth Drive,
Broadstone
(18) 6204 yards

Came Down G.C.
(030 581) 2531
Came Down, Dorchester
(18) 6121 yards

Christchurch G.C.
(0202) 473817
Iford Bridge, Christchurch
(9) 4824 yards

East Dorset G.C.
(0929) 472244
Hyde, Wareham
(18) 6108 yards

Ferndown G.C.
(0202) 874602
119 Golf Links Road,
Ferndown
(18) 6442 yards (Old Course)
(9) 5604 yards (New Course)

Highcliffe Castle G.C.
(04252) 272210
107 Lymington Road,
Highcliffe-on-Sea
(18) 4732 yards

Isle of Purbeck G.C.
(0929) 44361
Studland, Swanage
(18) 6248 yards
(9) 2022 yards

Knighton Heath G.C.
(0202) 572633
Francis Avenue, West Howe,
Bournemouth
(18) 6206 yards

Lakey Hill G.C.
(0929) 471776
Hyde, Wareham
(18) 6146 yards

Lyme Regis G.C.
(02974) 2963
Timber Hill, Lyme Regis
(18) 6262 yards

Meyrick Park G.C.
(0202) 290871
Central Drive, Bournemouth
(18) 5878 yards

Parkstone G.C.
(0202) 707138
Links Road, Parkstone
(18) 6250 yards

Sherborne G.C.
(0935) 814431
Higher Clatcombe, Sherborne
(18) 5768 yards

Weymouth G.C.
(0305) 773981
Links Road, Westham,
Weymouth
(18) 5985 yards

DURHAM

Aycliffe G.C.
(0325) 310820
Newton Aycliffe
(9) 6054 yards

Barnard Castle G.C.
(0833) 38355
Marmire Road, Barnard
Castle
(18) 5838 yards

Beamish Park G.C.
(091) 3701382
Beamish, Stanley
(18) 6205 yards

Birtley G.C.
(091) 4102207
Portobello Road, Birtley
(9) 5154 yards

Bishop Auckland G.C.
(0388) 663648
Durham Road, Bishop
Auckland
(18) 6420 yards

Blackwell Grange G.C.
(0325) 464464
Briar Close, Blackwell,
Darlington
(18) 5609 yards

Brancepeth Castle G.C.
(091) 3780075
Brancepeth Village, Durham
(18) 6300 yards

Chester-le-Street G.C.
(091) 3883218
Lumley Park,
Chester-le-Street
(18) 6054 yards

Consett & District G.C.
(0207) 502186
Elmfield Road, Consett
(18) 6001 yards

Crook G.C.
(0388) 762429
Low Job's Hill, Crook
(18) 6089 yards

Darlington G.C.
(0325) 463936
Haughton Grange,
Darlington
(18) 6272 yards

Dinsdale Spa G.C.
(0325) 332297
Middleton St. George,
Darlington
(18) 6078 yards

Durham City G.C.
(091) 3780069
Langley Moor, Durham
(18) 6118 yards

Mount Oswald G.C.
(091) 3867527
South Road, Durham
(18) 6009 yards

Roseberry Grange G.C.
(091) 3700660
Grange Villa,
Chester-le-Street
(18) 5628 yards

Seaham G.C.
(091) 5812354
Dawdon, Seaham
(18) 5972 yards

South Moor G.C.
(0207) 232848
The Middles, Craghead,
Stanley
(18) 6445 yards

Stressholme G.C.
(0325) 461002
Snipe Lane, Darlington
(18) 6511 yards

EAST SUSSEX

Ashdown Forest Hotel G.C.
(034282) 4866
Chapel Lane, Forest Row
(18) 5433 yards

Brighton and Hove G.C.
(0273) 556482
Dyke Road, Brighton
(9) 5722 yards

Cooden Beach G.C.
(04243) 2040
Cooden, Bexhill
(18) 6411 yards

Crowborough Beacon G.C.
(08926) 61511
Beacon Road, Crowborough
(18) 6279 yards

Dale Hill G.C.
(0580) 200112
Ticehurst, Wadhurst
(18) 6035 yards

The Dyke G.C.
(079156) 296
Dyke Road, Brighton
(18) 6557 yards

Eastbourne Downs G.C.
(0323) 20827
East Dean Road, Eastbourne
(18) 6635 yards

East Brighton G.C.
(0273) 603989
Roedean Road, Brighton
(18) 6291 yards

East Sussex National G.C.
(0825) 75577
Little Horsted, Uckfield
(18) 7112 yards (East)
(18) 7202 yards (West)

Hastings G.C.
(0424) 52981
Battle Road, St. Leonards-on-Sea
(18) 6073 yards

Highwoods G.C.
(0424) 212625
Ellerslie Lane, Bexhill-on-Sea
(18) 6218 yards

Hollingbury Park G.C.
(0273) 552010
Ditching Road, Brighton
(18) 6415 yards

Horam Park G.C.
(04353) 3477
Chiddingly Road, Horam
(9) 2600 yards

Lewes G.C.
(0273) 473074
Chapel Hill, Lewes
(18) 5951 yards

Peacehaven G.C.
(0273) 514049
Brighton Road, Newhaven
(9) 5235 yards

Piltdown G.C.
(082572) 2033
Piltdown, Uckfield
(18) 6059 yards

Pyecombe G.C.
(07918) 5372
Clayton Hill, Pyecombe
(18) 6234 yards

Royal Ashdown Forest G.C.
(034282) 2018
Chapel Lane, Forest Row
(18) 6439 yards

Royal Eastbourne G.C.
(0323) 29738
Paradise Drive, Eastbourne
(18) 6084 yards
(9) 2147 yards

Rye G.C.
(0797) 225241
Camber, Near Rye
(18) 6301 yards
(18) 6141 yards (Jubilee)

Seaford G.C.
(0323) 892442
East Blatchington, Seaford
(18) 6241 yards

Seaford Head G.C.
(0323) 894843
Southdown Road, Seaford
(18) 5812 yards

Waterhall G.C.
(0273) 508658
Mill Road, Brighton
(18) 5615 yards

West Hove G.C.
(0273) 419738
Old Shoreham Road, Hove
(18) 6130 yards

Willingdon G.C.
(0323) 410981
Southdown Road,
Eastbourne
(18) 6049 yards

ESSEX

Abridge G. & C.C.
(04028) 396
Stapleford Tawney, Abridge
(18) 6703 yards

Ballards Gore G.C.
(0702) 258917
Gore Road, Canewdon,
Rochford
(18) 7062 yards

Basildon G.C.
(0268) 533297
Clay Hill Lane, Basildon
(18) 6122 yards

Belfairs Park G.C.
(0702) 525345
Eastwood Road,
Leigh-on-Sea
(18) 5871 yards

Belhus Park G.C.
(0708) 854260
Belhus Park, South Ockendon
(18) 5501 yards

Bentley G.C.
(0277) 373179
Ongar Road, Brentwood
(18) 6709 yards

Birch Grove G.C.
(0206) 34276
Layer Road, Colchester
(9) 2828 yards

Boyce Hill G.C.
(0268) 793625
Vicarage Hill, South Benfleet
(18) 5882 yards

Braintree G.C.
(0376) 24117
Kings Lane, Stisted, Braintree
(18) 6026 yards

Bunsay Downs G.C.
(024541) 2648
Woodham Walter, Maldon
(18) 5826 yards

Burnham-on-Crouch G.C.
(0621) 782282
Creeksea, Burnham-on-Crouch
(9) 5866 yards

Canon's Brook G.C.
(0279) 21482
Elizabeth Way, Harlow
(18) 6745 yards

Royal North Devon.

Channels G.C.
(0245) 440005
Belsteads Farm Lane, Little
Waltham, Chelmsford
(18) 6033 yards

Chelmsford G.C.
(0245) 256483
Widford, Chelmsford
(18) 5912 yards

Clacton G.C.
(0255) 421919
West Road, Clacton-on-Sea
(18) 6217 yards

Colchester G.C.
(0206) 853396
Braiswick, Colchester
(18) 6319 yards

Forrester Park G.C.
(0621) 891406
Great Totham, Maldon
(9) 5350 yards

Frinton G.C.
(02556) 4618
Esplanade, Frinton-on-Sea
(18) 6259 yards

Harwich & Dovercourt G.C.
(0255) 503616
Parkeston, Harwich
(9) 5692 yards

Havering G.C.
(0708) 22942
Lower Bedfords Road,
Romford
(18) 5687 yards

Maldon G.C.
(0621) 53212
Beeleigh Landford, Maldon
(9) 6197 yards

Maylands G. & C.C.
(04023) 73080
Harold Park, Romford
(18) 6351 yards

Orsett G.C.
(0375) 891352
Brentwood Road, Orsett
(18) 6575 yards

Pipps Hill G.C.
(0268) 23456
Cranes Farm Road, Basildon
(9) 5658 yards

Quietwaters G.C.
(0621) 860410
Colchester Road, Tolleshunt
D'Arcy
(18) 6201 yards
(18) 6855 yards

Rochford Hundred G.C.
(0702) 544302
Rochford Hall, Rochford
(18) 6255 yards

Romford G.C.
(0708) 740986
Gidea Park, Romford
(18) 6377 yards

Saffron Walden G.C.
(0799) 22786
Windmill Hill, Saffron
Walden
(18) 6608 yards

Skips G.C.
(04023) 48234
Tysea Hill, Stapleford
Abbotts
(18) 6146 yards

Stoke-by-Nayland G.C.
(0206) 262836
Leavenheath, Colchester
(18) 6471 yards
(Gainsborough)
(18) 6498 yards (Constable)

Theydon Bois G.C.
(0378) 3054
Theydon Road, Epping
(18) 5472 yards

East Sussex National.

Thorndon Park G.C.
(0277) 811666
Ingrave, Brentwood
(18) 6455 yards

Thorpe Hall G.C.
(0702) 582205
Thorpe Hall Avenue, Thorpe Bay
(18) 6259 yards

Three Rivers G. & C.C.
(0621) 828631
Stow Road, Purleigh
(18) 6609 yards (Kings)
(9) 2142 yards

Toot Hill G.C.
(0277) 365523
Toot Hill, Ongar
(18) 6000 yards

Towerlands G.C.
(0376) 26802
Panfield Road, Braintree
(9) 5396 yards

Upminster G.C.
(04022) 22788
Hall Lane, Upminster
(18) 5926 yards

Warley Park G.C.
(0277) 224891
Little Warley, Brentwood
(18) 6261 yards
(9) 3166 yards

Warren G.C.
(024541) 3258
Woodham Walter, Maldon
(18) 6211 yards

GLOUCESTER-SHIRE

Cirencester G.C.
(0285) 652465
Cheltenham Road, Bagendon, Cirencester
(18) 6021 yards

Cleeve Hill G.C.
(0242) 672592
Cleeve Hill, Cheltenham
(18) 6217 yards

Cotswold Hills G.C.
(0242) 515264
Ullenwood, Cheltenham
(18) 6716 yards

Gloucester Hotel G. & C.C.
(0452) 25653
Robinswood Hill, Gloucester
(18) 6135 yards

Lilley Brook G.C.
(0242) 526785
Cirencester Road, Charlton Kings, Cheltenham
(18) 6226 yards

Lydney G.C.
(0594) 42614
Lakeside Avenue, Lydney
(9) 5382 yards

Minchinhampton G.C.
(045383) 3860 (New)
(045383) 3860 (Old)
Minchinhampton, Stroud
(18) 6295 yards (Old Course)
(18) 6675 yards (New Course)

Painswick G.C.
(0452) 812180
Painswick, Stroud
(18) 4780 yards

Royal Forest of Dean G.C.
(0594) 32583
Lords Hill, Coleford
(18) 5519 yards

Stinchcombe Hill G.C.
(0453) 2015
Stinchcombe Hill, Dursley
(18) 5710 yards

Tewkesbury Park Hotel G.C.
(0684) 295405
Lincoln Green Lane,
Tewkesbury
(18) 6533 yards

Westonbirt G.C.
(066) 688242
Westonbirt, Tetbury
(9) 4504 yards

GREATER LONDON

The Addington G.C.
(081) 777 6057
Shirley Church Road,
Croydon
(18) 6242 yards

Addington Court G.C.
(081) 657 0281
Featherbed Lane,
Addington, Croydon
(18) 5577 yards (Old)
(18) 5513 yards (New)

Addington Palace G.C.
(081) 654 3061
Gravel Hill, Addington,
Croydon
(18) 6262 yards

Arkley G.C.
(081) 449 0394
Rowley Green Road, Barnet
(9) 6045 yards

Aquarius G.C.
(081) 693 1626
Marmora Road, Honor Oak
SE22
(9) 5035 yards

Ashford Manor G.C.
(0784) 252049
Fordbridge Road, Ashford
(18) 6343 yards

Banstead Downs G.C.
(081) 642 2284
Burdon Lane, Belmont,
Sutton
(18) 6169 yards

Beckenham Place Park G.C.
(081) 658 5374
Beckenham Hill Road,
Beckenham
(18) 5722 yards

Bexley Heath G.C.
(081) 303 6951
Mount Road, Bexley Heath
(9) 5239 yards

Brent Valley G.C.
(081) 567 1287
Church Road, Hanwell W7
(18) 5426 yards

Bushey G.C.
(081) 950 2215
High Street, Bushey
(9) 6000 yards

Bush Hill Park G.C.
(081) 360 5738
Winchmore Hill, N21
(18) 5809 yards

Chigwell G.C.
(081) 500 2059
High Road, Chigwell
(18) 6279 yards

Chingford G.C.
(081) 529 5708
Station Road, Chingford E4
(18) 6136 yards

Chislehurst G.C.
(081) 467 2782
Camden Place, Chislehurst
(18) 5128 yards

Coombe Hill G.C.
(081) 942 2284
Golf Club Drive,
Kingston Hill
(18) 6286 yards

Coombe Wood G.C.
(081) 942 0388
George Road, Kingston Hill
(18) 5210 yards

Coulsdon Court G.C.
(081) 660 0468
Coulsdon Road, Coulsdon
(18) 6030 yards

Crews Hill G.C.
(081) 363 6674
Cattlegate Road, Crews Hill
(18) 6208 yards

Croham Hurst G.C.
(081) 657 2075
Croham Road,
South Croydon
(18) 6274 yards

Cuddington G.C.
(081) 393 0952
Banstead Road, Banstead
(18) 6282 yards

Dulwich & Sydenham Hill G.C.
(081) 693 3961
College Road, SE21
(18) 6051 yards

Dyrham Park G.C.
(081) 440 3361
Galley Lane, Barnet
(18) 6369 yards

Ealing G.C.
(081) 997 0937
Perivale Lane, Greenford
(18) 6216 yards

Elstree G.C.
(081) 953 6115
Watling Street, Elstree
(18) 5245 yards

Eltham Warren G.C.
(081) 850 4477
Bexley Road, Eltham SE9
(9) 5840 yards

Enfield G.C.
(081) 363 3970
Old Park Road South,
Windmill Hill, Enfield
(18) 6137 yards

Fairlop Waters G.C.
(081) 500 9911
Barkingside, Ilford
(18) 6288 yards

Finchley G.C.
(081) 346 2436
Frith Lane, NW7
(18) 6411 yards

Fulwell G.C.
(081) 977 2733
Hampton Hill
(18) 6490 yards

Greenford G.C.
(081) 578 3949
Rockware Avenue, Greenford
(9) 4418 yards

Grim's Dyke G.C.
(081) 428 4539
Oxhey Lane, Hatch End,
Pinner
(18) 5598 yards

Hadley Wood G.C.
(081) 449 4328
Beech Hill, Hadley Wood
(18) 6473 yards

Hainault Forest G.C.
(081) 500 0385
Chigwell Row, Hainault
Forest
(18) 5754 yards (No. 1)
(18) 6445 yards (No. 2)

Hampstead G.C.
(081) 455 7089
Winnington Road, N2
(9) 5812 yards

Harefield Place G.C.
(0895) 31169
The Drive, Harefield Place,
Uxbridge
(18) 5711 yards

Hartsbourne G. & C.C.
(081) 950 1113
Bushey Heath
(18) 6305 yards
(9) 5432 yards

Haste Hill G.C.
(09274) 22877
The Drive, Northwood
(18) 5794 yards

Hatfield London C.C.
(0707) 42624
Bedwell Park, Essendon
(18) 6878 yards

Hendon G.C.
(081) 346 6023
Devonshire Road, NW7
(18) 6241 yards

Highgate G.C.
(081) 340 3745
Denewood Road,
Highgate N6
(18) 5964 yards

Hillingdon G.C.
(0895) 233956
Dorset Way, Hillingdon
(9) 5469 yards

Home Park G.C.
(081) 977 2423
Hampton Wick, Kingston
(18) 6497 yards

Horsenden Hill G.C.
(081) 902 4555
Woodland Rise, Greenford
(9) 1618 yards

Hounslow Heath G.C.
(081) 570 5271
Staines Road, Hounslow
(18) 5820 yards

Ilford G.C.
(081) 554 0094
Wanstead Park Road, Ilford
(18) 5710 yards

Langley Park G.C.
(081) 658 6849
Barnfield Wood Road,
Beckenham
(18) 6488 yards

Lime Trees G.C.
(081) 845 3180
Ruislip Road, Northolt
(9) 5815 yards

London Scottish G.C.
(081) 788 0135
Windmill Enclosure,
Wimbledon Common SW19
(18) 5486 yards

Magpie Hall Lane G.C.
(081) 462 7014
Magpie Hall Lane, Bromley
(9) 5538 yards

Malden G.C.
(081) 942 0654
Traps Lane, New Malden
(18) 6315 yards

Mill Hill G.C.
(081) 959 2339
Barnet Way, Mill Hill NW7
(18) 6294 yards

Mitcham G.C.
(081) 648 4197
Carshalton Road, Mitcham
Junction
(18) 5931 yards

Muswell Hill G.C.
(081) 888 1764
Rhodes Avenue, Wood Green
N22
(18) 6470 yards

North Middlesex G.C.
(081) 445 1604
Friern Barnet Lane, N20
(18) 5611 yards

Northwood G.C.
(09274) 21384
Rickmansworth Road,
Northwood
(18) 6464 yards

Oaks Park Sports Centre G.C.
(081) 643 8363
Woodmansterne Road,
Carshalton
(18) 5873 yards

Old Ford Manor G.C.
(081) 440 9185
Hadley Green, Barnet
(18) 6449 yards

Perivale Park G.C.
(081) 575 8655
Ruislip Road East, Greenford
(9) 5334 yards

Picketts Lock G.C.
(081) 803 3611
Picketts Lock Lane,
Edmonton
(9) 2496 yards

Pinner Hill G.C.
(081) 866 0963
South View Road, Pinner Hill
(18) 6293 yards

Purley Downs G.C.
(081) 657 8347
Purley Downs Road, Purley
(18) 6237 yards

Richmond G.C.
(081) 940 4351
Sudbrook Park, Richmond
(18) 5965 yards

Richmond Park G.C.
(081) 876 1795
Richmond Park, SW15
(18) 5940 yards (Dukes)
(18) 5969 yards (Princes)

Roehampton G.C.
(081) 876 5505
Roehampton Lane
(18) 6057 yards

Royal Blackheath G.C.
(081) 850 1795
Court Road, Eltham
(18) 6216 yards

Royal Epping Forest G.C.
(081) 529 2195
Forest Approach, Chingford
(18) 6220 yards

Royal Mid-Surrey G.C.
(081) 940 1894
Old Deer Park, Richmond
(18) 6331 yards (Outer)
(18) 5446 yards (Inner)

Royal Wimbledon G.C.
(081) 946 2125
29 Camp Road, Wimbledon
(18) 6300 yards

Ruislip G.C.
(0895) 638835
Ickenham Road, Ruislip
(18) 5235 yards

Sandy Lodge G.C.
(09274) 25429
Sandy Lodge Lane,
Northwood
(18) 6340 yards

Selsdon Park Hotel G.C.
(081) 657 8811
Addington Road,
Sanderstead
(18) 6402 yards

Shirley Park G.C.
(081) 654 1143
Addiscombe Road, Croydon
(18) 6210 yards

Shooters Hill G.C.
(081) 854 6368
Eaglesfield Road,
Shooters Hill
(18) 5736 yards

Shortlands G.C.
(081) 460 2471
Meadow Road, Shortlands,
Bromley
(9) 5261 yards

Sidcup G.C.
(081) 300 2150
Hurst Road, Sidcup
(9) 5692 yards

South Herts G.C.
(081) 445 2035
Links Drive, Totteridge
(18) 6470 yards

Stanmore G.C.
(081) 954 2599
Gordon Avenue, Stanmore
(18) 5982 yards

Strawberry Hill G.C.
(081) 894 0165
Wellesley Road, Twickenham
(9) 4762 yards

Sudbury G.C.
(081) 902 3713
Bridgewater Road, Wembley
(18) 6282 yards

Sundridge Park G.C.
(081) 460 0278
Garden Road, Bromley
(18) 6410 yards (East)
(18) 6027 yards (West)

Surbiton G.C.
(081) 398 3101
Woodstock Lane,
Chessington
(18) 6211 yards

Thames Ditton & Esher G.C.
(081) 398 1551
Portsmouth Road, Esher
(9) 5415 yards

Trent Park G.C.
(081) 366 7432
Bramley Road, Southgate
(18) 6008 yards

Twickenham G.C.
(081) 892 5579
Staines Road, Twickenham
(9) 6014 yards

Wanstead G.C.
(081) 989 3938
Overton Drive, Wanstead
(18) 6211 yards

West Essex G.C.
(081) 529 7558
Stewardstonebury, Chingford
(18) 6289 yards

West Middlesex G.C.
(081) 574 3450
Greenford Road, Southall
(18) 6242 yards

Whitewebbs G.C.
(081) 363 4458
Clay Hill, Enfield
(18) 5755 yards

Wimbledon Common G.C.
(081) 946 7571
Camp Road, Wimbledon Common
(18) 5486 yards

Wimbledon Park G.C.
(081) 946 1250
Home Park Road, Wimbledon
(18) 5465 yards

Woodcote Park G.C.
(081) 668 2788
Meadow Hill, Coulsdon
(18) 6624 yards

Woodford G.C.
(081) 504 3330
Sunset Avenue, Woodford Green
(9) 5806 yards

Wyke Green G.C.
(081) 560 8777
Syon Lane, Isleworth
(18) 6242 yards

GREATER MANCHESTER

Altrincham Municipal G.C.
(061) 928 0761
Stockport Road, Timperley, Altrincham
(18) 6204 yards

Ashton-in-Makerfield G.C.
(0942) 727745
Gardwood Park, Liverpool Road, Ashton-in-Makerfield
(18) 6160 yards

Ashton-on-Mersey G.C.
(061) 973 3220
Church Lane, Sale
(9) 6242 yards

Ashton-under-Lyne G.C.
(061) 330 1537
Kings Road, Ashton-under-Lyne
(18) 6157 yards

Blackley G.C.
(061) 643 3812
Victoria Avenue East, Blackley
(18) 6235 yards

Bolton G.C.
(0204) 43067
Lostock Park, Bolton
(18) 6215 yards

Bolton Municipal G.C.
(0204) 42336
Links Road, Lostock, Bolton
(18) 6012 yards

Bolton Old Links G.C.
(0204) 42307
Chorley Old Road, Bolton
(18) 6406 yards

Brackley G.C.
(061) 790 6076
Bullows Road, Little Hulton
(9) 6006 yards

Bramhall G.C.
(061) 439 6092
Ladythorn Road, Bramhall
(18) 6293 yards

Bramhall Park G.C.
(061) 485 3119
Manor Road, Bramhall
(18) 6214 yards

Breightmet G.C.
(0204) 27381
Redbridge, Ainsworth
(9) 6407 yards

Brookdale G.C.
(061) 681 4534
Woodhouses, Failsworth
(18) 5878 yards

Bury G.C.
(061) 766 2213
Blackford Bridge, Bury
(18) 5961 yards

Castle Hawk G.C.
(0706) 40841
Castleton, Rochdale
(18) 6316 yards

Cheadle G.C.
(061) 428 2160
Shiers Drive, Cheadle
(9) 5006 yards

Chorlton-Cum-Hardy G.C.
(061) 881 5830
Barlow Hall Road, Chorlton
(18) 6004 yards

Crompton & Royton G.C.
(061) 624 2154
High Barn, Royton, Oldham
(18) 6121 yards

Davyhulme Park G.C.
(061) 748 2260
Gleneagles Road, Davyhulme
(18) 6237 yards

Deane G.C.
(0204) 651808
Junction Road, Deane, Bolton
(18) 5511 yards

Denton G.C.
(061) 336 3218
Manchester Road, Denton
(18) 6290 yards

Didsbury G.C.
(061) 998 2811
Ford Lane, Northenden
(18) 6273 yards

Disley G.C.
(0663) 62071
Jackson's Edge, Disley
(18) 5977 yards

Dukinfield G.C.
(061) 338 2669
Yew Tree Lane, Dukinfield
(18) 5544 yards

Dunham Forest G. & C.C.
(061) 928 2605
Oldfield Lane, Altrincham
(18) 6636 yards

Dunscar G.C.
(0204) 53321
Bromley Cross, Bolton
(18) 5995 yards

Ellesmere G.C.
(061) 790 7108
Old Clough Lane, Worsley
(18) 5957 yards

Fairfield G. & S.C.
(061) 370 2292
Booth Road, Andenshaw
(18) 5664 yards

Flixton G.C.
(061) 748 2116
Church Road, Flixton, Urmston
(9) 6441 yards

Gathurst G.C.
(02575) 2432
Shevington
(9) 6308 yards

Gatley G.C.
(061) 437 2091
Styal Road, Heald Green
(9) 5934 yards

Great Lever & Farnworth G.C.
(0204) 72550
Lever Edge Lane, Bolton
(18) 5859 yards

Greenmount G.C.
(020488) 3712
Greenmount, Bury
(9) 4920 yards

Hale G.C.
(061) 980 4225
Rappax Road, Hale
(9) 5734 yards

Harwood G.C.
(0204) 28028
Harwood, Bolton
(9) 6028 yards

Hazel Grove G.C.
(061) 483 7272
Buxton Road, Hazel Grove
(18) 6300 yards

Heaton Moor G.C.
(061) 432 6458
Heaton Mersey, Stockport
(18) 5876 yards

Heaton Park G.C.
(061) 798 0295
Heaton Park, Prestwich
(18) 5849 yards

Horwich G.C.
(0204) 696298
Horwich, Bolton
(9) 5404 yards

Houldsworth G.C.
(061) 224 4571
Wingate House, Levenshulme
(18) 6078 yards

Lowes Park G.C.
(061) 764 1231
Walmersley, Bury
(9) 6003 yards

Manchester G.C.
(061) 643 3202
Rochdale Road, Middleton
(18) 6450 yards

Marple G.C.
(061) 427 2311
Hawk Green, Marple, Stockport
(18) 5506 yards

Mellor & Townscliffe G.C.
(061) 427 2208
Mellor, Stockport
(18) 5925 yards

Mirrlees G.C.
(061) 483 1000
Bramhall Moor Lane, Hazel Grove
(9) 6102 yards

North Manchester G.C.
(061) 643 9033
Manchester Old Road, Middleton
(18) 6542 yards

Northenden G.C.
(061) 998 4738
Palatine Road, Northenden
(18) 6435 yards

Oldham G.C.
(061) 624 4986
Lees New Road, Oldham
(18) 5045 yards

Pike Fold G.C.
(061) 740 1136
Cooper Lane, Victoria Avenue, Blackley
(9) 5789 yards

Prestwich G.C.
(061) 773 2544
Hilton Lane, Prestwich M25
(18) 4712 yards

Reddish Vale G.C.
(061) 480 2359
Southcliffe Road, Reddish, Stockport
(18) 6048 yards

Ringway G.C.
(061) 980 2630
Hale Barns, Altrincham
(18) 6494 yards

Rochdale G.C.
(0706) 43818
Bagslate, Rochdale
(18) 5981 yards

Romiley G.C.
(061) 430 7257
Goosehouse Green, Romiley
(18) 6357 yards

Saddleworth G.C.
(04577) 3653
Uppermill, Oldham
(18) 5961 yards

Sale G.C.
(061) 973 1638
Golf Road, Sale
(18) 6351 yards

Springfield Park G.C.
(0706) 49801
Marland, Rochdale
(18) 5209 yards

Stamford G.C.
(04575) 4829
Huddersfield Road, Stalybridge
(18) 5619 yards

Stand G.C.
(061) 766 2388
Ashbourne Grove, Whitefield
(18) 6411 yards

Stockport G.C.
(061) 427 4425
Offerton Road, Offerton, Stockport
(18) 6319 yards

Swinton Park G.C.
(061) 794 0861
East Lanes Road, Swinton
(18) 6675 yards

Tunshill G.C.
(0706) 342095
Milnrow, Rochdale
(9) 5812 yards

Turton G.C.
(0204) 852235
Bromley Cross, Bolton
(9) 5805 yards

Walmersley G.C.
(061) 764 0018
Garretts Close, Walmersley
(9) 6114 yards

Werneth G.C.
(061) 624 1190
Garden Suburb, Oldham
(18) 5296 yards

Werneth Low G.C.
(061) 368 7388
Werneth Low, Hyde
(9) 5734 yards

Westhoughton G.C.
(0942) 811085
Westhoughton, Bolton
(9) 5834 yards

Whitefield G.C.
(061) 766 2904
Higher Lane, Whitefield
(18) 6106 yards

Wigan G.C.
(0257) 421360
Arley Hall, Haigh, Wigan
(9) 6058 yards

Wigan Metropolitan G.C.
(0942) 401107
Haigh Hall Park, Wigan
(18) 6423 yards

William Wroe G.C.
(061) 748 8680
Pennybridge Lane, Flixton
(18) 4395 yards

Withington G.C.
(061) 445 9544
Palatine Road, West Didsbury
(18) 6411 yards

Worsley G.C.
(061) 789 4202
Monton Green, Eccles
(18) 6217 yards

HAMPSHIRE

Alresford G.C.
(0962) 733746
Cheriton Road, Alresford
(18) 5986 yards

Alton G.C.
(0420) 82042
Old Odiham Road, Alton
(9) 5699 yards

Ampfield Par Three G.C.
(0794) 68480
Winchester Road, Ampfield
(18) 2478 yards

Andover G.C.
(0264) 58040
Winchester Road, Andover
(9) 5933 yards

Army G.C.
(0252) 540638
Laffans Road, Aldershot
(18) 6579 yards

Barton-on-Sea G.C.
(0425) 615308
Marine Drive, Barton-on-Sea
(18) 5565 yards

Basingstoke G.C.
(0256) 465990
Kempshott Park, Basingstoke
(18) 6309 yards

Basingstoke Hospitals G.C.
(0256) 20347
Aldermaston Road, Basingstoke
(9) 5480 yards

Bishopswood G.C.
(0734) 815213
Bishopswood Lane, Tadley, Basingstoke
(9) 6474 yards

Blackmoor G.C.
(04203) 2775
Golf Lane, White Hill, Bordon
(18) 6213 yards

Bramshaw G.C.
(0703) 813433
Brook, Lyndhurst
(18) 6233 yards (Manor)
(18) 5774 yards (Forest)

Brokenhurst Manor G.C.
(0590) 23332
Sway Road, Brokenhurst
(18) 6216 yards

Burley G.C.
(04253) 2431
Burley, Ringwood
(9) 6224 yards

Corhampton G.C.
(0489) 877279
Sheeps Pond Lane, Droxford, Southampton
(18) 6088 yards

Dibden G.C.
(0703) 845596
Dibden, Southampton
(18) 6206 yards

Dunwood Manor G.C.
(0794) 40549
Shootash Hill, Romsey
(18) 5959 yards

Fleming Park G.C.
(0703) 612797
Magpie Lane, Eastleigh
(18) 4436 yards

Gosport and Stokes Bay G.C.
(0705) 527941
Haslar, Gosport
(9) 5806 yards

Great Salterns G.C.
(0705) 664549
Eastern Road, Portsmouth
(18) 5970 yards

Hartley Wintney G.C.
(025126) 4211
London Road, Hartley Wintney
(9) 6096 yards

Hayling G.C.
(0705) 464446
Ferry Road, Hayling Island
(18) 6489 yards

Hockley G.C.
(0962) 713165
Twyford, Winchester
(18) 6260 yards

Lee-on-the-Solent G.C.
(0705) 551170
Brune Lane, Lee-on-the-Solent
(18) 6022 yards

Liphook G.C.
(0428) 723785
Wheatsheaf Enclosure, Liphook
(18) 6207 yards

Meon Valley Hotel G. & C.C.
(0329) 833455
Sandy Lane, Shedfield
(18) 6519 yards

New Forest G.C.
(042128) 2450
Lyndhurst
(18) 5748 yards

North Hants G.C.
(0252) 616443
Minley Road, Fleet
(18) 6257 yards

Old Thorns Hotel & G.C.
(0428) 724555
Longmoor Road, Liphook
(18) 6447 yards

Petersfield G.C.
(0730) 62386
Heath Road, Petersfield
(18) 5751 yards

Portsmouth G.C.
(0705) 372210
Crookhorn Lane, Woodley, Portsmouth
(18) 6259 yards

Romsey G.C.
(0703) 732218
Nursling, Southampton
(18) 5752 yards

Rowlands Castle G.C.
(070541) 2784
Links Lane, Rowlands Castle
(18) 6627 yards

Royal Winchester G.C.
(0962) 52462
Sarum Road, Winchester
(18) 6218 yards

Southampton G.C.
(0703) 768407
Golf Course Road, Bassett, Southampton
(18) 6218 yards
(9) 2391 yards

Southwick Park G.C.
(0705) 380131
Pinsley Drive, Southwick
(18) 5970 yards

Southwood G.C.
(0252) 548700
Ively Road, Farnborough
(18) 5553 yards

Stoneham G.C.
(0703) 769272
Bassett, Southampton
(18) 6310 yards

Tylney Park G.C.
(0256) 722079
Rotherwick, Basingstoke
(18) 6150 yards

Waterlooville G.C.
(0705) 263388
Idsworth Road, Cowplain, Portsmouth
(18) 6647 yards

HEREFORD & WORCESTER

Abbey Park G. & C.C.
(0527) 63918
Dagnell End Road, Redditch
(18) 6400 yards

Belmont House G.C.
(0432) 277445
Belmont, Hereford
(18) 6448 yards

Blackwell G.C.
(021) 445 1994
Blackwell, Bromsgrove
(18) 6105 yards

Broadway G.C.
(0386) 853683
Willersey Hill, Broadway
(18) 6211 yards

Churchill & Blakedown G.C.
(0562) 700200
Blakedown, Kidderminster
(9) 5399 yards

Droitwich G. & C.C.
(0905) 774344
Ford Lane, Droitwich
(18) 6036 yards

Evesham G.C.
(0386) 860395
Fladbury Cross, Pershore
(9) 6418 yards

Habberley G.C.
(0562) 745756
Habberley, Kidderminster
(9) 5440 yards

Herefordshire G.C.
(0432) 71219
Wormsley, Hereford
(18) 6036 yards

Kidderminster G.C.
(0562) 822303
Russell Road, Kidderminster
(18) 6156 yards

Kington G.C.
(0544) 230340
Bradnor Hill, Kington
(18) 5830 yards

Leominster G.C.
(0568) 2863
Ford Bridge, Leominster
(18) 6084 yards

Little Lakes G.C.
(0299) 266385
Lye Head, Bewdley
(9) 6204 yards

Redditch G.C.
(0527) 43309
Callow Hill, Redditch
(18) 6671 yards

Ross-on-Wye G.C.
(098982) 267
Gorsley, Ross-on-Wye
(18) 6500 yards

Tolladine G.C.
(0905) 21074
Tolladine Road, Worcester
(9) 5630 yards

Worcester G. & C.C.
(0905) 422555
Boughton Park, Worcester
(18) 5890 yards

Worcestershire G.C.
(0684) 575992
Wood Farm, Malvern Wells
(18) 6449 yards

HERTFORDSHIRE

Aldenham G. & C.C.
(0923) 853929
Radlett Road, Aldenham
(18) 6455 yards

Ashridge G.C.
(044284) 2244
Little Gaddesden, Berkhamsted
(18) 6508 yards

Batchwood Hall G.C.
(0727) 33349
Batchwood Drive,
St. Albans
(18) 6463 yards

Berkhamsted G.C.
(0442) 865832
The Common, Berkhamsted
(18) 6568 yards

Bishop's Stortford G.C.
(0279) 654715
Dunhow Road,
Bishop's Stortford
(18) 6440 yards

Boxmoor G.C.
(0442) 42434
Box Lane,
Hemel Hempstead
(9) 4854 yards

Brickendon Grange G.C.
(099286) 258
Brickendon, Hertford
(18) 6315 yards

Brookman's Park G.C.
(0707) 52487
Golf Club Road, Hatfield
(18) 6438 yards

Bushey Hall G.C.
(0923) 225802
Bushey Hall Drive,
Bushey
(18) 6071 yards

Chadwell Springs G.C.
(0920) 463647
Hertford Road, Ware
(9) 6418 yards

Cheshunt Park G.C.
(0992) 24009
Park Lane, Cheshunt
(18) 6608 yards

Chorleywood G.C.
(09278) 2009
Common Road, Chorleywood
(9) 5676 yards

East Herts G.C.
(0920) 821978
Hammels Park, Buntingford
(18) 6449 yards

Hanbury Manor G.C.
(0920) 487722
Thundridge, Ware
(18) 6500 yards

Harpenden G.C.
(0582) 712580
Hammonds End, Harpenden
(18) 6363 yards

Harpenden Common G.C.
(0582) 712856
East Common, Harpenden
(18) 5613 yards

Knebworth G.C.
(0438) 812752
Deards End Lane, Knebworth
(18) 6428 yards

Letchworth G.C.
(0462) 683203
Letchworth Lane, Letchworth
(18) 6082 yards

Little Hay G.C.
(0442) 833798
Bovingdon,
Hemel Hempstead
(18) 6610 yards

Mid Herts G.C.
(058283) 2242
Gustard Wood, Wheathampstead
(18) 6094 yards

Moor Park G.C.
(0923) 773146
Moor Park, Rickmansworth
(18) 6713 yards (High)
(18) 5815 yards (West)

Panshanger G.C.
(0707) 333350
Herns Lane,
Welwyn Garden City
(18) 6538 yards

Porters Park G.C.
(0923) 854127
Shenley Hill, Radlett
(18) 6313 yards

Potters Bar G.C.
(0707) 52020
Darkes Lane, Potters Bar
(18) 6273 yards

Redbourn G.C.
(0582) 793493
Kingsbourne Green Lane,
Redbourn
(18) 6407 yards

Rickmansworth G.C.
(0923) 773163
Moor Lane, Rickmansworth
(18) 4412 yards

Royston G.C.
(0763) 42696
Baldock Road, Royston
(18) 6032 yards

Stevenage G.C.
(043888) 424
Aston, Stevenage
(18) 6451 yards

Verulam G.C.
(0727) 53327
London Road, St Albans
(18) 6432 yards

Welwyn Garden City G.C.
(0707) 325243
High Oaks Road,
Welwyn Garden City
(18) 6200 yards

West Herts G.C.
(0923) 224264
Cassiobury Park, Watford
(18) 6488 yards

Whipsnade Park G.C.
(044284) 2330
Studham Lane, Dagnall
(18) 6812 yards

HUMBERSIDE

Beverley & East Riding G.C.
(0482) 869519
The Westwood, Beverley
(18) 5937 yards

Boothferry G.C.
(0430) 430364
Spaldington, Goole
(18) 6651 yards

Bridlington G.C.
(0262) 606367
Belvedere Road, Bridlington
(18) 6320 yards

Brough G.C.
(0482) 667374
Cave Road, Brough
(18) 6012 yards

Cleethorpes G.C.
(0472) 812059
Kings Road, Cleethorpes
(18) 6015 yards

Driffield G.C.
(0377) 44069
Sunderlandwick, Driffield
(18) 6227 yards

Elsham G.C.
(0652) 680291
Barton Road, Elsham
(18) 6420 yards

Flamborough Head G.C.
(0262) 850333
Flamborough, Bridlington
(18) 5438 yards

Ganstead Park G.C.
(0482) 811280
Coniston, Hull
(9) 5769 yards

Grimsby G.C.
(0472) 356981
Littlecoates Road, Grimsby
(18) 6058 yards

Hainsworth Park G.C.
(0964) 542362
Driffield
(9) 5350 yards

Hessle G.C.
(0482) 650171
Cottingham, Hull
(18) 6638 yards

Holme Hall G.C.
(0724) 862078
Bottesford, Scunthorpe
(18) 6475 yards

Hornsea G.C.
(0964) 534989
Rolston Road, Hornsea
(18) 6470 yards

Hull G.C.
(0482) 658919
Packman Lane, Kirk Ella,
Hull
(18) 6242 yards

Immingham G.C.
(0469) 75493
Church Lane, Immingham
(18) 5809 yards

Normanby Hall G.C.
(0724) 720226
Normanby Park, Scunthorpe
(18) 6398 yards

Scunthorpe G.C.
(0724) 866561
Burringham Road,
Scunthorpe
(18) 6281 yards

Sutton Park G.C.
(0482) 74242
Holderness Road, Hull
(18) 6251 yards

Withernsea G.C.
(0964) 612214
Chesnut Avenue,
Withernsea
(9) 5112 yards

ISLE OF MAN

Castletown G.C.
(0624) 822201
Fort Island, Castletown
(18) 6804 yards

Douglas G.C.
(0624) 75952
Pulrose Road, Douglas
(18) 6080 yards

Howstrake G.C.
(0624) 20430
Grondle Road, Onchan
(18) 5367 yards

Peel G.C.
(0624) 843456
Rheast Lane, Peel
(18) 5914 yards

Ramsey G.C.
(0624) 812244
Brookfield Avenue, Ramsey
(18) 6019 yards

Rowany G.C.
(0624) 834108
Rowany Drive, Port Erin
(18) 5813 yards

ISLE OF WIGHT

Cowes G.C.
(0983) 292303
Crossfield Avenue, Cowes
(9) 5880 yards

Freshwater Bay G.C.
(0983) 752955
Afton Downs,
Freshwater Bay
(18) 5628 yards

Newport G.C.
(0983) 525076
St. George's Down,
Newport
(9) 5704 yards

Osborne G.C.
(0983) 295421
Osborne, East Cowes
(9) 6286 yards

Ryde G.C.
(0983) 614809
Binstead Road, Ryde
(9) 5220 yards

Shanklin & Sandown G.C.
(0983) 403217
The Fairway, Sandown
(18) 6000 yards

Ventnor G.C.
(0983) 853326
Steephill Down Road, Ventnor
(9) 5910 yards

KENT

Ashford G.C.
(0233) 622655
Sandyhurst Lane, Ashford
(18) 6246 yards

Barnehurst G.C.
(0322) 523746
Mayplace Road, East Barnehurst
(9) 5320 yards

Bearsted G.C.
(0622) 38198
Ware Street, Bearsted, Maidstone
(18) 6253 yards

Broome Park G. & C.C.
(0227) 831701
Barham, Canterbury
(18) 6610 yards

Canterbury G.C.
(0227) 453532
Scotland Hills, Canterbury
(18) 6209 yards

Cherry Lodge G.C.
(0959) 72250
Jail Lane, Biggin Hill
(18) 6908 yards

Chestfield G.C.
(022779) 3569
Chestfield, Whitstable
(18) 6126 yards

Cobtree Manor Park G.C.
(0622) 53276
Chatham Road, Boxley, Maidstone
(18) 5701 yards

Cranbrook G.C.
(0580) 712833
Benenden Road, Cranbrook
(18) 6128 yards

Cray Valley G.C.
(0689) 37909
Sandy Lane, St Paul's Cray, Orpington
(18) 6338 yards

Darenth Valley G.C.
(09592) 2922
Station Road, Shoreham
(18) 6356 yards

Dartford G.C.
(0322) 26455
Dartford Heath, Dartford
(18) 5914 yards

Deangate Ridge G.C.
(0634) 251180
Hoo, Rochester
(18) 6300 yards

Edenbridge G. & C.C.
(0732) 865097
Crouch House Road, Edenbridge
(18) 6635 yards

Faversham G.C.
(079589) 561
Belmont Park, Faversham
(18) 5979 yards

Gillingham G.C.
(0634) 53017
Woodlands Road, Gillingham
(18) 5911 yards

Hawkhurst G.C.
(0580) 752396
High Street, Hawkhurst
(9) 5769 yards

Herne Bay G.C.
(0227) 373964
Eddington, Herne Bay
(18) 5466 yards

High Elms G.C.
(0689) 58175
High Elms Road, Downe
(18) 6210 yards

Holtye G.C.
(034286) 635
Holtye Common, Cowden, Edenbridge
(9) 5289 yards

Hythe Imperial G.C.
(0303) 67554
Princes Parade, Hythe
(9) 5583 yards

Knole Park G.C.
(0732) 452150
Seal Hollow Road, Sevenoaks
(18) 6249 yards

Lamberhurst G.C.
(0892) 890241
Church Road, Lamberhurst
(18) 6277 yards

Leeds Castle G.C.
(0622) 880467
Leeds Castle, Maidstone
(9) 6017 yards

Littlestone G.C.
(0679) 63355
St Andrews Road, Littlestone, New Romney
(18) 6417 yards

Lullingstone Park G.C.
(0959) 34542
Park Gate, Chelsfield, Orpington
(18) 6674 yards
(9) 2432 yards

Mid Kent G.C.
(0474) 568035
Singlewell Road, Gravesend
(18) 6206 yards

Nevill G.C.
(0892) 25818
Benhall Mill Road, Tunbridge Wells
(18) 6336 yards

North Foreland G.C.
(0843) 62140
Convent Road, Broadstairs
(18) 6382 yards

Poult Wood G.C.
(0732) 364039
Higham Lane, Tonbridge
(18) 5569 yards

Prince's G.C.
(0304) 613797
Sandwich Bay, Sandwich
(18) 6923 yards
(9) 3134 yards

Rochester & Cobham Park G.C.
(047482) 3411
Park Dale, Rochester
(18) 6467 yards

Royal Cinque Ports G.C.
(0304) 374007
Golf Road, Deal
(18) 6744 yards

Royal St George's G.C.
(0304) 613090
Sandwich
(18) 6857 yards

Ruxley G.C.
(0689) 71490
St Paul's Cray, Orpington
(18) 5017 yards

St Augustine's G.C.
(0843) 590333
Cliffsend, Ramsgate
(18) 5138 yards

Sene Valley G.C.
(0303) 268514
Sene, Folkestone
(18) 6320 yards

Sheerness G.C.
(0795) 662585
Powe Station Road, Sheerness
(18) 6500 yards

Sittingbourne & Milton Regis G.C.
(0795) 842261
Newington, Sittingbourne
(18) 6121 yards

Tenterden G.C.
(05806) 3987
Woodchurch Road, Tenterden
(9) 5119 yards

Tudor Park C.C.
(0622) 34334
Ashford Road, Bearsted
(18) 6041 yards

Tunbridge Wells G.C.
(0892) 23034
Langton Road,
Tunbridge Wells
(9) 4684 yards

Walmer & Kingsdown G.C.
(0304) 373256
Kingsdown, Deal
(18) 6451 yards

Westgate & Birchington G.C.
(0843) 31115
Domneva Road,
Westgate-on-Sea
(18) 4926 yards

West Kent G.C.
(0689) 51323
Downe, Orpington
(18) 6392 yards

West Malling G.C.
(0732) 844785
Addington, Maidstone
(18) 6142 yards

Whitstable & Seasalter G.C.
(0227) 272020
Collingwood Road,
Whitstable
(18) 5276 yards

Wildernesse G.C.
(0732) 61199
Seal, Sevenoaks
(18) 6478 yards

Woodlands Manor G.C.
(09592) 3806
Woodlands, Sevenoaks
(18) 5858 yards

Wrotham Heath G.C.
(0732) 884800
Comp, Sevenoaks
(9) 5823 yards

LANCASHIRE

Accrington & District G.C.
(0254) 35070
West End, Oswaldtwistle,
Accrington
(18) 5954 yards

Ashton & Lea G.C.
(0772) 720374
Blackpool Road, Lea, Preston
(18) 6286 yards

Bacup G.C.
(0706) 873170
Maden Road, Bacup
(9) 5652 yards

Baxenden & District G.C.
(0254) 34555
Top o' th' Meadow,
Baxenden,
Accrington
(9) 5740 yards

Beacon Park G.C.
(0695) 622700
Dalton, Up Holland, Wigan
(18) 5996 yards

Blackburn G.C.
(0254) 55942
Beardwood Brow, Blackburn
(18) 6099 yards

Blackpool North Shore G.C.
(0253) 52054
Devonshire Road, Blackpool
(18) 6440 yards

Blackpool Park G.C.
(0253) 31004
North Park Drive, Blackpool
(18) 6060 yards

Burnley G.C.
(0282) 24328
Glen View, Burnley
(18) 5891 yards

Chorley G.C.
(0257) 480263
Charnock, Chorley
(18) 6277 yards

Clitheroe G.C.
(0200) 22292
Whalley Road, Clitheroe
(18) 6311 yards

Colne G.C.
(0282) 863391
Skipton Old Road, Colne
(9) 5961 yards

Darwen G.C.
(0254) 771675
Winter Hill, Darwen
(18) 5752 yards

Dean Wood G.C.
(0695) 622219
Lafford Lane, Up Holland,
Skelmersdale
(18) 6097 yards

Duxbury Park G.C.
(02572) 65380
Duxbury Park, Chorley
(18) 6390 yards

Fairhaven G.C.
(0253) 736741
Lytham Hall Park, Ansdell,
Lytham St Annes
(18) 6883 yards

Fishwick Hall G.C.
(0772) 796866
Farringdon Park, Preston
(18) 6203 yards

Fleetwood G.C.
(03917) 3661
Princes Way, Fleetwood
(18) 6437 yards

Green Haworth G.C.
(0254) 37580
Green Haworth, Accrington
(9) 5513 yards

Heysham G.C.
(0254) 51011
Trumacar Park, Heysham
(18) 6224 yards

Hindley Hall G.C.
(0942) 55991
Hall Lane, Hindley
(18) 5875 yards

Ingol G. & S.C.
(0772) 734556
Ingol, Preston
(18) 6345 yards

Knott End G.C.
(0253) 810576
Wyreside, Knott End on Sea,
Blackpool
(18) 5852 yards

Lancaster G. & C.C.
(0524) 751247
Ashton-with-Stodday,
Lancaster
(18) 6442 yards

Lansil G.C.
(0524) 67143
Caton Road, Lancaster
(9) 5608 yards

Leyland G.C.
(0772) 436457
Wigan Road, Leyland
(18) 6105 yards

Longridge G.C.
(0772) 783291
Jeffrey Hill, Longridge
(18) 5678 yards

Lytham Green Drive G.C.
(0253) 737390
Ballam Road, Lytham
(18) 6043 yards

Marsden Park G.C.
(0282) 67525
Townhouse Road, Nelson
(18) 5806 yards

Morecambe G.C.
(0254) 412841
Bare, Morecambe
(18) 5766 yards

Nelson G.C.
(0282) 64583
Brierfield, Nelson
(18) 5961 yards

Ormskirk G.C.
(0695) 72227
Lathom, Ormskirk
(18) 6333 yards

Penwortham G.C.
(0772) 744630
Penworth, Preston
(18) 5915 yards

Pleasington G.C.
(0254) 22177
Pleasington, Blackburn
(18) 6445 yards

Poulton-le-Fylde G.C.
(0253) 892444
Breck Road, Poulton-le-Fylde
(9) 5752 yards

Preston G.C.
(0772) 700011
Fulwood, Preston
(18) 6249 yards

Rishton G.C.
(0254) 884442
Eachill Links, Rishton
(9) 6094 yards

Rossendale G.C.
(0706) 213616
Haslinden, Rossendale
(18) 6267 yards

Royal Lytham & St Annes G.C.
(0253) 724206
Links Gate, Lytham St Annes
(18) 6673 yards

St Annes Old Links G.C.
(0253) 723597
Highbury Road, St Annes, Lytham
(18) 6616 yards

Shaw Hill G. & C.C.
(02572) 69221
Whittle-le-Woods, Chorley
(18) 6467 yards

Silverdale G.C.
(0524) 701300
Redbridge Lane, Silverdale, Carnworth
(9) 5262 yards

Todmorden G.C.
(070681) 2986
Stone Road, Todmorden
(9) 5818 yards

Towneley G.C.
(0282) 38473
Towneley Park, Burnley
(9) 5840 yards

Whalley G.C.
(025482) 2236
Whalley, Blackburn
(9) 5953 yards

Whittaker G.C.
(0706) 78310
Whittaker Lane, Littleborough
(9) 5636 yards

Wilpshire G.C.
(0254) 48276
Wilpshire, Blackburn
(18) 5911 yards

LEICESTERSHIRE

Birstall G.C.
(0533) 674322
Station Road, Birstall, Leicester
(18) 6203 yards

Charnwood Forest G.C.
(0509) 890259
Breakback Lane, Woodhouse Eaves
(9) 6202 yards

Cosby G.C.
(0533) 864759
Chapel Lane, Cosby
(18) 6277 yards

Enderby G.C.
(0533) 849388
Mill Lane, Enderby
(9) 4356 yards

Glen Gorse G.C.
(0533) 714159
Glen Road, Oadby, Leicester
(18) 6641 yards

Hinckley G.C.
(0455) 615014
Leicester Road, Hinckley
(18) 6578 yards

Humberstone Heights G.C.
(0533) 764674
Gipsy Lane, Leicester
(18) 6444 yards

Kibworth G.C.
(0533) 792301
Weir Road,
Kibworth Beauchamp
(18) 6282 yards

Kirby Muxloe G.C.
(0533) 393457
Kirby Muxloe, Leicester
(18) 6303 yards

Leicestershire G.C.
(0533) 738825
Evington Lane, Leicester
(18) 6312 yards

Lingdale G.C.
(0509) 890035
Joe Moores Lane, Woodhouse Eaves
(18) 6114 yards

Longcliffe G.C.
(0509) 239129
Snell's Nook Lane, Loughborough
(18) 6551 yards

Luffenham Heath G.C.
(0780) 720205
Ketton, Stamford
(18) 6254 yards

Lutterworth G.C.
(0455) 552532
Rugby Road, Lutterworth
(18) 5570 yards

Market Harborough G.C.
(0858) 63684
Oxenden Road, Market Harborough
(9) 6080 yards

Melton Mowbray G.C.
(0664) 62118
Waltham Road, Melton Mowbray
(9) 6168 yards

Oadby G.C.
(0533) 709052
Leicester Road, Oadby
(18) 6228 yards

Rothley Park G.C.
(0533) 302809
Westfield Lane, Rothley
(18) 6487 yards

R.A.F. North Luffenham
(0780) 720041
North Luffenham, Oakham
(18) 5629 yards

Rushcliffe G.C.
(050982) 2959
Stocking Lane, East Leake, Loughborough
(18) 6057 yards

Scraptoft G.C.
(0533) 419000
Beeby Road, Scraptoft
(18) 6166 yards

Ullesthorpe G.C.
(0455) 209023
Ullesthorpe, Lutterswoth
(18) 6048 yards

Western Park G.C.
(0533) 872339
Scudmore Road, Leicester
(18) 6532 yards

Whetstone G.C.
(0533) 861424
Cosby, Leicester
(18) 5795 yards

Willesley Park G.C.
(0530) 414596
Tamworth Road, Ashby-de-la-Zouch
(18) 6310 yards

LINCOLNSHIRE

Belton Woods Hotel & C.C.
(0476) 593200
Londonthorpe Road, Grantham
(9) 6412 yards
(9) 6101 yards
(9) 5857 yards

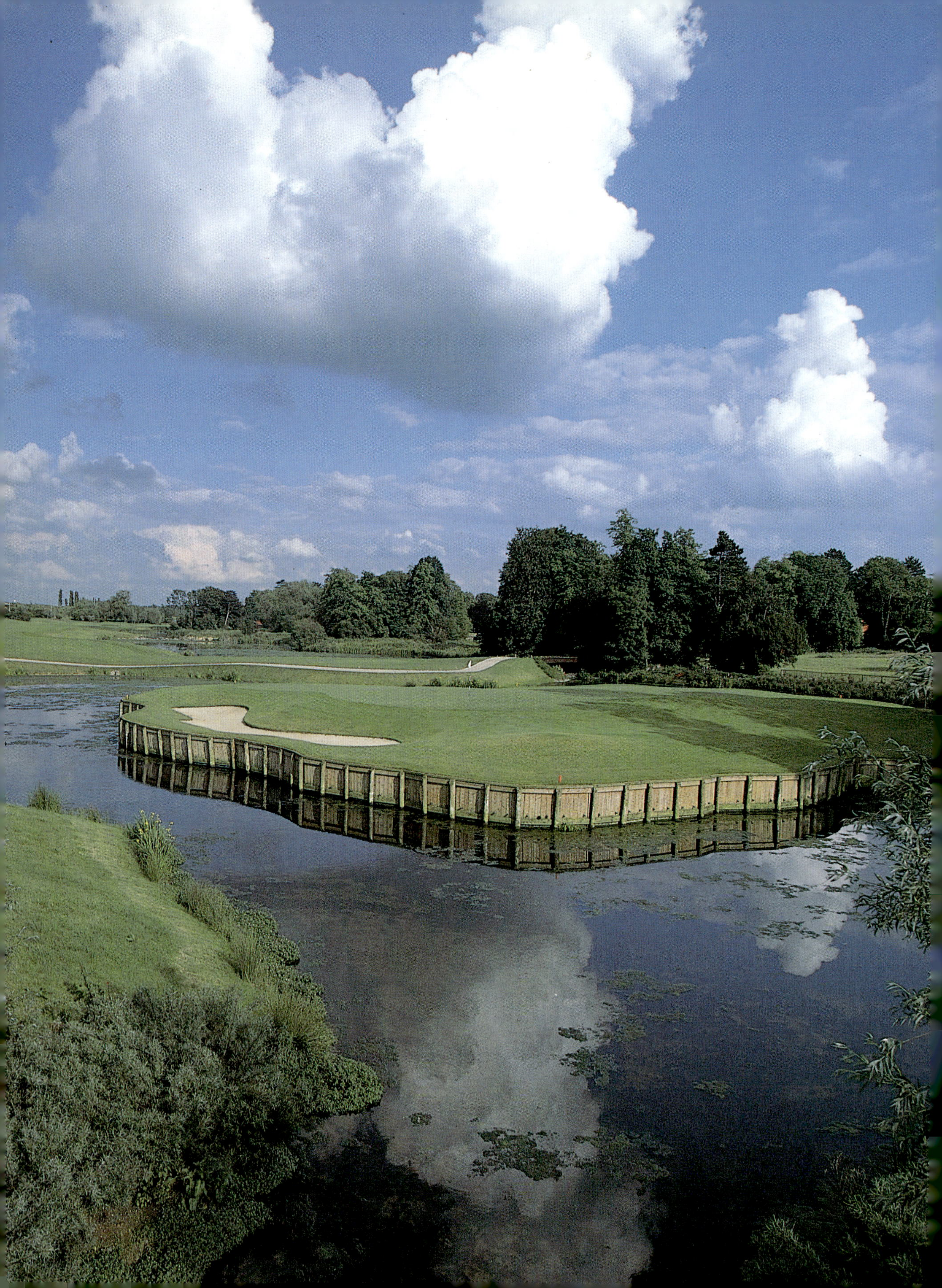

Ganton, North Yorkshire.

Blankney G.C.
(0526) 20202
Blankney, Lincoln
(18) 6232 yards

Boston G.C.
(0205) 350589
Horncastle Road,
Boston
(18) 5795 yards

Burghley Park G.C.
(0780) 53789
Stamford
(18) 6133 yards

Canwick Park G.C.
(0522) 22166
Canwick Park, Lincoln
(18) 6257 yards

*Collingtree Park,
Nr Northampton.*

Carholme G.C.
(0522) 33263
Carholme Road, Lincoln
(18) 6086 yards

Lincoln G.C.
(042771) 721
Torksey, Lincoln
(18) 6400 yards

Louth G.C.
(0507) 603681
Crowtree Lane, Louth
(18) 6502 yards

Market Rasen and District G.C.
(0673) 842416
Legsby Road, Market Rasen
(18) 6031 yards

North Shore G.C.
(0754) 3298
North Shore Road, Skegness
(18) 6134 yards

Sandilands G.C.
(0507) 441334
Sandilands, Mablethorpe
(18) 5995 yards

Seacroft G.C.
(0754) 3020
Seacroft, Skegness
(18) 6478 yards

Sleaford G.C.
(05298) 273
South Rauceby, Sleaford
(18) 6443 yards

Spalding G.C.
(077585) 386
Surfleet, Spalding
(18) 5807 yards

Stoke Rochford G.C.
(047683) 275
Stoke Rochford, Grantham
(18) 6204 yards

Sutton Bridge G.C.
(0406) 350323
Sutton Bridge, Spalding
(9) 5850 yards

Thonock G.C.
(0427) 3088
Thonock, Gainsborough
(18) 5824 yards

Toft Hotel G.C.
(0778) 33616
Toft, Nr. Bourne
(18) 6539 yards

Woodhall Spa G.C.
(0526) 52511
The Broadway,
Woodhall Spa
(18) 6899 yards

MERSEYSIDE

Allerton Municipal G.C.
(051) 428 1046
Allerton, Liverpool
(18) 5459 yards

Alt G.C.
(0704) 35268
Park Road West, Southport
(18) 5939 yards

Arrowe Park G.C.
(051) 677 1527
Arrow Park, Woodchurch,
Birkenhead
(18) 6377 yards

Bidston G.C.
(051) 630 6650
Leasowe, Wirral
(18) 6207 yards

Bootle G.C.
(051) 928 1371
Dunningsbridge Road, Bootle
(18) 6362 yards

Bowring G.C.
(051) 489 5985
Roby Road, Huyton
(9) 5592 yards

Brackenwood G.C.
(051) 608 3093
Bebington, Wirral
(18) 6285 yards

Bromborough G.C.
(051) 334 2978
Raby Hall Road,
Bromborough
(18) 6650 yards

Caldy G.C.
(051) 625 1818
Links Hey Road,
Caldy, Wirral
(18) 6665 yards

Childwall G.C.
(051) 487 9871
Naylor's Road,
Liverpool
(18) 6425 yards

Eastham Lodge G.C.
(051) 327 3003
Ferry Road, Eastham,
Wirral
(15) 5826 yards

Formby G.C.
(07048) 72164
Golf Road, Formby
(18) 6871 yards

Formby Ladies G.C.
(07048) 73493
Golf Road, Formby
(18) 5374 yards

Grange Park G.C.
(0744) 26318
Prescot Road, St Helens
(18) 6480 yards

Haydock Park G.C.
(09252) 6944
Golborne Park,
Newton-le-Willows
(18) 6014 yards

Hesketh G.C.
(0704) 36897
Cambridge Road,
Southport
(18) 6478 yards

Heswall G.C.
(051) 342 1237
Cottage Lane, Heswall,
Wirral
(18) 6472 yards

Hillside G.C.
(0704) 67169
Hastings Road,
Southport
(18) 6850 yards

Hoylake Municipal G.C.
(051) 632 2956
Carr Lane, Hoylake
(18) 6312 yards

Huyton & Prescot G.C.
(051) 489 3948
Hurst Park, Huyton
(18) 5738 yards

Leasowe G.C.
(051) 677 5852
Leasowe Road, Moreton,
Wirral
(18) 6204 yards

Lee Park G.C.
(051) 487 3882
Childwall Valley Road,
Liverpool
(18) 6024 yards

Liverpool Municipal G.C.
(051) 546 5435
Ingoe Lane, Kirkby
(18) 6571 yards

Prenton G.C.
(051) 608 1053
Golf Links Road, Prenton,
Birkenhead
(18) 6379 yards

Royal Birkdale G.C.
(0704) 67920
Waterloo Road, Southport
(18) 6968 yards

Royal Liverpool G.C.
(051) 632 3101
Meols Drive, Hoylake,
Wirral
(18) 6780 yards

Sherdley Park G.C.
(0744) 813149
Elton Road, St. Helens
(18) 5941 yards

Southport & Ainsdale G.C.
(0704) 78000
Bradshaws Lane,
Ainsdale,
Southport
(18) 6603 yards

Southport Municipal G.C.
(0704) 35286
Park Road West,
Southport
(18) 6253 yards

Southport Old Links G.C.
(0704) 24294
Moors Lane, Southport
(9) 6486 yards

Wallasey G.C.
(051) 691 1024
Bayswater Road, Wallasey
(18) 6607 yards

Warren G.C.
(051) 639 5730
Grove Road, Wallasey
(9) 5914 yards

West Derby G.C.
(051) 228 1034
Yew Tree Lane, West Derby,
Liverpool
(18) 6333 yards

West Lancashire G.C.
(051) 924 1076
Hall Road West,
Blundellsands,
Liverpool
(18) 6756 yards

Wirral Ladies G.C.
(051) 652 1255
Budston Road, Oxon,
Birkenhead
(18) 4966 yards

Woolton G.C.
(051) 486 2298
Doe Park, Woolton,
Liverpool
(18) 5706 yards

NORFOLK

Barnham Broom Hotel G.C.
(060545) 393
Honingham Road,
Barnham Broom
(18) 6470 yards (Valley)
(18) 6628 yards (Hill)

Bawburgh G.C.
(0603) 746390
Long Lane, Bawburgh
(9) 5278 yards

Dereham G.C.
(0362) 693122
Quebec Road, Dereham
(9) 6255 yards

Diss G.C.
(0379) 642847
Stuston, Diss
(9) 5900 yards

Eaton G.C.
(0603) 51686
Newmarket Road, Norwich
(18) 6125 yards

Fakenham G.C.
(0328) 2867
The Racecourse, Fakenham
(9) 5879 yards

Gorleston G.C.
(0493) 661911
Warren Road, Gorleston
Great Yarmouth
(18) 6279 yards

Great Yarmouth & Caister G.C.
(0493) 728699
Beach House, Caister-on-Sea
(18) 6235 yards

Hunstanton G.C.
(0485) 532811
Golf Course Road,
Old Hunstanton
(18) 6670 yards

Kings Lynn G.C.
(0533) 987654
Castle Rising, Kings Lynn
(18) 6552 yards

Links Country Park Hotel & G.C.
(026375) 691
West Runton
(9) 4814 yards

Mundesley G.C.
(0263) 720095
Mundesley, Norwich
(9) 5376 yards

Royal Cromer G.C.
(0263) 512884
Overstrand Road, Cromer
(18) 6508 yards

Royal Norwich G.C.
(0603) 429928
Hellesdon, Norwich
(18) 6603 yards

Royal West Norfolk G.C.
(0485) 210087
Brancaster
(18) 6302 yards

Ryston Park G.C.
(0366) 382133
Denver, Downham Market
(9) 6292 yards

Sheringham G.C.
(0263) 823488
Weybourne Road,
Sheringham
(18) 6430 yards

Sprowston Park G.C.
(0603) 410657
Wroxham Road, Sprowston,
Norwich
(18) 5985 yards

Swaffham G.C.
(0760) 21611
Clay Road, Swaffham
(9) 6252 yards

Thetford G.C.
(0842) 752169
Brandon Road, Thetford
(18) 6504 yards

NORTH YORKSHIRE

Aldwark Manor G.C.
(03473) 8146
Alne, York
(18) 5172 yards

Bedale G.C.
(0677) 22568
Leyburn Road, Bedale
(18) 5599 yards

Bentham G.C.
(0468) 61018
Robin Lane, Bentham
(9) 5752 yards

Catterick Garrison G.C.
(0748) 833268
Leyburn Road, Catterick Garrison
(18) 6336 yards

Easingwold G.C.
(0347) 21486
Stillington Road,
Easingwold
(18) 6222 yards

Filey G.C.
(0723) 513293
West Avenue, Filey
(18) 6030 yards

Fulford G.C.
(0904) 413579
Heslington Lane,
Fulford, York
(18) 6779 yards

Ganton G.C.
(0944) 70329
Ganton, Scarborough
(18) 6720 yards

Ghyll G.C.
(0282) 842466
Ghyll Brow, Barnoldswick
(9) 5708 yards

Harrogate G.C.
(0423) 862999
Starback, Harrogate
(18) 6183 yards

Heworth G.C.
(0904) 424618
Mancastergate, York
(11) 6078 yards

Kirkbymoorside G.C.
(0751) 31525
Manor Vale, Kirkbymoorside
(18) 5958 yards

Knaresborough G.C.
(0423) 862690
Boroughbridge Road,
Knaresborough
(18) 6281 yards

Malton & Norton G.C.
(0653) 697912
Norton, Malton
(18) 6411 yards

Masham G.C.
(0765) 89379
Masham, Ripon
(9) 5338 yards

Oakdale G.C.
(0423) 67162
Oakdale, Harrogate,
(18) 6456 yards

Pannal G.C.
(0423) 872628
Follifoot Road, Pannal,
Harrogate
(18) 6659 yards

Pike Hills G.C.
(0904) 708756
Copmanthorpe, York
(18) 6048 yards

Richmond G.C.
(0748) 4775
Bend Hagg, Richmond
(18) 5704 yards

Ripon City G.C.
(0765) 700411
Palace Road, Ripon
(9) 5752 yards

Scarborough North Cliff G.C.
(0723) 360786
Burniston Road, Scarborough
(18) 6425 yards

Scarborough South Cliff G.C.
(0723) 374737
Deepdale Avenue,
Scarborough
(18) 6085 yards

Selby G.C.
(0757) 228785
Mill Lane, Selby
(18) 6246 yards

Settle G.C.
(07292) 3912
Giggleswick, Settle
(9) 4900 yards

Skipton G.C.
(0756) 792128
Grassington Road, Skipton
(18) 6087 yards

Thirsk & Northallerton G.C.
(0845) 22170
Thornton-le-Street, Thirsk
(9) 6087 yards

Whitby G.C.
(0947) 600660
Low Straggleton, Whitby
(18) 5710 yards

York G.C.
(0904) 490304
Lords Manor Lane, Strensall, York
(18) 6275 yards

NORTHAMPTONSHIRE

Cherwell Edge G.C.
(0295) 711591
Chacombe, Nr. Banbury
(18) 5925 yards

Cold Ashby G.C.
(0604) 740548
Cold Ashby
(18) 5957 yards

Collingtree Park G.C.
(0604) 700000
Windingbrook Lane, Northampton
(18) 6692 yards

Daventry & District G.C.
(0327) 702829
Norton Road, Daventry
(9) 5555 yards

Delapre G.C.
(0604) 764036
Nene Valley Way, Northampton
(18) 6293 yards

Farthingstone Hotel G.C.
(032736) 291
Farthingstone, Towcester
(18) 6330 yards

Kettering G.C.
(0536) 511104
Headlands, Kettering
(18) 6035 yards

Kingsthorpe G.C.
(0604) 710610
Kingsley Road, Northampton
(18) 6006 yards

Northampton G.C.
(0604) 719453
Kettering Road, Northampton
(18) 6002 yards

Northamptonshire County G.C.
(0604) 843025
Church Brampton, Northampton
(18) 6503 yards

Oundle G.C.
(0832) 273267
Oundle
(18) 5507 yards

Priors Hall G.C.
(0536) 67546
Stamford Road, Weldon
(18) 6677 yards

Rushden & District G.C.
(0933) 312197
Kimbolton Road, Chelveston
(9) 6381 yards

Staverton Park G.C.
(0327) 705911
Staverton, Daventry
(18) 6634 yards

Wellingborough G.C.
(0933) 677234
Harrowden Hall, Wellingborough
(18) 6604 yards

NORTHUMBERLAND

Allendale G.C.
(091) 2675875
Allendale, Hexham
(9) 4488 yards

Alnmouth G.C.
(0665) 830368
Foxton Hall, Alnmouth
(18) 6414 yards

Alnmouth Village G.C.
(0665) 830370
Marine Road, Alnmouth
(9) 6078 yards

Alnwick G.C.
(0665) 602499
Swansfield Park, Alnwick
(9) 5379 yards

Arcot Hall G.C.
(091) 236 2794
Dudley, Cramlington
(18) 6389 yards

Bamburgh Castle G.C.
(06684) 321
Bamburgh
(18) 5465 yards

Bedlingtonshire G.C.
(0670) 822457
Acorn Bank, Bedlington
(18) 6825 yards

Bellingham G.C.
(0660) 20530
Boggle Hole, Bellingham
(9) 5226 yards

Berwick-upon-Tweed G.C.
(0289) 87348
Goswick, Berwick-upon-Tweed
(18) 6399 yards

Blyth G.C.
(0670) 356514
New Delaval, Blyth
(18) 6533 yards

Dunstanburgh Castle G.C.
(066576) 562
Embleton
(18) 6357 yards

Hexham G.C.
(0434) 603072
Spital Park, Hexham
(18) 6272 yards

Magdalene Fields G.C.
(0289) 306384
Berwick-upon-Tweed
(18) 6551 yards

Morpeth G.C.
(0670) 512065
The Common, Morpeth
(18) 6215 yards

Newbiggin-by-the-Sea G.C.
(0670) 817833
Newbiggin-by-the-Sea
(18) 6444 yards

Prudhoe G.C.
(0661) 32466
Eastwood Park, Prudhoe
(18) 5812 yards

Rothbury G.C.
(0669) 20718
Old Race Course, Rothbury
(9) 5650 yards

Seahouses G.C.
(0665) 720794
Bednell Road, Seahouses
(18) 5399 yards

Slaley Hall G & C.C.
(0434) 673691
Slaley, Hexham
(18) 6995 yards

Stocksfield G.C.
(0661) 843041
New Ridley, Stocksfield
(18) 5594 yards

Tynedale G.C.
(0434) 605701
Tyne Green, Hexham
(9) 5706 yards

Warkworth G.C.
(0665) 711596
Warkworth, Morpeth
(9) 5817 yards

NOTTINGHAMSHIRE

Beeston Fields G.C.
(0602) 257062
Beeston Fields, Nottingham
(18) 6404 yards

Bulwell Forest G.C.
(0602) 278008
Hucknall Road, Bulwell,
Nottingham
(18) 5606 yards

Bulwell Hall Park G.C.
(0602) 278021
Lawton Drive, Bulwell
(18) 6218 yards

Chilwell Manor G.C.
(0602) 258958
Meadow Lane, Chilwell,
Nottingham
(18) 6379 yards

Coxmoor G.C.
(0623) 557359
Coxmoor Road, Sutton-in-Ashfield
(18) 6501 yards

Edwalton Municipal G.C.
(0602) 234775
Edwalton, Nottingham
(9) 3336 yards

Kilton Forest G.C.
(0909) 486563
Blyth Road, Worksop
(18) 6569 yards

Lindrick G.C.
(0909) 475282
Lindrick Common, Worksop
(18) 6377 yards

Mansfield Woodhouse G.C.
(0623) 23521
Leeming Lane, Mansfield
(9) 2150 yards

Mapperley C.C.
(0602) 265611
Mapperley Plains,
Nottingham
(18) 6224 yards

Newark G.C.
(0636) 626241
Coddington, Newark
(18) 6486 yards

Notts G.C.
(0623) 753225
Hollinwell, Derby Road,
Kirby-in-Ashfield
(18) 7020 yards

Oxton G.C.
(0602) 653545
Oxton, Southwell
(18) 6630 yards

Radcliffe-on-Trent G.C.
(0602) 332500
Cropwell Road, Radcliffe-on-Trent
(18) 6423 yards

Retford G.C.
(0777) 703733
Ordsall, Retford
(9) 6230 yards

Sherwood Forest G.C.
(0623) 26689
Eakring Road, Mansfield
(18) 6709 yards

Stanton-on-the-Wolds G.C.
(06077) 2044
Stanton-on-the-Wolds,
Keyworth
(18) 6379 yards

Wollaton Park G.C.
(0602) 787574
Wollaton Park, Nottingham
(18) 6494 yards

Worksop G.C.
(0909) 477731
Windmill Lane, Worksop
(18) 6651 yards

OXFORDSHIRE

Badgemore Park G.C.
(0491) 572206
Henley-on-Thames
(18) 6112 yards

Burford G.C.
(099 382) 2583
Burford
(18) 6405 yards

Chesterton County G.C.
(0869) 241204
Chesterton, Bicester
(18) 6496 yards

Chipping Norton G.C.
(0608) 642383
Southcombe,
Chipping Norton
(9) 5280 yards

Frilford Heath G.C.
(0865) 390865
Frilford Heath, Abingdon
(18) 6768 yards (Red)
(18) 6006 yards (Green)

Henley G.C.
(0491) 575742
Harpsden,
Henley-on-Thames
(18) 6329 yards

Huntercombe G.C.
(0491) 641207
Nuffield, Henley-on-Thames
(18) 6257 yards

North Oxford G.C.
(0865) 54924
Banbury Road, Oxford
(18) 5805 yards

Southfield G.C.
(0865) 242158
Hill Top Road, Oxford
(18) 6230 yards

Tadmarton Heath G.C.
(0608) 737278
Wiggington, Banbury
(18) 5917 yards

SHROPSHIRE

Bridgnorth G.C.
(07462) 2400
Stanley Lane, Bridgnorth
(18) 6673 yards

Church Stretton G.C.
(0694) 722281
Trevor Hill, Church Stretton
(18) 5008 yards

Hawkstone Park Hotel & G.C.
(093924) 611
Weston-under-Redcastle,
Shrewsbury
(18) 6465 yards (Hawkstone)
(18) 5368 yards (Weston)

Hill Valley G. & C.C.
(0948) 3584
Terrick Road, Whitchurch
(18) 6884 yards
(9) 5106 yards

Lilleshall Hall G.C.
(0952) 604776
Lilleshall, Newport
(18) 5891 yards

Llanymynech G.C.
(0691) 830542
Pant, Oswestry
(18) 6114 yards

Ludlow G.C.
(058477) 285
Bromfield, Ludlow
(18) 6239 yards

Market Drayton G.C.
(0630) 2266
Sutton, Market Drayton
(18) 6170 yards

Meole Brace G.C.
(0743) 64050
Meole Brace
(9) 5830 yards

Oswestry G.C.
(069188) 535
Aston Park, Oswestry
(18) 6046 yards

Patshull Park G.C.
(0902) 700342
Pattingham
(18) 6412 yards

Shifnal G.C.
(0952) 460330
Decker Hill, Shifnal
(18) 6422 yards

Shrewsbury G.C.
(074372) 2976
Condover, Shrewsbury
(18) 6212 yards

Telford Hotel G. & C.C.
(0952) 585642
Greay Hay, Telford
(18) 6228 yards

Wrekin G.C.
(0952) 44032
Wellington, Telford
(18) 5699 yards

SOMERSET

Brean G.C.
(027875) 467
Brean, Burnham-on-Sea
(18) 5566 yards

Burnham and Berrow G.C.
(0278) 785760
St Christopher's Way, Burnham-on-Sea
(18) 6547 yards
(9) 6550 yards

Enmore Park G.C.
(027867) 481
Enmore, Bridgewater
(18) 6443 yards

Minehead and West Somerset G.C.
(0643) 2057
The Warren, Minehead
(18) 6131 yards

Taunton and Pickeridge G.C.
(082342) 240
Corfe, Taunton
(18) 5927 yards

Vivary Park G.C.
(0823) 333875
Taunton
(18) 4620 yards

Wells G.C.
(0749) 72868
East Horrington Road, Wells
(18) 5288 yards

Windwhistle G. & S.C.
(046030) 231
Cricket St Thomas, Chard
(18) 6055 yards

Yeovil G.C.
(0935) 22965
Sherborne Road, Yeovil
(18) 6139 yards

SOUTH YORKSHIRE

Abbeydale G.C.
(0742) 360763
Twentywell Lane, Dore, Sheffield
(18) 6419 yards

Austerfield Park G.C.
(0302) 710850
Cross Lane, Austerfield
(18) 6824 yards

Barnsley G.C.
(0226) 382954
Staincross, Barnsley
(18) 6048 yards

Beauchief Municipal G.C.
(0742) 367274
Abbey Lane, Sheffield
(18) 5428 yards

Birley Wood G.C.
(0742) 389198
Birley Lane, Sheffield
(18) 6275 yards

Concord Park G.C.
(0742) 456806
Shiregreen Lane, Sheffield
(18) 4280 yards

Crookhill Park G.C.
(0709) 863466
Conisbrough, Doncaster
(18) 5846 yards

Doncaster G.C.
(0302) 868404
Bescarr, Doncaster
(18) 6230 yards

Doncaster Town Moor G.C.
(0302) 535458
Belle Vue, Doncaster
(18) 6081 yards

Dore & Totley G.C.
(0742) 369872
Broadway Road, Sheffield
(18) 6301 yards

Grange Park G.C.
(0709) 559497
Upper Wortley Road, Rotherham
(18) 6461 yards

Hallamshire G.C.
(0742) 302153
Sandygate, Sheffield
(18) 6396 yards

Hallowes G.C.
(0246) 413734
Hallowes Lane, Dronfield, Sheffield
(18) 6366 yards

Hickleton G.C.
(0709) 895170
Hickleton, Doncaster
(18) 6401 yards

Hillsborough G.C.
(0742) 349151
Worrall Road, Sheffield
(18) 6100 yards

Lees Hall G.C.
(0742) 552900
Hemsworth Road, Norton, Sheffield
(18) 6137 yards

Phoenix G.C.
(0709) 370759
Brinsworth, Rotherham
(18) 6170 yards

Rotherham G.C.
(0709) 850812
Thrybergh Park, Rotherham
(18) 6324 yards

Serlby Park G.C.
(0777) 818268
Serlby, Doncaster
(18) 5325 yards

Silkstone G.C.
(0226) 790328
Field Head, Silkstone, Barnsley
(18) 6045 yards

Sitwell Park G.C.
(0709) 541046
Shrogswood Road, Rotherham
(18) 6203 yards

Stocksbridge & District G.C.
(0742) 882408
Royd Lane, Townend, Deepcar
(15) 5055 yards

Tankersley Park G.C.
(0742) 468247
High Green, Sheffield
(18) 6241 yards

Tinsley Park G.C.
(0742) 560237
Darnall, Sheffield
(18) 6045 yards

Wath G.C.
(0709) 878677
Abdy Rawmarsh, Rotherham
(9) 5606 yards

Wheatley G.C.
(0302) 831655
Armthorpe Road, Doncaster
(18) 6345 yards

Wortley G.C.
(0742) 885294
Hermit Hill Lane, Wortley, Sheffield
(18) 5960 yards

STAFFORDSHIRE

Alsager G. & C.C.
(0270) 875700
Alsager Road, Alsager
(18) 6192 yards

Beau Desert G.C.
(05438) 2626
Hazel Slade, Cannock
(18) 6285 yards

Branston G.C.
(0283) 43207
Branston, Burton-on-Trent
(18) 6480 yards

Brocton Hall G.C.
(0785) 661901
Brocton, Stafford
(18) 6095 yards

Burslem G.C.
(0782) 837006
High Lane, Tunstall,
Stoke-on-Trent
(9) 5354 yards

Craythorne G.C.
(0283) 64329
Stretton, Burton-on-Trent
(18) 5230 yards

Drayton Park G.C.
(0827) 251139
Drayton Park, Tamworth
(18) 6414 yards

Greenway Hall G.C.
(0782) 503158
Stockton Brook,
Stoke-on-Trent
(18) 5676 yards

Ingestre Park G.C.
(0889) 270845
Ingestre, Weston,
Stafford
(18) 6376 yards

Leek G.C.
(0538) 385889
Cheadle Road, Leek
(18) 6240 yards

Leek Westwood G.C.
(0538) 383060
Newcastle Road, Leek
(9) 5501 yards

Newcastle-under-Lyme G.C.
(0782) 617006
Whitmore Road, Newcastle
(18) 6450 yards

Newcastle Municipal G.C.
(0782) 627596
Keele Road, Newcastle
(18) 6301 yards

Stafford Castle G.C.
(0785) 3821
Newport Road, Stafford
(9) 6347 yards

Stone G.C.
(0785) 813103
Filleybrooks, Stone
(9) 6272 yards

Tamworth G.C.
(0827) 53850
Eagle Drive, Tamworth
(18) 6695 yards

Trentham G.C.
(0782) 658109
Barlaston Old Road,
Trentham,
Stoke-on-Trent
(18) 6644 yards

Trentham Park G.C.
(0782) 658800
Trentham Park,
Trentham,
Stoke-on-Trent
(18) 6403 yards

Uttoxeter G.C.
(08893) 4844
Wood Lane, Uttoxeter
(9) 5695 yards

Whittington Barracks G.C.
(0543) 432317
Tamworth Road, Lichfield
(18) 6457 yards

Wolstanton G.C.
(0782) 622413
Dimsdale Old Hall,
Newcastle
(18) 5807 yards

SUFFOLK

Aldeburgh G.C.
(0728) 452890
Saxmundham Road,
Aldeburgh
(18) 6330 yards
(9) 2114 yards

Beccles G.C.
(0502) 712479
The Common, Beccles
(9) 5392 yards

Bungay & Waveny Valley G.C.
(0986) 2337
Outney Common, Bungay
(18) 5944 yards

Bury St Edmunds G.C.
(0284) 755979
Tuthill,
Bury St Edmunds
(18) 6615 yards

Felixstowe Ferry G.C.
(0394) 286834
Ferry Road, Felixstowe
(18) 6042 yards

Flempton G.C.
(0284) 728291
Flempton,
Bury St Edmunds
(9) 6050 yards

Fornham Park G.C.
(0284) 706777
Fornham St. Martin,
Bury St. Edmunds
(18) 6212 yards

Haverhill G.C.
(0440) 61951
Coupals Road, Haverhill
(9) 5708 yards

Ipswich G.C.
(0473) 78941
Purdis Heath, Ipswich
(18) 6405 yards
(9) 3860 yards

Links G.C.
(0638) 663000
Cambridge Road,
Newmarket
(18) 6402 yards

Newton Green G.C.
(0787) 77501
Newton Green, Sudbury
(9) 5442 yards

Rookery Park G.C.
(0502) 560380
Carlton Colville,
Lowestoft
(18) 6649 yards

Royal Worlington & Newmarket G.C.
(0638) 712216
Worlington,
Bury St Edmunds
(9) 6218 yards

Rushmere G.C.
(0473) 75648
Rushmere Heath, Ipswich
(18) 6287 yards

Southwold G.C.
(0502) 723248
The Common, Southwold
(9) 6001 yards

Stowmarket G.C.
(04493) 473
Onehouse, Stowmarket
(18) 6119 yards

Thorpeness G.C.
(0728) 452176
Thorpeness
(18) 6241 yards

Waldringfield Heath G.C.
(0473) 726821
Waldringfield, Woodbridge
(18) 5837 yards

Woodbridge G.C.
(03943) 3213
Bromeswell Heath,
Woodbridge
(18) 6314 yards
(9) 4486 yards

SURREY

Barrow Hills G.C.
(0276) 72037
Longcross, Chertsey
(18) 3090 yards

Betchworth Park G.C.
(0306) 882052
Reigate Road, Dorking
(18) 6266 yards

Bramley G.C.
(0483) 892696
Godden Hill, Bramley
(18) 5910 yards

Burhill G.C.
(0932) 227345
Walton-on-Thames
(18) 6224 yards

Camberley Heath G.C.
(0276) 23258
Golf Drive, Camberley
(18) 6402 yards

Chipstead G.C.
(0737) 555781
How Lane, Coulsdon
(18) 5454 yards

Crondall G.C.
(0252) 850880
Oak Park, Heath Lane,
Crondall
(18) 6233 yards

Dorking G.C.
(0306) 886917
Chart Park, Dorking
(9) 5106 yards

Drift G.C.
(04865) 4641
The Drift, East Horsley
(18) 6404 yards

Effingham G.C.
(0372) 52203
Guildford Road,
Effingham
(18) 6488 yards

Epsom G.C.
(03727) 21666
Longdown Lane, Epsom
(18) 5725 yards

Farnham G.C.
(02518) 2109
The Sands, Farnham
(18) 6313 yards

Fernfell G. & C.C.
(0483) 276626
Barhatch Lane, Cranleigh
(18) 5236 yards

Foxhills G.C.
(093287) 2050
Stonehill Road, Ottershaw
(18) 6658 yards
(18) 6406 yards

**Gatton Manor Hotel
& G.C.**
(030679) 555
Ockley, Dorking
(18) 6902 yards

Guildford G.C.
(0483) 63941
High Path Road, Merrow,
Guildford
(18) 6080 yards

Hankley Common G.C.
(025125) 2493
Tilford, Farnham
(18) 6403 yards

Hindhead G.C.
(042873) 4614
Churt Road, Hindhead
(18) 6357 yards

Hoebridge G.C.
(0483) 722611
Old Woking Road,
Old Woking
(18) 6587 yards

Kingswood G.C.
(0737) 832188
Sandy Lane, Kingswood
(18) 6821 yards

Laleham G.C.
(09328) 564211
Laleham Reach, Chertsey
(18) 6203 yards

Leatherhead G.C.
(037284) 3966
Kingston Road, Leatherhead
(18) 6069 yards

Limpsfield Chart G.C.
(0883) 713097
Limpsfield, Oxted
(9) 5718 yards

Moore Place G.C.
(0372) 63533
Portsmouth Road, Esher
(9) 3512 yards

New Zealand G.C.
(0932) 345049
Woodham Lane, Woodham,
Weybridge
(18) 6012 yards

North Downs G.C.
(088385) 3004
Northdown Road,
Woldingham
(18) 5787 yards

Puttenham G.C.
(0483) 810498
Puttenham
(18) 5367 yards

R.A.C. Country Club
(0372) 276311
Woodcote Park, Epsom
(18) 6672 yards
(18) 5520 yards

Redhill & Reigate G.C.
(0737) 240777
Pendleton Road, Redhill
(18) 5193 yards

Reigate Heath G.C.
(0737) 242610
Reigate Heath, Reigate
(9) 5554 yards

St George's Hill G.C.
(0932) 847758
St George's Hill, Weybridge
(18) 6492 yards
(9) 4562 yards

Sandown Park G.C.
(0372) 63340
Moor Lane, Esher
(9) 5658 yards

Shillinglee Park G.C.
(0428) 53237
Chiddingfold, Godalming
(9) 2500 yards

Silvermere G.C.
(0932) 67275
Redhill Road, Cobham
(18) 6333 yards

Tandridge G.C.
(0883) 712733
Oxted
(18) 6260 yards

Tyrell's Wood G.C.
(0372) 376025
Tyrell's Wood, Leatherhead
(18) 6219 yards

Walton Heath G.C.
(073781) 2380
Tadworth
(18) 6813 yards (Old)
(18) 6659 yards (New)

Wentworth G.C.
(0344) 842201
Virginia Water
(18) 6945 yards (West)
(18) 6176 yards (East)
(18) 6979 yards (Edinburgh)

West Byfleet G.C.
(09323) 43433
Sheerwater Road,
West Byfleet
(18) 6211 yards

West Hill G.C.
(04867) 4365
Bagshot Road, Brookwood
(18) 6307 yards

West Surrey G.C.
(0483) 421275
Enton Green, Godalming
(18) 6247 yards

Wildwood G.C.
(0403) 753255
Alford, Cranleigh
(18) 6700 yards

Windlemere G.C.
(027685) 8727
Windlesham Road,
West End,
Woking
(9) 5346 yards

Woking G.C.
(04837) 60053
Pond Road, Hook Heath,
Woking
(18) 6322 yards

Worplesdon G.C.
(04867) 2277
Heath House Road, Woking
(18) 6422 yards

TYNE AND WEAR

Backworth G.C.
(091) 2681048
Backworth, Shiremoor
(9) 5930 yards

Boldon G.C.
(091) 536 5360
Dip Lane, East Boldon
(18) 6319 yards

City of Newcastle G.C.
(091) 2851775
Three Mile Bridge, Gosforth
(18) 6508 yards

Garesfield G.C.
(0207) 561278
Chopwell
(18) 6610 yards

Gosforth G.C.
(091) 285 3495
Broadway East, Gosforth
(18) 6030 yards

Gosforth Park G.C.
(091) 236 4480
High Gosforth Park,
Gosforth
(18) 6200 yards

Heworth G.C.
(0632) 692137
Heworth, Gateshead
(18) 6442 yards

Hobson Municipal G.C.
(0207) 70941
Hobson, Burnopfield
(18) 6502 yards

Houghton-le-Spring G.C.
(091) 584 1198
Copt Hill,
Houghton-le-Spring
(18) 6248 yards

Newcastle United G.C.
(091) 286 9998
Ponteland Road, Cowgate,
Newcastle
(18) 6498 yards

Northumberland G.C.
(091) 236 2498
High Gosforth Park,
Newcastle
(18) 6629 yards

Ponteland G.C.
(0661) 22689
Bell Villas, Ponteland,
Newcastle
(18) 6512 yards

Ravensworth G.C.
(091) 487 2843
Wrekenton, Gateshead
(18) 5872 yards

Ryton G.C.
(091) 413 3737
Clara Vale, Ryton
(18) 6034 yards

South Shields G.C.
(091) 456 8942
Cleadon Hills, South Shields
(18) 6264 yards

Tynemouth G.C.
(091) 257 4578
Spital Dean, Tynemouth,
North Shields
(18) 6351 yards

Tyneside G.C.
(091) 413 2742
Westfield Lane, Ryton
(18) 6055 yards

Wallsend G.C.
(091) 262 8989
Bigges Main, Wallsend
(18) 6601 yards

Washington G.C.
(091) 417 8346
Cellar Road, Washington
(18) 6604 yards

Wearside G.C.
(091) 534 2518
Coxgreen, Sunderland
(18) 6204 yards

Westerhope G.C.
(091) 286 9125
Westerhope, Newcastle
(18) 6468 yards

Whickham G.C.
(091) 488 7309
Hollinside Park, Newcastle
(18) 6129 yards

Whitburn G.C.
(091) 529 4210
Lizard Lane, South Shields
(18) 6035 yards

Whitley Bay G.C.
(091) 252 0180
Claremount Road,
Whitley Bay
(18) 6712 yards

WARWICKSHIRE

Atherstone G.C.
(0827) 713110
The Outwoods, Atherstone
(18) 6239 yards

Kenilworth G.C.
(0926) 58517
Crew Lane, Kenilworth
(18) 6408 yards

Leamington & Country G.C.
(0926) 28014
Whitnash, Leamington Spa
(18) 6430 yards

Newbold Comyn G.C.
(0926) 421157
Newbold Terrace East,
Leamington Spa
(18) 6430 yards

Nuneaton G.C.
(0203) 347810
Whitestone, Nuneaton
(18) 6368 yards

Purley Chase G.C.
(0203) 395 348
Ridge Lane, Nuneaton
(18) 6604 yards

Rugby G.C.
(0788) 75134
Clifton Road, Rugby
(18) 5457 yards

Stratford-upon-Avon G.C.
(0789) 205749
Tiddington Road,
Stratford
(18) 6309 yards

Warwick G.C.
(0926) 494316
The Racecourse, Warwick
(9) 5364 yards

Welcombe Hotel & G.C.
(0789) 295252
Warwick Road,
Stratford-upon-Avon
(18) 6202 yards

WEST MIDLANDS

The Belfry
(0675) 470301
Lichfield Road, Wishaw,
Sutton Coldfield
(18) 6975 yards (Brabazon)
(18) 6127 yards (Derby)

Bloxwich G.C.
(0922) 405724
Stafford Road, Bloxwich
(18) 6286 yards

Boldmere G.C.
(021) 354 3379
Monmouth Drive,
Sutton Coldfield
(18) 4463 yards

Brand Hall G.C.
(021) 552 2195
Heron Road, Oldbury, Warley
(18) 5813 yards

Brandon Wood G.C.
(0203) 543141
Wolston, Coventry
(18) 6530 yards

Calderfields G.C.
(0922) 32243
Aldridge Road, Walsall
(18) 6636 yards

City of Coventry G.C.
(0203) 85032
Brandon Lane, Coventry
(18) 6530 yards

Cocks Moor Woods G.C.
(021) 444 3584
Alcester Road South, Kings Heath, Birmingham
(18) 5888 yards

Copt Heath G.C.
(0564) 772650
Warwick Road, Knowle, Solihull
(18) 6504 yards

Coventry G.C.
(0203) 414152
Finham Park, Coventry
(18) 6613 yards

Dartmouth G.C.
(021) 588 2131
Vale Street, West Bromwich
(9) 6060 yards

Druids Heath G.C.
(0922) 55595
Stonnall Road, Aldridge
(18) 6914 yards

Dudley G.C.
(0384) 53719
Turners Hill, Dudley
(18) 5715 yards

Edgbaston G.C.
(021) 454 1736
Church Road, Edgbaston
(18) 6118 yards

Enville G.C.
(0384) 872074
Highgate Common, Stourbridge
(18) 6541 yards

Forest of Arden G. & C.C.
(0676) 22118
Maxstone Lane, Meriden, Coventry
(18) 6867 yards

Fulford Heath G.C.
(0564) 822806
Tanners Green Lane, Wythall
(18) 6256 yards

Gay Hill G.C.
(021) 430 8544
Alcester Road, Hollywood, Birmingham
(18) 6532 yards

Grange G.C.
(0203) 451465
Copeswood, Coventry
(9) 6002 yards

Great Barr G.C.
(021) 357 1232
Chapel Lane, Birmingham
(18) 6545 yards

Hagley C.C.
(0562) 883701
Wassell Grove, Stourbridge
(18) 6353 yards

Halesowen G.C.
(021) 501 3606
The Leasowes, Halesowen
(18) 5673 yards

Handsworth G.C.
(021) 554 0599
Sunningdale Close, Handsworth, Birmingham
(18) 6297 yards

Harborne G.C.
(021) 427 1728
Tennal Road, Harborne, Birmingham
(18) 6240 yards

Hatchford Brook G.C.
(021) 743 9821
Coventry Road, Sheldon, Birmingham
(18) 6164 yards

Hearsall G.C.
(0203) 713470
Beechwood Avenue, Coventry
(18) 5951 yards

Hill Top G.C.
(021) 554 4463
Park Lane, Handsworth, Birmingham
(18) 6200 yards

Himley Hall G.C.
(0902) 895207
Himley Hall Park, Dudley
(9) 3090 yards

Kings Norton G.C.
(0564) 822822
Brockhill Lane, Weatheroak, Alvechurch
(18) 6754 yards
(9) 3290 yards

Ladbrook Park G.C.
(05644) 2264
Poolhead Lane, Tanworth-in-Arden, Solihull
(18) 6407 yards

Lickey Hills G.C.
(021) 453 3159
Rednal, Birmingham
(18) 6010 yards

Little Aston G.C.
(021) 353 2066
Streetly, Sutton Coldfield
(18) 6724 yards

Maxstone Park G.C.
(0203) 64915
Castle Lane, Coleshill, Birmingham
(18) 6437 yards

Moor Hall G.C.
(021) 308 6130
Moor Hall Park, Sutton Coldfield
(18) 6249 yards

Moseley G.C.
(021) 444 4957
Springfield Road, Kings Heath, Birmingham
(18) 6227 yards

North Warwickshire G.C.
(0676) 22259
Hampton Lane, Meriden, Coventry
(9) 6362 yards

North Worcestershire G.C.
(021) 475 1047
Northfield, Birmingham
(18) 5919 yards

Olton G.C.
(021) 705 7296
Mirfield Road, Solihull
(18) 6229 yards

Oxley Park G.C.
(0902) 25445
Bushbury, Wolverhampton
(18) 6153 yards

Penn G.C.
(0902) 341142
Penn Common, Wolverhampton
(18) 6449 yards

Pype Hayes G.C.
(021) 353 4594
Walmley, Sutton Coldfield
(18) 5811 yards

Robin Hood G.C.
(021) 706 0061
St Bernards Road, Solihull
(18) 6609 yards

Sandwell Park G.C.
(021) 553 4637
Birmingham Road, West Bromwich
(18) 6470 yards

Shirley G.C.
(021) 744 6001
Stratford Road, Solihull
(18) 6445 yards

South Staffordshire G.C.
(0902) 751065
Danescourt Road, Tettenhall,
Wolverhampton
(18) 6538 yards

Stourbridge G.C.
(0384) 395566
Pedmore, Stourbridge
(18) 6178 yards

Sutton Coldfield G.C.
(021) 353 2014
Thornhill Road,
Sutton Coldfield
(18) 6541 yards

Walmley G.C.
(021) 373 0029
Wylde Green,
Sutton Coldfield
(18) 6340 yards

Walsall G.C.
(0922) 613512
The Broadway, Walsall
(18) 6232 yards

Warley G.C.
(021) 429 2440
Lightwood Hill, Warley
(9) 5212 yards

WEST SUSSEX

Bognor Regis G.C.
(0243) 821929
Downview Road, Felpham,
Bognor
Regis
(18) 6238 yards

Copthorne G.C.
(0342) 712508
Borers Arms Road,
Copthorne
(18) 6505 yards

Cottesmore G.C.
(0293) 28256
Buchan Hill, Crawley
(18) 6097 yards (North)
(18) 5321 yards (South)

Cowdray Park G.C.
(073081) 3599
Midhurst
(18) 6212 yards

Effingham Park G.C.
(0342) 716528
Copthorne
(9) 1749 yards

Goodwood G.C.
(0243) 774968
Goodwood, Chichester
(18) 6370 yards

Ham Manor G.C.
(0903) 783288
Angmering
(18) 6216 yards

Haywards Heath G.C.
(0444) 414457
High Beech Lane, Haywards
Heath
(18) 6202 yards

Hill Barn G.C.
(0903) 37301
Hill Barn Lane, Worthing
(18) 6224 yards

Ifield G. & C.C.
(0293) 20222
Rusper Road, Ifield, Crawley
(18) 6289 yards

Littlehampton G.C.
(0903) 717170
Rope Walk, Littlehampton
(18) 6202 yards

Mannings Heath G.C.
(0403) 210228
Goldings Lane,
Mannings Heath
(18) 6402 yards

Selsey G.C.
(0243) 602203
Golf Links Lane, Selsey
(9) 5932 yards

Tilgate Forest G.C.
(0293) 30103
Titmus Drive, Tilgate,
Crawley
(18) 6359 yards

West Chiltington G.C.
(0798) 813574
Broadford Road,
West Chiltington
(18) 5969 yards

West Sussex G.C.
(0798) 872563
Pulborough
(18) 6156 yards

Worthing G.C.
(0903) 60801
Links Road, Worthing
(18) 6519 yards (Lower)
(18) 5243 yards (Upper)

WEST YORKSHIRE

Alwoodley G.C.
(0532) 681680
Wigton Lane, Alwoodley,
Leeds
(18) 6686 yards

Baildon G.C.
(0274) 595162
Baildon, Shipley
(18) 6085 yards

Ben Rhydding G.C.
(0943) 608759
Ben Rhydding, Ilkley
(9) 4711 yards

Bingley St Ives G.C.
(0274) 562506
Harden, Bingley
(18) 6480 yards

Bradford G.C.
(0943) 75570
Hawksworth Lane, Guisley
(18) 6259 yards

Bradford Moor G.C.
(0274) 638313
Pollard Lane, Bradford
(9) 5854 yards

Bradley Park G.C.
(0484) 539988
Bradley Road, Huddersfield
(18) 6100 yards

Branshaw G.C.
(0535) 43235
Oakworth, Keighley
(18) 5790 yards

City of Wakefield G.C.
(0924) 360282
Luspet Park, Wakefield
(18) 6405 yards

Clayton G.C.
(0724) 880047
Thornton View Road,
Clayton,
Bradford
(9) 5527 yards

Cleckheaton & District G.C.
(0274) 877851
Bradford Road, Cleckheaton
(18) 5994 yards

Crosland Heath G.C.
(0484) 653262
Crosland Heath,
Huddersfield
(18) 5962 yards

Dewsbury District G.C.
(0924) 492399
Sands Lane, Mirfield
(18) 6226 yards

East Bierley G.C.
(0274) 681023
South View Road, Bierley,
Bradford
(9) 4692 yards

Elland G.C.
(0422) 372505
Leach Lane, Elland
(9) 5526 yards

Fulneck G.C.
(0532) 565191
Pudsey
(9) 5432 yards

Garforth G.C.
(0532) 863308
Long Lane, Garforth, Leeds
(18) 6327 yards

Gott's Park G.C.
(0532) 638232
Armley Ridge Road, Leeds
(18) 4449 yards

Halifax G.C.
(0422) 244171
Union Lane, Ogden, Halifax
(18) 6038 yards

Halifax Bradley Hall G.C.
(0422) 70231
Holywell Green, Halifax
(18) 6213 yards

Hanging Heaton G.C.
(0924) 461729
Bennett Lane, Dewsbury
(9) 5874 yards

Headingley G.C.
(0532) 679573
Back Church Lane, Adel, Leeds
(18) 6238 yards

Headley G.C.
(0274) 833481
Thornton, Bradford
(9) 4918 yards

Horsforth G.C.
(0532) 585200
Horsforth, Leeds
(18) 6293 yards

Howley Hall G.C.
(0924) 472432
Scotchman Lane, Morley, Leeds
(18) 6209 yards

Huddersfield G.C.
(0484) 426203
Fixby Hall, Huddersfield
(18) 6424 yards

Ilkley G.C.
(0943) 600214
Myddleton, Ilkley
(18) 6249 yards

Keighley G.C.
(0535) 604778
Howden Park, Keighley
(18) 6139 yards

Leeds G.C.
(0532) 658775
Elmete Lane, Roundhay, Leeds
(18) 6097 yards

Lightcliffe G.C.
(0422) 202459
Knowle Top Road, Lightcliffe
(9) 5888 yards

Longley Park G.C.
(0484) 422304
Maple Street, Huddersfield
(9) 5269 yards

Low Laithes G.C.
(0924) 274667
Flushdyke, Ossett
(18) 6440 yards

Marsden G.C.
(0484) 844253
Hemplow, Marsden
(9) 5702 yards

Meltham G.C.
(0484) 850227
Meltham, Huddersfield
(18) 6145 yards

Middleton Park G.C.
(0532) 700449
Middleton Park, Leeds
(18) 5233 yards

Moor Allerton G.C.
(0532) 661154
Coal Road, Wike, Leeds
(9) 3242 yards
(9) 3138 yards
(9) 3441 yards

Moortown G.C.
(0532) 686521
Harrogate Road, Leeds
(18) 6544 yards

Mount Skip G.C.
(0422) 842896
Wadsworth, Hebden Bridge
(9) 5114 yards

Normanton G.C.
(0924) 220134
Syndale Road, Normanton
(9) 5284 yards

Northcliffe G.C.
(0274) 596731
High Bank Lane
(18) 6093 yards

Otley G.C.
(0943) 463403
West Busk Lane, Otley
(18) 6225 yards

Outlane G.C.
(0422) 74762
Outlane, Huddersfield
(18) 5590 yards

Painthorpe G.C.
(0924) 255083
Crigglestone, Wakefield
(9) 4108 yards

Phoenix Park G.C.
(0274) 667178
Phoenix Park, Thornbury
(9) 4982 yards

Pontefract & District G.C.
(0977) 792115
Park Lane, Pontefract
(18) 6227 yards

Queensbury G.C.
(0274) 882155
Brighouse Road, Queensbury
(9) 5102 yards

Rawdon G.C.
(0532) 506040
Rawdon, Leeds
(9) 5964 yards

Riddlesden G.C.
(0535) 602148
Riddleston, Keighley
(18) 4247 yards

Roundhay G.C.
(0532) 661686
Park Lane, Leeds
(9) 5166 yards

Sand Moor G.C.
(0532) 683925
Alwoodley Lane, Leeds
(18) 6429 yards

Scarcroft G.C.
(0532) 892311
Skye Lane, Leeds
(18) 6426 yards

Shipley G.C.
(0274) 568652
Cottingley Bridge, Bingley
(18) 6203 yards

Silsden G.C.
(0535) 52998
Silsden, Keighley
(14) 4780 yards

South Bradford G.C.
(0274) 676911
Odsal, Bradford
(9) 6004 yards

South Leeds G.C.
(0532) 771676
Gipsy Lane, Leeds
(18) 5835 yards

Temple Newsam G.C.
(0532) 645624
Temple Newsam Road, Leeds
(18) 6448 yards
(18) 6029 yards

Wakefield G.C.
(0924) 255380
Sandal, Wakefield
(18) 6626 yards

West Bowling G.C.
(0274) 393207
Rooley Lane, Bradford
(18) 5756 yards

West Bradford G.C.
(0274) 542767
Haworth Road, Bradford
(18) 5752 yards

West End G.C.
(0422) 363293
Highroad Well, Halifax
(18) 6003 yards

Wetherby G.C.
(0937) 62527
Linton Lane, Wetherby
(18) 6244 yards

Sunningdale.

Whitwood G.C.
(0997) 558596
Whitwood, Castleford
(9) 6176 yards

Woodhall Hills G.C.
(0532) 554594
Calverley, Rudsey
(18) 6102 yards

Woodsome Hall G.C.
(0484) 602971
Fenay Bridge, Huddersfield
(18) 6068 yards

WILTSHIRE

Bremhill Park G.C.
(0793) 782946
Shrivenham, Swindon
(18) 6040 yards

Brinkworth G.C.
(066641) 277
Brinkworth,
Chippenham
(18) 6086 yards

Broome Manor G.C.
(0793) 532403
Pipers Way, Swindon
(18) 6359 yards
(9) 5610 yards

Chippenham G.C.
(0249) 652040
Malmesbury Road,
Chippenham
(18) 5540 yards

High Post G.C.
(0722) 73356
Great Durnford, Salisbury
(18) 6267 yards

Kingsdown G.C.
(0225) 73219
Kingsdown, Corsham
(18) 6445 yards

Marlborough G.C.
(0672) 52147
The Common, Marlborough
(18) 6440 yards

North Wilts G.C.
(0380) 860627
Bishops Cannings, Devizes
(18) 6450 yards

R.A.F. Upavon G.C.
(0980) 630787
R.A.F. Upavon, Pewsey
(9) 5597 yards

Salisbury & South Wilts G.C.
(0722) 742645
Netherhampton, Salisbury
(18) 6189 yards
(9) 4848 yards

Shrivenham Park G.C.
(0793) 782946
Shrivenham, Swindon
(18) 5622 yards

Swindon G.C.
(067284) 287
Ogbourne St George,
Marlborough
(18) 6226 yards

Tidworth Garrison G.C.
(0980) 42321
Bulford Road, Tidworth
(18) 5990 yards

West Wilts G.C.
(0985) 212110
Elm Hill, Warminster
(18) 5701 yards

SCOTLAND

BORDERS

Duns G.C.
(0361) 82717
Hardens Road, Duns
(9) 5826 yards

Eyemouth G.C.
(08907) 50551
Gunsgreen Road, Eyemouth
(9) 5446 yards

Galashiels G.C.
(0896) 3724
Ladhope Recreation Ground, Galashiels
(18) 5309 yards

Hawick G.C.
(0450) 72293
Vertish Hill, Hawick
(18) 5929 yards

Innerliethen G.C.
(0896) 830951
Innerliethen Water
(9) 5820 yards

Jedburgh G.C.
(0835) 63587
Dunion Road, Jedburgh
(9) 5520 yards

Kelso G.C.
(0573) 23009
Racecourse Road, Kelso
(18) 6066 yards

Lauder G.C.
(05782) 409
Galashiels Road, Lauder
(9) 6002 yards

Melrose G.C.
(089682) 2855
Dingleton, Melrose
(9) 5464 yards

Minto G.C.
(0450) 72267
Minto Village, Denholm, Hawick
(18) 5460 yards

Peebles G.C.
(0721) 20153
Kirkland Street, Peebles
(18) 6137 yards

St Boswells G.C.
(0835) 22359
St Boswells
(9) 5054 yards

Selkirk G.C.
(0750) 20621
The Hill, Selkirk
(9) 5560 yards

Torwoodle G.C.
(0896) 2260
Edinburgh Road, Galashiels
(9) 5720 yards

West Linton G.C.
(0968) 60256
West Linton
(18) 5835 yards

CENTRAL

Aberfoyle G.C.
(087 72) 441
Braval, Aberfoyle, Stirling
(18) 5205 yards

Alloa G.C.
(0259) 722745
Schawpark, Sauchie, Alloa
(18) 6230 yards

Alva G.C.
(0259) 60431
Beauclerc Street, Alva
(9) 4574 yards

Bonnybridge G.C.
(0324) 812645
Larbert Road, Bonnybridge
(9) 6058 yards

Braehead G.C.
(0259) 722078
Cambus, Alloa
(18) 6013 yards

Bridge of Allan G.C.
(0786) 832332
Sunnylaw, Bridge of Allan
(9) 4932 yards

Buchanan Castle G.C.
(0360) 60307
Drymen
(18) 6032 yards

Callander G.C.
(0877) 30090
Aveland Road, Callander
(18) 5125 yards

Dollar G.C.
(02594) 2400
Brewlands House, Dollar
(18) 5144 yards

Dunblane New G.C.
(0786) 823711
Perth Road, Dunblane
(18) 5878 yards

Falkirk G.C.
(0324) 611061
Stirling Road, Falkirk
(18) 6090 yards

Falkirk Tryst G.C.
(0324) 562091
Burnhead Road, Larbert
(18) 6053 yards

Glenbervie G.C.
(0324) 562605
Stirling Road, Larbert
(18) 6452 yards

Grangemouth G.C.
(0324) 711500
Polmont, Falkirk
(18) 6339 yards

Muckhart G.C.
(025981) 423
Dramburn Road, Muckhart, Dollar
(18) 6115 yards

Polmont G.C.
(0324) 711277
Maddison, Falkirk
(9) 6088 yards

Stirling G.C.
(0786) 64098
Queens Road, Stirling
(18) 6409 yards

Tillicoultry G.C.
(0259) 50741
Alva Road, Tillicoultry
(9) 5256 yards

Tulliallan G.C.
(0259) 30897
Alloa Road, Kincardine, Alloa
(18) 5982 yards

DUMFRIES & GALLOWAY

Castle Douglas G.C.
(0556) 2801
Abercromby Road, Castle Douglas
(9) 5408 yards

Colvend G.C.
(055663) 398
Sandyhills, Dalbeattie
(9) 4208 yards

Dumfries & County G.C.
(0387) 62045
Edinburgh Road, Dumfries
(18) 5914 yards

Dumfries & Galloway G.C.
(0387) 63848
Laurieston Avenue, Dumfries
(18) 5782 yards

Kirkcudbright G.C.
(0557) 30542
Stirling Crescent, Kirkcudbright
(18) 5598 yards

Langholm G.C.
(0541) 80429
Langholm
(9) 2872 yards

Lochmaben G.C.
(038781) 0552
Castlehill Gate, Lochmaben
(9) 5338 yards

Lockerbie G.C.
(05762) 2165
Currie Road, Lockerbie
(18) 5228 yards

Moffat G.C.
(06833) 20020
Coateshill, Moffat
(18) 5218 yards

Newton Stewart G.C.
(0671) 2172
Newton Stewart
(9) 5512 yards

Portpatrick (Dunskey) G.C.
(077681) 273
Portpatrick, Stranraer
(18) 5644 yards

Powfoot G.C.
(04612) 2866
Cummertrees, Annan
(18) 6283 yards

Sanquhar G.C.
(0659) 50577
Old Barr Road, Sanquhar
(9) 5144 yards

Southerness G.C.
(038788) 677
Southerness
(18) 6554 yards

Stranraer G.C.
(0776) 3539
Creachmore, Stranraer
(18) 6300 yards

Thornhill G.C.
(0848) 30546
Blacknest, Thornhill
(18) 6011 yards

Wigtown & Bladnoch G.C.
(09884) 3354
Wigtown
(9) 5462 yards

Wigtownshire County G.C.
(05813) 420
Mains of Park, Glenluce
(9) 5826 yards

FIFE

Aberdour G.C.
(0383) 860353
Seaside Place, Aberdour
(18) 5469 yards

Anstruther G.C.
(0333) 312055
Anstruther
(9) 4504 yards

Auchterderran G.C.
(0592) 721579
Woodend Road, Cardenden
(9) 5250 yards

Balbirnie Park G.C.
(0592) 752006
Balbirnie Park, Markinch,
Glenrothes
(18) 6444 yards

Ballingry G.C.
(0592) 860086
Crosshill, Lochgelly
(9) 6244 yards

Burntisland Golf House Club
(0592) 874093
Dodhead, Burntisland
(18) 5871 yards

Canmore G.C.
(0383) 726098
Venturefair Avenue, Dunfermline
(18) 5474 yards

Crail Golfing Society
(0333) 50278
Balcomie Clubhouse,
Fifeness,
Crail
(18) 5720 yards

Cupar G.C.
(0334) 53549
Cupar
(9) 5074 yards

Dunfermline G.C.
(0383) 723534
Pitfirrane, Crossford,
Dunfermline
(18) 6271 yards

Dunnikier Park G.C.
(0592) 267462
Dunnikier Way, Kirkcaldy
(18) 6601 yards

Glenrothes G.C.
(0592) 758686
Golf Course Road,
Glenrothes
(18) 6444 yards

Golf House Club (Elie)
(0333) 330301
Elie, Leven
(18) 6241 yards

Kinghorn G.C.
(0592) 890345
Macduff Crescent, Kinghorn
(18) 5269 yards

Kirkcaldy G.C.
(0592) 203258
Balwearie Road, Kirkcaldy
(18) 6007 yards

Ladybank G.C.
(0337) 30814
Annsmuir, Ladybank
(18) 6617 yards

Leslie G.C.
Leslie 741449
Balsillie Laws, Leslie
(9) 4686 yards

Leven Links
(0333) 23509
Links Road, Leven
(18) 6434 yards

Leven Municipal
(0333) 27057
Leven Links
(18) 5403 yards

Lochgelly G.C.
(0592) 780174
Cartmore Road, Lochgelly
(18) 5491 yards

Lundin Links
(0333) 320202
Golf Road, Lundin Links
(18) 6377 yards

Lundin Ladies G.C.
(0333) 320022
Woodiela Road,
Lundin Links
(9) 4730 yards

Pitreavie G.C.
(0383) 722591
Queensferry Road,
Dunfermline
(18) 6086 yards

St Andrews
(0334) 75757
St Andrews
(18) 6933 yards (Old)
(18) 6604 yards (New)
(18) 6284 yards (Jubilee)
(18) 5971 yards (Eden)

St Michaels G.C.
(033483) 365
Leuchars
(9) 5510 yards

Saline G.C.
(0383) 852591
Kineddar Hill, Saline
(9) 5302 yards

Scotscraig G.C.
(0382) 730880
Golf Road, Tayport
(18) 6486 yards

Thornton G.C.
(0592) 771111
Station Road, Thornton
(18) 6177 yards

GRAMPIAN

Aboyne G.C.
(03398) 86328
Formaston Park, Aboyne
(18) 5330 yards

Auchinblae G.C.
Auchinblae
(9) 4748 yards

Auchmill G.C.
(0224) 642121
Auchmill, Aberdeen
(9) 5500 yards

Ballater G.C.
(03397) 55567
Ballater
(18) 6106 yards

Balnagesk G.C.
(0224) 876407
St. Fittick's Road, Aberdeen
(18) 5975 yards

Banchory G.C.
(03302) 2365
Kinneskie, Banchory
(18) 5271 yards

Braemar G.C.
(033083) 618
Cluniebank, Braemar
(18) 5011 yards

Buckpool G.C.
(0542) 35368
Barhill Road, Buckie
(18) 6257 yards

Cruden Bay G.C.
(0779) 812285
Aulton Road, Cruden Bay
(18) 6401 yards (Championship)
(9) 4710 yards (St. Olaf)

Cullen G.C.
(0542) 40685
The Links, Cullen
(18) 4610 yards

Deeside G.C.
(0224) 867697
Bieldside, Aberdeen
(18) 5972 yards

Duff House Royal G.C.
(02612) 2062
Barnyards, Banff
(18) 6161 yards

Dufftown G.C.
(0340) 20325
Dufftown
(9) 4556 yards

Elgin G.C.
(0343) 542338
Birnie Road, Elgin
(18) 6401 yards

Fraserburgh G.C.
(0346) 28287
Philarth, Fraserburgh
(18) 6217 yards

Hazelhead G.C.
(0224) 317336
Hazelhead Park, Aberdeen
(18) 6595 yards
(9) 5205 yards

Huntly G.C.
(0466) 2643
Cooper Park, Huntly
(18) 5399 yards

Inverallochy G.C.
(03465) 2324
Inverallochy, Fraserburgh
(18) 5137 yards

Inverurie G.C.
(0467) 24080
Blackhall Road, Inverurie
(18) 5703 yards

Keith G.C.
(05422) 2469
Fife Park, Keith
(18) 5745 yards

Kings Links
(0224) 632269
Kings Links, Aberdeen
(18) 6520 yards

Kintore G.C.
(0467) 32631
Kintore, Inverurie
(9) 5240 yards

McDonald G.C.
(0358) 20576
Hospital Road, Ellon
(18) 5986 yards

Moray G.C.
(034381) 2018
Stotfield Road, Lossiemouth
(18) 6258 yards (New)
(18) 6643 yards (Old)

Murcar G.C.
(0224) 704370
Bridge of Don, Aberdeen
(18) 6240 yards

Newburgh-on-Ythan G.C.
(03586) 389
Millend, Newburgh
(9) 6404 yards

Old Meldrum G.C.
(06512) 2212
Old Meldrum
(9) 5252 yards

Peterhead G.C.
(0779) 72149
Craigewan Links, Peterhead
(18) 6070 yards

Royal Aberdeen G.C.
(0224) 702221
Balgownie, Bridge of Don, Aberdeen
(18) 6372 yards
(18) 4003 yards

Royal Tarlair G.C.
(0261) 32897
Buchan Street, Macduff
(18) 5866 yards

Spey Bay G.C.
(0343) 820424
Spey Bay, Fochabers
(18) 6059 yards

Stonehaven G.C.
(0569) 62124
Cowie, Stonehaven
(18) 5103 yards

Strathiene G.C.
(0542) 31798
Buckie
(18) 5957 yards

Tarland G.C.
(033981) 413
Tarland, Aboyne
(9) 5812 yards

Torphine G.C.
(033982) 493
Golf Road, Torphine
(9) 2330 yards

Turriff G.C.
(0888) 62745
Rosehall, Turriff
(18) 6105 yards

Westhill G.C.
(0224) 740159
Westhill, Skene
(18) 5866 yards

HIGHLAND

Abernethy G.C.
(047982) 637
Nethybridge
(9) 2484 yards

Alness G.C.
(0349) 883877
Ardross Road, Alness
(9) 4718 yards

Boat-of-Garten G.C.
(047983) 282
Boat-of-Garten
(18) 5720 yards

Bonar Bridge G.C.
(054982) 248
Bonar Bridge
(9) 4616 yards

Brora G.C.
(0408) 21475
Golf Road, Brora
(18) 6110 yards

Carrbridge G.C.
(047984) 674
Carrbridge
(9) 5250 yards

Buchanan Castle.

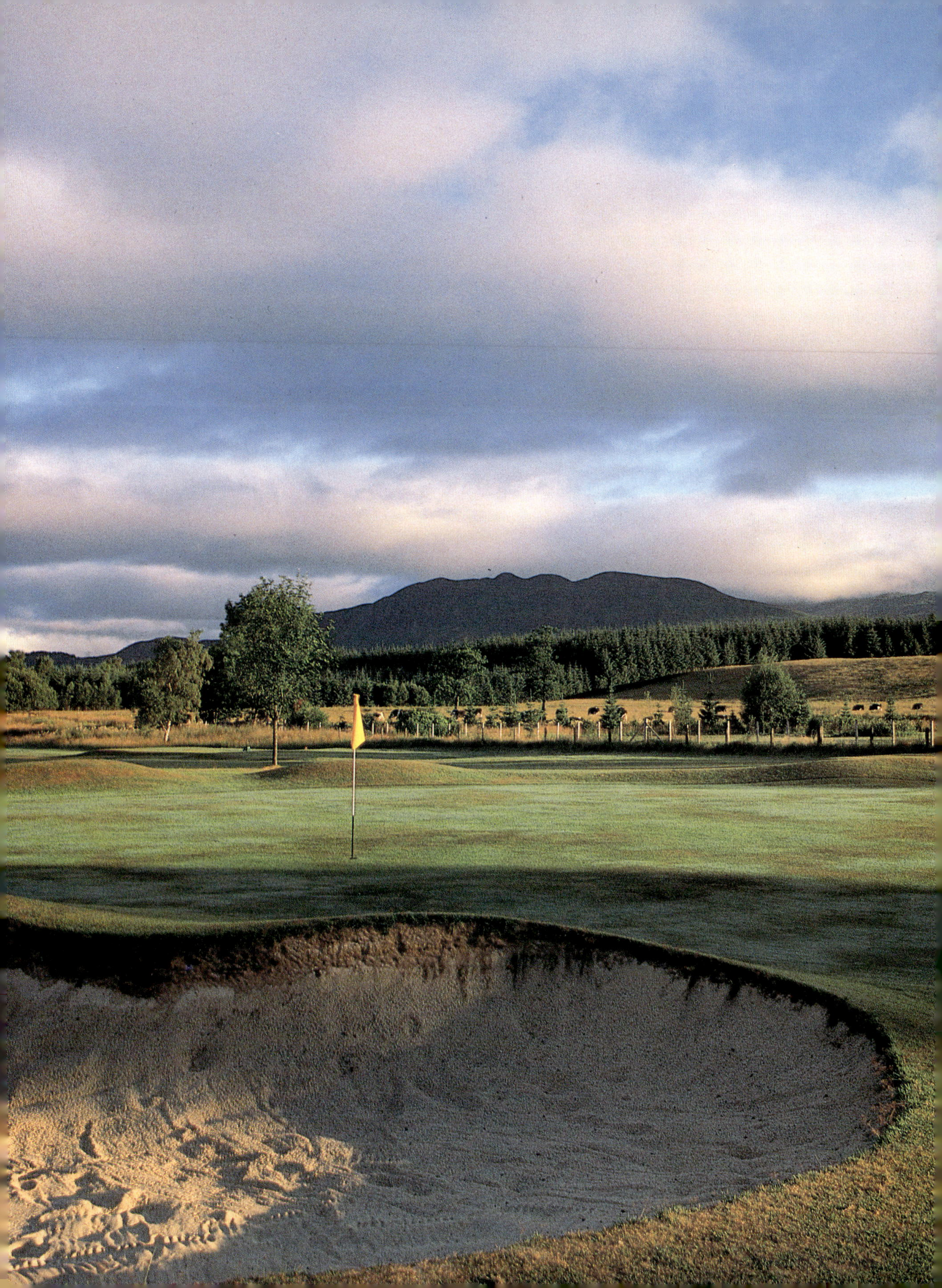

Forres G.C.
(0309) 72949
Muiryshade, Forres
(18) 6141 yards

Fort Augustus G.C.
(0320) 6460
Markethill, Fort Augustus
(9) 5454 yards

Fortrose & Rosemarkie G.C.
(0381) 20529
Ness Road East, Fortrose
(18) 5964 yards

Fort William G.C.
(0397) 4464
North Road, Fort William
(18) 5640 yards

Gairloch G.C.
(0445) 2407
Gairloch
(9) 4186 yards

Garmouth & Kingston G.C.
(034387) 388
Garmouth Road, Fochabers
(18) 5649 yards

Golspie G.C.
(04083) 3266
Ferry Road, Golspie
(18) 5763 yards

Grantown-on-Spey G.C.
(0479) 2667
Golf Course Road, Grantown-on-Spey
(18) 5672 yards

Hopeman G.C.
(0348) 830578
Hopeman
(18) 5439 yards

Invergordon G.C.
(0349) 852116
Cromlet Drive, Invergordon
(9) 6028 yards

Inverness G.C.
(0463) 239882
Culcabock Road, Inverness
(18) 6226 yards

Kingussie G.C.
(0540) 661600
Bynack Road, Kingussie
(18) 5466 yards

Lybster G.C.
(05932) 359
Main Street, Lybster
(9) 3770 yards

Muir of Ord G.C.
(0463) 870825
Great Northern Road, Muir of Ord
(18) 5022 yards

Nairn G.C.
(0667) 53208
Seabank Road, Nairn
(18) 6452 yards

Nairn Dunbar G.C.
(0667) 52741
Lochloy Road, Nairn
(18) 6431 yards

Newtonmore G.C.
(05403) 328
Golf Course Road, Newtonmore
(18) 5890 yards

Orkney G.C.
(0856) 2457
Grainbank, Kirkwall, Orkney
(18) 5406 yards

Reay G.C.
(084781) 288
Reay, Thurso
(18) 5876 yards

Royal Dornoch G.C.
(0862) 810902
Golf Road, Dornoch
(18) 6577 yards
(9) 2485 yards

Sconser G.C.
(0478) 2364
Sconser, Isle of Skye
(9) 4796 yards

Shetland G.C.
(059584) 369
Dale, Shetland
(18) 5791 yards

Stornoway G.C.
(0851) 2240
Lady Lever Park, Stornoway, Isle of Lewis
(18) 5119 yards

Strathpeffer Spa G.C.
(0997) 21219
Strathpeffer
(18) 4813 yards

Stromness G.C.
(0856) 850772
Ness, Stromness, Orkney
(18) 4665 yards

Tain G.C.
(0862) 2314
Tain
(18) 6222 yards

Tarbat G.C.
(086287) 519
Portmahomack
(9) 4656 yards

Thurso G.C.
(0847) 63807
Newlands of Geise, Thurso
(18) 5818 yards

Torvean G.C.
(0463) 237543
Glenurquart Road, Inverness
(18) 4308 yards

Wick G.C.
(0955) 2726
Reiss, Wick
(18) 5976 yards

LOTHIAN

Baberton G.C.
(031) 453 4911
Juniper Green, Edinburgh
(18) 6098 yards

Bathgate G.C.
(0506) 630505
Edinburgh Road, Bathgate
(18) 6326 yards

Braids United G.C.
(031) 447 6666
Braids Hill Approach, Edinburgh
(18) 5731 yards (No. 1)
(18) 4832 yards (no. 2)

Broomieknowe G.C.
(031) 663 9317
Golf Course Road, Bonnyrigg
(18) 6046 yards

Bruntsfield Links Golfing Society
(031) 336 1479
Barnton Avenue, Edinburgh
(18) 6407 yards

Craigmillar Park G.C.
(031) 667 2837
Observatory Road, Edinburgh
(18) 5846 yards

Dalmahoy Hotel G. & C.C.
(031) 333 4105
Dalmahoy, Kirknewton
(18) 6664 yards (East)
(18) 5212 yards (West)

Deer Park G. & C.C.
(0506) 38843
Livingston
(18) 6636 yards

Duddingston G.C.
(031) 661 7688
Duddingston Road, Edinburgh
(18) 6647 yards

Dunbar G.C.
(0368) 62317
East Links, Dunbar
(18) 6426 yards

Dundas Park G.C.
(031) 331 3090
South Queensferry
(9) 6026 yards

East Links G.C.
(0620) 2340
East Links, North Berwick
(18) 6079 yards

Gifford G.C.
(062081) 267
Station Road, Gifford
(9) 6138 yards

Glencorse G.C.
(0968) 77189
Milton Bridge, Penicuik
(18) 5205 yards

Greenburn G.C.
(0501) 70292
Bridge Street, Fauldhouse
(18) 6210 yards

Gullane G.C.
(0620) 842255
Gullane
(18) 6479 yards (No. 1)
(18) 6127 yards (No. 2)
(18) 5035 yards (No. 3)

Honourable Company of Edinburgh Golfers (Muirfield)
(0620) 842123
Muirfield, Gullane
(18) 6941 yards

Kilspindie G.C.
(0875) 358
Aberlady
(18) 5410 yards

Kingsknowe G.C.
(031) 441 1145
Lanark Road, Edinburgh
(18) 5979 yards

Linlithgow G.C.
(0506) 842585
Braehead, Linlithgow
(18) 5858 yards

Longniddry G.C.
(0875) 52141
Links Road, Longniddry
(18) 6210 yards

Lothianburn G.C
(031) 445 2288
Biggar Road, Edinburgh
(18) 5671 yards

Luffness New G.C.
(0620) 843336
Aberlady
(18) 6085 yards

Merchants of Edinburgh G.C.
(031) 447 1219
Craighill Gardens, Edinburgh
(18) 4889 yards

Mortonhall G.C.
(031) 447 6974
Braid Road, Edinburgh
(18) 6557 yards

Murrayfield G.C.
(031) 337 3478
Murrayfield Road, Edinburgh
(18) 5727 yards

Muirfield (see Hon. Co. of Edinburgh Golfers)

Musselburgh G.C.
(031) 665 2005
Monktonhall, Musselburgh
(18) 6623 yards

Newbattle G.C.
(031) 663 2123
Abbey Road, Dalkeith
(18) 6012 yards

North Berwick G.C.
(0620) 2135
West Links, Beach Road, North Berwick
(18) 6298 yards

Prestonfield G.C.
(031) 667 9665
Piestfield Road North, Edinburgh
(18) 6216 yards

Ratho Park G.C.
(031) 333 1752
Ratho, Newbridge
(18) 6028 yards

Royal Burgess Golfing Society
(031) 339 2075
Whitehouse Road, Barton, Edinburgh
(18) 6604 yards

Royal Musselburgh G.C.
(0875) 810276
Prestongrange House, Prestonpans
(18) 6204 yards

Silverknowes G.C.
(031) 336 5359
Silverknowes, Parkway, Edinburgh
(18) 6210 yards

Swanston G.C.
(031) 445 2239
Swanston Road, Edinburgh
(18) 5024 yards

Torphin Hill G.C.
(031) 441 1100
Torphin Road, Colinton, Edinburgh
(18) 5030 yards

Turnhouse G.C.
(031) 339 7701
Turnhouse Road, Edinburgh
(18) 6171 yards

Uphall G.C.
(0506) 856404
Uphall
(18) 5567 yards

West Lothian G.C.
(0506) 826030
Airngath Hill, Linlithgow
(18) 6629 yards

Winterfield G.C.
(0368) 62564
North Road, Dunbar
(18) 5053 yards

STRATHCLYDE

Airdrie G.C.
(0236) 62195
Rochsoles, Airdrie
(18) 6004 yards

Alexandra Park Municipal G.C.
(041) 556 3711
Alexandra Parade, Glasgow
(9) 4562 yards

Annanhill G.C.
(0563) 21644
Irvine Road, Kilmarnock
(18) 6269 yards

Ardeer G.C.
(0294) 64035
Greenhead, Stevenston
(18) 6630 yards

Ayr Belleisle G.C.
(0292) 41258
Belleisle Park, Ayr
(18) 6540 yards (Belleisle)
(18) 5244 yards (Seafield)

Ayr Dalmilling G.C.
(0292) 263893
Westwood Avenue, Ayr
(18) 5401 yards

Ballochmyle G.C.
(0290) 50469
Ballochmyle, Mauchline
(18) 5952 yards

Balmore G.C.
(041) 332 0392
Balmore, Torrance
(18) 5735 yards

Barshaw G.C.
(041) 884 2533
Barshaw Park, Paisley
(18) 5703 yards

Bearsden G.C.
(041) 942 2351
Thorn Road, Bearsden, Glasgow
(9) 5977 yards

Beith G.C.
(05055) 2011
Bigholm, Beith
(9) 5488 yards

Bellshill G.C.
(0698) 745124
Orbiston, Bellshill
(18) 6607 yards

Biggar G.C.
(0899) 20618
Broughton Road, Biggar
(18) 5256 yards

Bishopbriggs G.C.
(041) 772 1810
Brackenbrae Road, Bishopbriggs, Glasgow
(18) 6041 yards

Blairbeth G.C.
(041) 634 3355
Rutherglen, Glasgow
(18) 5448 yards

Blairmore & Strone G.C.
(036984) 217
Blairmore, Argyll
(9) 4224 yards

Bonnyton G.C.
(03553) 2256
Eaglesham, Glasgow
(18) 6252 yards

Bothwell Castle G.C.
(0698) 853177
Blantyre Road, Bothwell, Glasgow
(18) 6432 yards

Brodick G.C.
(0770) 2513
Brodick, Isle of Arran
(18) 4404 yards

Bute G.C.
(0700) 83242
Kilchaltan Bay, Bute
(9) 5594 yards

Calderbraes G.C.
(0698) 813425
Roundknowe Road, Uddingston
(9) 5186 yards

Caldwell G.C.
(050585) 616
Uplawnmoor
(18) 6102 yards

Cambuslang G.C.
(041) 641 3130
Westburn Drive, Cambuslang, Glasgow
(9) 6072 yards

Campsie G.C.
(0360) 310244
Crow Road, Lennoxtown, Glasgow
(18) 5517 yards

Caprington G.C.
(0563) 23702
Ayr Road, Kilmarnock
(18) 5718 yards

Cardross G.C.
(0389) 841350
Main Road, Cardross, Dumbarton
(18) 6466 yards

Carluke G.C.
(0555) 71070
Hallcraig, Carluke
(18) 5805 yards

Carnwath G.C.
(0555) 840251
Main Street, Carnwath
(18) 5860 yards

Carradale G.C.
(05833) 387
Carradale, Argyll
(9) 4774 yards

Cathcart Castle G.C.
(041) 638 9449
Mearns Road, Clarkston, Glasgow
(18) 5832 yards

Cathkin Braes G.C.
(041) 634 4007
Cathkin Road, Rutherglen, Glasgow
(18) 6266 yards

Cawder G.C.
(041) 772 7101
Cadder Road, Bishopbriggs, Glasgow
(18) 6229 yards (Cawder)
(18) 5877 yards (Keir)

Clober G.C.
(041) 956 1685
Craigton Road, Milngavie
(18) 5068 yards

Clydebank & District G.C.
(0389) 73289
Hardgate, Clydebank
(18) 5815 yards

Clydebank Municipal G.C.
(041) 952 6372
Overtoun Road, Clydebank
(18) 5349 yards

Cochrane Castle G.C.
(0505) 20146
Craigston, Johnstone
(18) 6226 yards

Colonsay G.C.
(09512) 316
Isle of Colonsay
(18) 4775 yards

Colville Park G.C.
(0698) 63017
Jerviston Estate, Motherwell
(18) 6208 yards

Corrie G.C.
(077081) 223
Corrie, Isle of Arran
(9) 3896 yards

Cowal G.C.
(0396) 5673
Kirn, Dunoon
(18) 5820 yards

Cowglen G.C.
(041) 632 0556
Barhead Road, Glasgow
(18) 5976 yards

Crow Wood G.C.
(041) 779 1943
Muirhead, Chryston
(18) 6209 yards

Cumbernauld Municipal G.C.
(02367) 28138
Cumbernauld
(18) 6412 yards

Dougalston G.C.
(041) 956 5750
Milngavie, Glasgow
(18) 6683 yards

Douglas Park G.C.
(041) 942 2220
Hillfoot, Bearsden, Glasgow
(18) 5957 yards

Douglas Water G.C.
(0555) 2295
Douglas Water, Lanark
(9) 5832 yards

Drumpellier G.C.
(0236) 24139
Drumpellier, Coatbridge
(18) 6227 yards

Dullatur G.C.
(02367) 27847
Dullatur, Glasgow
(18) 6253 yards

Dumbarton G.C.
(0389) 32830
Broadmeadow, Dumbarton
(18) 5981 yards

Dunaverty G.C.
(No tel.)
Southend, Campbeltown, Argyll
(18) 4597 yards

Easter Moffat G.C.
(0236) 21864
Mansion House, Plains, Airdrie
(18) 6221 yards

East Kilbride G.C.
(03552) 47728
Chapelside Road, Nerston, East Kilbride
(18) 6419 yards

East Renfrewshire G.C.
(03555) 258
Pilmuir, Newton Mearns, Glasgow
(18) 6097 yards

Eastwood G.C.
(03555) 280
Muirshield, Newton Mearns, Glasgow
(18) 5864 yards

Elderslie G.C.
(0505) 23956
Main Road, Elderslie
(18) 6004 yards

Erskine G.C.
(0505) 2302
Bishopston
(18) 6287 yards

Fereneze G.C.
(041) 881 1519
Fereneze Avenue, Barrhead,
Glasgow
(18) 5821 yards

Girvan G.C.
(0465) 4272
Golf Course Road, Girvan
(18) 5075 yards

Glasgow Gailes G.C.
(0294) 311347
Gailes, Irvine
(18) 6447 yards

Glasgow Killermont G.C.
(041) 942 2011
Killermont, Glasgow
(18) 5968 yards

Gleddoch G. & C.C.
(047554) 711
Langbank
(18) 6200 yards

Glencruitten G.C.
(0631) 62868
Glencruitten, Oban
(18) 4452 yards

Gourock G.C.
(0475) 33696
Cowal View, Gourock
(18) 6492 yards

Greenock G.C.
(0475) 20793
Forsyth Street, Greenock
(18) 5838 yards

Greenock Whinhill G.C.
(0475) 210641
Beith Road, Greenock
(18) 5454 yards

Haggs Castle G.C.
(041) 427 1157
Drumbreck Road, Glasgow
(18) 6464 yards

Hamilton G.C.
(0698) 282872
Riccarton, Ferniegair,
Hamilton
(18) 6264 yards

Hayston G.C.
(041) 775 0882
Campsie Road, Kirkintilloch,
Glasgow
(18) 6042 yards

Helensburgh G.C.
(0436) 74173
East Abercromby Street,
Helensburgh
(18) 6058 yards

Hollandbush G.C.
(0555) 893484
Lesmahagow, Coalburn
(18) 6110 yards

Innellan G.C.
(0369) 3546
Innellan, Argyll
(9) 4878 yards

Irvine (Bogside) G.C.
(0294) 75979
Bogside, Irvine
(18) 6450 yards

Irvine Ravenspark G.C.
(0294) 79550
Kidsneuk Road, Irvine
(18) 6496 yards

Kilbirnie Place G.C.
(050582) 683398
Largs Road, Kilbirnie
(18) 5479 yards

Kilmacolm G.C.
(050587) 2695
Porterfield, Kilmacolm
(18) 5964 yards

Kilmarnock (Barassie) G.C.
(0292) 311077
Hillhouse Road, Barassie,
Troon
(18) 6473 yards

Kilsyth Lennox G.C.
(0236) 822190
Tak-Ma-Doon Road, Kilsyth,
Glasgow
(9) 5944 yards

Kirkhill G.C.
(041) 641 8499
Greenlees Road,
Cambuslang,
Glasgow
(18) 5889 yards

Kirkintilloch G.C.
(041) 776 1256
Todhill, Campsie Road,
Kirkintilloch
(18) 5269 yards

Knightswood G.C.
(041) 959 2131
Lincoln Avenue,
Knightswood,
Glasgow
(9) 2717 yards

Kyles of Bute G.C.
(0700) 811355
Tighnabruaich, Argyll
(9) 4758 yards

Lamlash G.C.
(07706) 296
Lamlash, Isle of Arran
(18) 4681 yards

Lanark G.C.
(0555) 3219
The Moor, Lanark
(18) 6416 yards

Landoun G.C.
(0563) 821993
Edinburgh Road, Galston
(18) 5824 yards

Largs G.C.
(0475) 672497
Irvine Road, Largs
(18) 6257 yards

Larkhall G.C.
(0698) 881113
Burnhead Road, Larkhall
(9) 6236 yards

Leadhills G.C.
(0659) 74222
Leadhills, Biggar
(9) 4062 yards

Lenzie G.C.
(041) 776 1535
Crosshill Road, Lenzie,
Glasgow
(18) 5982 yards

Lethamhill G.C.
(041) 770 6220
Cumbernauld Road, Glasgow
(18) 6073 yards

Linn Park G.C.
(041) 637 5871
Simshill Road, Glasgow
(18) 4832 yards

Littlehill G.C.
(041) 772 1916
Auchinairn Road,
Bishopbriggs,
Glasgow
(18) 6199 yards

Lochranza G.C.
(077083) 273
Brodick, Isle of Arran
(9) 3580 yards

Lochwinnoch G.C.
(0505) 842153
Burnfoot Road,
Lochwinnoch
(18) 6223 yards

Machrie Hotel and G.C.
(0496) 2310
Machrie Hotel, Port Ellen,
Isle of Islay
(18) 6226 yards

Machrie Bay G.C.
(077084) 258
Machrie Bay, Isle of Arran
(9) 4246 yards

Machrihanish G.C.
(058681) 277
Machrihanish,
Campbeltown,
Argyll
(18) 6228 yards

Maybole G.C.
(0292) 281511
Memorial Park,
Maybole
(9) 5270 yards

Millport G.C.
(0475) 530485
Golf Road, Millport,
Isle of Cumbrae
(18) 5831 yards

Milngavie G.C.
(041) 956 1619
Laigh Park, Milngavie,
Glasgow
(18) 5818 yards

Mount Ellen G.C.
(0236) 782277
Johnston House, Gartcosh,
Glasgow
(18) 5525 yards

Paisley G.C.
(041) 884 2292
Braehead, Paisley
(18) 6424 yards

Pollok G.C.
(041) 632 4351
Barrhead Road, Glasgow
(18) 6257 yards

Port Bannatyne G.C.
(0700) 2009
Port Bannatyne, Isle of Bute
(13) 4654 yards

Port Glasgow G.C.
(0475) 704181
Port Glasgow
(18) 5712 yards

Prestwick G.C.
(0292) 77404
Links Road, Prestwick
(18) 6544 yards

Prestwick St Cuthbert G.C.
(0292) 79120
East Road, Prestwick
(18) 6470 yards

Prestwick St Nicholas G.C.
(0292) 77608
Grangemuir Road, Prestwick
(18) 5926 yards

Raiston G.C.
(041) 882 1349
Raiston, Paisley
(18) 6100 yards

Ranfurly Castle G.C.
(0505) 612609
Golf Road, Bridge of Weir
(18) 6284 yards

Renfrew G.C.
(041) 886 6692
Blythswood Estate,
Inchinnan Road, Renfrew
(18) 6818 yards

Rothesay G.C.
(0700) 2244
Rothesay, Isle of Bute
(18) 5358 yards

Routenburn G.C.
(0475) 674289
Largs
(18) 5650 yards

Royal Troon G.C.
(0292) 311555
Craigend Road, Troon
(18) 6641 yards (Old)
(18) 6274 yards (Portland)

Sandyhills G.C.
(041) 778 1179
Sandyhills Road, Glasgow
(18) 6253 yards

Shiskine G.C.
(077086) 293
Blackwaterfoot, Isle of Arran
(12) 3000 yards

Shotts G.C.
(0501) 20431
Blairhead, Shotts
(18) 6125 yards

Skelmorlie G.C.
(0475) 520152
Skelmorlie
(13) 5056 yards

Strathaven G.C.
(0357) 20421
Overton Avenue,
Glasgow Road,
Strathaven
(18) 6226 yards

Strathclyde Park G.C.
(0698) 66155
Motel Hill, Hamilton
(9) 6294 yards

Tarbert G.C.
(08802) 565
Kilberry Road, Tarbert,
Argyll
(9) 4460 yards

Torrance House G.C.
(03552) 33451
Strathaven Road,
East Kilbride,
Glasgow
(18) 6640 yards

Troon Municipal G.C.
(0292) 312464
Harling Drive, Troon
(18) 6687 yards (Lochgreen)
(18) 6327 yards (Darley)
(18) 4784 yards (Fullarton)

Turnberry Hotel
(0655) 31000
Turnberry Hotel, Turnberry
(18) 6956 yards (Ailsa)
(18) 6276 yards (Arran)

Vaul G.C.
(08792) 566
Scarinish, Isle of Tiree, Argyll
(9) 6246 yards

Western Gailes G.C.
(0294) 311649
Gailes, Irvine
(18) 6614 yards

Western Isles G.C.
(0688) 2020
Tobermory, Isle of Mull
(9) 4920 yards

Westerwood Hotel & G.C.
(0236) 725281
St Andrews Drive,
Cumbernauld
(18) 6800 yards

West Kilbride G.C.
(0294) 823911
Fullerton Drive,
West Kilbride
(18) 6348 yards

Whitecraigs G.C.
(041) 639 4530
Ayr Road, Giffnock, Glasgow
(18) 6230 yards

Whiting Bay G.C.
(07707) 487
Whiting Bay, Isle of Arran
(18) 4405 yards

Williamwood G.C.
(041) 637 2715
Clarkeston Road, Netherlee,
Glasgow
(18) 5878 yards

Windyhill G.C.
(041) 942 7157
Baljaffray Road, Bearsden,
Glasgow
(18) 6254 yards

Wishaw G.C.
(0698) 372869
Cleland Road, Wishaw
(18) 6134 yards

TAYSIDE

Aberfeldy G.C.
(0887) 20203
Taybridge Road, Aberfeldy
(9) 5466 yards

Alyth G.C.
(08283) 2411
Pitcrocknie, Alyth
(18) 6226 yards

Arbroath G.C.
(0241) 72666
Elliot, Arbroath
(18) 6078 yards

Auchterarder G.C.
(07646) 2804
Auchterarder
(18) 5737 yards

Bishopshire G.C.
(0592) 860379
Kinnesswood
(9) 4360 yards

Blair Atholl G.C.
(079681) 274
Blair Atholl
(9) 5710 yards

Blairgowrie G.C.
(0250) 3116
Rosemount, Blairgowrie
(18) 6592 yards (Rosemount)
(18) 6865 yards (Lansdowne)
(9) 4614 yards (Wee)

Brechin G.C.
(03562) 2383
Trinity, Brechin
(18) 5267 yards

Caird Park G.C.
(0382) 44003
Mains Loan, Dundee
(18) 6303 yards

Camperdown (Municipal) G.C.
(0382) 68340
Camperdown Park, Dundee
(18) 6561 yards

Carnoustie
(0241) 53789
Links Parade, Carnoustie
(18) 6931 yards (Championship)
(18) 5935 yards (Burnside)
(18) 6445 yards (Buddon Links)

Comrie G.C.
(0764) 70544
Polinard, Comrie
(9) 5966 yards

Craigie Hill G.C.
(0738) 22644
Cherrybank, Perth
(18) 5379 yards

Crieff G.C.
(0764) 2909
(18) 6363 yards (Ferntower)
(9) 4772 yards (Dornock)

Dalmunzie Hotel G.C.
(025085) 224
Spittal of Glenshee,
Blairgowrie
(9) 4458 yards

Downfield G.C.
(0382) 825595
Turnberry Avenue, Dundee
(18) 6899 yards

Dunkeld & Birnam G.C.
(03502) 524
Fungarth, Dunkeld
(9) 5264 yards

Dunning G.C.
(076484) 398
Rollo Park, Dunning
(9) 4836 yards

Edzell G.C.
(03564) 7283
High Street, Edzell, Brechin
(18) 6299 yards

Forfar G.C.
(0307) 63773
Cunninghill, Arbroath Road,
Forfar
(18) 6255 yards

Glenalmond G.C.
(073888) 270
Trinity College, Glenalmond
(9) 5812 yards

Gleneagles Hotel
(0764) 63543
Gleneagles Hotel,
Auchterarder
(18) 6452 yards (King's)
(18) 5964 yards (Queen's)

Green Hotel G.C.
(0577) 63467
Green Hotel, Kinross
(18) 6339 yards
(18) 5000 yds

Killin G.C.
(05672) 312
Killin
(9) 5016 yards

King James VI G.C.
(0738) 32460
Moncrieffe Island, Perth
(18) 6037 yards

Kirriemuir G.C.
(0575) 73317
23 Bank Street, Kirriemuir,
Angus
(18) 5591 yards

Letham Grange G. & C.C.
(0241) 89373
Letham Grange, Collistonby,
Arbroath
(18) 6290 yards

Milnathort G.C.
(0577) 64069
South Street, Milnathort
(9) 5918 yards

Monifieth Golf Links
(0382) 533300
Ferry Road, Monifieth
(18) 6657 yards (Medal)
(18) 5123 yards (Ashludie)

Montrose Links
(0674) 72932
Trail Drive, Montrose
(18) 6451 yards (Medal)
(18) 4815 yards (Broomfield)

Murrayshall Hotel & G.C.
(0738) 52784
Murrayshall, New Scone
(18) 6416 yards

Muthill G.C.
(0764) 3319
Peat Road, Muthill, Crieff
(9) 4742 yards

Panmure G.C.
(0241) 53120
Burnside Road, Barry
(18) 6302 yards

Pitlochry G.C.
(0796) 2792
Golf Course Road, Pitlochry
(18) 5811 yards

St Fillans G.C.
(076485) 312
St Fillans
(9) 5268 yards

Taymouth Castle G.C.
(08873) 228
Kenmore, Aberfeldy
(18) 6066 yards

WALES

CLWYD

Abergele & Pensarn G.C.
(0745) 824034
Tan-y-Goppa Road, Abergele
(18) 6500 yards

Denbigh G.C.
(074571) 4159
Henllan Road, Denbigh
(18) 5650 yards

Flint G.C.
(0352) 732186
Cornist Park, Flint
(9) 5829 yards

Hawarden G.C.
(0244) 531447
Groomsdale Lane, Hawarden
(9) 5735 yards

Holywell G.C.
(0352) 710040
Brynford, Holywell
(9) 6484 yards

Mold G.C.
(0352) 740318
Pantmywyn, Nr. Mold
(18) 5521 yards

Old Colwyn G.C.
(0492) 515581
Old Colwyn, Colwyn Bay
(9) 5268 yards

Old Padeswood G.C.
(0244) 547401
Station Road, Padeswood, Mold
(18) 6728 yards

Padeswood & Buckley G.C.
(0244) 543636
Station Lane, Padeswood
(18) 5746 yards

Prestatyn G.C.
(07456) 4320
Marine Road East, Prestatyn
(18) 6714 yards

Rhuddlan G.C.
(0745) 590675
Rhuddlan, Rhyl
(18) 6038 yards

Rhyl G.C.
(0745) 35317
Coast Road, Rhyl
(9) 6153 yards

Ruthin-Pwllglas G.C.
(08242) 4658
Ruthin-Pwllglas, Ruthin
(9) 5306 yards

St Melyd G.C.
(07456) 4405
Melyden Road, Prestatyn
(9) 5805 yards

Vale of Llangollen G.C.
(0978) 860050
Holyhead Road, Llangollen
(18) 6617 yards

Wrexham G.C.
(0978) 364268
Holt Road, Wrexham
(18) 6038 yards

DYFED

Aberystwyth G.C.
(0970) 615104
Bryn-y-Mor, Aberystwyth
(18) 5868 yards

Ashburnham G.C.
(05546) 2269
Cliff Terrace, Burry Port
(18) 6916 yards

Borth and Ynyslas G.C.
(097081) 202
Borth
(18) 6094 yards

Cardigan G.C.
(0239) 612035
Gwbert-on-Sea
(18) 6207 yards

Carmarthen G.C.
(0267) 214
Blaenycoed Road, Carmarthen
(18) 6212 yards

Cilgywn G.C.
(0570) 45286
Llangybi
(9) 5318 yards

Glynhir G.C.
(0269) 850472
Glynhir Road, Llandybie, Nr. Ammanford
(18) 6090 yards

Haverfordwest G.C.
(0437) 68409
Arnolds Down, Haverfordwest
(18) 5945 yards

Milford Haven G.C.
(0646) 692368
Milford Haven
(18) 6235 yards

Newport (Pembs) G.C.
(0239) 820244
Newport
(9) 6178 yards

St David's City G.C.
(0437) 720403
Whitesands Bay, St Davids
(9) 5695 yards

South Pembrokeshire G.C.
(0646) 682035
Defensible Barracks, Pembroke Dock
(9) 5804 yards

Tenby G.C.
(0834) 2978
The Burrows, Tenby
(18) 6232 yards

GWENT

Blackwood G.C.
(0495) 223152
Cwmgelli, Blackwood
(9) 5304 yards

Caerleon G.C.
(0633) 420342
Caerleon, Newport
(9) 6184 yards

Greenmeadow G.C.
(06333) 626262
Treherbert Road, Cwmbran
(9) 6128 yards

Llanwern G.C.
(0633) 415233
Tennyson Avenue, Llanwern
(18) 6202 yards
(9) 5674 yards

Monmouth G.C.
(0600) 2212
Leasebrook Lane, Monmouth
(9) 5434 yards

Monmouthshire G.C.
(0873) 2606
Llanfoist, Abergavenny
(18) 6045 yards

Newport G.C.
(0633) 892643
Great Oak, Rogerstone, Newport
(18) 6370 yards

Pontnewydd G.C.
(0633) 32170
West Pontnewydd, Cwmbran
(10) 5321 yards

Pontypool G.C.
(0495) 763655
Trevethyn, Pontypool
(18) 6070 yards

North Wales G.C.

Rolls of Monmouth G.C.
(0600) 5353
The Hendre, Monmouth
(18) 6723 yards

St Mellons G.C.
(0633) 680401
St Mellons, Nr. Cardiff
(18) 6225 yards

St Pierre G. & C.C.
(0291) 625261
St Pierre Park, Chepstow
(18) 6700 yards (Old)
(18) 5762 yards (New)

Tredegar Park G.C.
(0633) 894433
Bassaleg Road, Newport
(18) 6044 yards

Tredegar and Rhymney G.C.
(0685) 894433
Rhymney
(9) 5564 yards

West Monmouthshire G.C.
(0495) 310233
Pond Road, Nantyglo
(18) 6097 yards

GWYNEDD

Aberdovey G.C.
(065472) 493
Aberdovey
(18) 6445 yards

Abersoch G.C.
(075881) 2622
Pwllheli, Abersoch
(9) 5722 yards

Bala G.C.
(0678) 520359
Penlan, Bala
(10) 4934 yards

Betws-y-Coed G.C.
(0690) 710556
Betws-y-Coed
(9) 5030 yards

Caernarfon G.C.
(0286) 2642
Llanfaglan, Caernarfon
(18) 5859 yards

Caernarvonshire G.C.
(0492) 592423
Conway
(18) 6901 yards

Criccieth G.C.
(0766) 522697
Ednyfed Hill, Criccieth
(18) 5755 yards

Dolgellau G.C.
(0341) 422603
Pencefn Road, Dolgellau
(9) 4662 yards

Ffestiniog G.C.
(0766) 831829
Blaenau Ffestiniog
(9) 4536 yards

Llandudno (Maesdu) G.C.
(0492) 76450
Hospital Road, Llandudno
(18) 6513 yards

Llanfairfechan G.C.
(0248) 680144
Llanfairfechan
(9) 6238 yards

Nefyn and District G.C.
(0758) 720966
Morfa Nefyn
(18) 6294 yards

North Wales G.C.
(0492) 75325
Bryniau Road, West Shore, Llandudno
(18) 6132 yards

Penmaenmawr G.C.
(0492) 622085
Conway Old Road,
Penmaenmawr
(9) 5031 yards

Portmadog G.C.
(0766) 513828
Morfa Bychan, Portmadog
(18) 5728 yards

Pwllheli G.C.
(0758) 612520
Golf Road, Pwllheli
(18) 6110 yards

Royal St David's G.C.
(0766) 780361
Harlech
(18) 6495 yards

St Deiniol G.C.
(0248) 353098
Bangor
(18) 5545 yards

ISLE OF ANGLESEY

Anglesey G.C.
(0407) 810219
Rhosneigr
(18) 6204 yards

Baron Hill G.C.
(0248) 810231
Beaumaris
(9) 5564 yards

Bull Bay G.C.
(0407) 830960
Almwch
(18) 6160 yards

Holyhead G.C.
(0407) 763279
Trearddur Bay, Holyhead
(18) 6090 yards

MID GLAMORGAN

Aberdare G.C.
(0685) 878735
Abernant, Aberdare
(18) 5875 yards

Bargoed G.C.
(0443) 830143
Hoelddu, Bargoed
(18) 6012 yards

Bryn Meadows G. & C.C.
(0495) 221905
The Bryn, Nr. Hengoed
(18) 5963 yards

Caerphilly G.C.
(0222) 863441
Mountain Road, Caerphilly
(14) 6063 yards

Castell Heights G.C.
(0222) 861128
Caerphilly
(9) 5376 yards

Creigiau G.C.
(0222) 890263
Creigiau
(18) 5736 yards

Llantrisant and Pontyclun G.C.
(0443) 228169
Talbot Green, Llantrisant
(12) 5712 yards

Maesteg G.C.
(0656) 732037
Mount Pleasant, Maesteg
(18) 5845 yards

Merthyr Tydfil G.C.
(0685) 3063
Cilsanws Mountain,
Cefn Coed,
Merthyr Tydfil
(9) 5794 yards

Morlais Castle G.C.
(0685) 2822
Pant Dowlais,
Merthyr Tydfil
(9) 6356 yards

Mountain Ash G.C.
(0443) 472265
Cefnpennar
(18) 5535 yards

Mountain Lakes G.C.
(0222) 861128
Caerphilly
(18) 6815 yards

Pontypridd G.C.
(0443) 402359
Tygwyn Road,
Pontypridd
(18) 5650 yards

Pyle and Kenfig G.C.
(0656) 783093
Kenfig
(18) 6655 yards

Rhondda G.C.
(0443) 433204
Pontygwaith, Rhondda
(18) 6428 yards

Royal Porthcawl G.C.
(0656) 782251
Porthcawl
(18) 6691 yards

Southerndown G.C.
(0656) 880476
Ewenny, Bridgend
(18) 6615 yards

Whitehall G.C.
(0443) 740245
Nelson, Treharris
(9) 5750 yards

POWYS

Brecon G.C.
(0874) 2004
Llanfaes, Brecon
(9) 5218 yards

Builth Wells G.C.
(0982) 553296
Builth Wells
(9) 5458 yards

Cradoc G.C.
(0874) 3658
Penoyre Park, Cradoc
(18) 6318 yards

Llandrindod Wells G.C.
(0597) 2059
Llandrindod Wells
(18) 5759 yards

Machynlleth G.C.
(0654) 2000
Machynlleth
(9) 5734 yards

St Giles G.C.
(0686) 25844
Pool Road, Newtown
(9) 5864 yards

St Idloes G.C.
(05512) 2205
Penrhalt, Llanidloes
(9) 5210 yards

Welshpool G.C.
(0938) 3377
Golfa Hill, Welshpool
(18) 5708 yards

SOUTH GLAMORGAN

Brynhill G.C.
(0446) 733660
Port Road, Barry
(18) 6000 yards

Cardiff G.C.
(0222) 754772
Sherborne Avenue, Cyncoed,
Cardiff
(18) 6015 yards

Dinas Powis G.C.
(0222) 512727
Old High Walls, Dinas Powis
(18) 5377 yards

Glamorganshire G.C.
(0222) 701185
Lavernock Road, Penarth
(18) 6150 yards

Llanishen G.C.
(0222) 752205
Cwm-Lisvane, Cardiff
(18) 5296 yards

Royal Porthcawl.

Radyr G.C.
(0222) 842408
Drysgol Road, Radyr
(18) 6031 yards

Wenvoe Castle G.C.
(0222) 594371
Wenvoe Castle, Cardiff
(18) 6411 yards

Whitchurch G.C.
(0222) 614660
Pantmawr Road,
Whitchurch,
Cardiff
(18) 6245 yards

WEST GLAMORGAN

Clyne G.C.
(0792) 401989
Owls Lodge Lane,
Mayals, Swansea
(18) 6312 yards

Fairwood Park G. & C.C.
(0792) 203648
Upper Killay, Swansea
(18) 6606 yards

Glynneath G.C.
(0639) 720679
Pontneathvaughan
(9) 5742 yards

Inco G.C.
(0792) 844216
Clydach, Swansea
(18) 5976 yards

Langland Bay G.C.
(0792) 66023
Langland Bay, Swansea
(18) 5812 yards

Morriston G.C.
(0792) 796528
Claremont Road, Morriston,
Swansea
(18) 5722 yards

Neath G.C.
(0639) 643615
Cadoxton, Neath
(18) 6460 yards

Palleg G.C.
(0639) 842524
Lower Cwmtwrch, Swansea
(9) 3209 yards

Pennard G.C.
(044128) 3131
Southgate Road, Southgate
(18) 6266 yards

Pontardawe G.C.
(0792) 863118
Cefn Llan, Pontardawe
(18) 6061 yards

Swansea Bay G.C.
(0792) 812198
Jersey Marine, Neath
(18) 6302 yards

NORTHERN IRELAND

CO. ANTRIM

Ballycastle G.C.
(026) 5762536
Ballycastle
(18) 5902 yards

Ballyclare G.C.
(09603) 22051
Springvale Road, Ballyclare
(9) 6708 yards

Ballymena G.C.
(026) 6861487
Raceview Road, Ballymena
(18) 5168 yards

Bushfoot G.C.
(026) 5731317
Portballintrae, Bushmills
(9) 5572 yards

Cairndhu G.C.
(0574) 83324
Coast Road, Ballygally, Larne
(18) 6112 yards

Carrickfergus G.C.
(09603) 63713
North Road, Carrickfergus
(18) 5789 yards

Cushendall G.C.
(026) 6771318
Shore Road, Cushendall
(9) 4678 yards

Dunmurry G.C.
(0232) 621402
Dunmurry Lane, Dunmurry, Belfast
(18) 5832 yards

Greenisland G.C.
(0232) 862236
Upper Road, Greenisland
(9) 5951 yards

Larne G.C.
(09603) 72043
Ferris Bay, Islandmagee, Larne
(9) 6114 yards

Lisburn G.C.
(08462) 77216
Eglantine Road, Lisburn
(18) 6255 yards

Massereene G.C.
(08494) 62096
Lough Road, Antrim
(18) 6554 yards

Royal Portrush G.C.
(0265) 822311
Bushmills Road, Portrush
(18) 6810 yards (Dunluce)
(18) 6259 yards (Valley)

Whitehead G.C.
(09603) 72792
McCrae's Brae, Whitehead
(18) 6412 yards

CO. ARMAGH

County Armagh G.C.
(0861) 522501
Newry Road, Armagh
(18) 6184 yards

Craigavon Golf & Ski Centre
(07622) 6606
Silverwood, Lurgan
(18) 6496 yards

Lurgan G.C.
(0762) 322087
Lurgan
(18) 6380 yards

Portadown G.C.
(0762) 335356
Carrickblacker, Portadown
(18) 6119 yards

Tandragee G.C.
(0762) 840727
Tandragee, Craigavon
(18) 6084 yards

BELFAST

Balmoral G.C.
(0232) 381514
Lisburn Road, Belfast
(18) 6250 yards

Belvoir Park G.C.
(0232) 491693
Newtown, Breda, Belfast
(18) 6476 yards

Cliftonville G.C.
(0232) 744158
Westland Road, Belfast
(9) 6240 yards

Fortwilliam G.C.
(0232) 771770
Downview Avenue, Belfast
(18) 5642 yards

The Knock G.C.
(02318) 3825
Summerfield, Dundonald, Belfast
(18) 6292 yards

Malone G.C.
(0232) 612695
Upper Malone Road, Dunmurry
(18) 6433 yards

Ormeau G.C.
(0232) 641069
Ravenhill Road, Belfast
(9) 5306 yards

Shandon Park G.C.
(0232) 797859
Shandon Park, Belfast
(18) 6252 yards

CO. DOWN

Ardglass G.C.
(0396) 841219
Castle Place, Ardglass
(18) 6500 yards

Banbridge G.C.
(08206) 22342
Huntly Road, Banbridge
(12) 5879 yards

Bangor G.C.
(0247) 270922
Broadway, Bangor
(18) 6450 yards

Carnalea G.C.
(0247) 270368
Carnalea
(18) 5513 yards

Clandeboye G.C.
(0247) 271767
Conlig, Newtownards
(18) 6650 yards (Dufferin)
(18) 5634 yards (Ava)

Donaghadee G.C.
(0237) 883624
Warren Road, Donaghadee
(18) 6099 yards

Downpatrick G.C.
(0396) 2152
Saul Road, Downpatrick
(18) 6196 yards

Helen's Bay G.C.
(0247) 852601
Helen's Bay, Bangor
(9) 5638 yards

Holywood G.C.
(02317) 2138
Nuns Walk, Demesne Road, Holywood
(18) 5885 yards

Kilkeel G.C.
(069) 3762296
Mourne Park, Ballyardle
(9) 6000 yards

Kirkistown Castle G.C.
(02477) 71233
Cloughey, Newtownards
(18) 6157 yards

Royal County Down.

Mahee Island G.C.
(0238) 541234
Comber, Belfast
(9) 5580 yards

Royal Belfast G.C.
(0232) 428165
Holywood, Craigavad
(18) 6205 yards

Royal County Down G.C.
(03967) 23314
Newcastle
(18) 6692 yards
(18) 4100 yards

Scrabo G.C.
(0247) 812355
Scrabo Road,
Newtownards
(18) 6000 yards

The Spa G.C.
(0238) 562365
Grove Road, Ballynahinch
(9) 5770 yards

Warrenpoint G.C.
(06937) 73695
Lower Dromore Road,
Warrenpoint
(18) 6215 yards

CO. FERMANAGH

Enniskillen G.C.
(0365) 25250
Enniskillen
(18) 5476 yards

CO. LONDON-DERRY

Castlerock G.C.
(0265) 848314
Circular Road, Castlerock
(18) 6694 yards

City of Derry G.C.
(0504) 46369
Victoria Road, Londonderry
(18) 6362 yards (Prehen)
(9) 4708 yards (Dunhugh)

Kilrea G.C.
(026) 653 397
Drumagarner Road, Kilrea
(9) 4326 yards

Moyola Park G.C.
(0648) 68830
Shanemullagh, Castledawson
(18) 6517 yards

Portstewart G.C.
(026) 5832015
Strand Road, Portstewart
(18) 6784 yards
(Championship)
(18) 4733 yards (Town)
(9) (Blue)

CO. TYRONE

Dungannon G.C.
(08687) 22098
Mullaghmore, Dungannon
(18) 5914 yards

Fintona G.C.
(0662) 841480
Fintona
(9) 6250 yards

Killymoon G.C.
(06487) 62254
Killymoon, Cookstown
(18) 6000 yards

Newtownstewart G.C.
(06626) 61466
Golf Course Road,
Newtownstewart
(18) 6100 yards

Omagh G.C.
(0662) 3160
Dublin Road, Omagh
(18) 5800 yards

Strabane G.C.
(0504) 882271
Ballycolman, Strabane
(18) 6100 yards

IRELAND

CO. CARLOW

Borris G.C.
(0503) 73143
Borris
(9) 6026 yards

Carlow G.C.
(0503) 31695
Carlow
(18) 6347 yards

CO. CAVAN

Belturbet G.C.
(049) 22287
Belturbet
(9) 5180 yards

Blacklion G.C.
(0017) 53024
Toam, Blacklion
(9) 6000 yards

County Cavan G.C.
(049) 31283
Drumelis
(18) 6037 yards

Virginia G.C.
(049) 44103
Virginia
(9) 4520 yards

CO. CLARE

Dromoland Castle G.C.
(061) 71144
Newmarket-on-Fergus
(9) 6098 yards

Ennis G.C.
(065) 24074
Drumbiggle Road, Ennis
(18) 5714 yards

Kilkee G.C.
(Kilkee) 48
East End, Kilkee
(9) 6058 yards

Kilrush G.C.
(Kilrush) 138
Parknamoney, Kilrush
(9) 5478 yards

Lahinch G.C.
(065) 81003
Lahinch
(18) 6515 yards (Championship)
(18) 5450 yards (Castle)

Shannon G.C.
(061) 61020
Shannon Airport
(18) 6480 yards

Spanish Point G.C.
(065) 84198
Miltow, Malbay
(9) 6248 yards

CO. CORK

Bandon G.C.
(023) 41111
Castlebernard, Bandon
(18) 6101 yards

Bantry G.C.
(027) 50579
Donemark, Bantry
(9) 6436 yards

Charleville G.C.
(063) 257
Charleville
(18) 6380 yards

Cobh G.C.
(021) 811372
Ballywilliam, Cobh
(9) 4800 yards

Cork G.C.
(021) 353451
Little Island
(18) 6600 yards

Doneraile G.C.
(022) 24137
Doneraile
(9) 5528 yards

Douglas G.C.
(021) 291086
Douglas
(18) 5651 yards

Dunmore G.C.
(023) 33352
Clonakilty, Dunmore
(9) 4180 yards

East Cork G.C.
(021) 631687
Gortacrue, Midleton
(18) 5602 yards

Fermoy G.C.
(025) 31472
Fermoy
(18) 5884 yards

Glengarriff G.C.
(027) 63150
Glengarriff
(9) 4328 yards

Kanturk G.C.
(029) 50181
Fairy Hill, Kanturk
(9) 5918 yards

Kinsale G.C.
(021) 772197
Ringnanean, Belgooly, Kinsale
(9) 5580 yards

Macroom G.C.
(026) 41072
Lackaduve, Macroom
(9) 5850 yards

Mallow G.C.
(022) 22465
Balleyellis, Mallow
(18) 6559 yards

Mitchelstown G.C.
(025) 24072
Gurrane, Mitchelstown
(9) 5550 yards

Monkstown G.C.
(021) 841225
Parkgarriffe, Monkstown
(18) 6000 yards

Muskerry G.C.
(021) 85297
Carrigrohane
(18) 6350 yards

Skibbereen G.C.
(028) 21227
Skibbereen
(9) 5890 yards

Youghal G.C.
(024) 2787
Knockaverry, Youghal
(18) 6206 yards

CO. DONEGAL

Ballybofey & Stranorlar G.C.
(074) 31093
Ballybofey
(18) 5913 yards

Ballyliffin G.C.
(077) 74417
Ballyliffin, Clonmany
(18) 6524 yards

Bundoran G.C.
(072) 41302
Great Northern Hotel, Bundoran
(18) 6328 yards

Donegal G.C.
(073) 22166
Murvagh, Donegal
(18) 6842 yards

Dunfanaghy G.C.
(074) 36238
Dunfanaghy
(18) 5572 yards

Greencastle G.C.
(077) 81013
Greencastle
(9) 2693 yards

Gweedore G.C.
(075) 31140
Derrybeg, Letterkenny
(9) 6234 yards

Letterkenny G.C.
(074) 21150
Barnhill, Letterkenny
(18) 6299 yards

Nairn & Portnoo G.C.
(075) 45107
Nairn & Portnoo
(18) 5950 yards

North West G.C.
(077) 61027
Lisfannon, Fahan
(18) 5895 yards

Otway G.C.
(074) 58319
Saltpans, Rathmullen
(9) 4134 yards

Portsalon G.C.
(074) 59102
Portsalon
(18) 5949 yards

Rosapenna G.C.
(074) 55301
Rosapenna
(18) 6254 yards

CO. DUBLIN

Balbriggan G.C.
(01) 412173
Blackhall, Balbriggan
(9) 5952 yards

Ballinascorney G.C.
(01) 512516
Ballinascorney
(18) 5500 yards

Beaverstown G.C.
(01) 436439
Beaverstown, Donabate
(18) 6000 yards

Beech Park G.C.
(01) 580522
Johnstown, Rathcoole
(18) 5600 yards

Corballis G.C.
(01) 450583
Donabate
(18) 4898 yards

Carrickmines G.C.
(01) 895 676
Carrickmines, Dublin
(9) 6044 yards

Castle G.C.
(01) 904207
Rathfarnham, Dublin
(18) 6240 yards

Clontarf G.C.
(01) 315085
Malahide Road, Dublin
(18) 5608 yards

Deerpark G.C.
(01) 322624
Deerpark Hotel, Howth
(18) 6647 yards

Donabate G.C.
(01) 436059
Balcarrick, Donabate
(18) 6187 yards

Dublin Sport G.C.
(01) 895418
Kilternan, Dublin
(18) 5413 yards

Dun Laoghaire G.C.
(01) 801055
Eglinton Park,
Dun Laoghaire,
Dublin
(18) 5950 yards

Edmonstown G.C.
(01) 931082
Rathfarnham, Dublin
(18) 6177 yards

Elm Park G.C.
(01) 693014
Donnybrook, Dublin
(18) 5485 yards

Forrest Little G.C.
(01) 401183
Cloghran
(18) 6400 yards

Foxrock G.C.
(01) 895668
Foxrock, Torquay Road,
Dublin
(9) 5699 metres

Grange G.C.
(01) 932832
Whitechurch, Rathfarnham,
Dublin
(18) 5517 yards

Hermitage G.C.
(01) 264549
Lucan
(18) 6000 yards

Howth G.C.
(01) 323055
Carrickbrae Road, Sutton,
Dublin
(18) 6168 yards

The Island G.C.
(01) 436205
Corballis, Donabate
(18) 6320 yards

Killiney G.C.
(01) 851983
Killiney
(9) 6201 yards

Lucan G.C.
(01) 280246
Lucan
(9) 6287 yards

Malahide G.C.
(01) 450248
Coast Road, Malahide
(9) 5568 yards

Milltown G.C.
(01) 976090
Lower Churchtown Road,
Dublin
(18) 6275 yards

Newlands G.C.
(01) 593157
Clondalkin, Dublin
(18) 6184 yards

Portmarnock G.C.
(01) 323082
Portmarnock
(18) 7103 yards

Rathfarnham G.C.
(01) 931201
Newtown, Dublin
(9) 6250 yards

Royal Dublin G.C.
(01) 336477
Bull Island, Dollymount,
Dublin
(18) 6858 yards

Rush G.C.
(01) 437548
Rush
(9) 5655 yards

St Anne's G.C.
(01) 336471
Bull Island, Dublin
(9) 6104 yards

Skerries G.C.
(01) 491204
Skerries
(18) 6300 yards

Slade Valley G.C.
(01) 582207
Lynch Park, Brittas
(18) 5800 yards

Woodbrook G.C.
(01) 824799
Bray
(18) 6541 yards

CO. GALWAY

Athenry G.C.
(091) 94466
Derrydonnell, Oranmore
(9) 5448 yards

Ballinasloe G.C.
(0905) 42126
Ballinasloe
(18) 5844 yards

Connemara G.C.
(095) 23502
Ballyconneely, Nr. Clifden
(18) 7100 yards

Galway G.C.
(091) 22169
Blackrock, Salthill
(18) 6193 yards

Gort G.C.
(091) 31336
Gort
(9) 5688 yards

Loughrea G.C.
(091) 41049
Loughrea
(9) 5798 yards

Mount Bellew G.C.
(0905) 79259
Mount Bellow
(9) 5564 yards

Oughterard G.C.
(091) 82131
Gurteeva, Oughterard
(9) 6356 yards

Portumna G.C.
(0509) 41059
Portumna
(9) 5776 yards

Tuam G.C.
(093) 24354
Barnacurragh, Tuam
(18) 6321 yards

CO. KERRY

Ballybunion G.C.
(068) 27146
Ballybunion
(18) 6529 yards (Old)
(18) 6477 yards (New)

Ceann Sibeal G.C.
(066) 51657
Ballyferriter, Tralee
(9) 6222 yards

Dooks G.C.
(066) 68205
Glenbeigh, Dooks
(18) 5850 yards

Kenmare G.C.
(064) 41291
Kenmare
(9) 5900 yards

Killarney Golf & Fishing Club
(064) 31034
O'Mahony's Point, Killarney
(18) 6677 yards (Mahony's Point)
(18) 6798 yards (Killeen)

Parknasilla G.C.
(064) 45122
Parknasilla
(9) 5000 yards

Tralee G.C.
(066) 36379
West Barrow, Ardfert
(18) 6900 yards

Waterville G.C.
(0667) 4545
Waterville
(18) 7146 yards

CO. KILDARE

Athy G.C.
(0607) 31727
Geraldine, Athy
(9) 6158 yards

Bodenstown G.C.
(045) 97096
Bodenstown, Sallins
(18) 7031 yards

Cill Dara G.C.
(045) 21433
Cilldara, Kildare Town
(9) 6196 yards

Clongowes G.C.
(045) 68202
Clongowes Wood, College Naas
(9) 5743 yards

Curragh G.C.
(045) 41238
Curragh
(18) 6565 yards

Naas G.C.
(045) 97509
Kerdiffstown, Naas
(9) 6233 yards

CO. KILKENNY

Callan G.C.
(056) 25136
Geraldine, Callan
(9) 5844 yards

Castlecomer G.C.
(056) 41139
Castlecomer
(9) 6985 yards

Kilkenny G.C.
(056) 22125
Glendine, Kilkenny
(18) 6374 yards

Mount Juliet Hotel & G.C.
(056) 24455
Thomastown
(18) 7000 yards

CO. LAOIS

Abbey Leix G.C.
(0502) 31450
Abbey Leix, Portlaoise
(9) 5680 yards

Heath G.C.
(0502) 46622
Portlaoise
(18) 6247 yards

Mountrath G.C.
(0502) 32558
Mountrath
(9) 5492 yards

Portarlington G.C.
(0502) 23115
Garryhinch, Portarlington
(9) 5700 yards

Rathdowney G.C.
(0505) 46170
Rathdowney
(9) 5416 yards

CO. LEITRIM

Ballinamore G.C.
(078) 44346
Ballinamore
(9) 5680 yards

Carrick-on-Shannon G.C.
(078) 20157
Carrick-on-Shannon
(9) 5922 yards

CO. LIMERICK

Adare Manor G.C.
(061) 86204
Adare
(9) 5430 yards

Castleroy G.C.
(061) 335753
Castleroy
(18) 6089 yards

Limerick G.C.
(061) 44083
Ballyclough, Limerick
(18) 5767 yards

Newcastle West G.C.
(069) 62015
Newcastle West
(9) 5482 yards

CO. LONGFORD

Co. Longford G.C.
(043) 46310
Dublin Road, Longford
(18) 6028 yards

CO. LOUTH

Ardee G.C.
(041) 53227
Town Parks, Ardee
(18) 5833 yards

Ballyliffin, Co. Donegal.

County Louth G.C.
(041) 22329
Baltray, Drogheda
(18) 6728 yards

Dundalk G.C.
(042) 21731
Blackrock, Dundalk
(18) 6740 yards

Greenore G.C.
(042) 73212
Greenore
(18) 6300 yards

CO. MAYO

Achill Island G.C.
(098) 43202
Keel, Achill Island
(9) 5420 yards

Ballina G.C.
(096) 21050
Mosgrove, Shanaghy, Ballina
(9) 5182 yards

Ballinrobe G.C.
(092) 41659
Ballinrobe
(9) 2895 yards

Ballyhaunis G.C.
(0907) 30014
Coolnaha, Ballyhaunis
(9) 5852 yards

Belmullet G.C.
(097) 81093
Belmullet
(9) 5714 yards

Castlebar G.C.
(094) 21649
Rocklands, Castlebar
(18) 6109 yards

Claremorris G.C.
(094) 71527
Claremorris
(9) 5898 yards

Mulrany G.C.
(098) 36185
Mulrany, Westport
(9) 6380 yards

Swinford G.C.
(094) 51378
Swinford
(9) 5230 yards

Westport G.C.
(098) 25113
Carrowholly, Westport
(18) 6950 yards

CO. MEATH

Headfort G.C.
(046) 40148
Kells
(18) 6393 yards

Laytown & Bettystown G.C.
(041) 27534
Bettystown, Drogheda
(18) 6254 yards

Royal Tara G.C.
(046) 25244
Bellinter, Navan
(18) 6343 yards

Trim G.C.
(046) 31463
Newtownmoynagh, Trim
(9) 6266 yards

CO. MONAGHAN

Clones G.C.
(Scotshouse) 17
Hiton Park, Clone
(9) 550 yards

Nuremore G.C.
(042) 61438
Nuremore, Carrickmacross
(9) 6032 yards

Rossmore G.C.
(047) 81316
Rossmore Park, Monaghan
(9) 5859 yards

CO. OFFALY

Birr G.C.
(0509) 20082
The Glenns, Birr
(18) 6216 yards

Edenberry G.C.
(0405) 31072
Boherbree, Edenberry
(9) 5791 yards

Tullamore G.C.
(0506) 21439
Brookfield, Tullamore
(18) 6314 yards

CO. ROSCOMMON

Athlone G.C.
(0902) 2073
Hodson Bay, Athlone
(18) 6000 yards

Ballaghaderreen G.C.
(No tel.)
Ballaghaderreen
(9) 5686 yards

Boyle G.C.
(079) 62594
Roscommon Road, Boyle
(9) 5728 yards

Castlerea G.C.
(0907) 20068
Clonalis, Castlerea
(9) 5466 yards

Roscommon G.C.
(0903) 6382
Mote Park, Roscommon
(9) 6215 yards

CO. SLIGO

Ballymote G.C.
(071) 3460
Ballymote
(9) 5032 yards

County Sligo G.C.
(071) 77134
Rosses Point
(18) 6600 yards

Enniscrone G.C.
(096) 36297
Enniscrone
(18) 6511 yards

Strandhill G.C.
(071) 68188
Strandhill
(18) 5523 yards

CO. TIPPERARY

Cahir Park G.C.
(062) 41474
Kilcommon, Cahir
(9) 6262 yards

Carrick-on-Suir G.C.
(051) 40047
Garravoone, Garrick-on-Suir
(9) 5948 yards

Clonmel G.C.
(052) 21138
Lyreanearle, Clonmel
(18) 6330 yards

Nenagh G.C.
(067) 31476
Beechwood, Nenagh
(18) 5911 yards

Roscrea G.C.
(0505) 21130
Roscrea
(9) 6059 yards

Thurles G.C.
(0504) 21983
Thurles
(18) 6230 yards

Tipperary G.C.
(062) 51119
Rathanny, Tipperary
(9) 6074 yards

CO. WATERFORD

Dungarvon G.C.
(058) 41605
Ballinacourty, Dungarvan
(9) 6282 yards

Lismore G.C.
(058) 54026
Lismore
(9) 5460 yards

Tramore G.C.
(051) 81247
Tramore
(18) 6408 yards

Waterford G.C.
(051) 74182
Newrath, Waterford
(18) 6237 yards

Waterford Castle
(051) 78203
The Island, Waterford
(18) 6700 yards

CO. WESTMEATH

Moate G.C.
(0902) 31271
Moate
(9) 5348 yards

Mullingar G.C.
(044) 48629
Belvedere, Mullingar
(18) 6370 yards

CO. WEXFORD

Courtown G.C.
(055) 25166
Courtown Harbour, Gorey
(18) 6398 yards

Enniscorthy G.C.
(055) 33191
Knockmarshall, Enniscorthy
(9) 6220 yards

New Ross G.C.
(051) 21433
Tinneranny, New Ross
(9) 6102 yards

Rosslare G.C.
(053) 32113
Strand, Rosslare
(18) 6485 yards

Wexford G.C.
(053) 42238
Mulgannon, Wexford
(9) 6038 yards

CO. WICKLOW

Arklow G.C.
(0402) 32401
Arklow
(18) 5770 yards

Baltinglass G.C.
(0508) 81350
Baltinglass
(9) 6070 yards

Blainroe G.C.
(0404) 68168
Blainroe
(18) 6681 yards

Bray G.C.
(01) 862484
Ravenswell Road, Bray
(9) 6250 yards

Coollattin G.C.
(055) 29125
Coollattin, Shillelagh
(9) 5966 yards

Delgany G.C.
(0404) 874536
Delgany
(18) 5249 yards

Greystones G.C.
(01) 876624
Greystones
(18) 5900 yards

Wicklow G.C.
(0404) 67379
Dunbar Road, Wicklow
(9) 5536 yards

Woodenbridge G.C.
(0402) 5202
Arklow
(9) 6104 yards